AF411842

Blues for Smoke

Organized by Bennett Simpson

The Museum of Contemporary Art, Los Angeles

DelMonico Books • Prestel

Munich London New York

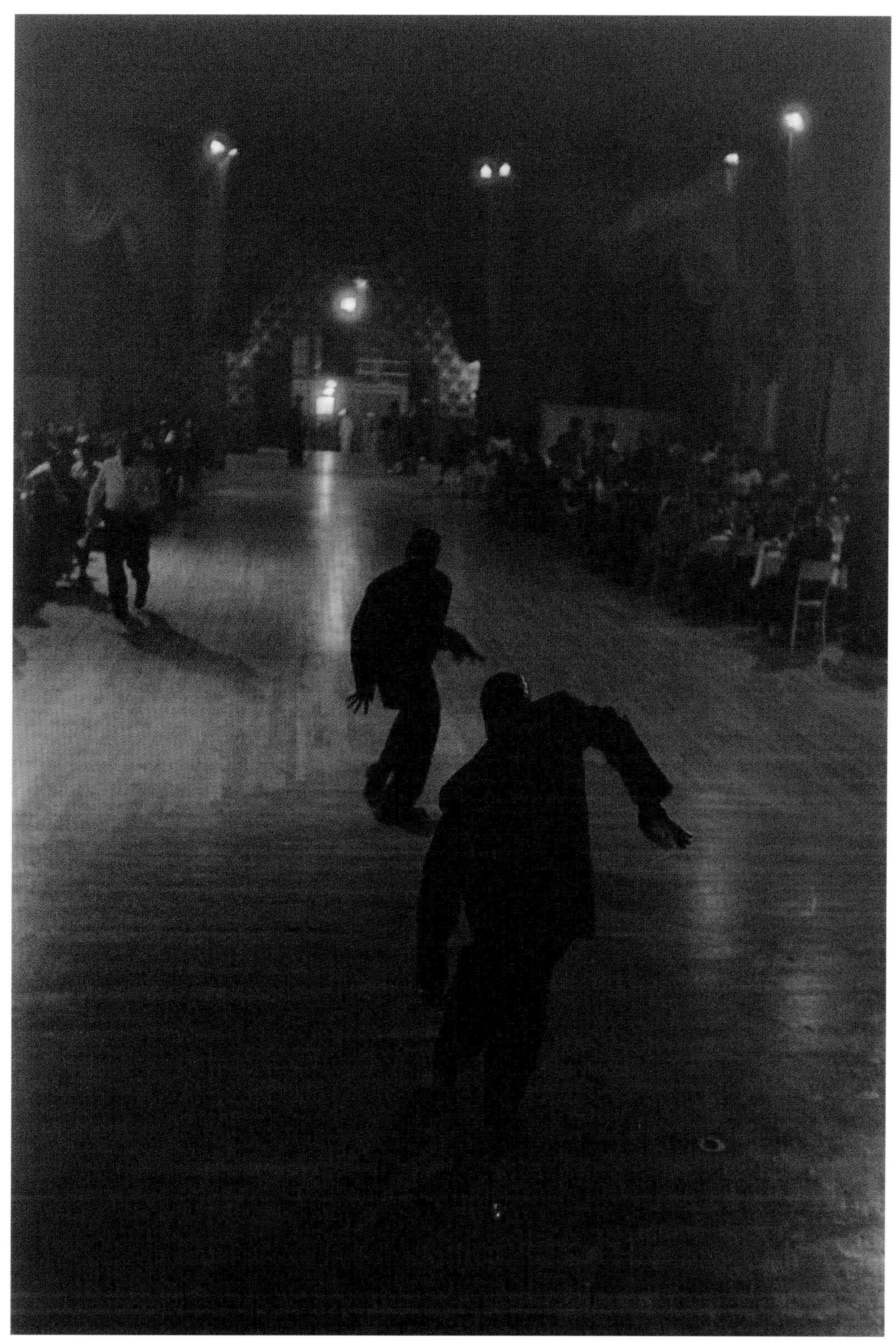

Roy DeCarava
Dancers, New York, 1956

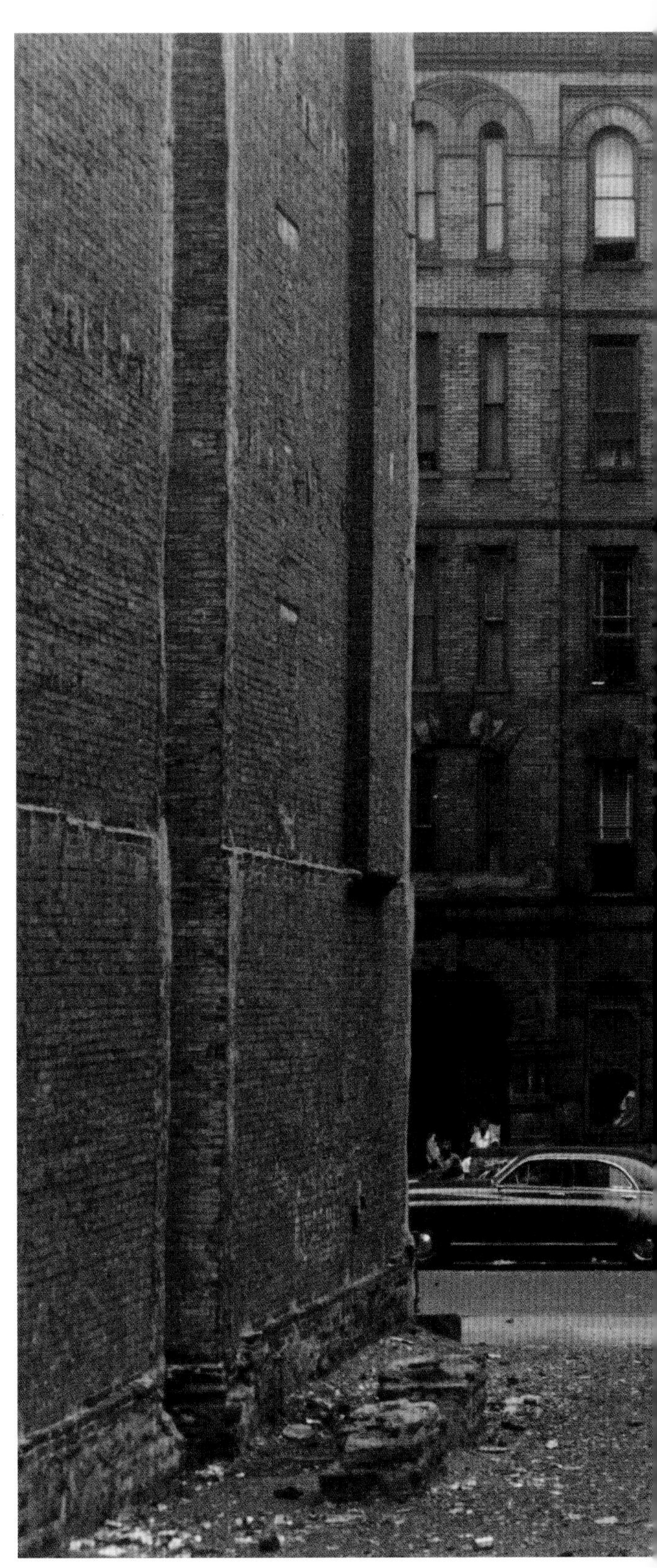

Roy DeCarava
117th Street, 1951

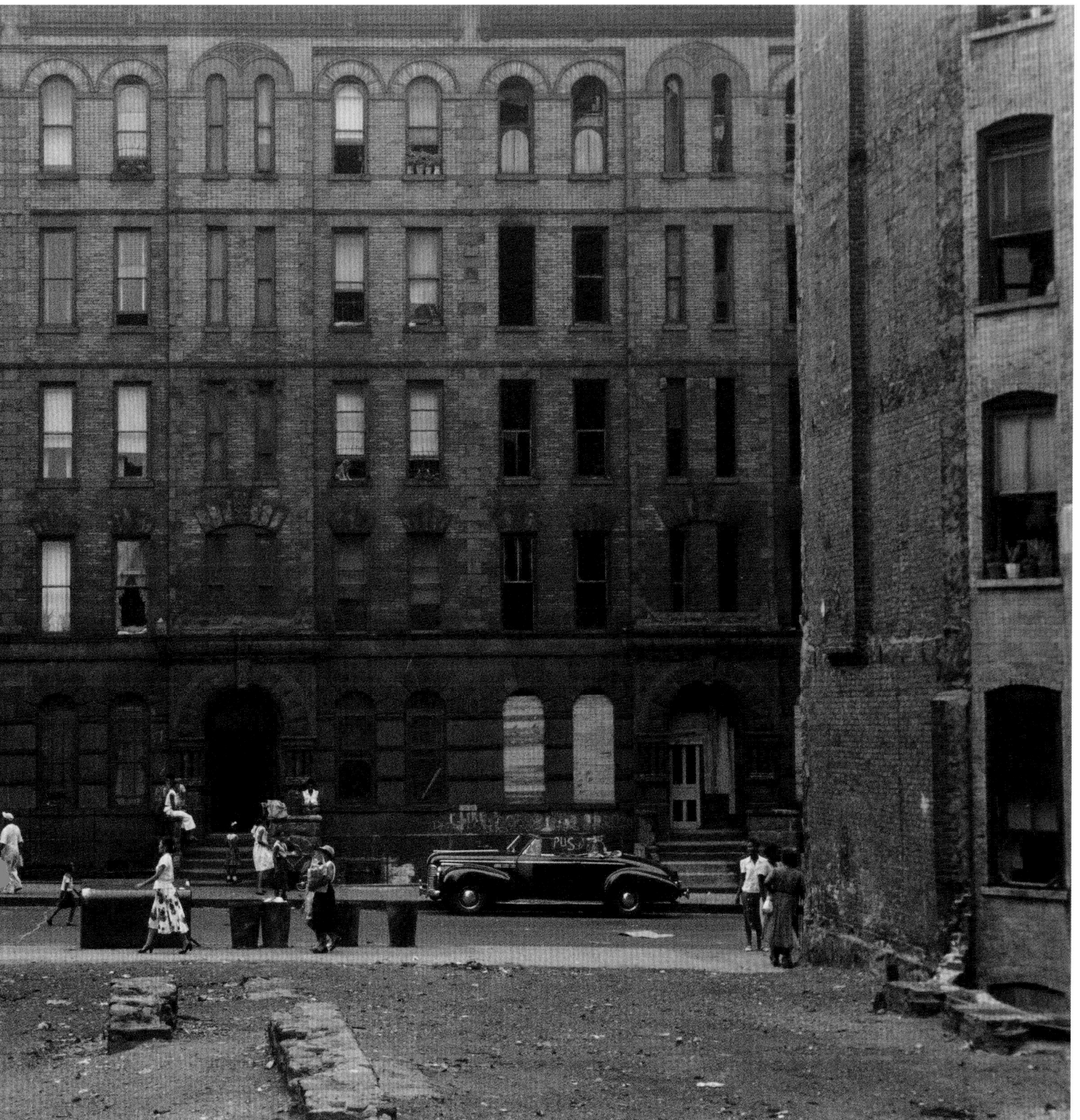

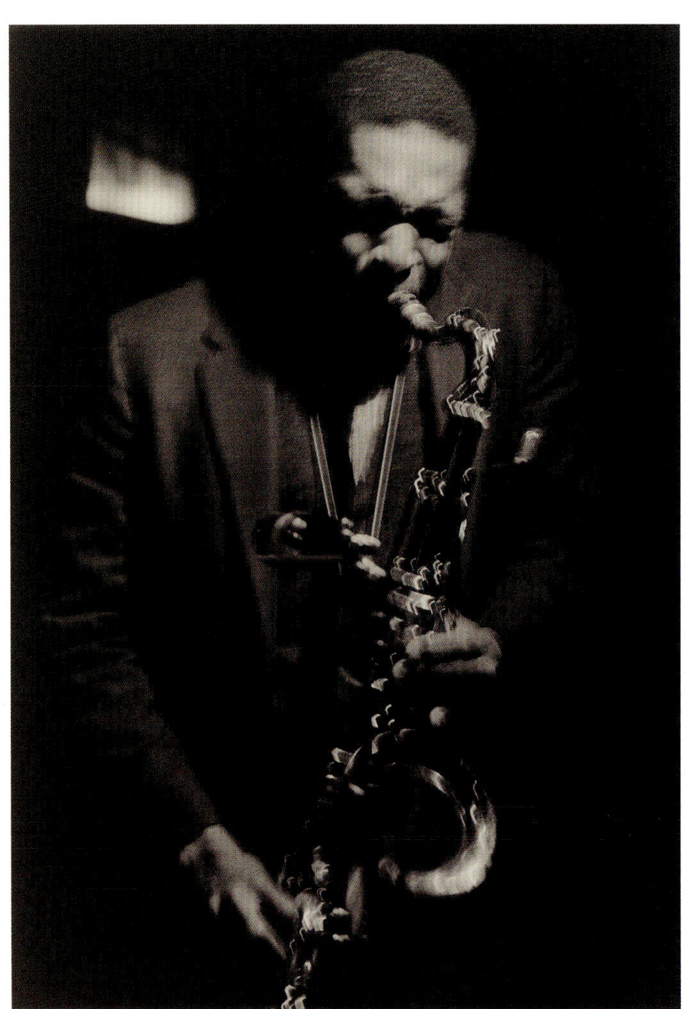

Coltrane playing, 1961

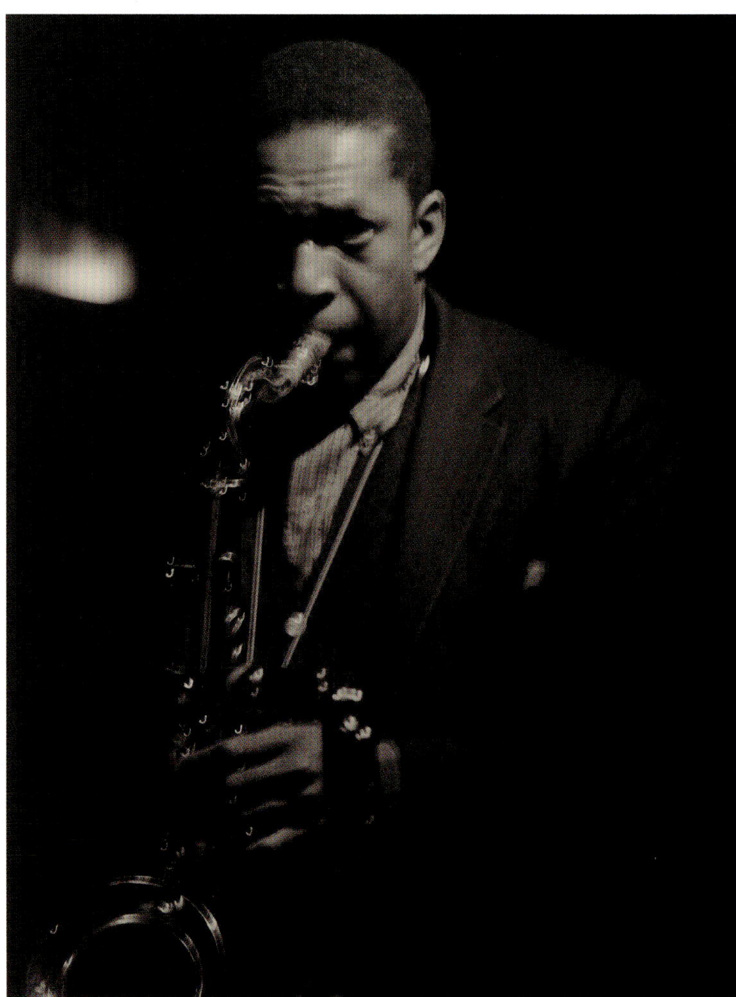

Coltrane looking, 1961

Roy DeCarava

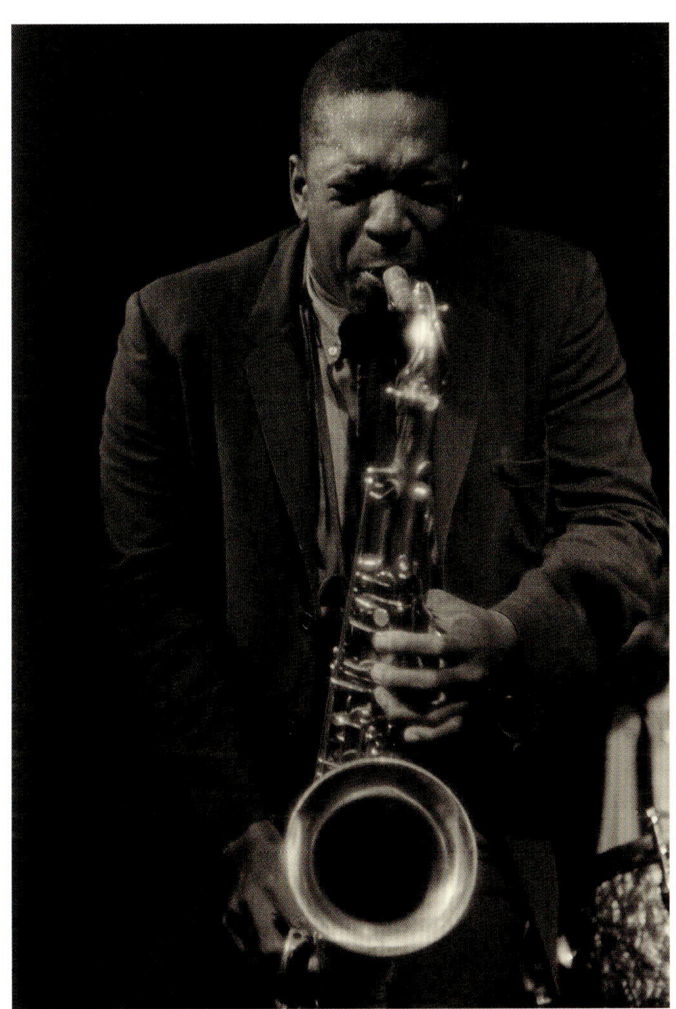

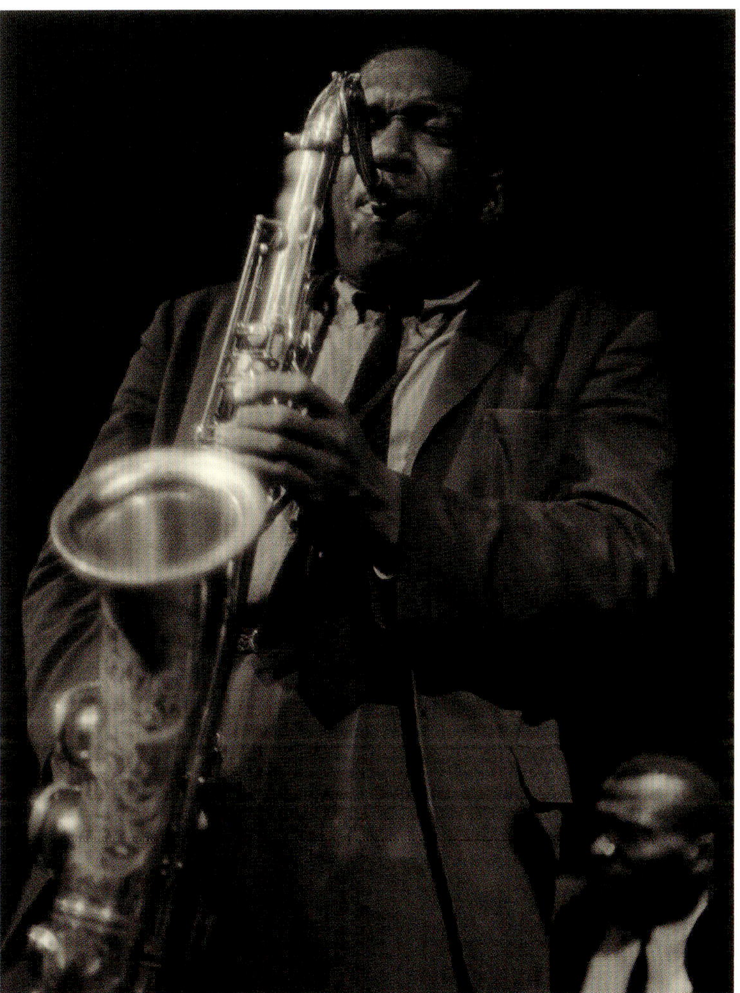

Roy DeCarava
Coltrane #27, 1961

Coltrane #24, 1961

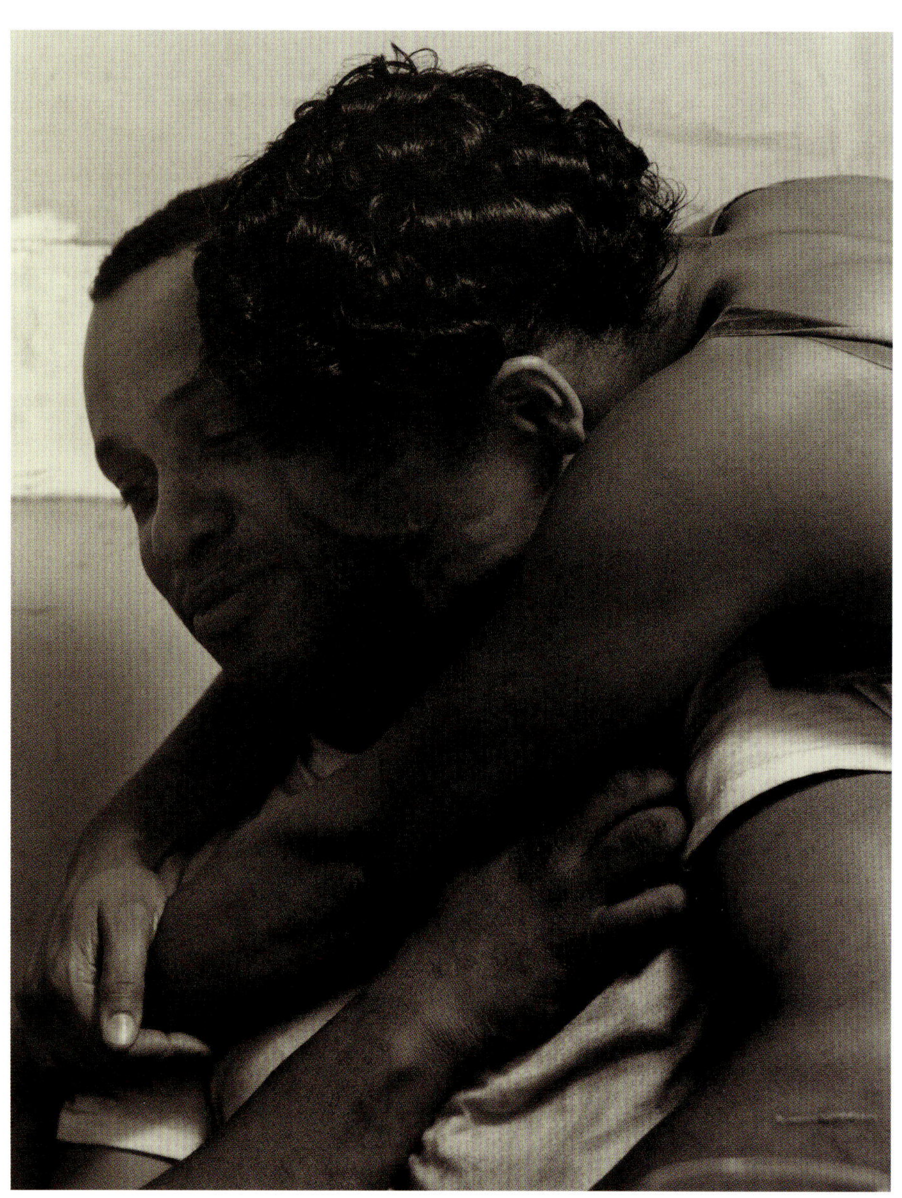

Roy DeCarava
Shirley embracing Sam, 1952

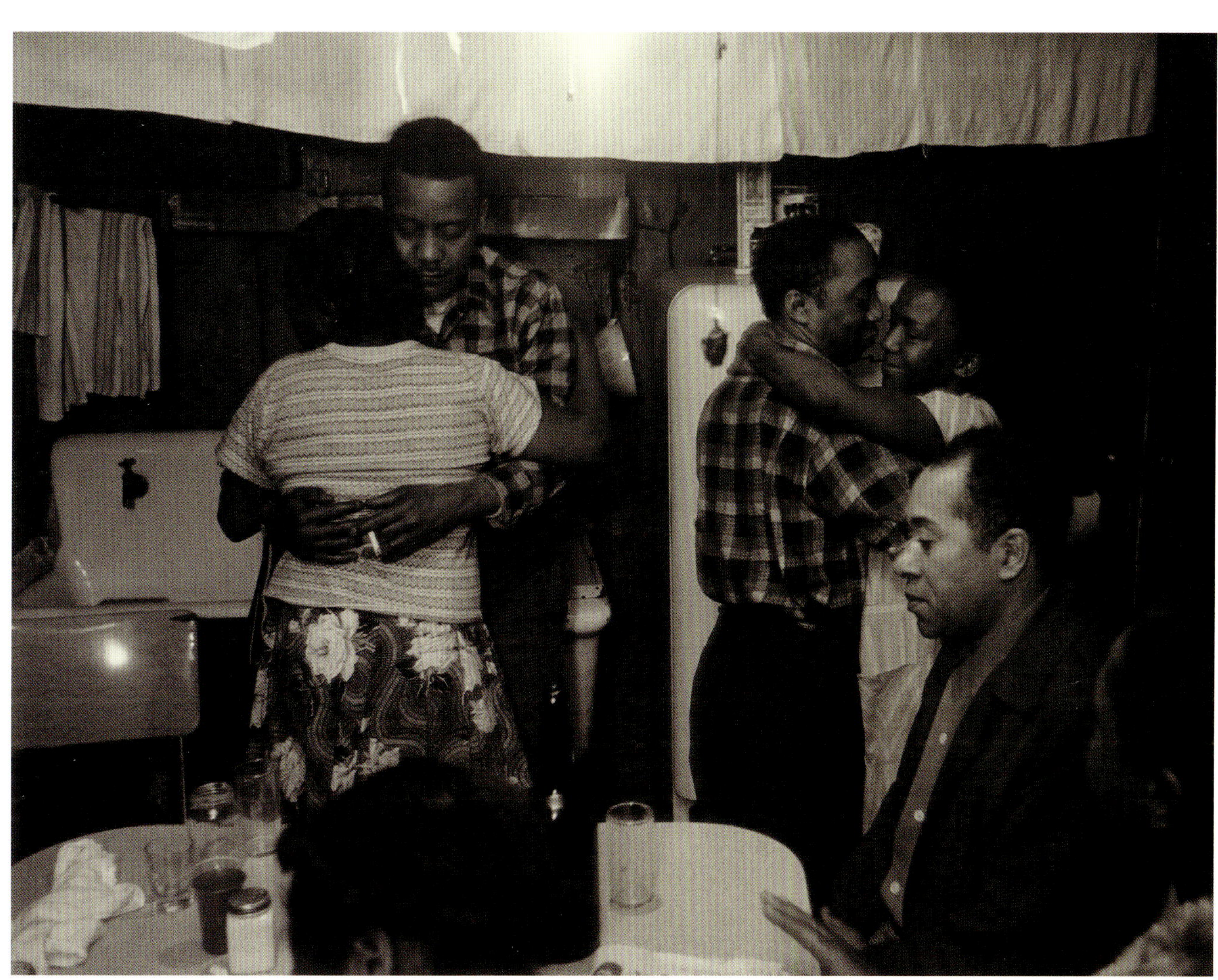

Roy DeCarava
Two couples dancing, group at table, 1953

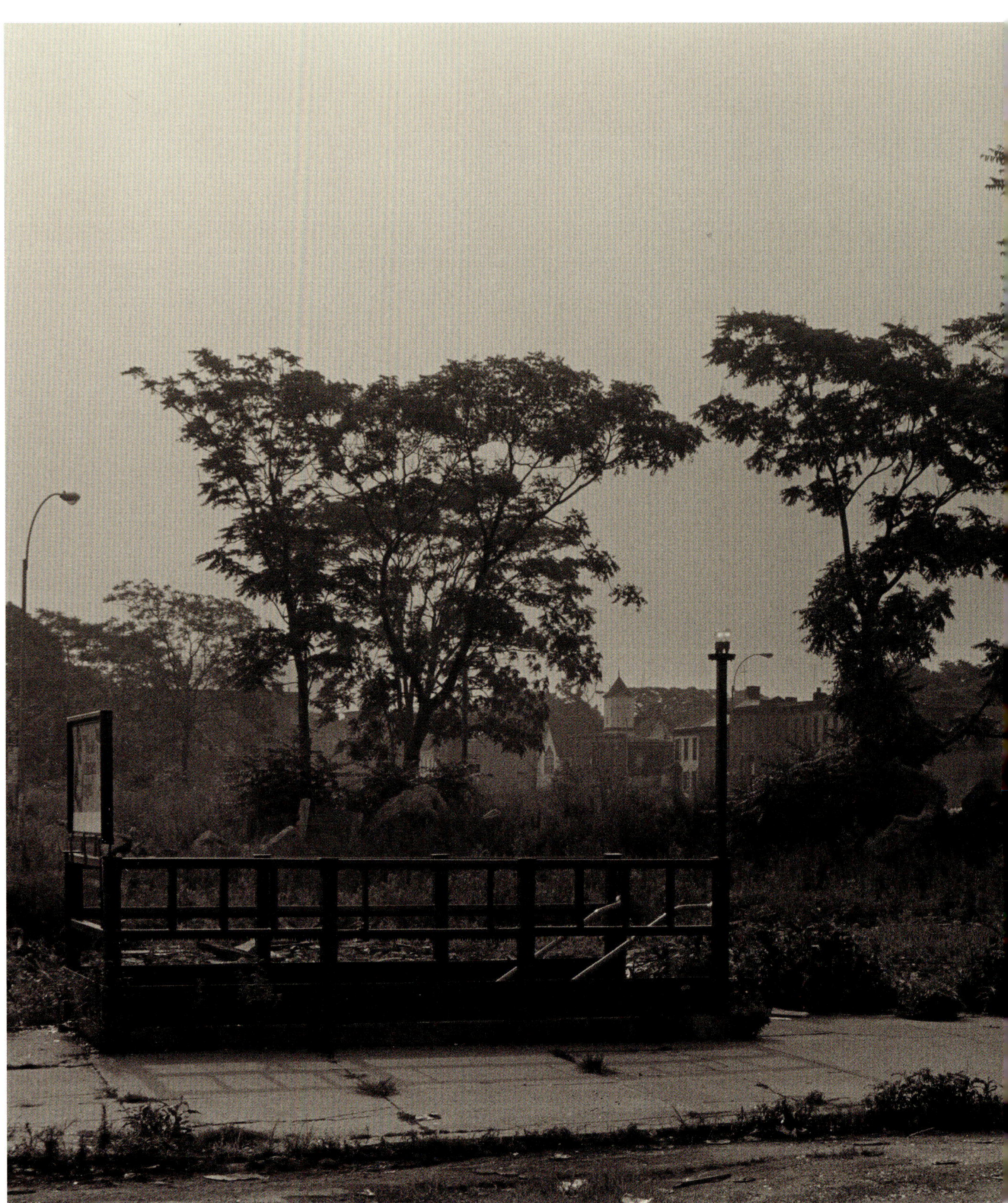

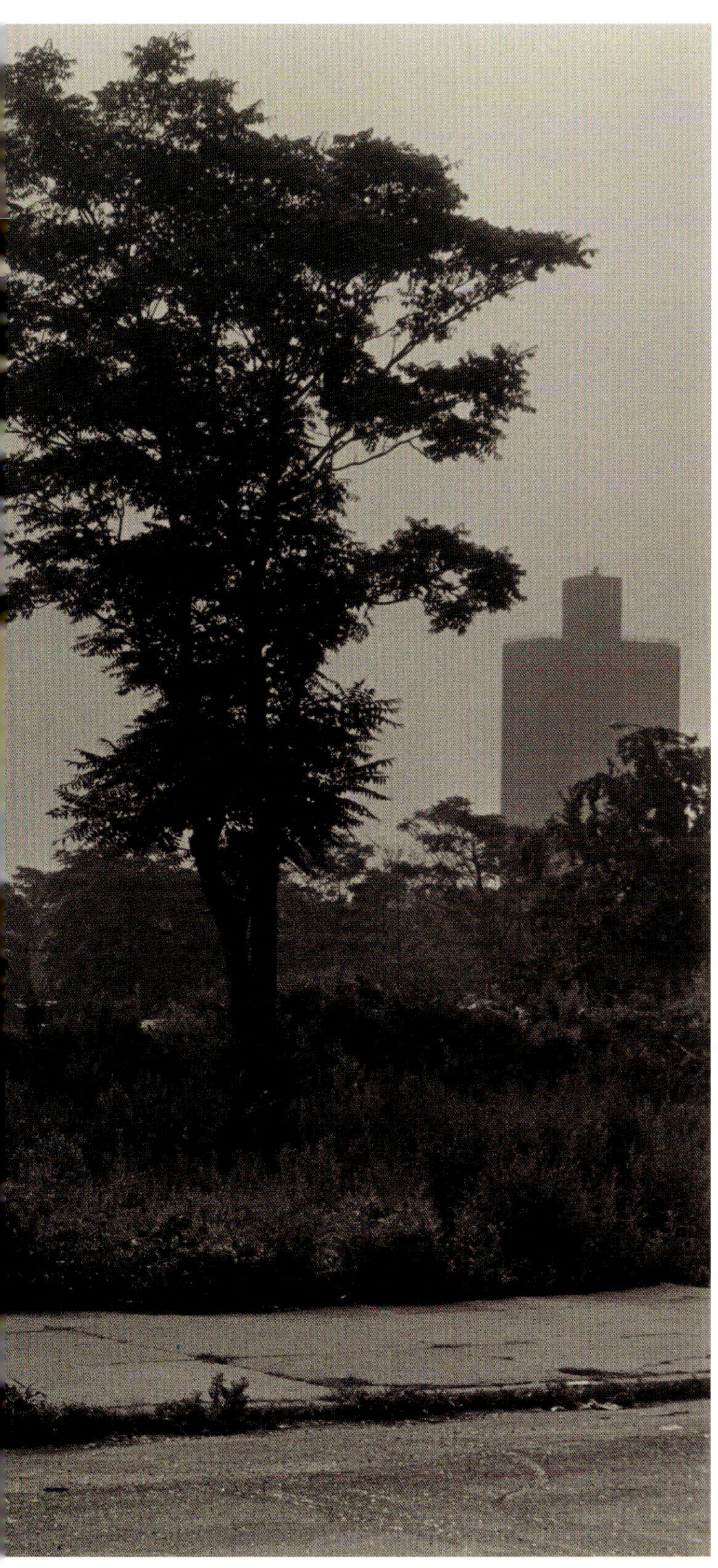

Roy DeCarava
Trees and subway entrance, 1979

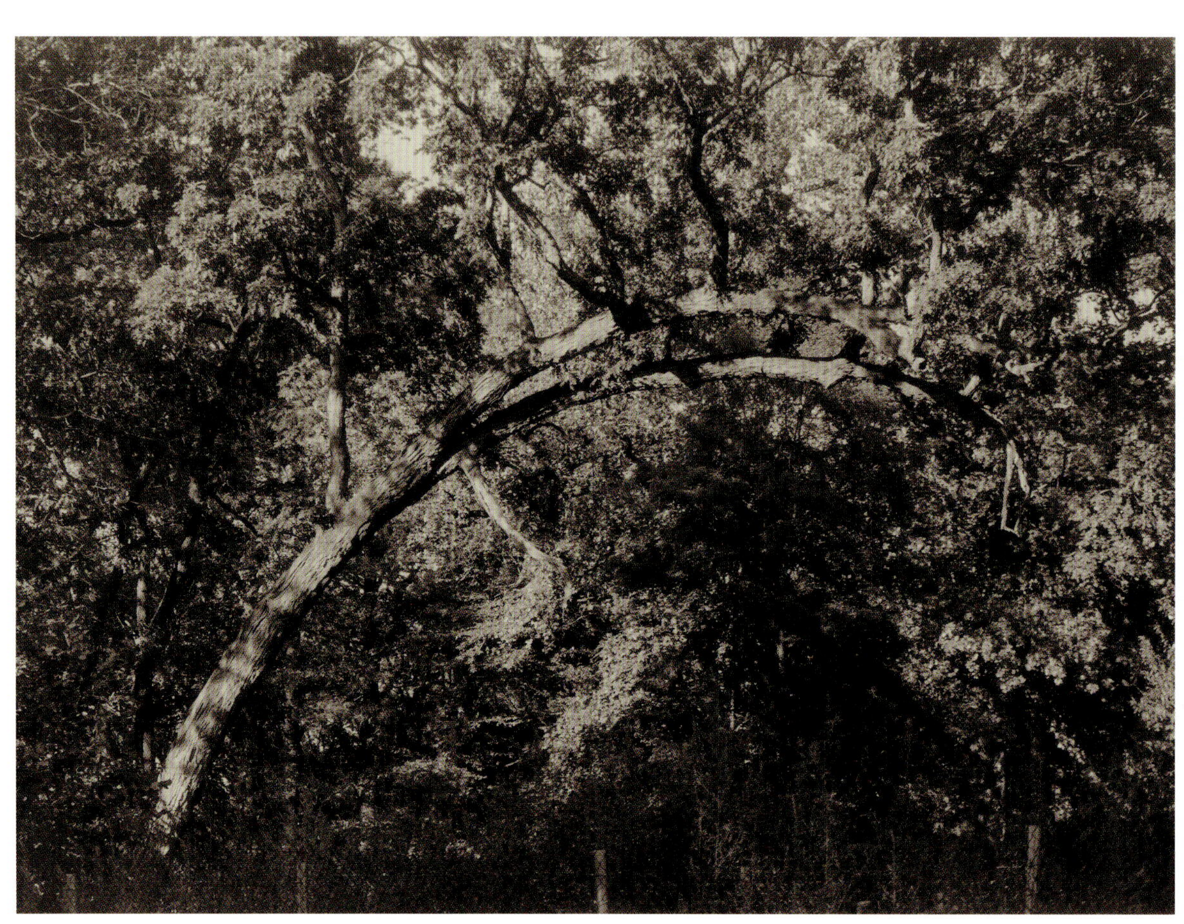

Roy DeCarava
Curved branch, 1994

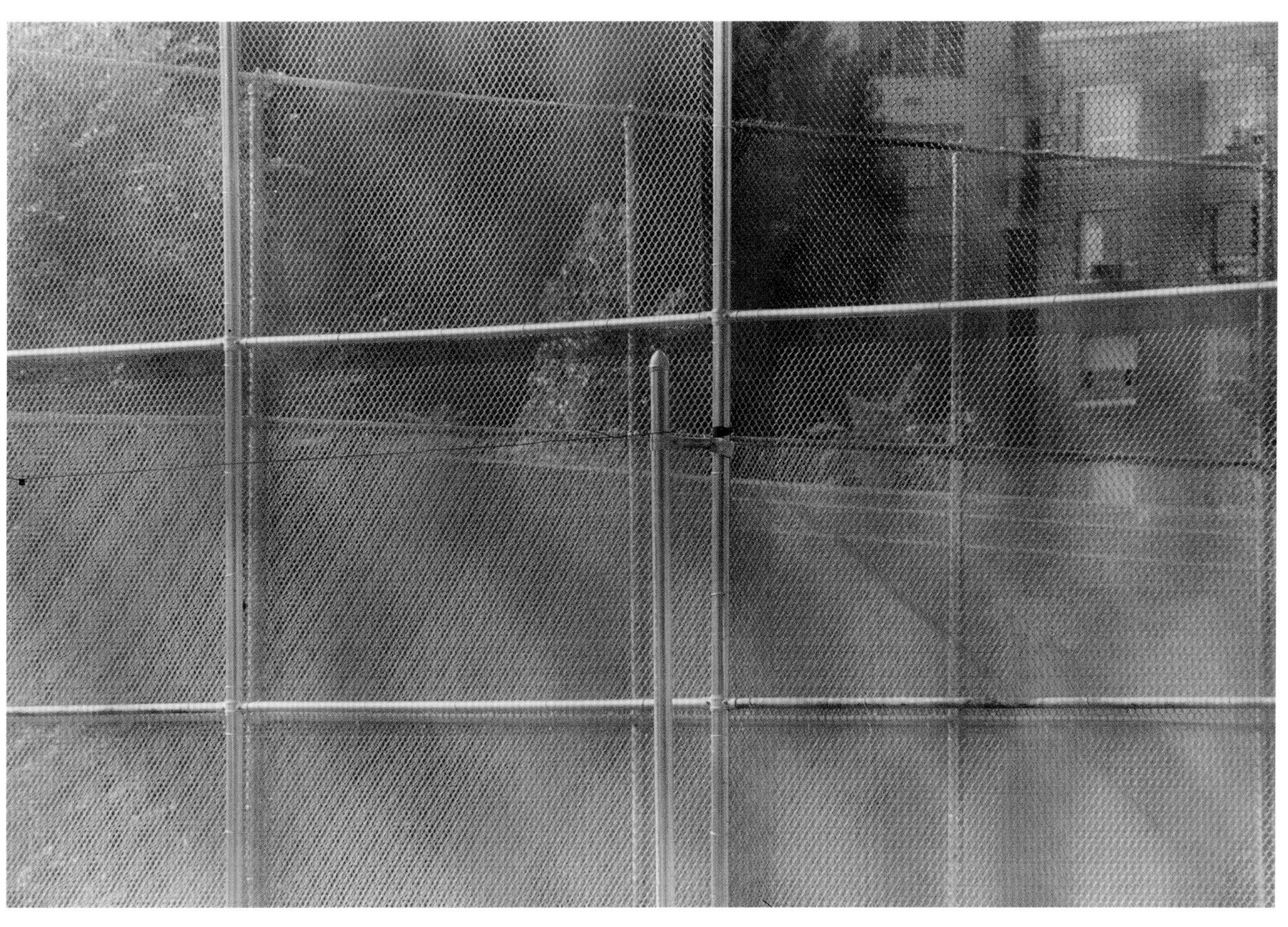

Roy DeCarava
Silver fence, 1983

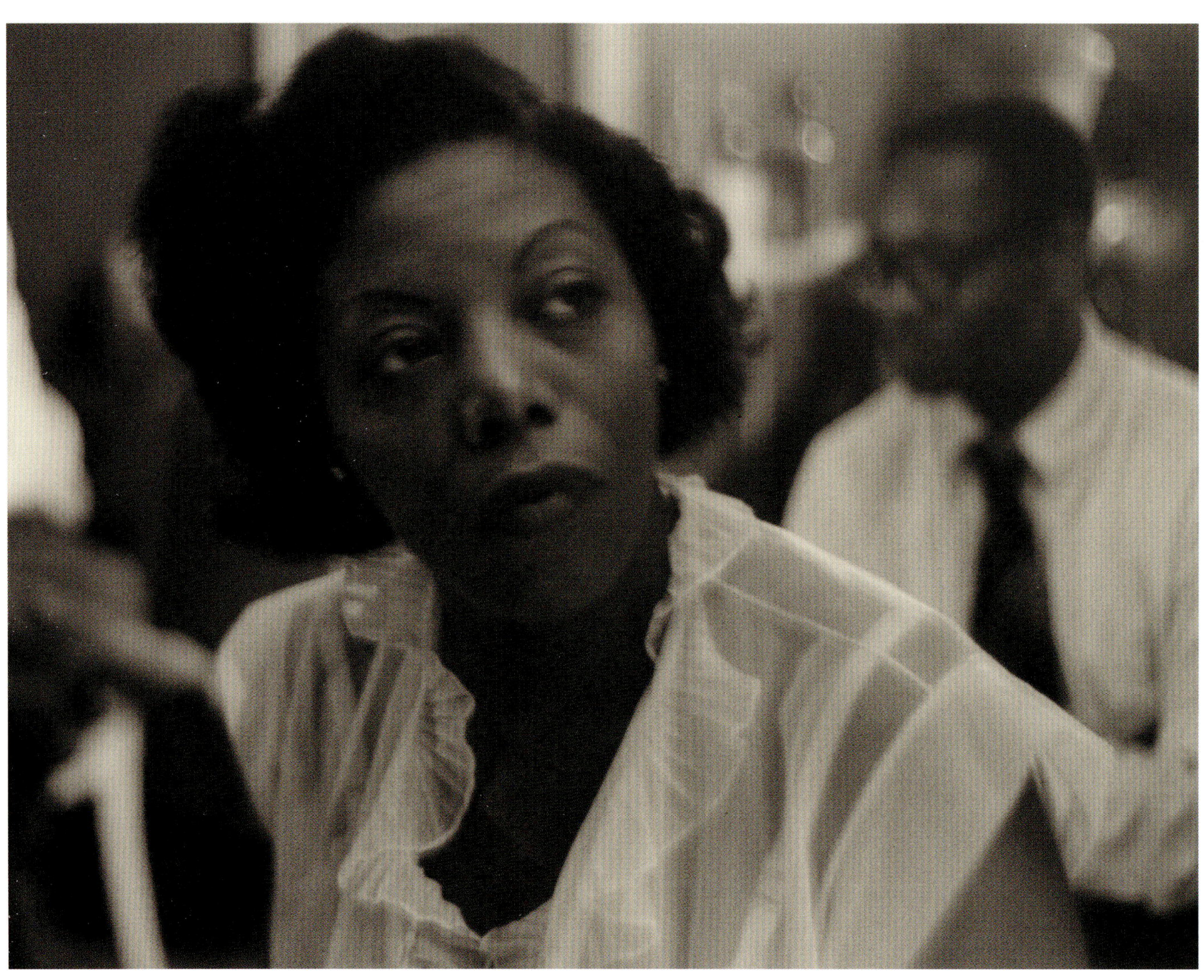

Roy DeCarava
Mary Lou Williams, 1952

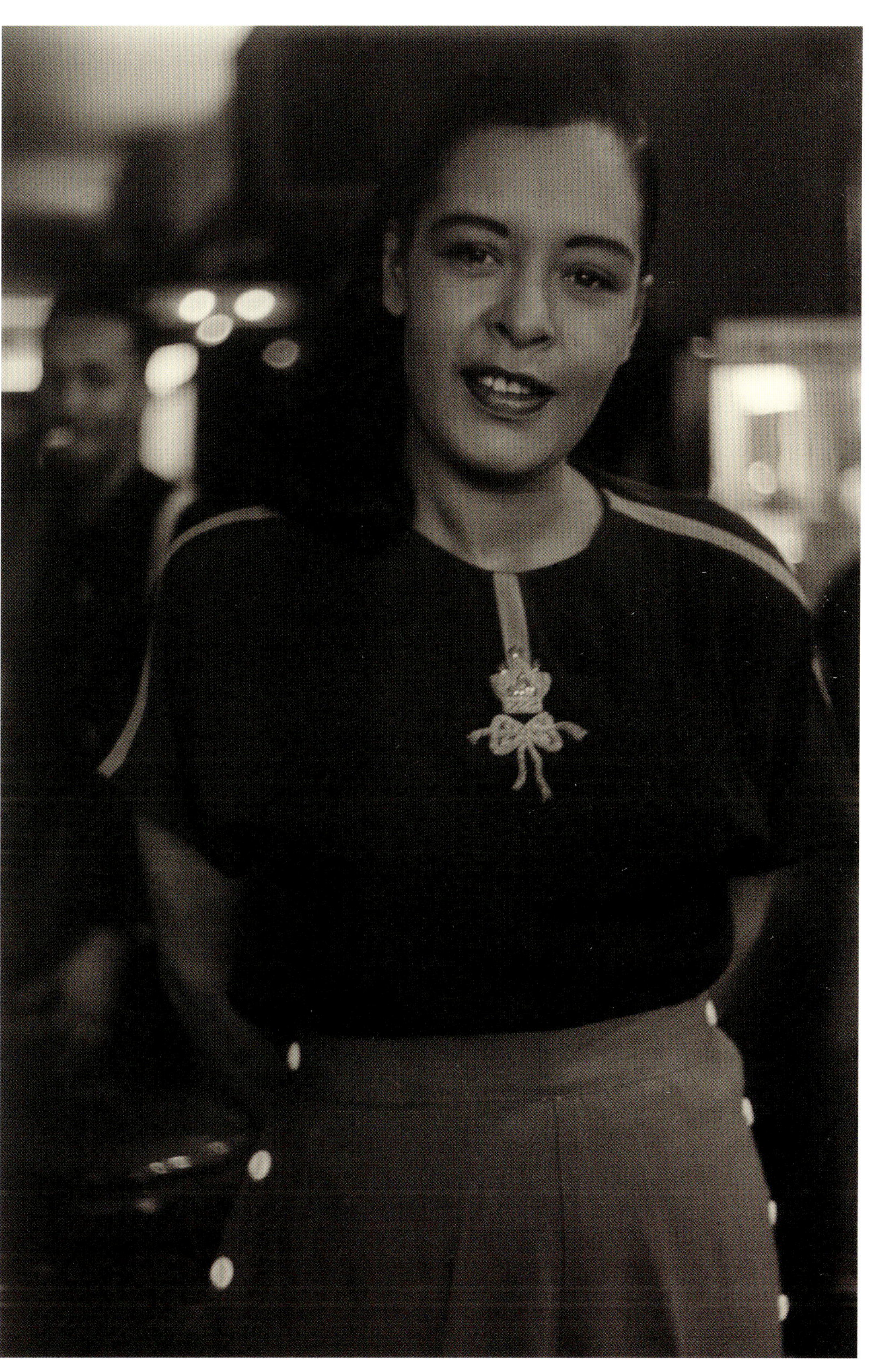

Roy DeCarava
Billie Holiday, 1952

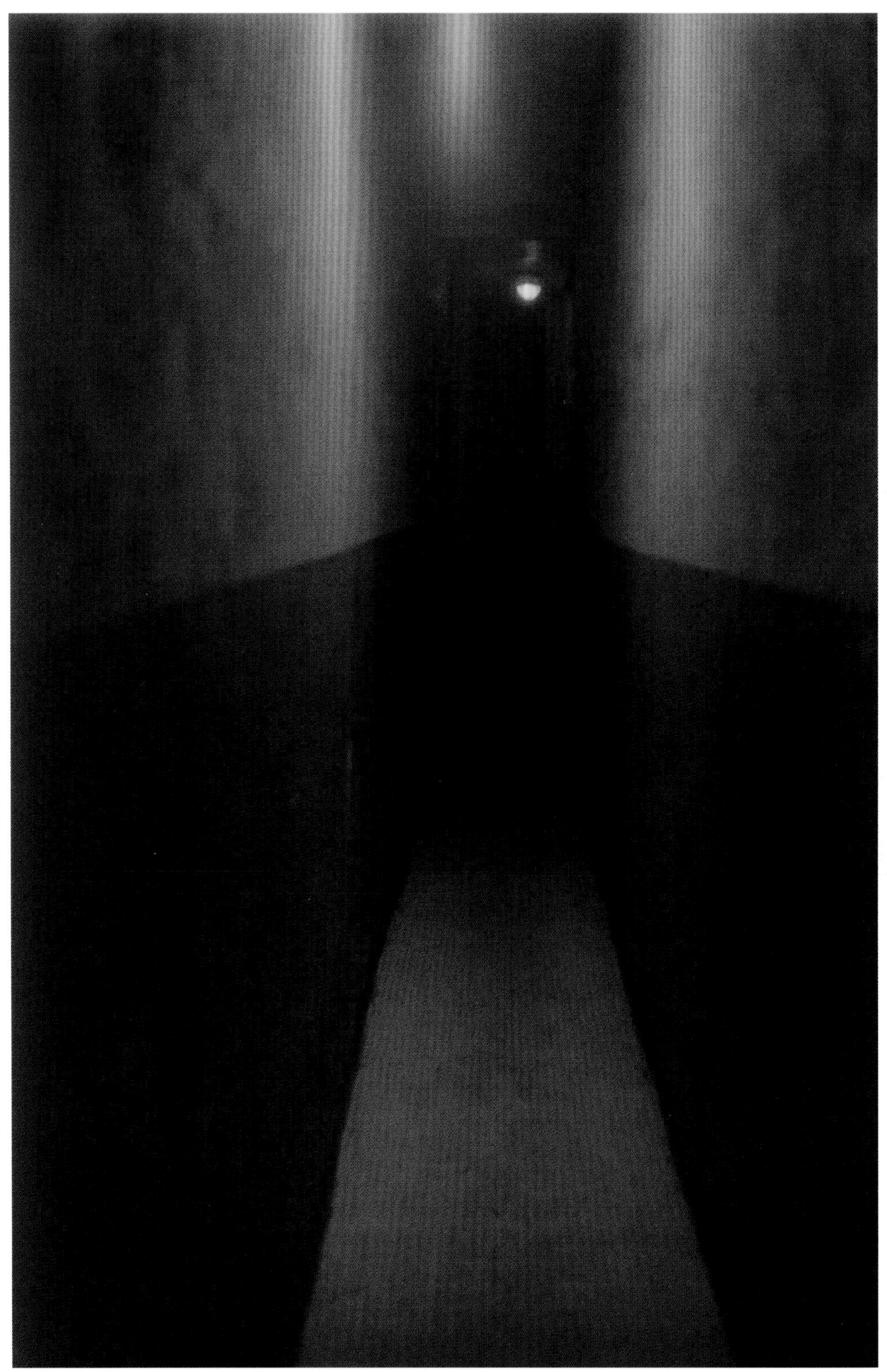

Roy DeCarava
Hallway, New York, 1953

CONTENTS

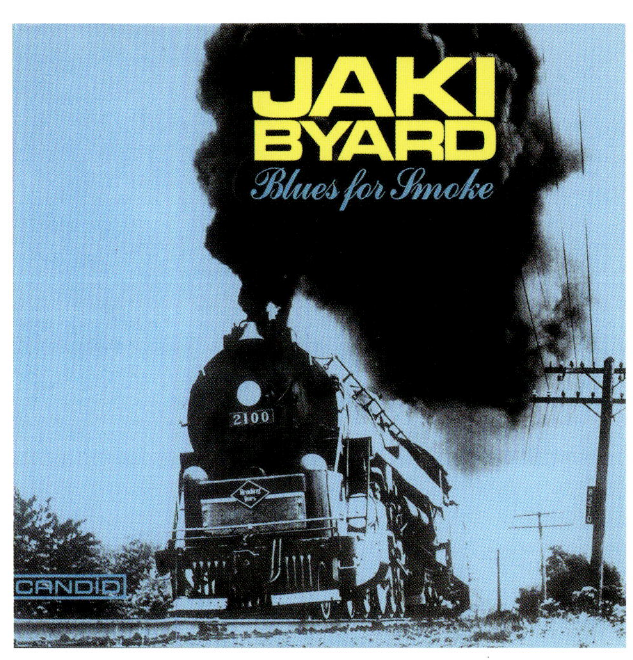

CANDID Printed in West Germany CCD 79018

JAKI BYARD (piano)
BLUES FOR SMOKE

1. **EXCERPTS FROM EUROPEAN EPISODE**
   a) Journey / Hollis Stomp   b) Milan To Lyon
   (Byard) BMI . . . . Time: 5'57
2. **ALUMINUM BABY**
   (Byard) BMI . . . . Time: 4'32
3. **PETE AND THOMAS** (TRIBUTE TO THE TICKLERS)
   (Byard) BMI . . . . Time: 3'41
4. **SPANISH TINGE No. 1**
   (Byard) BMI . . . . Time: 4'12
5. **FLIGHT OF THE FLY**
   (Byard) BMI . . . . Time: 5'44
6. **BLUES FOR SMOKE**
   (Byard) BMI . . . . Time: 4'52
7. **JAKI'S BLUES NEXT**
   (Byard) BMI . . . . Time: 2'07
8. **DIANE'S MELODY**
   (Byard) . . . . Time: 5'05
9. **ONE TWO FIVE**
   (Byard) . . . . Time: 2'40

Front and back covers of Jaki Byard's album *Blues for Smoke* (Candid, 1960)

Jaki Byard: *Blues for Smoke*

Fred Moten

---

excerpts from european episode. the history of the soloist who is not one, opening onto something other than that, the other way that's out from that, aperture's stray horn tested out through a crack in the wall, the narrows between the open mouth of the wall, the decreasing permanence of the wall in open air, up under the gun tower, spilled in pipespace, embalmed, little brother's barrel, her platform, her impossible upper room and rolling stone, the extraminimal syntax of her flesh, the underconceptual presence of her hammond, playing nothing which is where she coming from, taking nothing for her journey now, covering the recovery of her eyes and ears in exhausted standing, outside and below are something more and less than judging, anorchestral jurisdiction, devoted to smoke, which can't be shown,

but you weren't there before it woke you. the history of the form of double life, after hours, hollis stomp apollo stump is an early riser, a fury, locomotive organizing sculpture breaking tools, abusive equipment tore up into vapor, whose monolithic skin has many skins, each worn different than the other and itself, all disorganized in being worn, that cube on the makeshift bandstand, just a circle they made on the floor, a little inside squabble, the sound of love without a terminal, his tinny, tinkling breaking apart that's right on time, strode rode off into off-stride in freddie webster's mystery, the movement that got started in a distillate, quickening they can't shoot out of us, harlan stoop holcomb step, that hole on that hill that's on top of the world,

the particles are still on tour. the history of the slurred voice, no voice without the common slur of owing, underwritten big road in chicago arkansas, discomposed in an open recipe, a breath of string on the edge of aroma, lyonnaise, milanese, the merely culinary expression that moves between them, in the homelessness of that same old place that if you can't love who do you love, when the dissonance is freed and i know why, abandoned every time they say one more time, an encore of alternative fingers, what parlan brings when he comes as something missing, can you feel what you can't hold, to see if you can hear the missive skip as code, decarava's fade, as smoke, for blue, which can be shown.

---

aluminum baby. the relation between loss and discovery is how to think about (how everything is in) it. the child troubles things. his murmurs bury things to uncover them. he makes things prettier than everything. he misunderstands things. he formed an association of things that look like this, moving critical as this stiff flow, this paranalysis, he's aluminum. an autist gives you flowers with a sound on edge to the jitney stand, by the giant eagle, across from ventos. to engineer a brittle sentence in a thick surround, and aluminum, who been mixing shade all day, who they say is a brawler. in kansas city there's a still, out the corner of your eye, on the edge of the other side, a flower with a balm inside, her eyes covered and her ears shut down, thinking how to get across, in theory, like memphis minimal.

pete and thomas (tribute to the ticklers). abelard and tallis had an affair, evidently. they met at a rent party underneath an alley and fell in love. they never went to sleep. they spanned time like they were in buffalo. back to back they played the beast with two fronts. other stuff got held back but not this, which was most tough, too. they had a bad habit of playing patty fingers, riding around in strange habit and carriage as if the old days had old days that harnessed chargers and plowers, all fucked up from having to work together, smuggled around like a rhythm section. i mean, rhythm sections smuggle, generally, as part of their duties. they're domestic in a foreign sense and if you don't believe me ask susie ibarra. this is about love, as you know. what they don't forbid they overlook, which is worse, as i'm sure you know. but one never knows, do one. all you can do is take care of the one, who keeps your time good, fold him in a basin of marble, fluted water, hope some letters survive.

spanish tinge no. 1. it's all about speed, now, for the marronage. iberian note blacking on the loosaphone. when ferdinand started thinking on expansion, wondering where the surplus would come from, wondering what the surplus was, wary as all his cups began to fade, the theory of itinerant note blacking and line worrying is celebrating a thousand years, bursting from the writing of its practice like a star. it was already there as something else from someplace else always. when it arrives, as the difference you always move to be, from someplace else always you never been, welcome it like a tight chemise dropped in a boarding house on amsterdam. the venereal nation under our feet only has kings for a day. the spanish quarter, the latin quarter, the french quarter, the mill quarters, and the barrack yards. a buried city we touch sometimes and gone.

flight of the fly. the servants of the hardest time are the next spring. this is my sky song. the books in my cell are a jackson in your house. see how idle chat gathers around things, that wood 22 is chopping, his axe? miss thing chats fragile kit shake. the social life of things beside themselves, laughing through alan lomax. a lot of times, just sitting around, people be talking about the work it comes from. a lot of times people be sitting around talking about how some people think it only comes from sitting around. mosquito fucked that all up just by turning up the music by the river. she turned it up so loud that she could hear all that endlessly beginning segue in c. she wrote it so the count-off comes back in eastern man alone as evil nigger, rough-hewn, mean. the shit is deep, that open joint, that mill. parchman's general intellect is a blues for charles tyler and julius eastman. basically, gayl jones is the countess of the blues.

blues for smoke. and the velocity of waiting, which is right next to the philosophy of waiting, most famously articulated in a blues called why we can't wait. the ensemble of particulate articulation—between black and flew, razing and cantwaite, all the way to court and spark and flynt—is still on fire. it's a slow train you can look at from along the track to see every car pulse. when repetition is uncoordinated, off abstraction. the sentence has a degenerative condition, a developmental disorder. it associates with loneliness for the multiple. sometimes they grow and sometimes they just curl, then fade, till the next episode. her ashes are in anything folded over us in the cold. for the exhausted to return, oh for the new thing to come, come on with me while we make another run.

jaki's blues next. just calling, just lining out while they sell that flour. here come presence out of nowhere. the social hum of movement is the essence of it, "because that is Black Power, that is one of the elements, a sitting down together to reason, to 'ground' as the Brothers say. we have to 'ground together,'" in a gully, in a dungle, in the jungle, on an oil drum, till the furniture move. the history of the undergrounding is our orchard hill, our clyde woods, our way of shearing, the sound of residue in spacing, like a bare living room in the morning air. when he's ready to get up and do his thing, when he wants to get into it, man, it's paramilitary theory. the good foot is a blues march. the screamers are lost in thought, to prepare the song they pare, like a next machine, man. marshall allen is so close you can hear his people drumming we are nowhere, here, we are elsewhere, moving, doing it, you know, to escape the bell, down slow, sounding, diving, tell her the shape i'm in.

diane's melody. air for daughter number two is lovingly submitted as an intersection of rainbows. somebody was talking about a yellow cymbal, the way a teacher might hold your hand, holding your face between my hands and we name the colors we hear. the club must have been a haven for a family man, providing in the heavy air. back off in the woods was full with the love of children, the terror of blues for children. how many generations in that room above the club? how many stories whispered in the groove of storyville? all them little babies wrapped up in the corner. the relation between next (episode, breath, string, world) and our long night's festival is blue, the sound we make so we can see, that broken chroma at the end, daddy, play my song again.

one two five. jaki byard was a sociologist. he was concerned with the "evident incalculability in human action." if a pattern were to emerge it would only be in re-fits and re-starts, "the sudden rise at a given tune" that keeps withdrawing. his hesitation was a singularity that became our engine. our engine was that continual propulsive chant that can't be said alone. the history of the ones who go off by themselves to make us say it. make me say it again. make me say it again, girl. see, this slight dehiscence is what i mean. it's got to go there, to the interlocking questions of all and need, so we can hold our preferential option. the broken logic of our line and run keeps that in reserve for us, if we want it, but it's hard to want, it's so violent and beautiful.

Notes

jaki's blues next: Walter A. Rodney, *The Groundings with My Brothers* (London: Bogle-L'Ouverture Publications, 1969; reprint, Chicago: Research Associate School Times, 2001), 63–64.

one two five: W. E. B. DuBois, "Sociology Hesitant," *Boundary 2: An International Journal of Literature and Culture* 27, no. 3 (Fall 2000): 41, 44.

This Air

Bennett Simpson

Praise then the interruption of our composure, the image that comes to fit
we cannot account for, the juncture in the music that appears discordant.
—Robert Duncan, *Bending the Bow*, 1968

The blues-oriented observer (the *trained* critic) necessarily "heats up" the
observational space by his or her very presence.
—Houston A. Baker, *Blues, Ideology, and Afro-American Literature*, 1984

I.

The blues I want is for the future. Or it's about now, the smoke in this air. The
future I want has the blues in its air. Has the blues not as smoke, but clear. This
exhibition anticipates a time when the blues is seen better, when the invention and experiment of African American cultural traditions are not thought to
linger or to languish on the side lots of what is modern, at the fringes of the
perceived avant-garde, in the side-ways of critical discourse, removed from the
center (because if one looks around, such an impression could be had), but are
valued *as* central, exemplary, and real to experience. This may be the messianic
inflection of that most significant blues figure, the crossroads: the transition or
juncture that must be met, to move.

> (Culture makes smoke, makes unclear what is seen.
> Culture makes the center. But art makes culture otherwise and
> clarifies the air.)

"Blues for Smoke" is not about the past—though the blues has the past all in
it. The presence of the past in the blues in this show serves to offset the current
moment: to frame and to mobilize, to create differential space. Actually, I am
not entirely interested in the past of the blues. I mean, I'm not entirely invested
in telling a story of the blues as it has existed. This is not revival. There was no
death. There are other stories that need telling, that can be more useful (we
need stories we can use to keep us engaged, unless, of course, we like how
things are)—stories that bring a knowledge to the present. That, for instance,
can admit and reflect the continual displacement of race and sex and identity
and affect (that grammar of the blues) from the art of this time. Stories about
stories that were not told or heard, or were thought to be one thing, but weren't.

I turned to the blues—and to these artworks that invoke it—because many of
the contexts and meanings it grants us access to remain unsettled. Because

the blues is unsettling. What could this turn permit us to think about? *Because that thinking feels necessary today.* Though it may go unspoken in the happy grind of the popular imagination, is not the blues a territory burdened with ambiguous subjects (does it not also unburden these subjects)? First among them: subjects of the social (in blues structure, does not the social precede and produce the subject?). These might start with the collision and hesitant assimilation of African American culture in this country, but could, if we let them, illuminate other collisions and other identities. (Isn't a kind of queering implicit in the blues? Isn't the blues also always sexual?) To speak about these subjects is to acknowledge discourses oriented to expression—whether autobiographical or collective—despite "our" "postmodern" "uneasiness" with authorship, the lyrical, and voice. To deal with the blues is to come in close to affect, to come in near one's feelings and those of others, sometimes embarrassingly close, "to allow suffering to speak," Cornell West says, turning Theodor Adorno, "as a condition of truth."[1] This affect may be stated: my baby left me. Nothing feels right. Or it may be intuited, attenuated, projected through form. (Isn't so much of what the blues makes one feel conveyed as form: repetition that gets you out, gets you on. A break or a massing—congestion—that brings you up. The "abstract truth" of the blues is the opposite of pictures.) In the blues, do we not find an idea of formal experiment that is both tethered to and defiant of an experience of limitation? Such that innovation entangles with endurance and basic responses to life encompass or enable improvisation? I do not step into the space of these questions with a desire to chart a history or to lend definition to an established aesthetic. The blues is too many things for that. Rather, I move toward the blues with a hope of opening certain areas of art (an art that might respond to our care for it) to a tension that seems productive—and, as tension, seems true.

I need to make a distinction about my use of the term "the blues" in this text. Rarely does it signify, in any exclusive sense, the specific forms of music commonly referred to as "blues music." When music is implied (as opposed to a broader blues ethos or sensibility), I tend to mean a kind of tradition, something akin to the "Great Black Music" idea that the Art Ensemble of Chicago began to circulate at the end of the 1960s. As slogan and as worldview, Great Black Music (with or without its modifier "Ancient to the Future") developed out of an avant-garde jazz context that embraced "roots" and "experiment" as twin ciphers of a critical imagination. It proposed an embrace of African American music, its genres and motivations, that situated individual examples within a continuum, what Horace Tapscott might have called "the dark tree," some foundation or trunk of which can be seen in the blues and gospel, with branches outward in jazz, R&B, reggae and dub, funk, hip-hop, and rock. Refusing to discriminate between what, in effect, were music industry rubrics rather than reflections of musical practice or popular taste, the Art Ensemble's broad inclusion of African American invention exploded canons both musical and social. Though in age and style he predates that group by a generation, the virtuoso pianist Jaki Byard, in his own way, was as bold a student of Great Black Music

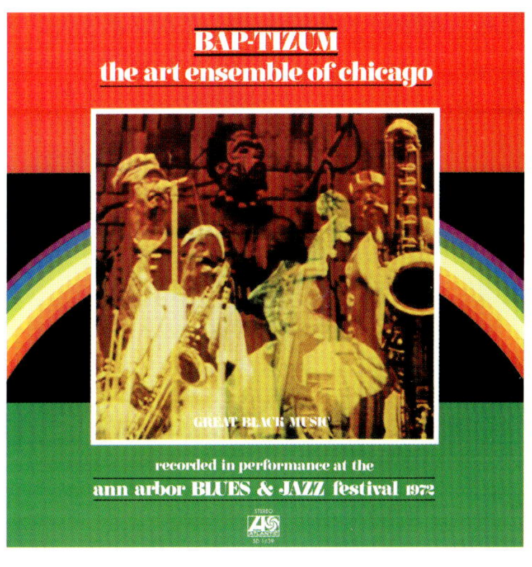

Cover of the Art Ensemble of Chicago's album *Bap-Tizum* (Atlantic, 1973)

as anyone. His debut solo recording *Blues for Smoke* (1960), after which this exhibition is named, was a poignant and playful example of the transgenre experimentation with blues form that had been a part of jazz since the early years of Louis Armstrong and Duke Ellington. Reverent of the music's origins in ragtime, blues, and boogie-woogie, Byard was equally propelled by approaches to composition and improvisation that would become characteristic of the 1960s "free jazz" revolution. In his joyful and restless push against boundaries, "postmodern" before the fact, he is as much the blues to me as are Lightnin' Hopkins, Big Mama Thornton, James Brown, Funkadelic, and the Bad Brains. While all examples are specific, Byard's shows us, as George E. Lewis once wrote about Wadada Leo Smith, "just how richly variegated … a blues aesthetic can be when it is released from any limits imposed from without."[2]

With Byard in mind, "Blues for Smoke" presents an uncommon heterogeneity of subject matter, art historical contexts, formal and conceptual inclinations, genres, and disciplines. It holds artists and art worlds together that are often kept apart, within and across lines of race and generation. It resists telling a single story based on the assumed self-evidence of a category or culture, but maintains the urgency for a "multiple-meter" of ostensibly divergent stories.[3] And yet, if its mix is particular, hedging toward a "weird music" in its own right,[4] it is not random, nor simply indulgent or melancholy (a mood). Rather, it is animated by an idea, articulated most importantly by literary historian Houston A. Baker in *Blues, Ideology, and Afro-American Literature: A Vernacular Theory* (1984), but present in much of the great blues literature of the 1960s and 70s, from Amiri Baraka's (writing as LeRoi Jones) *Blues People: Negro Music in White America* (1963) to Albert Murray's *Stomping the Blues* (1976), that to properly apprehend the blues is to view it as a "matrix" or amalgam of forms, sensibilities, and artistic and cultural phenomena. For these critics, the blues figures as a characteristic idiom and ethos of African Americans in the twentieth century, simultaneously reflecting and transcending the realities and institutions of a postslavery, preequality nation. As Baker has it:

> The blues are a synthesis (albeit one always synthesizing rather than one already hypostatized). Combining work songs, group seculars, field hollers, sacred harmonies, proverbial wisdom, folk philosophy, political commentary, ribald humor, elegiac lament, and much more, they constitute an amalgam that seems always to have been in motion in America—always becoming, shaping, transforming, displacing the peculiar experiences of Africans in the New World.[5]

This view departs from a sense of the blues as simply a genre or style of music— most reductively, the "country" blues of the 1920s–40s, or the Chicago sound of the 1950s–60s. While it seems pointless to deny the importance of *these* blues, given their wellspring of innovation and efflorescence of national and individual psyche (which clearly have lasting appeal),[6] the accompanying temptation to locate the blues within established historical and geocultural coordinates ("back

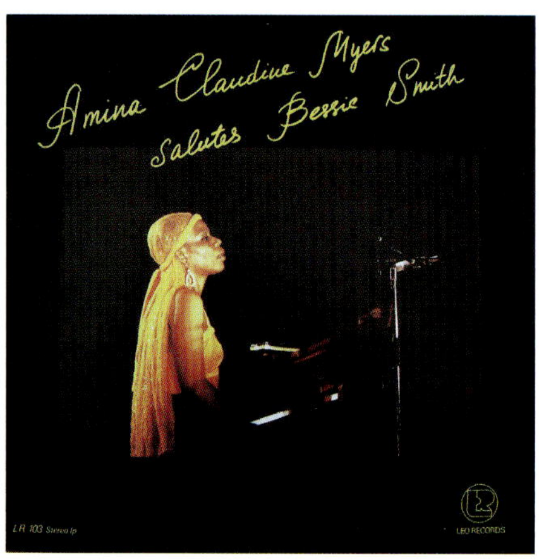

Cover of Amina Claudine Myers's album
Amina Claudine Myers Salutes Bessie Smith (**Leo, 1980**)

there" or "down there") often isolates its potential within revival, fantasy, and nostalgia. What is crucial to parse in Baker's sentences is not that the blues *is* work songs, group seculars, etc. (which, indeed, can be codified and placed), but that it *does* to them. The blues is a sensibility or stance shaping culture. The "always" present participle of synthesizing, combining, becoming, and displacing recalls the "form of diversion" Murray identified as "the nature and function" of the blues.[7] And it is what Lewis implies when he writes elsewhere in this book: "criticality is what the blues is all about."[8]

In his 1989 exhibition "The Blues Aesthetic: Black Culture and Modernism," art historian Richard J. Powell argued that the familiar vernacular of the blues— what he called "basic, twentieth century Afro-American culture"—could be seen as either representation or inspiration in the work of a wide range of African American artists.[9] "Beyond its obvious impact on other Afro-American musical forms (i.e., jazz, gospel, rhythm and blues, etc.), the blues provides much contemporary literature, theater, dance, and visual arts with the necessary elements for defining these various art forms as intrinsically 'Afro-American.'"[10] Powell's concern for describing "intrinsic" characteristics of black culture and aesthetics extended certain tendencies that had been active throughout the twentieth century, but were increasingly urgent after the mid-1960s, most notably in the ideologies of the Black Arts Movement, to claim and define an autonomous, authentic space and history for African American culture. In situating the work of black artists squarely within a holistic notion of that culture, one in which the blues figures as presiding ethos or spirit, Powell followed writers like Baraka and Baker in a process of recovery, validation, and expansion that applied not just to artists, but to imagination and memory in the largest sense.

While certain territories approached by Powell's "blues aesthetics" are also relevant to the artworks included here—musical images and motifs, a cultural and formal liberation born of dissent, questions of the subject or identity, models of performativity—the parameters and goals of the present exhibition diverge significantly. For starters, intrinsicality and African American cultural unification are not my objects. To be sure, naming the blues as a lens onto contemporary art asserts the authority of African American traditions within a discursive and historical field where these have often been denied. Yet, despite the identitarian claims made on the blues at different times, some major aspect of its power, as I take it, extends from the ambiguity to which it submits terms of feeling and self. In its breaks, cuts, jumps, riffs, runs, slurs, and asides, its proliferation of interrupting signifiers, the blues creates a space of waves and residual movement, demanding and containing multiplicity. Alternately, it saturates and coats, so that when blues objects touch other objects these also turn blue—a rubbing-off—until before long the pure products are the crazy ones, holding on to fictions. No doubt, the blues comes from black culture, carries it on and out. But in its examples other cultures and contexts also reflect. These lessons are, need to be, a larger part of the knowledge art seeks, both in the addresses it makes to its histories and in its construction, theoretical and actual, of a more equal present.

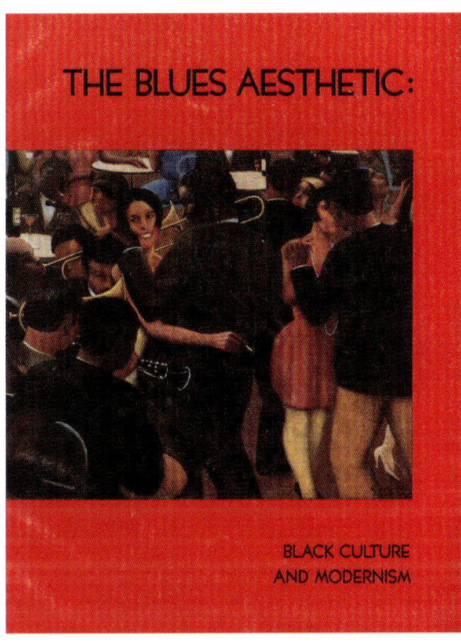

Cover of Richard J. Powell's exhibition catalogue *The Blues Aesthetic: Black Culture and Modernism* (Washington, D.C.: Washington Project for the Arts, 1989)

Problems Today

When I began to conceive of this exhibition in 2006, I did so with a feeling, alternately vague and pointed, that some conversation in art was not happening or could no longer be placed. To name this placeless conversation "identity" would be true, and it would be misleading at the same time. For it was as much the interruption and disavowal of identity, as any positive attribution or negotiation, that suddenly seemed at stake. Even before America elected its first black president, many people spoke of our "postidentity" moment, in which older categorizations of race, sex, and gender were no longer supposed to matter. This could be rejected as wishful thinking (and actual repression) when it came from politicians or the media, but it was also obvious that many artists no longer had much use for the "cheering fictions" of representation and uplift held dear by previous generations.[11] This was a time in which curator Thelma Golden could joke that "post-black was the new black."[12] In which queer artists and critics were embracing collectivity, affect, and dissonance, not instead of but *as* politics. On Facebook and YouTube, new paradigms of the distributed self were looming and spreading. Destabilizing performance, hide-and-seek persona, and ambivalent, ambiguous forms were the order of the day.

Two of the most prominent names in the art imagination of the 2000s, for instance, David Hammons and Martin Kippenberger, had careers that stretched back decades but were increasingly, spectacularly present. From some perspective, this visibility could be construed as ironic, given the dizzying and deeply provocative double movement of identity deferral and objectification that marks each artist's work. We see this in sculptures like Hammons's *Rocky* (1990), an impassive, diminutive "stone head" adorned with barbershop clippings of real, kinky black hair, or Kippenberger's portrait of self-deprecation *Martin, ab in die Ecke und schäm dich* (Martin, Into the Corner, You Should Be Ashamed of Yourself, 1992). These works make a display of themselves, performing and mediating subjectivity as hypervisible and socially loaded. Hammons's head, poised on its cast-iron stand, could be the representation of a black Everyman, generalized and racially profiled. Or it could be an emblem of endurance, "hard-headed" witness to Fred Moten's observation that "the history of blackness is testament to the fact that objects can and do resist."[13] Similarly, the Kippenberger could be a simple joke—a parody of discipline offered to the many critics who (once anyway) claimed he had gone too far. Or it could be a figure of real shame, an alienated symptom of the mobility and publicness of the artist's legendary persona.

In some sense, the outsized visibility of Hammons and Kippenberger was symptomatic of the time. Everywhere one looked, artists were spazzing, burrowing, leaking, and fading, in and out of view before our gaze. There were cults of "nonproduction," overproduction, and refusal (Josef Strau, Merlin Carpenter, Bernadette Corporation, Tino Sehgal); submersions into network relations and archives (R. H. Quaytman, Seth Price, Leslie Hewitt); struggles with social

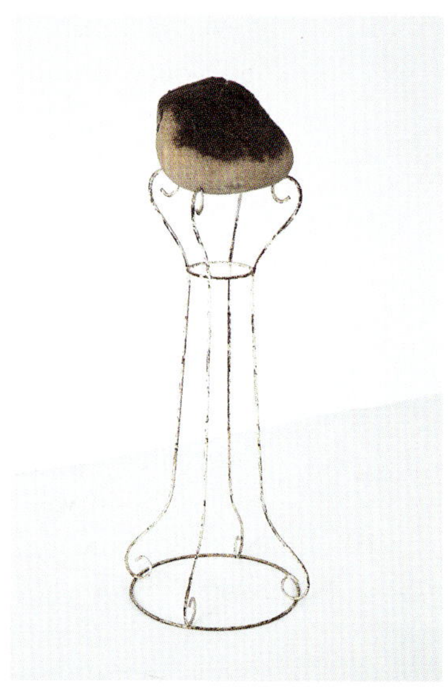

David Hammons
Rocky, **1990**

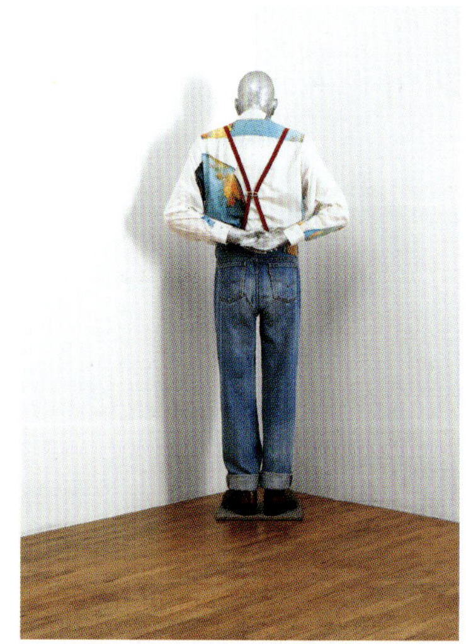

Martin Kippenberger
Martin, ab in die Ecke und schäm dich
**(Martin, Into the Corner, You Should Be
Ashamed of Yourself), 1992**

visibility and utility (Dave McKenzie, Andrea Fraser); a vogue for artists who had opted out of or circumvented conventional career formations (Cady Noland, Hammons); a hunger for work that had been overlooked, lost in history, or not yet translated (William Leavitt, Lorraine O'Grady, Jack Whitten, Maria Lassnig); and a full-blown celebration of ephemeral performance (Marina Abramović, Lady Gaga, Performa).[14] As both anxiety and affirmation, this fitful landscape suggested the extent to which the institutions of art—from its markets to its museums and media—increasingly registered the currency and meaning of artistic subjects as social, professional, and financial.[15] If, as Fraser claimed, artists have "become the poster girls, and boys, for the joys of insecurity, flexibility, deferred economic rewards [and] social alienation," for the most part her skepticism was rare.[16] The elevation of subjectivity to a possibly (though in reality likely not) lucrative career choice reflected a universalizing of exchange value over and above all else.

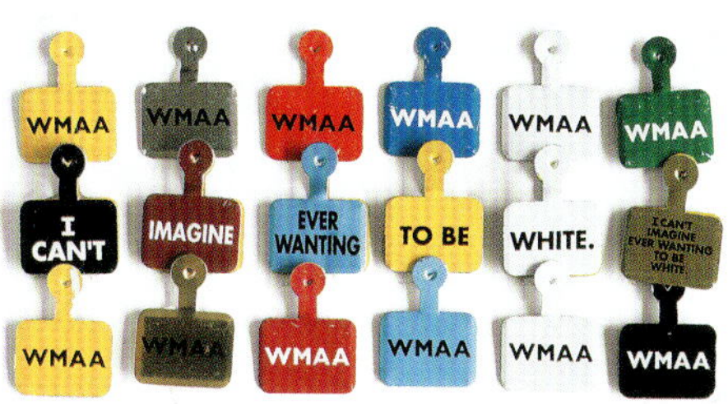

Daniel Joseph Martinez, *I Can't Imagine Ever Wanting to Be White*, 1993

It also contributed to the already active displacing of the conflict and particularity of the "identity politics" debates of the 1980s and 90s. Certainly, by the beginning of the millennium, multiculturalism's emphases on social and cultural retribution, critical and art historical inclusion, canon revision, and celebrations of pride and heritage no longer expressed the kinds of polemical fire as they had, say, in 1993, when visitors to that year's Whitney Biennial received Daniel Joseph Martinez's headline-grabbing admission pins announcing "I Can't Imagine Ever Wanting to Be White." Similarly, the notion of the self as historically and discursively situated, performed, and contested, a hallmark of 1980s and 90s American feminism, postcolonialism, and queer and critical race theory, appeared to abruptly cede the stage to the collective social subject of the "multitude" that animated the effectively European discourse of globalization and Empire.[17]

Within this period of discursive flux, the afterlife of identity politics found pointed expression in the emergence of post-black, an artistic sensibility and set of motivating concerns announced by Golden in her 2001 exhibition "Freestyle" at the Studio Museum in Harlem. As she put it then, "post-black artists are adamant about not being labeled 'black' artists, though their work [is] steeped, in fact deeply interested, in redefining complex notions of blackness."[18] On one level, post-black acknowledged a younger generation's desire for works of art to be viewed free of what the writer Nathaniel Mackey has called "assumptions of representationality."[19] That is, free from a racially or biographically deterministic horizon of interpretation—even when a given work made explicit reference to race, culture, or other facets of identity.[20] On another level, with its rejection of an "on message" content-orientation, the formulation suggested a perception that an older expectation internal to definitions of black art had become a kind of burden. "We must confront the neo-traditionalism that has taken hold of late," Mackey wrote in 1993, as if in anticipation, "with a counter-tradition of marronage, divergence, flight, fugitive tilt."[21] Needless to say, the arrival of post-black, assumed by some to announce an end to politics, was itself highly divisive. A younger generation's complexity was an older generation's giving

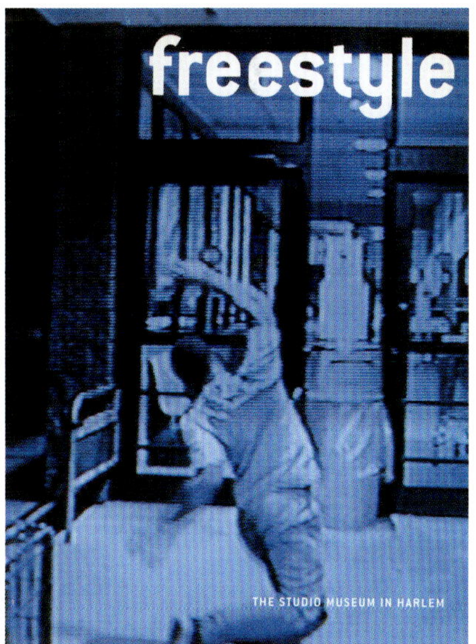

Cover of Thelma Golden's exhibition catalogue *Freestyle* (New York: The Studio Museum in Harlem, 2001)

up the fight. Newfound mobility clashed with hard-fought responsibility. That such discord came in a moment of economic expansion in art, which brought increased opportunities for artists of color in a globalizing marketplace, only hastened apprehensions of selling out and trading in. The flush times also made it easy to deny any problem at all.

We might propose a stronger reading for the politics of post-black, however, not merely as a symptom of conflict between generations or as some evidence of a trend toward universalized subjectivity, but as an extension of the critical distinguishing and self-reflection that characterized the best instances of the identity politics legacy. In decoupling black artists from a construction of intrinsic blackness and identifying a divergence from or contrast with normative representations of "what black artists do," whether externally or internally construed, post-black opens the door to acknowledging the rupture and injunction that have accompanied previous moments in the history of art made by African Americans.[22] Recalling the unstable ontologies parodied by William Pope.L's *Skin Set Drawings* (2001–5), post-black asks us to see the racializing of aesthetic judgment as contingent, if not somehow surreal. But, it also implies that *any art* might be seen as a territory of inclusion and exclusion. Some definition of Abstract Expressionism, for instance, upheld a purity that in both theory and practice excluded women and artists of color (despite the innovative work of artists such as Edward Clark, Alma Thomas, and Joan Mitchell). Minimalism could build a philosophy of energized participatory experience based on serial form and industrial material, but could essentially ignore the deep connection of repetition and labor implicit in the history of African American music.[23] The white critic Rosalind Krauss could opine, in Adrian Piper's words, that if any "non-formalist, ethnically diverse art … didn't generate sufficient energy to 'bring itself to one's attention,' then it probably didn't exist."[24] Such "aversions of the gaze," as Moten via Piper calls them, fundamentally shape the history of twentieth-century art: moments when power, whether white or male or straight, chooses not to acknowledge the visibility of other forms and subjects by looking away, but in so doing reveals itself to be socially visible.[25]

II.

"Blues for Smoke" proposes that art has always *othered*, made manifest, what is meant by the blues. Rather than charting these displacements as an evolution, however, the exhibition proceeds topographically, producing an array of forms and contexts in which the potential of an idiom opens onto the contemporary. Many of the works included here prompt a need for analyses capable of viewing formal and cultural experimentation within and against each other. In his ever trenchant study *Discrepant Engagement: Dissonance, Cross-Culturality, and Experimental Writing* (1993), Mackey observes that this need becomes especially great in relation to art made by African Americans, in whose work formal and aesthetic concerns have often been perceived as secondary to the legibility of cultural content:

> That black writers have been experimentally engaged with the medium, addressing issues of form as well as issues of content, tends to be ignored. The ability to influence the course of the medium, to *move* the medium, entails an order of animacy granted only to whites when it comes to writing. The situation with regard to music is a bit better, black musicians having been acknowledged to be innovators, even though their white imitators enjoy commercial success and critical acclaim greatly disproportionate to their musical contributions. The non-recognition of black artistic othering is symptomatic of the social othering to which black people are subjected, particularly in light of the celebration accorded artistic othering practiced by whites.[26]

Within the groupings of artists and individual works that structure this show, form, subject matter, history, and cultural position intersect in ways I hope will encourage a broader and more imaginative reception. If these groupings appear heterodox, they mean to interrupt and fly—to approach an expanded idea of what the experimental and cultural might entail. I recognize that the exhibition leaves itself open to the criticism that it has ignored familiar and beloved aspects of the blues for examples or contrasts that may strike some viewers as tendentious. I accept that its bent notes, unfamiliar juxtapositions, and historical blurs might be considered an exercise in the subjective. But I also hope that its divergences can be interpreted, as Baker writes about his own work, "not as a sign of myopic exclusiveness, but as an invitation to inventive play."[27] I am not naïve to the flare of cultural ownership—of who gets "to play" with what—but if we consider how rarely curators and critics engage across lines of race or how deeply separated this hesitation has kept discourses and histories, we may also begin to respect transgression rather than fear it.[28]

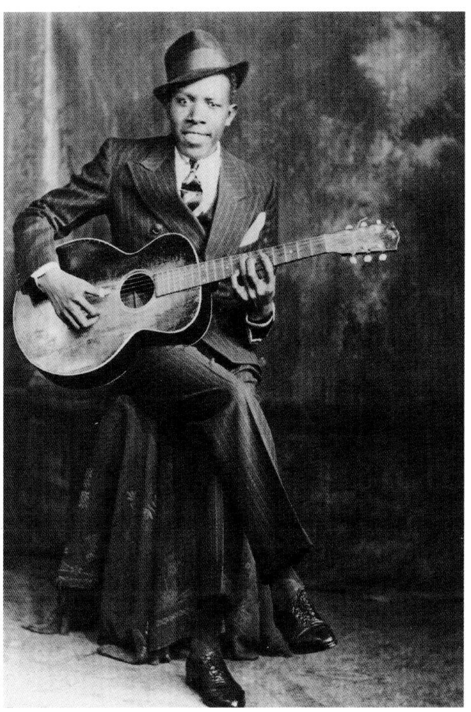

Studio portrait of Robert Johnson, Hooks Brothers, Memphis, c. 1935

Crossroads

In blues mythology, no figure of place is more prominent than "the crossroads." One can go to Mississippi, drive down the lonesome lanes—despite (or because of) the tourists, they are always lonesome—and find no fewer than three intersections claiming provenance to Robert Johnson's midnight barter with the Devil. The crossroads, which may also be a train junction, a clearing between farms, or really anywhere worlds and times collide, is indelibly coded as a site of transformation: the place one waits for the future to come, the place one watches it pass by, the place one leaves from or winds up. The existential and historical valence of the metaphor can be grasped in Jean-Michel Basquiat's epic, five-panel masterpiece *Undiscovered Genius of the Mississippi Delta*

(1983), a painting in which the artist's signature style of fragmented expressionism and bop-jive scrawl submits the fetish for blues discovery to a caustic archeological signifying. Presented as a kind of timeline or deep history—ironic, in itself, given its title—the work takes as its point of departure an unnamed Delta "genius," depicted at far left in the possibly Johnsonesque visage labeled, pseudo-scientifically, "Fig. 23." Moving back in time as it moves right, through a visual and taxonomic landscape ("THE DEEP SOUTH 1912–1936–1951©") scattered with agricultural motifs, overseeing white men ("Mark Twain"), and references to prices and crops (cotton and human), the narrative culminates, or begins, depending on how one thinks of it, with the word "NEGROES" scratched three times in red oil stick—as if blackness, both genius and genus, were the "undiscovery" discovered by the work.

A crossroads liminality informs many of the places depicted by artists in this exhibition. William Eggleston's pioneering color photographs of the 1970s and 80s, taken around his native Memphis, Tennessee, or in nearby Mississippi show a world caught between its rural past, where plantations sink into the earth and kudzu smothers wasted trees, and a melancholy and strangely creeping contemporary life. Romare Bearden's allegorical collages ricochet from scenes of Southern waiting and watching to jazz-sped visions of Harlem, or in *Uptown Looking Downtown* (1965), between idealized bohemian coordinates, whereas Kippenberger's *New York von der Bronx ausgesehen* (New York Seen from the Bronx, 1985) is characteristically mordant about the prospect of looking across boundaries. His view of a Manhattan skyscraper, rendered as a cast-metal desk organizer perched atop a tall plinth, puns on a foreigner's mis-association: bronze for Bronx. *Garden of Music* (1960), a seminal painting by Bob Thompson, pictures an otherworldly, Eden-like landscape populated or somehow prophesied by a group of jazz musicians. Historians have identified Thompson's figures as the ensemble led by Ornette Coleman, which at the time of the painting was ushering music toward a freedom, a "New Thing," that would fundamentally alter its horizons.[29] Marked by strange colors (exaggerating the diversity of an apparently multiracial audience surrounding the group) and an expressionism that is equally haunting and sweet, the work beatifies music as a bridge or conduit to transcendence.

"Traditionally," Albert Murray writes, "the highest praise given a blues musician has been the declaration that he can make a dance hall rock and roll like a downhome church during revival time. But then many of the elements of blues music seem to have been derived from the downhome church in the first place."[30] In *From Asterisks in Dockery* (2012), a room-scale installation made especially for this exhibition, Rodney McMillian constructs a "downhome church" replete with pews, altar, pulpit, and choir. The ambiguous title suggests a modification or footnote to one of the sacred homes of blues mythology: the Delta plantation Dockery Farms, often cited as "the birthplace of the blues," owing to the many legendary musicians (Charlie Patton, Muddy Waters, Lonnie Johnson) who lived and worked there during the sharecropping days of the

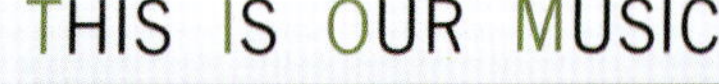
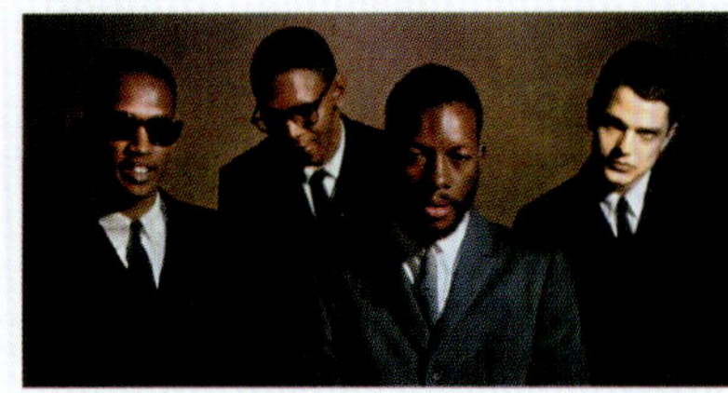

Cover of The Ornette Coleman Quartet's album
This Is Our Music (Atlantic, 1961)

1920s and 30s. The irreverence of McMillian's work can be sensed immediately, as every surface of his interior—floor, walls, ceiling—has been covered or draped by a patchwork of crimson vinyl, a "blues" material if ever there was one. Hand-stitched and multitextured, seething and salacious, the overheated room recovers some aspect of lived contradiction from the sepia-toned (white) remove of blues lore. The true origin of the blues, McMillian seems to say, is that sweaty, troubled space between Saturday night and Sunday morning.

Between-ness can be ascertained in several other works that take the form of archives. Or rather an archival impulse can put us in the space of the blues, which, recalling Baker's matrix idea, is often one of displacement, translation, becoming, and memory. In practical fact, the blues has always had a complicated relation to the archival. If the popularity of a certain kind of blues music in the postwar period, in particular its popularity among whites, owes greatly to the interpretations or appropriations of white musicians like Elvis, Dylan, or the Rolling Stones, such musicians were themselves often indebted to translators or mediators—the Sam Phillipses and Alan Lomaxes and John Faheys—who sought out and circulated, with intentions both commercial and ethnographic, the vast wealth of black musical culture.[31] On the other hand, blues-oriented music is itself often archival—an index of daily life, current events, local lore, and the range of inhabitable realities that the performer or the receiver might know. Further, blues compositions and forms are frequently recombinant, down to their basic elements, so that one finds multiple versions or interpretations of popular numbers performed by different people, not unlike the way particular chord changes, dubs, or beats proliferate across the histories and practices of jazz, reggae, and hip-hop. In this way, the blues has always carried an archival impulse. Its specific examples are always in relation to its larger body, implying a culture that takes shape actively and consciously through participation and reception.

Initially produced for her Museum of Contemporary Art, Los Angeles, exhibition "World Tour" in 1993 and included in the Whitney Biennial of the same year, Renée Green's large-scale installation *Import/Export Funk Office* (1992–93) is a landmark critical reflection upon the culture of the archive vis-à-vis black music. Resembling a walk-in media library or "office" (the latter term perhaps better suited to the agency of mediation the work prioritizes), the installation focuses on the "import/export" of African American popular culture within Germany, a country in which Green traveled frequently during this time. The materials collected in the work reference widely, from Angela Davis and Adorno to the Black Power movement and the 1960s "discovery" of the blues to the then recent embrace of hip-hop. Taken together they form a social and intellectual field that allows Green to play observer to another culture's translations and to mistranslations of her own—a role most keenly viewed in a series of video interviews between Green and the critic Diedrich Diederichsen, deftly cast as the work's "native informant." The mutual fascination that accompanies this inversion of traditional ethnographic positions (European observer/Black observed) propels the work beyond polemic into a realm of cultural exchange that, while certainly complex, becomes navigable through a subtle mix of poetry and analysis. *Import/Export Funk Office*, and Green's practice generally, contributed to the rise of so-called context art in the 1990s, joining work by Andrea Fraser, Christian Philipp Müller, and Mark Dion, among others, in locating the site of the art object not just within the architectural or art historical space of the gallery or museum, but within the political and discursive parameters of culture.

Out Moves

Like *Import/Export Funk Office*, Stan Douglas's masterful video installation *Hors-champs* (1992) is one of the best examples of the critical negotiation of culture and black expressive practice to come out of the early 1990s. A world apart from the facile polemics of the identity politics era, the work is a prism of contrasts and discrepancies, lyrically potent and analytically precise. Translated from the French as "out of field" or more colloquially as "off-camera," its title borrows from the terminology of film theory, referring to the role of images that create a sense of narrative space beyond what is immediately shown by the camera—the way, for instance, a close-up of a limp hand suggests that a death has occurred. Douglas's work is a meditation on the politics and histories, the ambiguities and promises, that lie "outside" the representations of his film. What one sees "inside" the work is a concert—a performance session staged and recorded in a Paris television studio, in which four musicians render an interpretation of *Spirits Rejoice* (1965), one of the seminal compositions of 1960s free jazz, by the iconoclastic American saxophonist and bandleader Albert Ayler.[32] Alternately wobbling and soaring, plaintive and ecstatic, the music's fluid field of reference and feeling moves from the moan of the blues and gospel praise to emphatic refrains of the French national anthem, all in a tangle of virtuosic soloing and collective improvisation.

Yet even as it transports, the music is an object of Douglas's and our reflection, provoking consideration of relationships among images, sounds, cultures, and aesthetic practices. We might think about the setting of the performance: a neutral backdrop bathed in shadow and soft light, in which the performers appear unencumbered in open space, vessels of pure expression—so familiar as a way in which jazz has been pictured on television. How could such a space contain this music? We might think about Douglas's installation, which positions a single screen floating in a gallery but projects a different edit of the session onto each side, so that a viewer cannot "see" or "know" the entirety of the performance from any one vantage. We might also think about the music Douglas has his musicians perform, how its own sonic and referential contrasts mirror the trouble of real history, create a matrix or archive of that trouble: the America of the mid-twentieth century, choked by racial prejudice and exclusion; the France of *liberté, egalité, fraternité*, a beacon to black artists seeking release; the deep love and admiration of the tradition of the Spirituals; the fire

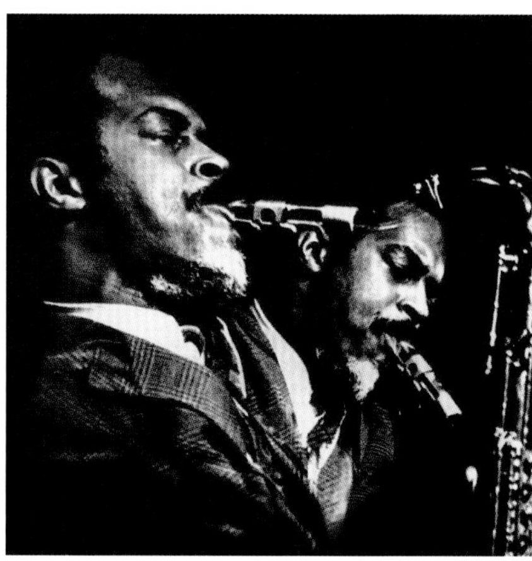

Cover of Albert Ayler's album
Spirits Rejoice (Calibre, 1965)

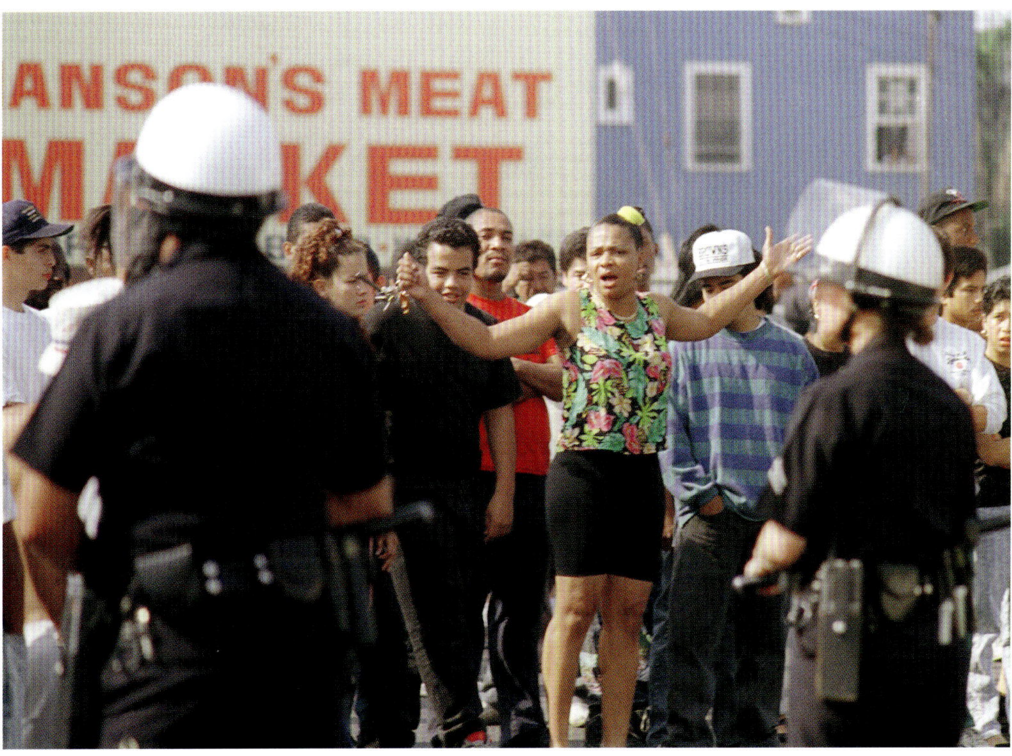

A woman yells at Los Angeles police officers who stand guard outside a shopping center, April 30, 1992. The acquittal of four police officers in the beating of Rodney King led to widespread anger and rioting.

and tortured need to transcend expressed by the honking, calling, testifying interplay of sounds. We might further pressure the historical frame and find a relation between the signified time of the work—the turbulent 1960s—and the actual moment of its creation. Douglas once wrote that *Hors-champs* was "dedicated to the people of South Central Los Angeles"[33]—to a people and place which, in 1992, were seized by the turmoil, trauma, and uprising of the Rodney King verdict. By holding together the shown and the unshown, the known and the sensed, "those other times" and its own, *Hors-champs* departs from absolutes to find a more ethical space of communication and reverie. "At some moment," Douglas writes, "polyphonic music in general, and ensemble pieces in particular, always say 'we'—and, therefore, can always suggest possibilities, unimagined ways in which individuals can collectively inhabit time."[34]

The blues teaches us that movement and anticipation are closely linked. To hop a train or repeat refrains, to bend a note or improvise, is to imagine time and place stretching, is to instantiate and enact this stretching, beyond *whatever* time and place, the fixity of which may be unbearable. If, as George E. Lewis once wrote, "the truth of improvisation involves survival,"[35] the boxcarlike sequence of battered blue suitcases in Zoe Leonard's *1961* (2002–ongoing; titled after the year of the artist's birth) suffuses the linearity of Minimalism with memorial recognition of life's transience and burden. Hammons's installation

Chasing the Blue Train (1989) may, likewise, suggest a reflection upon life and death, its title engine a figure of the movement and migration that defined a "blues people" throughout much of the twentieth century. With a soundtrack of John Coltrane ("Trane") and Thelonious Monk coming from multiple, simultaneously playing boom boxes, a sonic backdrop attuned to motion, change, continuance, and collective expansion mirrors a relation between music and labor, sound and survival, seen in the work's landscape of upturned piano lids and tunnels of coal. Hammons's installation suggests the essentially outward signification of the blues—a blues that must always be "chased" along the tracks. "At the junctures, the intersections of experience where roads cross and diverge," Baker writes, "… blues … performance[s] serve as codifiers, absorbing and transforming discontinuous experience into formal expressive instances…. Like signification itself, [the] blues are always nomadically wandering."[36]

In this sense, the visually explosive, hard-edge abstraction of William T. Williams's painting *Trane* (1969) can be considered in the same breath as Bearden's collage *Train Whistle Blues: II* (1964), as reflections on the social juncture and anticipation shaping African American modernity. A blues sensibility requires the critic to think beyond traditional categories of representation—abstraction and figuration, for instance—to grasp a cultural and conceptual confluence of signs, styles, and gestures. In the early 1970s, as an artist-in-residence at the Xerox Corporation, painter Jack Whitten began to experiment with new printing and imaging technologies, departing from the Abstract Expressionist idiom he had practiced early in his career. Like many artists of his generation, he was drawn to the "sheets of sound" he heard in the music of Coltrane, Cecil Taylor, and others, a music schooled in and reverent of the harmonic and rhythmic exploration pioneered by Duke Ellington and others. An important work from this period, *Black Table Setting (Homage to Duke Ellington)* (1974)—conceived years before Gerhard Richter began making his now-famous "squeegee" abstractions—was produced by raking or pulling devices Whitten called "developers" over a canvas layered with acrylic medium, so that the work's subtle color and light appear embedded by a gesture of speed and process.

A different type of movement is felt in *STOP* (1995–2012), a four-part, two-hour film and installation by Jeff Preiss. Edited from thousands of brief, one- or two-second shots taken on the artist's 16mm Bolex camera over the past seventeen years, the work consists of a densely lyrical flow of images and sounds that creates a cumulative, almost improvisational picture of the artist's own life, shaped toward narrative by a series of transformations effecting the New York world of his family, friends, and professional career as a commercial filmmaker. The most obvious of these, coming at the conclusion of the film's first section, is the upheaval of September 11, which *STOP* depicts, as it does all its subjects, with an objectivity that is both melancholy and fragmented. More emergent is a development unfolding with the artist's child, one of the work's principal characters, who appears to undergo a process of female-to-male gender transition across the duration of the film. Tender, polyrhythmic,

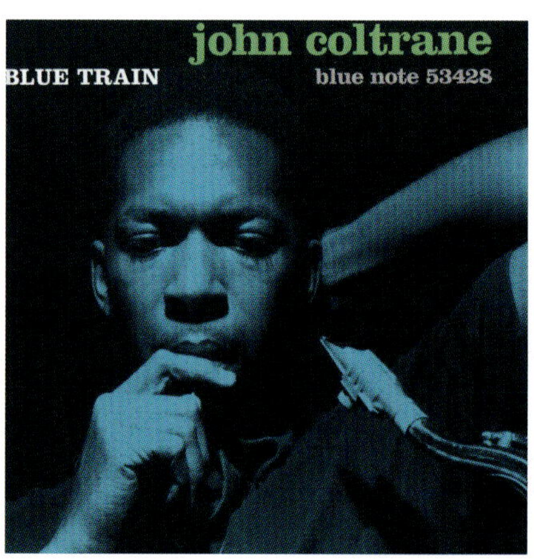

Cover of John Coltrane's album
Blue Train (Blue Note, 1957)

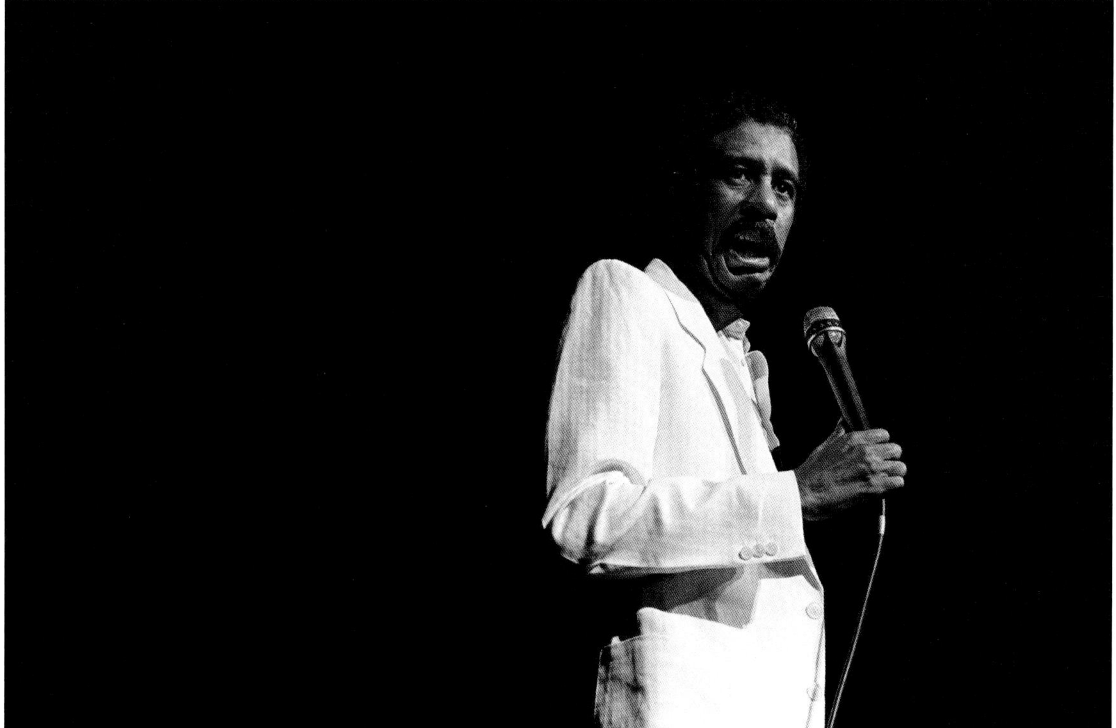

Richard Pryor on stage, 1983

and confusing, this coming to grips with an identity in flux, with a life increasingly oriented by the non-fit of a body, lends profound significance to the film's formal restlessness and drive. When the work does actually "stop," following the teenager's top surgery, it does so more with a sense of beginning (or ongoing becoming) than of conclusion.

Needless to say, blues movement is not always expansive, forward, or outward bound. It can be recursive as well, as in the tight circularity of the conveyor belt in Dave McKenzie's installation *Fear and Trembling* (2009) or the seemingly endless inner variation of algorithmic form in Charles Gaines's *Regression Series* drawings (1973–74). In Glenn Ligon's *No Room* paintings (2007), the transcendence of identity parodied by a Richard Pryor joke—"I was a nigger for twenty-three years. I gave that shit up. No room for, no room for advancement."—is further qualified by Ligon's serial reproduction of the comedian's words across multiple, identical canvases. Needless to say, Pryor is already a quintessential blues figure. He gave expression to the traumas of everyday life in a voice as accessible, lyrical, and affecting (abjecting) as any musician's. But Ligon also *turns him blue*, "blues" him (from noun to verb), in the songlike, ritualistic, and (com)plaintive refraining of his words. Repetition is essential to the blues as a figure of ongoingness: the constant coming-up-against that is life, the constant promise of overcoming, getting beyond, or getting free.

No Room finds what is painful and hopeful in the idea of black advancement—
what is painful and hopeful in Pryor—and gives it a form and a process that
are equally full of pain and hope. What may seem like foreclosure, the irony
of "advancement" repeated over and over, is also an opening onto existential
time: deliberation, simultaneity, reflection. Mackey says it better than anyone
(with props to Ellington) when he writes: "seriality's mix of utopic ongoingness
and recursive constraint is blutopic, an idealism shaped or shaded by blue, in-
between foreboding, blue, dystopic apprehension of the way the world is."[37]

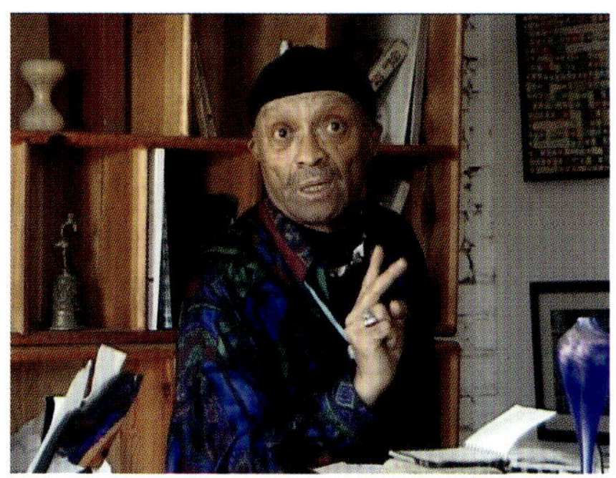

Cecil Taylor in the documentary
Cecil Taylor: All the Notes, **2006**

Total Area

If time and movement are one axis of the blues, space and affect are another.
Amiri Baraka once observed that the music of Ornette Coleman and Cecil
Taylor "depends for its form on the same references as primitive blues forms.
It considers the *total area* of its existence as a means to evolve…. This total
area is not merely the largely artificial considerations of bar lines and constantly stated chords, but the *more* musical considerations of rhythm, pitch,
timbre, and melody. All these are shaped by the emotional requirements of the
player."[38] Taylor himself wrote, "the player advances to the area, an unknown
totality, made whole thru self-analysis (improvisation), the conscious manipu-
lation of known material."[39] If the capaciousness of utterance, gesture, and
affect that Baraka distinguishes in the blues serves both to define the particularity of "the player," his or her voice or vision, and to provide a space of
identification and sympathy for the audience or viewer, it privileges subjectivity
as a primary space in which this work gets done. Which is to say it privileges
an intersubjective, collective space, what saxophonist Jackie McLean, speaking about the promise of free jazz, called "the big room."[40] Perhaps this is
one way to read the insistent, mantralike evocation of scale in Jutta Koether's
100% (Portrait Robert Johnson) (1990). Perhaps making sense of blues affect
requires an attention not just to the generic aspects of an artwork or piece of
music, but to the ways self reverberates and projects through form: in tone and
overtone, inflection, kinds of stylization and embellishment, emotional tempera-
ture, bodily propriety and impropriety, expressions of ecstasy and endurance,
choreographies of presentation and display, persona and self-staging. The over-
loaded, peculiar presence of formal signifiers in the blues, its shines and drones,
its creaking, rasping, limping echoes, creates affective space in the ambiguous
slippage between part and whole.

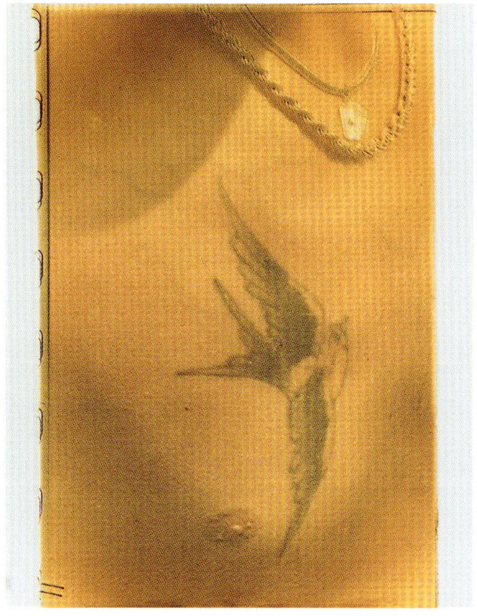

Mark Morrisroe
Untitled, **1988**

Like his fellow Boston School photographers Nan Goldin and David Armstrong,
Mark Morrisroe tended to focus his camera on his own life, depicting himself and
his friends in situations that are alternately intimate, defiant, and exaggeratedly
camp. And yet his images seem haunted by various forms of limit, whether that
be the social marginalization of sexuality or the reality of physical, bodily deterioration brought about by AIDS. In the face of limit, the restlessness and profound

lyricism of his invention become even more pronounced. Morrisroe's subjects—
his nudes, his drag divas, his Romantic still-life tableaux—are already theatrical,
but they become more so through the artist's darkroom experiments with negative sandwiching and retouching, which give a soft-focus, gauzy expressionism
to his images, or in his frequent use of a handwritten scribble, applied directly
to prints, which encodes photographs such as *Blow Both of Us, Gail Thacker
and Me, Summer 1978* and *Dismal Boston Skyline* (both 1986) with the elegiac
touch of personal signature and poignant humor. As a young man, scrapping his
way toward becoming an artist, hustling, taking pictures, and making things with
friends, Morrisroe adopted the nom de guerre "Mark Dirt," a punkish, Genet-like
affectation aligning him with the low, the outcast, and the afflicted. However
sentimental this posture may be (no less sentimental for its casual irony), the
ubiquitous presence of grain and texture in Morrisroe's images, their "mark of
dirt," suggests a foil for what is otherwise an exquisite, even lapidary beauty.
The allegory of bondage and freedom that plays out in the rope necklaces
and sparrow tattoo adorning a man's gold-hued breast in *Untitled* (1988), the
rouged lips and powdered cheeks of a drag queen's tossed-back head in *Sweet
Raspberry, Spanish Madonna* (1986), or the fetish of Tina Turner's placid face
in *Untitled* (c. 1981) in some basic sense dress up and reappropriate subjects
society has deemed ugly or strange, a masquerade that echoes with a blues
desire for subversion, private pleasure, and getting by.

In some ways, Morrisroe's photographs rhyme with earlier work by Roy DeCarava,
a photographer celebrated for his documentation of black life in Harlem beginning in the 1950s, which encompassed scenes of domestic intimacy, urban
landscapes, and heroic portraiture of jazz musicians, among other subjects.
Though it could not be said that DeCarava's pictures are "dirty" like Morrisroe's,
they are nonetheless suffused with a kind of lyrical haze, a propensity for dim
light and shadow, and suggest a language of the self rich in tone, feeling, and
abstraction. A series of portraits of John Coltrane (1961) show the legendary
saxophonist blowing on a darkened stage. Ecstatic, tortured, spiritual, his figure
seems to blast out or repudiate the suffocating *Hallway, New York* (1953) or the
broken city block of *117ᵗʰ Street* (1951). Later photographs such as *Silver fence*
(1983) and *Curved branch* (1994) dwell on patterns found in the urban landscape
with an "allover" attention to growth and diffusion. These works recall the cosmic
mingling of abstract form and figuration found in Beauford Delaney's portraits
of Jean Genet and James Baldwin, or Kira Lynn Harris's redirection of Light and
Space phenomenology toward utopian, science-fictional zones of sensation. Like
Cecil Taylor's "all the notes" keyboard runs or the buzz of Sun Ra's Wurlitzer,
these are blues of thresholds, full and flowing.

Numerous works in this exhibition witness the disrupting tension of the blues in
representations of the body. One of DeCarava's most iconic images, *Dancers,
New York* (1956), captures a scene in a Harlem ballroom as two figures "cut-
up" the expanse of a dance floor, their bodies gripped by a movement that is
ferocious, jubilant, and *stylized*. Not unlike Thelonious Monk, who was known to

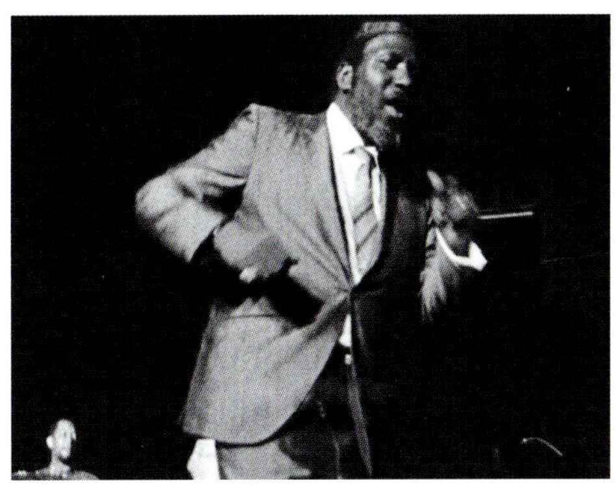

Thelonius Monk in the documentary
Thelonius Monk: Straight, No Chaser, **1988**

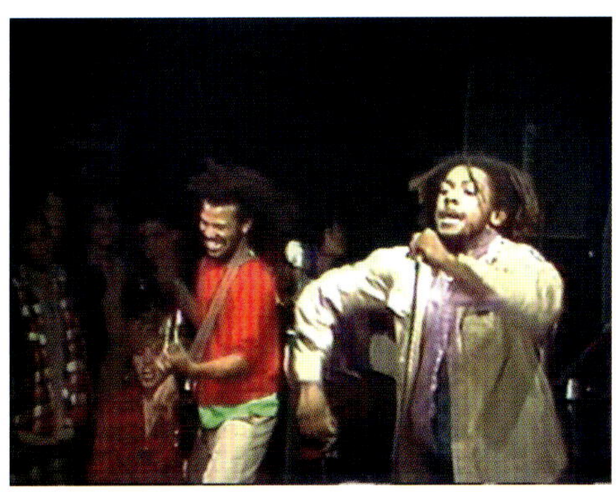

Bad Brains in concert footage from
Bad Brains: Live at CBGB 1982, **1982**

get up from the piano and strut around the stage when his band was really on, DeCarava's dancers suggest a conducting of the music from the inside, "compelling insinuation" (Zora Neale Hurston)[41] so that physicality becomes socially reflective as well as sensual. In a different way, the contingency of black bodily representation animates the painting *Blue Water Silver Moon (Mermaid)* (1991), Kerry James Marshall's portrait of a female nude luxuriating in the shallows of a marshy pool. Idealized and dreamlike, this image of black feminine beauty and self-possession speaks not simply to male desire or looking, but to the historical lack of such images in the canons and exemplary genres of Western art. Marshall's will in depicting what has been absented from or denied by imaginative standards finds an echo in Henry Taylor's *Emelda* (2011), a "from-life" rendering of a black female nude reclining face down on a cream-colored sofa. With its fast conjunction of angular body masses (outlined in watery indigo, as if the blues were leaking out) and the tongue-in-cheek presence of a black feline, the painting recalls the fascination with racialized otherness that runs through European modernism, from Édouard Manet's *Olympia* (1863) to the primitivist impulses of Henri Matisse and Pablo Picasso, but quotes from this tradition with a casualness that seems wholly contemporary.

In works by Melvin Edwards, Zoe Leonard, and Liz Larner the human body is seen in pieces, traumatized and deformed. *Write When You Can* and *Fire Blossom* (both 1991) belong to Edwards's long-running series of sculptures known as the *Lynch Fragments*, made since the mid-1960s, in which assemblages of welded metal parts—chains, bolts, torquing screws—memorialize the physical violence and bodily disfiguration of America's worst moments of racial conflict. Terrifying and strange, the wall reliefs recall Ralph Ellison's definition of the blues as "an impulse to keep the painful details and episodes of a brutal experience alive in one's aching consciousness, to finger its jagged grain, and to transcend it, not by the consolation of philosophy but by squeezing from it a near-tragic, near-comic lyricism."[42] A smaller version of her major *Strange Fruit* installation (1994), Leonard's *Untitled* (1994–97) presents a shelf display of desiccated orange and banana skins, emptied of their pulp and hand-sewn back together with rough thread. Titled after Billie Holiday's famous antilynching protest song, *Strange Fruit* was a dark lament to bodily and social loss—in this case, as the double entendre of her title suggests, to the physical ravages and withering homophobia accompanying the AIDS epidemic, the memory of which Leonard dwells in and processes through the repetitive act of suturing. Assembled six years after the initial installation, *Untitled* re-presents the fruit now darkened and shrunken—a deterioration mirroring grief in its passage. Though it does not share Edwards's and Leonard's direct reference to social tragedy, Larner's *No M, No D, Only S & B* (1990)—a title that might translate as "no mom, no dad, only sister and brother"—suggests a similar turmoil and deformity in its jumble of bulbous leather forms. Another work, *Lux Interior (gold plated)* (2010), resembles a disease-stricken and decayed heart, uncannily cast in lustrous gold. Not unlike Edwards's *Lynch Fragments*, Larner's gnarled mass seems to radiate with uncomfortable energy, its title an homage to Lux Interior, the recently passed lead singer of "psychobilly" pioneers the Cramps.[43]

In the work of Edwards and Larner a kind of formalism appears to slip away from itself, undo itself, through the affective pull of the social, psychological, and organic. The same could be said for the work of Amy Sillman, whose painting *DUEL* (2011) submerges a tangle of ghostly limbs beneath an acid surface of green-yellow fog. At the top center of the canvas, a pair of dainty ladies gloves—a feminized version of those objects dropped to commence a duel—sit astride a forceful black line shooting up and dividing the canvas from below, a kind of vaginal slit or bottom crack through which the abstraction of the work emerges awkwardly, if undeniably, in a nether realm of female sexuality. "I don't find it odd that [Abstract Expressionist] practices have now been vitally reinvigorated by a queered connection of the vulgar and the camp," Sillman writes. "I would argue that this is because AbEx already *had* something to do with the politics of the body, and that it was all the more tempting once it seemed to have been shut down by its own rhetoric, rendered mythically straight and male in quotation marks."[44]

The Clearing

In her collaged photo-diptych *Body/Ground (The Clearing: Or Cortez and La Malinche, Thomas Jefferson and Sally Hemmings, N. and Me)* (1991/2012), Lorraine O'Grady insists upon, rather than running from, the profound racial and sexual collisions that have shaped America from its origins. An allegory of miscegenation spanning multiple eras—from the colonial past to the contemporary present—the work depicts a trio of mixed-race couples set amidst a primeval forest clearing. On the right, a white male skeleton clad in conquistador chain mail appears to grope the naked breast of a black female figure, whose listless face turns toward the viewer. In the panel to the left, two children chase a ball toward a pile of discarded clothes (barely concealing a gun), their youth perhaps representing the early nation of Jefferson and Hemmings, while hovering in the sky overhead a white man and a black woman embrace in what appears to be reciprocal copulation. Taken together, the couples reflect the deep intermingling of pain, pleasure, abuse, and desire that gave birth to and continues to inform the peculiar hybridity of the New World. O'Grady's metaphors of complexity and "clearing" are not mutually exclusive, but dependent, the latter, really, an avowal of recognition, truth-telling, and vision that might cut through or open up the various tangles of prejudice that keep something like "America" in denial about its mixed identity. As the artist states:

> My attitude about hybridity is that it is essential to understanding what is happening here. People's reluctance to acknowledge it is part of the problem.… The argument for embracing the Other is

more realistic than what is usually argued for, which is an idealistic and almost romantic maintenance of difference. But I don't mean interracial sex literally. I'm really advocating for the kind of mis-cegenated *thinking* that's needed to deal with what we've already created here.[45]

"Blues for Smoke" is likewise motivated by some basic desire to create space—to find a clearing—so that the complexity of "what we've already created," our lived experience of culture and identity, might come into sharper relief. On one level, this desire can be sensed in the multiplicity of artists and artworks collected in the exhibition: in the presence of white artists placed in relation to black cultural contexts, in a framing of the blues to include questions of sexual and gender identity, and in the juxtaposition of historical tendencies that would seem "not to fit" with each other. Of the latter, one could point to the proximity created in the exhibition between artists who emerged in or exemplified an early 1990s "postconceptual" moment, with its emphasis on a critical poetics of cultural form, and artists identified with earlier and later moments. Though a viewer might often find works by Renée Green, Stan Douglas, David Hammons, Martin Kippenberger, Gregg Bordowitz, Jutta Koether, Zoe Leonard, Glenn Ligon, and Liz Larner exhibited together (whether contextualized according to generation, politics, or style), far less frequently will one see these artists alongside Beauford Delaney, Edward Clark, Alma Thomas, or Jack Whitten, whose aesthetic sensibilities were shaped in the 1950s, 60s, and 70s. Among the many ambitions of "Blues for Smoke" is to consider what happens to our discourses of form and culture when divergent contexts intersect—to take a first step, to slow down, to learn (or unlearn, as the case may be) from discrepancy. Is it not the case, for instance, that all of these artists, regardless of their historical moment, manifest a resistance to facile representations of identity?

This willful crossing of art historical boundaries takes its cue from, extends from, or mirrors the multiplicity of the blues as I have sought it out, and found it, in music. By way of conclusion, I should acknowledge the role that music plays in the actual installation of "Blues for Smoke." Beyond the many works that, themselves, contain or refer to song or sound, the exhibition includes an assortment of listening and viewing "stations" where music or video perfor-mance footage serves to punctuate or complement the displays of visual art. Here, for instance, one can encounter the musical art of Jaki Byard, the Art Ensemble of Chicago, Mary Lou Williams, Henry Flynt, Howlin' Wolf, Bukka White, the Bad Brains, Thelonious Monk, Trouble Funk, Susie Ibarra, Death Grips, Cannibal Ox, Muhal Richard Abrams, Amina Claudine Myers, and Duke Ellington, among many others. The point of this material is neither to provide shelter from the unfamiliar or troubling artifices of contemporary art nor to naturalize music in the face of the visual—for representations of music, as any fan knows, are often highly contrived—but to express one curator's sense of the diversity and legacy of the blues, its manifold imagination, past and future. Though the intermingling of racial, cultural, and artistic discourse remains by turns active, painful, surprising, unconsidered, revealing, affirming, frightening, symptomatic, and strange—though the blues itself suggests an aesthetics of delirious surplus—we might come to the world we find ourselves in with eyes and ears open to the possibility, as William Carlos Williams observed, that "dissonance / …leads to discovery."[46] We might neither fear this dissonance nor pass judgment on its noises, but instead simply listen and attempt to reflect. For "to lose a master desire," as Houston Baker once put it, "is to see a different America—singing."[47]

Notes

I dedicate this essay to the memory of my grandfather, The Rev. Dr. George Willis Bennett (1919–1994), and to my daughter, Esther Anastas Simpson.

1. See http://bigthink.com/ideas/17240. Cornell West states, "And so the blues people in America have been the leaven in the democratic loaf, because black people could have chosen counterterroristic tactics when they were lynched over and over and over again. They said no, we're not going to go out and lynch white folk. We would rather be defeated for the moment, with integrity, than win and be a gangster like them. That's a blues sensibility. That's a blues sensibility. So you let that love inside of you be expressed even though it's hard for it to be translated into love or justice on the ground. That's a great lesson in this age of terrorism and in the age of recession, you see. And so a bluesman like myself in the life of the mind, a jazzman in the world of ideas, says I want to tell the truth. The condition of truth is to allow suffering to speak. And as a Christian, I believe in unconditional love; that's why I love brother Larry Summers. I want him to have more joy in his life. It's hard to have a lot of arrogance and have a lot of joy at the same time. I want him to have more joy and less arrogance. But unconditional love is always tied to justice. Justice is love on legs, spilling over into the public sphere."

2. George E. Lewis, "Wadada Leo Smith's New World Music," liner notes, *Wadada Leo Smith, Kabell Years: 1971–1979*, Tzadik, 7610, 2004. It is often assumed that the "modernization" of the music categorized as jazz, beginning with the arrival of bebop in the early 1940s, led to a long, slow separation from the music's traditional blues origins. But, in fact, nearly every moment understood to be a radical departure

in jazz—that is, both a leap forward and a kind of death, a crossroads—has also witnessed a fluorescence of the blues. The music of Charlie Parker and Thelonious Monk, for instance, was steeped in the blues: a modernism built from hard-swinging Kansas City riffs (Parker) and the encounter of Harlem "stride" piano with the holy-rolling gospel of the Pentecostal church (Monk). A generation later, as attentive listeners began to sense a "New Thing" coming, Cecil Taylor's *Jazz Advance* (1956) moved on with "Charge 'em Blues"; Ornette Coleman's moanful "Lonely Woman" announced *The Shape of Jazz to Come* (1958), and "Blues Connotation" led off *This Is Our Music* (1961). Nearly everything Charles Mingus touched was blue: *Weary Blues* (1958), *Blues & Roots* (1959), *Mysterious Blues* (1960), "Hog-Callin' Blues" (1962). On *Blues for Smoke* (1960), Jaki Byard unfurled his future from a history of stride blues. The newness of John Coltrane's *Blue Train* (1957), *Coltrane Plays the Blues* (1962), and "Afro Blue" (1961) was bound to blue. The blues of Herman "Sonny" Blount, aka Sun Ra, radiated cosmic heat for decades before he released *Some Blues but Not the Kind That's Blue* (1977) and *Other Voices, Other Blues* (1978), but still has not been heard enough. As jazz traditions and forms continued to expand into the 1970s, many of the artists affiliated with Chicago's Association for the Advancement of Creative Music (AACM) made daringly original work faceted with blues forms and spirit, from Roscoe Mitchell's *Congliptious* (1968), the Art Ensemble of Chicago's *People in Sorrow* (1969), and Leo Smith's *Creative Music 1* (1971) to George Lewis's *Homage to Charles Parker* (1979), Air's *Air Lore* (1979), and Amina Claudine Myers's *Amina Claudine Myers Salutes Bessie Smith* (1980). AACM founder Muhal Richard Abrams frequently improvised on the blues, whether on

collaborations with Malachi Favors Maghostout (*Sightsong*, 1976) or Anthony Braxton (*Duets*, 1976), or as a group leader on *Blues Forever* (1982) or *Blu Blu Blu* (1991). Bobby Bradford and John Carter, in Los Angeles, played "The Sunday Afternoon Jazz Blues Society" on *Self-Preservation Music* (1970). On *Coon Bid'ness* (1975), Julius Hemphill, from St. Louis, played the "Hard Blues."

3. Robert Farris Thompson identified "a propensity for multiple-meter" as a hallmark of the black Atlantic visual tradition. See Thompson, *Flash of the Spirit: African and Afro-American Art and Philosophy* (New York: Vintage, 1984), iii.

4. W. C. Handy, a self-proclaimed "Father of the Blues," first encountered the music he would later popularize on a train platform in Tutwiler, Mississippi, in 1903. "A lean, loose-jointed Negro had commenced plunking a guitar beside me while I slept. His clothes were rags; his feet peeped out of his shoes. His face had on it some of the sadness of the ages. As he played, he pressed a knife on the strings of a guitar in a manner popularized by Hawaiian guitarists who used steel bars. The effect was unforgettable. His song, too, struck me instantly. 'Goin' where the Southern cross' the Dog.' The singer repeated the line three times, accompanying himself on the guitar with the weirdest music I ever heard." See W. C. Handy, *Father of the Blues: An Autobiography* (New York: Da Capo Press, 1969), 78.

5. Houston A. Baker, *Blues, Ideology, and Afro-American Literature: A Vernacular Theory* (Chicago: University of Chicago Press, 1984), 5.

6. Another indication of the enduring appeal of a certain vision of the blues can be found in the taste of American presidents. Starting with George H. W. Bush, whose campaign strategist and right-wing Svengali Lee Atwater became a friend of B. B. King and fashioned himself a

blues impresario, every president has hosted blues concerts at the White House and been photographed jamming with the band (we might add that Jimmy Carter, bless him, merely marveled when Cecil Taylor graced his stage).

7. Albert Murray, *Stomping the Blues* (1976; reprint, New York: Da Capo Press, 2000), 16.

8. Lewis, "The Timeless Blues," page 76 in this volume.

9. See Richard J. Powell, ed., *The Blues Aesthetic: Black Culture and Modernism*, exh. cat. (Washington, D.C.: Washington Project for the Arts, 1989), 21. Powell's exhibition focused primarily on black artists and black cultural artifacts, but did include the work of white artists such as Jackson Pollock, Larry Rivers, and Robert Frank to show the influence and broad significance of black culture throughout the century.

10. Ibid.

11. One need only consider the racial and social outcry surrounding the Trayvon Martin shooting in February 2012 or the pathos and desire of the Occupy slogan "We are the 99%" to grasp the fantasy of "postidentity." The phrase "cheering fictions" comes from the filmmaker Hanif Kureishi, but I first heard it used by the artist Glenn Ligon, who wrote that the work of David Hammons "has never been 'on point' because it's always too Fellini, too carnivalesque, too damn freaky-deke to be useful as a set of cheering fictions, an expression of an essential, unchanging blackness, or a standard-bearer for some multiculturalist agenda." Glenn Ligon, "Black Light: David Hammons and the Poetics of Emptiness," *Artforum* 43, no. 1 (September 2004): 244. See also Hanif Kureishi, "Dirty Washing," *Time Out* (London), October 14–20, 1985.

12. Thelma Golden, introduction to *Freestyle*, ed. Golden, exh. cat. (New York: Studio Museum in Harlem, 2001), 14.

13. Fred Moten, *In the Break: The Aesthetics of the Black Radical Tradition* (Minneapolis: University of Minnesota Press, 2003), 1.

14. The proliferation of artistic selves that burst forth and disappeared in the same moment—though, of course, some had the intent of sticking around—supplied ample possibility for the professional, economic, and critical rituals that bloomed and fizzled in art with increasing speed. The economic collapse of 2008, which forced museums to do less with less and galleries to rely heavily on a spiral of art fairs and globalized collectors, actually had the effect of reinforcing the fetish for transience and immateriality in art. In diminished times diminishment seemed to have a near magical appeal.

15. See Rhea Anastas, ed., "The Artist Is a Currency," roundtable with Gregg Bordowitz, Andrea Fraser, Jutta Koether, and Glenn Ligon, *Grey Room*, no. 24 (Summer 2006): 110–25.

16. See "Fantasies of the Unknowable Object: Andrea Fraser in Conversation with Bennett Simpson," *Purple*, no. 13 (Summer 2002): 145. Fraser's critique echoes similar analyses of the field of culture advanced by sociologist Pierre Bourdieu and the political economists Luc Boltanski and Eve Chiapello. See also Pierre Bourdieu, *The Field of Cultural Production: Essays on Art and Literature*, ed. Randal Johnson (New York: Columbia University Press, 1998), and Luc Boltanski and Eve Chiapello, *The New Spirit of Capitalism*, trans. Gregory Elliott (London and New York: Verso, 2005).

17. Okwui Enwezor's Documenta 11 (2002) was one argument for the ongoing validity of cultural discourse within globalization.

18. Golden, introduction to *Freestyle*, 14.

19. "We need more than content analyses based on assumptions of representationality," Mackey wrote. "The dislocating tilt of artistic othering, especially as practiced by African-American artists, deserves a great deal more attention than it has been given." See Nathaniel Mackey, "Other: From Noun to Verb," in *Discrepant Engagement: Dissonance, Cross-Culturality, and Experimental Writing* (Tuscaloosa: University of Alabama Press, 2000), 284–85.

20. The ambiguity of post-black representation was a major focus of Hamza Walker's important exhibition "Black Is, Black Ain't," presented at the Renaissance Society, Chicago, in 2008.

21. Mackey, "Other: From Noun to Verb," 285.

22. One thinks of the suppressed history of African American abstract painters of the 1960s and 70s or the political, linguistic terrain of novels such as Samuel Delany's *Dhalgren* (1975).

23. Dan Graham's Postminimalist works for magazine pages in the mid-to-late 1960s make a direct connection between the serial forms of suburban architecture and the propulsive oblivion of rock and roll (the Kinks, the Beatles, the Rolling Stones), but stop short of reading race into the culture of rock, turning instead to the Shakers as the music's ecstatic antecedent. The writings of Mike Kelley are likewise important in the sustained consideration of music's cultural politics.

24. Adrian Piper, "Critical Hegemony and Aesthetic Acculturation," *Noûs* 19, no. 1 (1985): 29–40. I became aware of this quote from Fred Moten's discussion of Piper's theatricality in Moten, *In the Break*, 299–300, note 1. Importantly, as Moten notes, "Piper discusses Krauss's formulation without naming Krauss, placing it within the framework of a larger critique of the convergence of ontological fallacy and socioeconomic presumption in the (construction of the) art world."

25. What blackness does to whiteness, or to discourses historically naturalized as "not-black" (for it is rare that whiteness actually calls itself white), how it shows these discourses to look in looking away, is a major subject of works such as Mackey's *Discrepant Engagement*; Lewis's *A Power Stronger than Itself*; and Moten's *In the Break*. Such writers effect a pause, if not a corrective, in the celebrated history of white artists looking to African and African American art and culture for inspiration. The names Picasso, Matisse, Mondrian, Pollock, Kerouac, and Rauschenberg are well known in this regard. Lesser or more problematically well known are Henry Flynt, Robert Watts, Martin Kippenberger, and Sam Durant, among many others.

26. Mackey, "Other: From Noun to Verb," 284–85.

27. Baker, *Blues, Ideology, and Afro-American Literature*, 14.

28. Though there is an assumption that race determines expertise, or that it might privilege certain areas or histories, is it not also the case that we rarely hesitate to assume that a black curator or critic might be interested in white art? Can we not begin to consider how culture is produced collectively, through exclusion and discrimination as much as through affirmation, and then take responsibility for each of our relations to this?

29. In addition to Coleman on his white plastic saxophone, the painting shows Don Cherry on trumpet, Ed Blackwell on drums, and Charlie Haden on bass. The ambiguous central figure has been guessed to be Sonny Rollins, though he was not a member of Coleman's group.

30. Murray, *Stomping the Blues*, 27.

31. The lingering stylistic prejudices of much contemporary white blues-based rock reflects the massive impact made by these encounters in the 1950s and 60s, such that the blues "discovered" in this time has become ingrained or frozen for generations hence.

32. Though Ayler was known as one of the most advanced improvisers of his time, championed by John Coltrane and other leaders of jazz's avant-garde in the 1960s, his huge tenor vibrato was, according to musician Roswell Rudd, "the epitome of gut." Rudd, quoted in John Kruth, "The Healing Force of the Universe: Albert Ayler's Life and Legacy (34 Years Hence)," *Signal to Noise* 36 (Winter 2005), available at http://www.johnkruth.com/ayler.html. Simultaneously earthy and spiritual, body and mind, Ayler's music was likened to a "Salvation Army band on LSD," and pulsed equally with blues drudge and ecstatic shimmer. Kruth, ibid. The arc of his too brief career began with a stint backing blues harmonica legend Little Walter in the mid-1950s. After a "high" period in the mid-1960s, during which he made a lasting impact on the sound and shape of collectively improvised music, Ayler in some ways returned to his "folk" beginnings, producing records like *New Grass* and *Music Is the Healing Power of the Universe* that embraced the propulsive rhythms of R&B, proto-funk, and blues. In 1970, Ayler's drowned body was found in New York's East River.

33. Stan Douglas, *Stan Douglas, Past Imperfect: Works, 1986–2007*, ed. Hans D. Christ and Iris Dressler, exh. cat. (Ostfildern, Germany: Hatje Cantz, 2008), 190.

34. Douglas, interviewed by Fetherstonhaugh Associates, 1998, http://www.fetherstonhaugh.com/about-us/art-resource/stan-douglas.

35. Lewis, "Wadada Leo Smith's New World Music."

36. Baker, *Blues, Ideology, and Afro-American Literature*, 8.

37. Mackey, preface to *Splay Anthem* (New York: New Directions, 2002), xiv.

38. See LeRoi Jones (Amiri Baraka), *Blues People: Negro Music in White America* (New York: Harper Collins, 1963), 226–27. Interestingly, about his own poetry, Baraka projected similar horizons: "MY POETRY is whatever I think I am.[…] I make a poetry with what I feel is useful & can be saved out of all the garbage of our lives. What I see, am touched by (CAN HEAR) … wives, gardens, jobs, cement yards where cats pee, all my interminable artifacts … ALL are poetry, & nothing moves (with any grace) pried apart from these things.[…] Everything must be made to fit into the poem." Baraka, "How You Sound??," in *The LeRoi Jones/Amiri Baraka Reader* (New York: Basic Books, 2009), 16.

39. Cecil Taylor, "Sound Structure of Subculture Becoming Major Breath/Naked Fire Gesture," liner notes, *Unit Structures*, Blue Note, LP 84237, 1966.

40. McLean's "big room," like Baraka's "total area," suggests a spatial metaphor that has long been operative in jazz. The groups assembled by Duke Ellington as early as the late 1920s were famous for their engineered, total sound, expressed not merely through traditional instrumentation but through the unique style and sound of individual players. Likewise, innovative musicians of the 1960s and 70s established expansion of sonic and performative space as central to the meaning and feeling of their art. To hear the intervallic leaps of bird song or baritone rumbling in Eric Dolphy and Anthony Braxton or the "little instruments" and incorporation of theatricality and pastiche in the Art Ensemble of Chicago is to hear space established through affective particularity.

41. "Negro dancing is dynamic suggestion. No matter how violent it may appear to the beholder, every posture gives the impression that the dancer will do much more. For example, the performer flexes one knee sharply, assumes a ferocious face mask, thrusts the upper part of the body forward with clenched fists, elbows taut as in hard running or grasping a thrusting blade. That is all. But the spectator himself adds the picture of ferocious assault, hears the drums and finds himself keeping time with the music and tensing himself for the struggle. It is compelling insinuation. That is the very reason the spectator is held so rapt. He is participating in the performance himself—carrying out the suggestions of the performer." Zora Neale Hurston, "Characteristics of Negro Expression" (1934), reprinted in *Folklore, Memoirs, and Other Writings* (New York: Library of America, 1995), 835.

42. Ralph Ellison, *Living with Music: Ralph Ellison's Jazz Writings*, ed. Robert G. O'Meally (New York: Modern Library, 2001), 103.

43. What would be uncomfortable about the Cramps? First heard in the punk heyday of the late 1970s, and continuing until Interior's death in 2009, the group's signature "psychobilly" sound was a toxic muck of Elvis-addled proto-rock, garage bombast, and Z-grade pop effluvia. Campy, spiteful, and preposterously gauche, the Cramps embraced a dismemberment of rock's sacred bodies—including, in some sense, its longstanding suppression of racial discrepancy. Though the group didn't exactly lionize Little Richard or Chuck Berry, it seems important to acknowledge that in gutting figures like record producer Sam Phillips and Elvis Presley, the Cramps' mockery was addressed, de facto, at a kind of whiteness: in particular, a Southern whiteness formed and deformed in an era of racial perversity.

44. Amy Sillman, "Ab-Ex and Disco Balls," *Artforum* 49, no. 10 (Summer 2011): 325.

45. Lorraine O'Grady, "New Worlds," exhibition press release, Alexander Gray Associates, New York, April 11–May 19, 2012, http://www.alexandergray.com/exhibitions/2012-04-11_lorraine-oand39grady.

46. William Carlos Williams, quoted in Mackey, *Discrepant Engagement*, 21.

47. Baker, *Blues, Ideology, and Afro-American Literature*, 202.

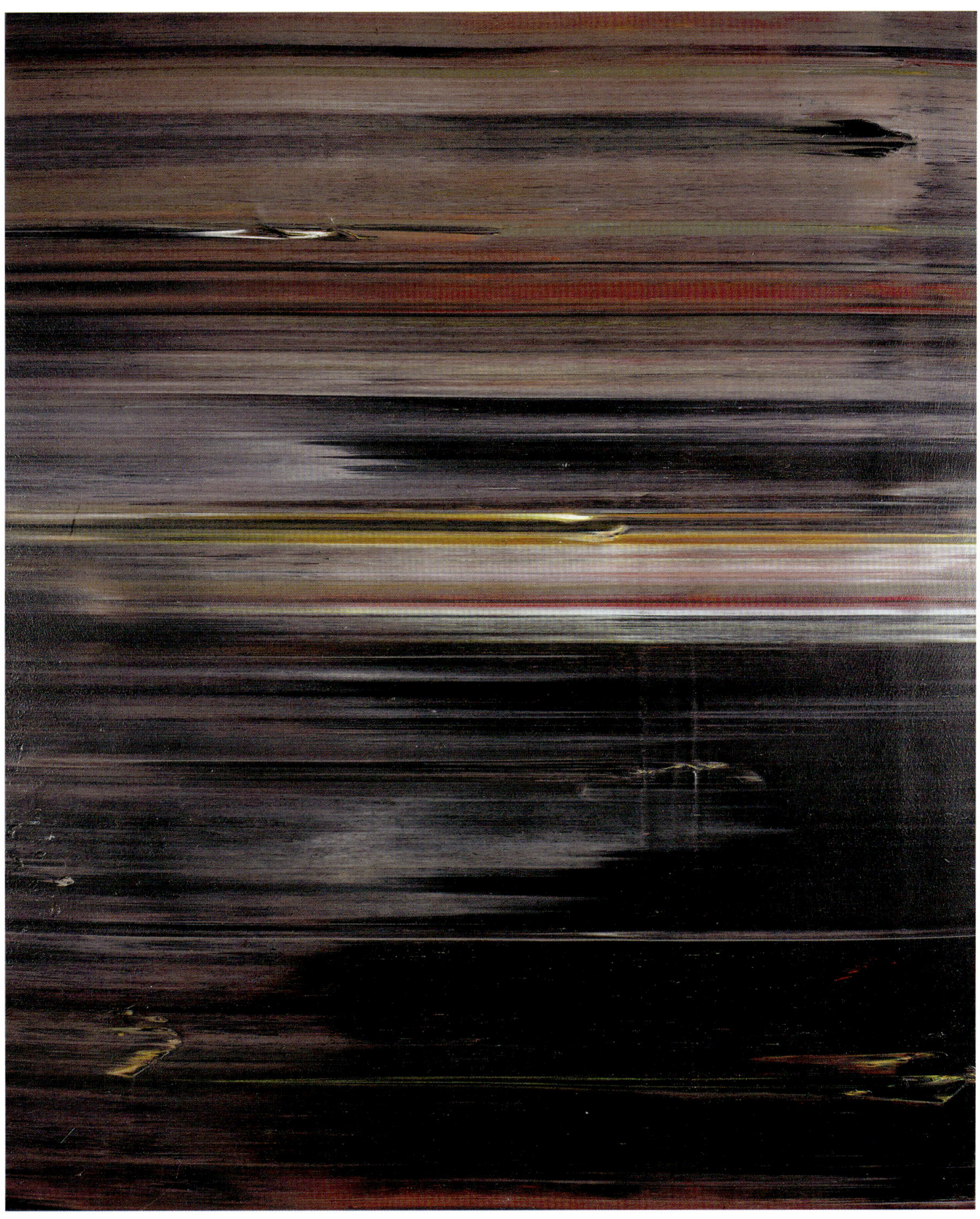

Jack Whitten
Black Table Setting (Homage to Duke Ellington), 1974

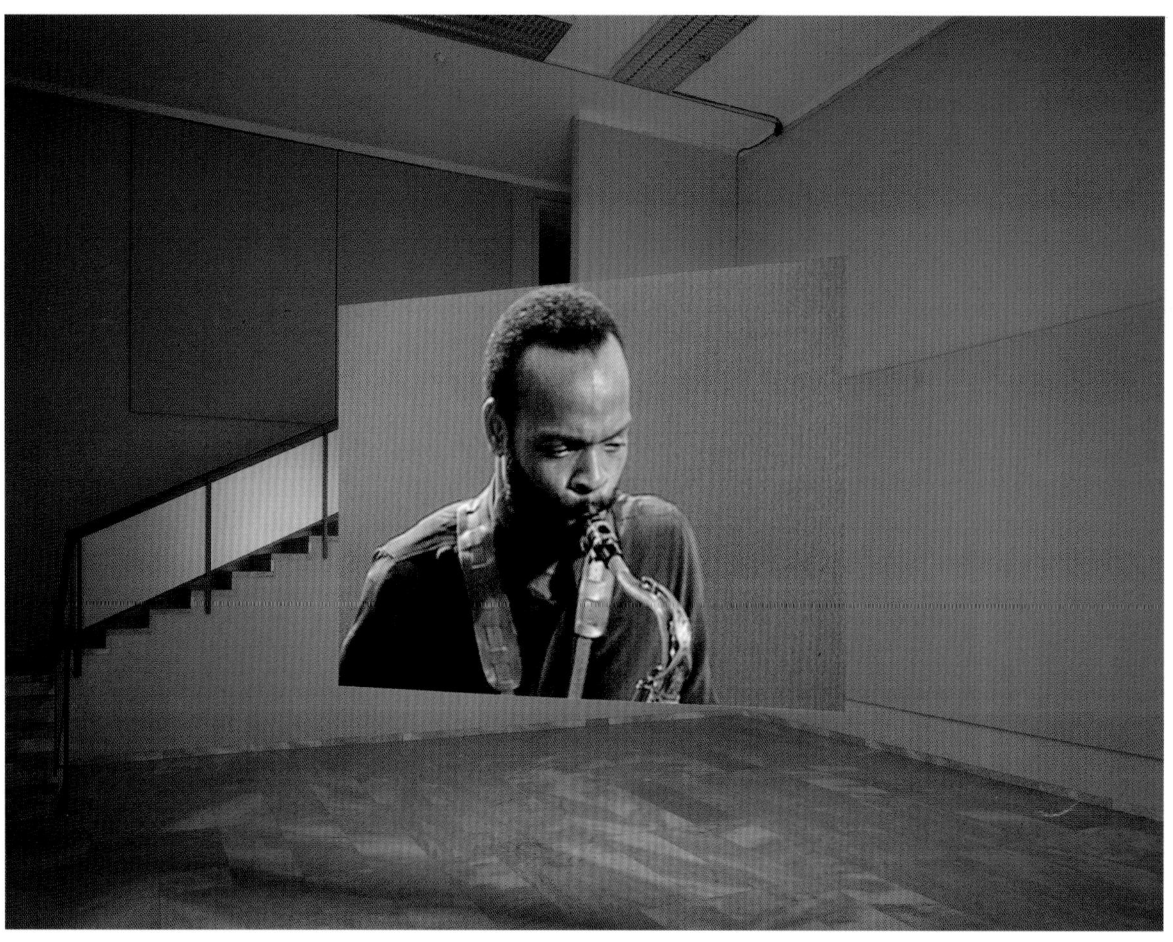

Stan Douglas
Hors-champs, 1992
Installation at Württembergischer Kunstverein, Stuttgart, Germany, 2007

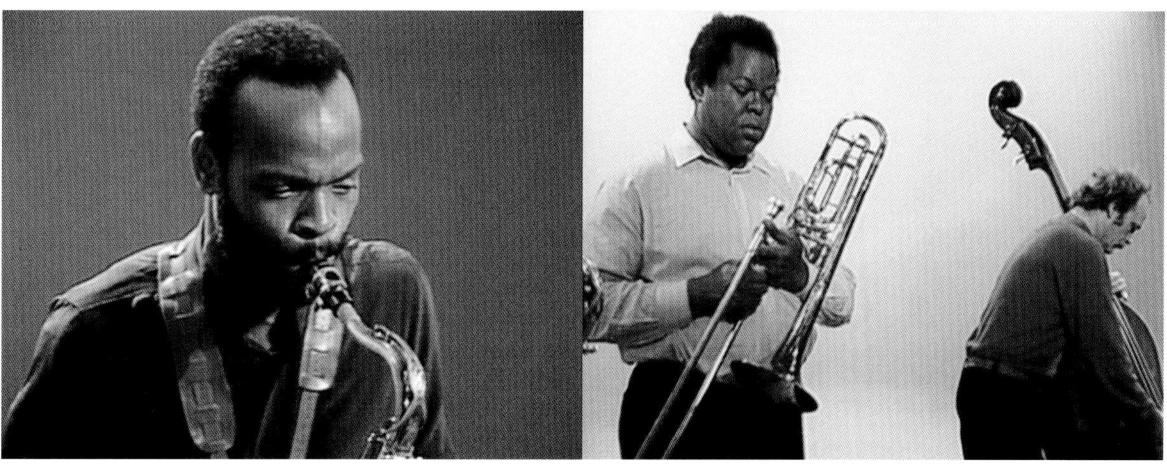

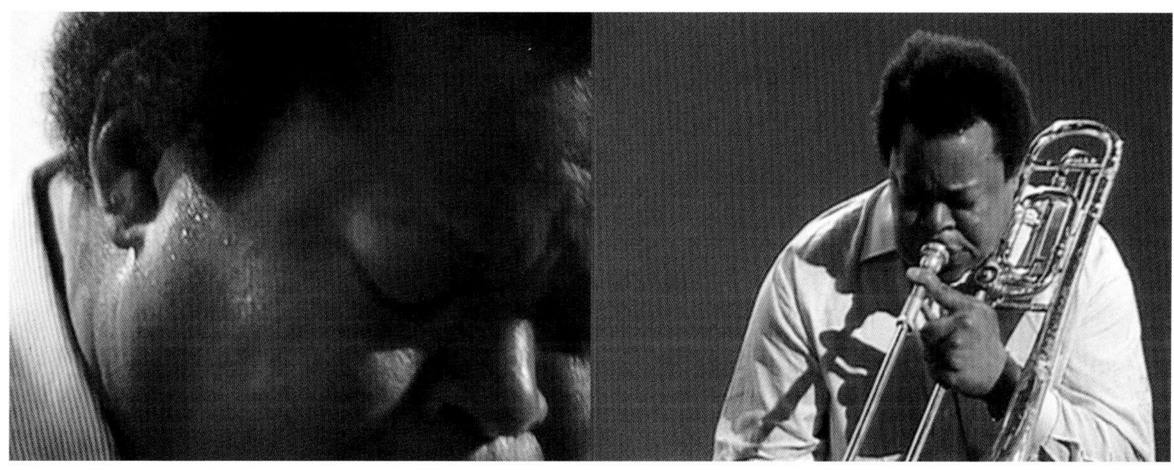

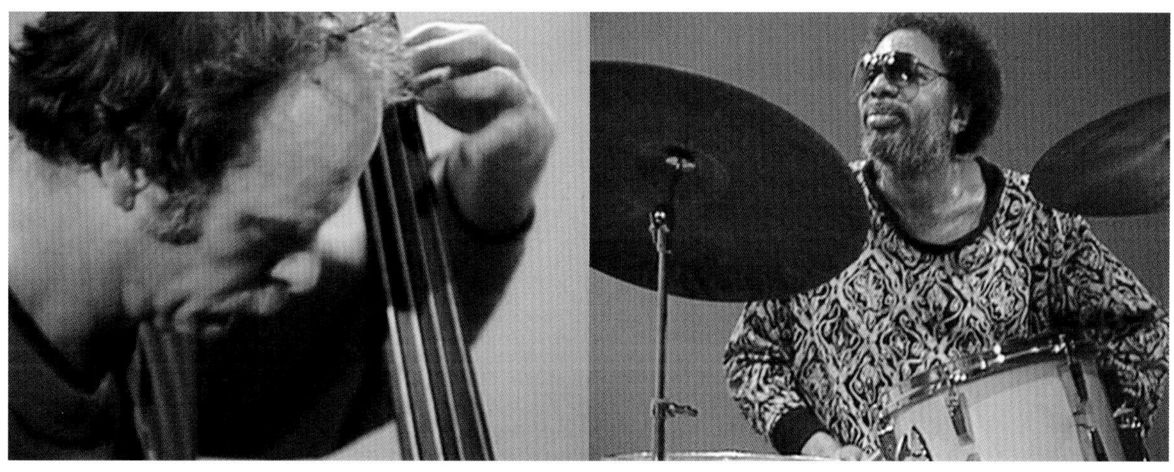

Stan Douglas
Stills from *Hors-champs*, 1992

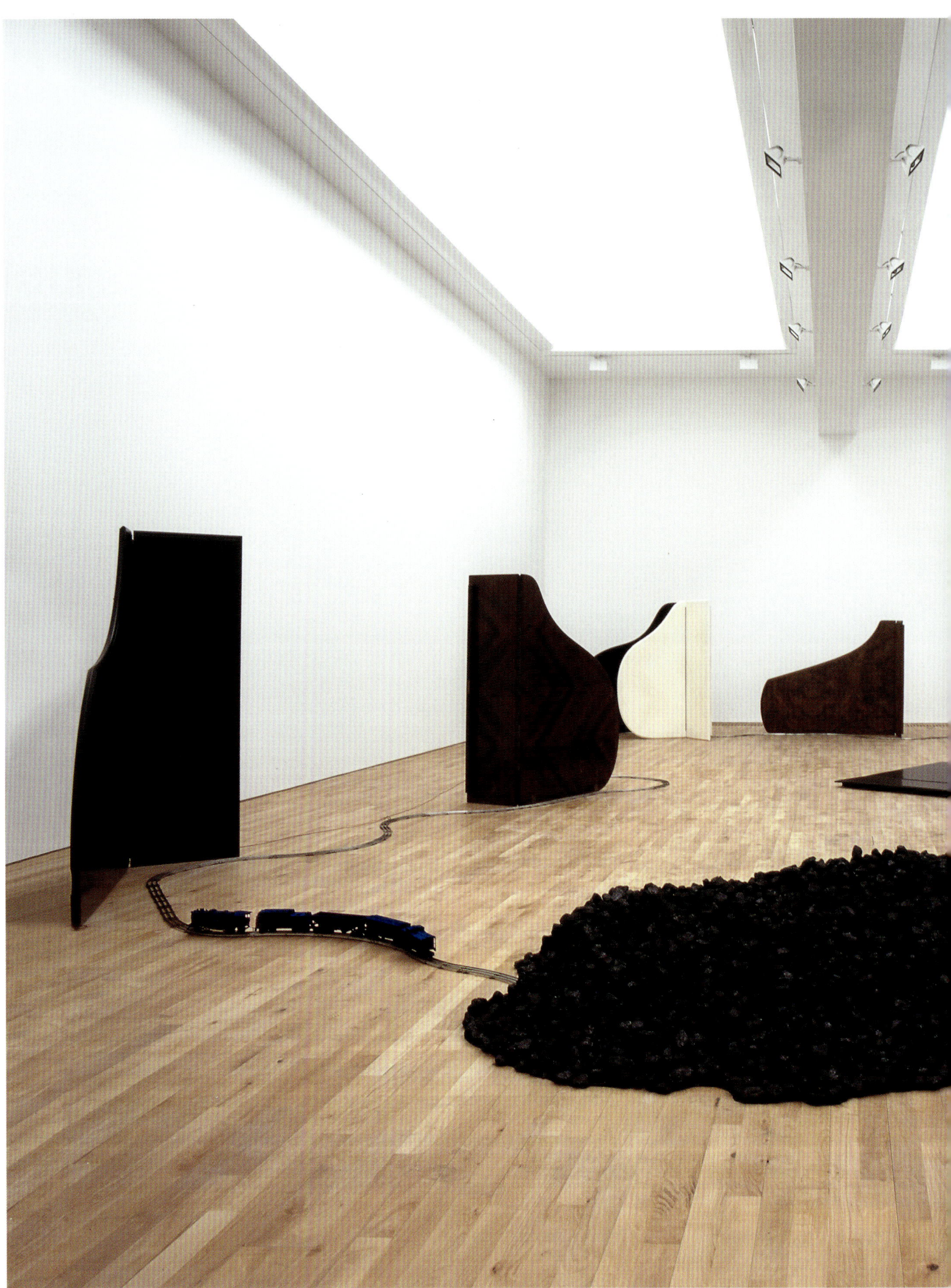

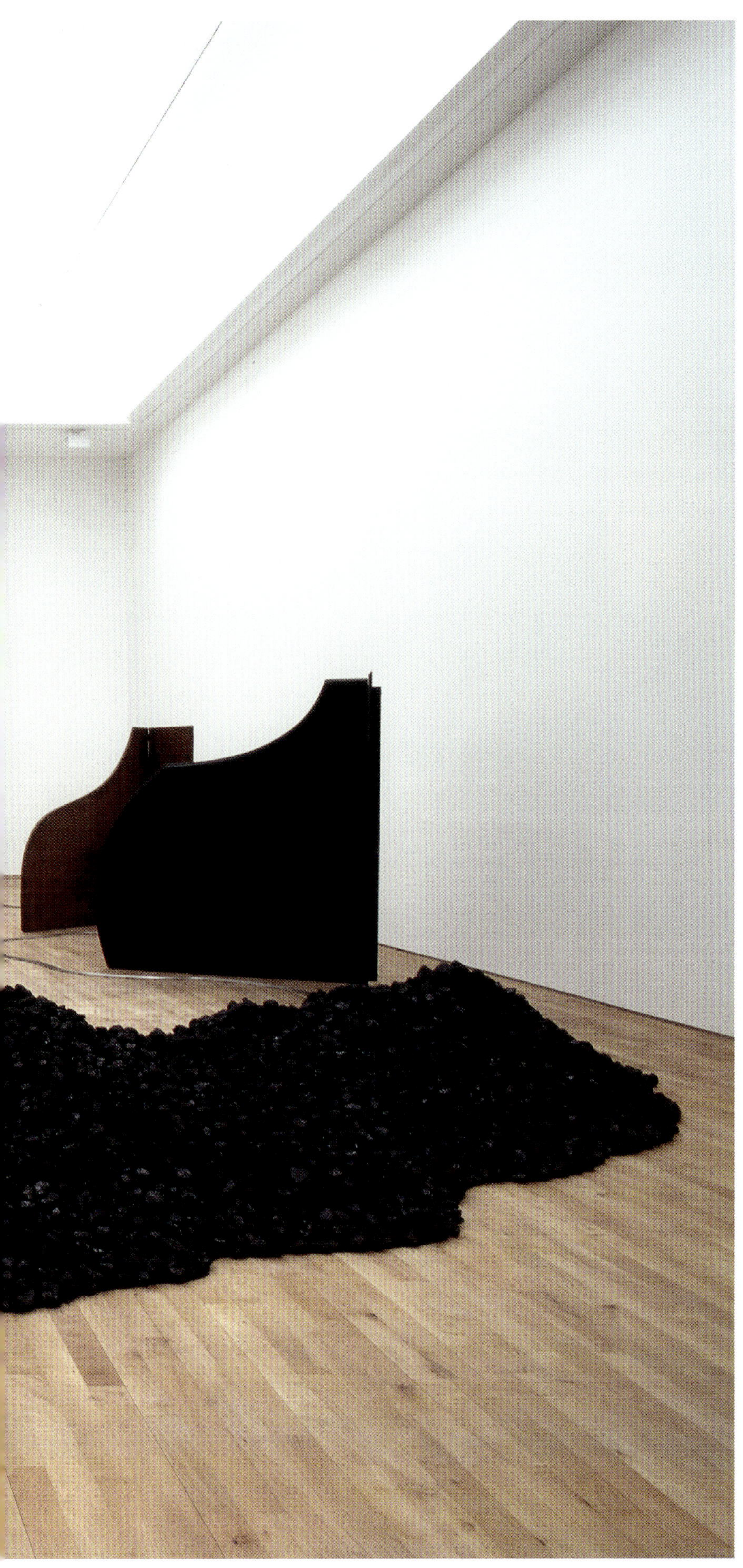

David Hammons
Chasing the Blue Train, 1989

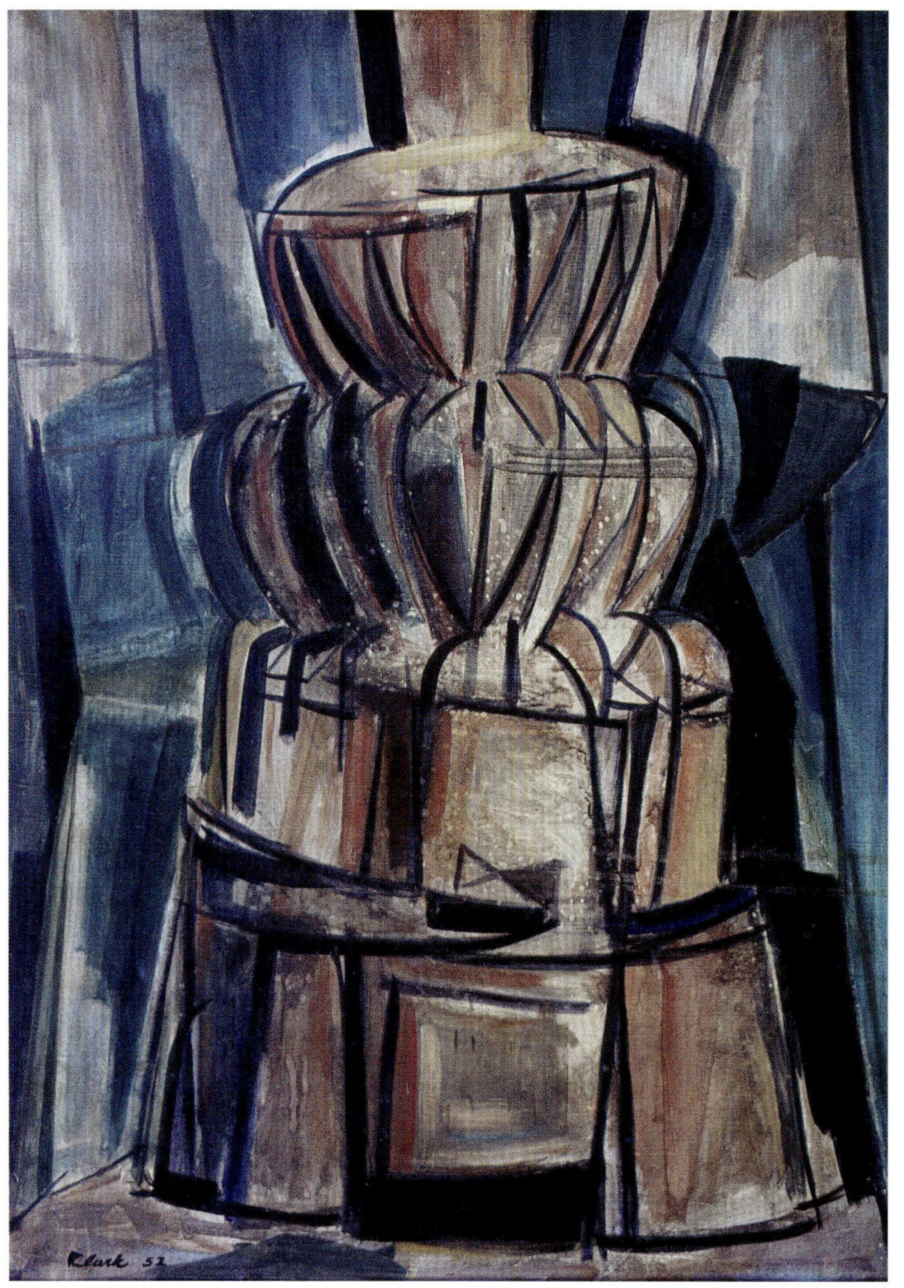

Edward Clark
The Stove, 1952

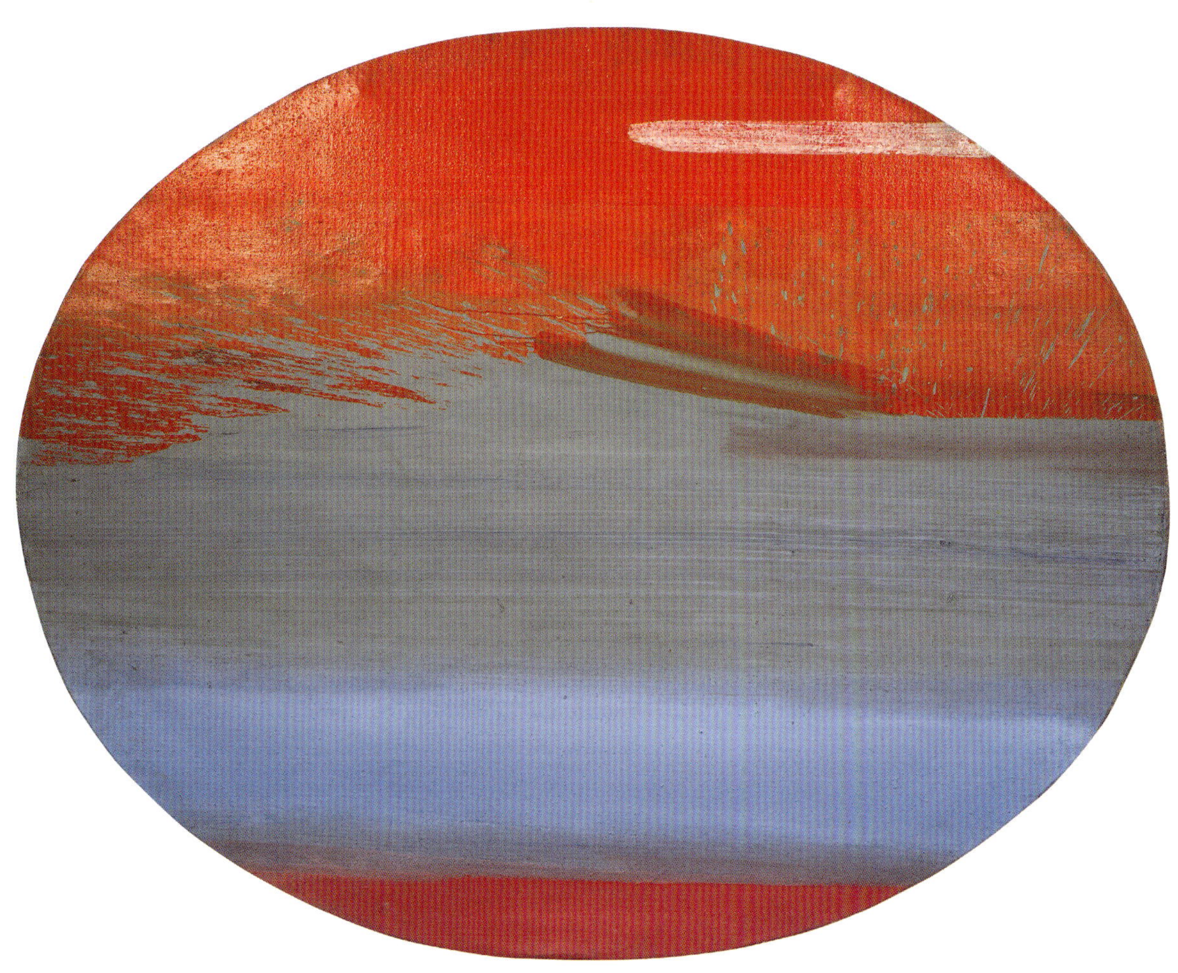

Edward Clark
The Big Egg (Vetheuil Series), 1968

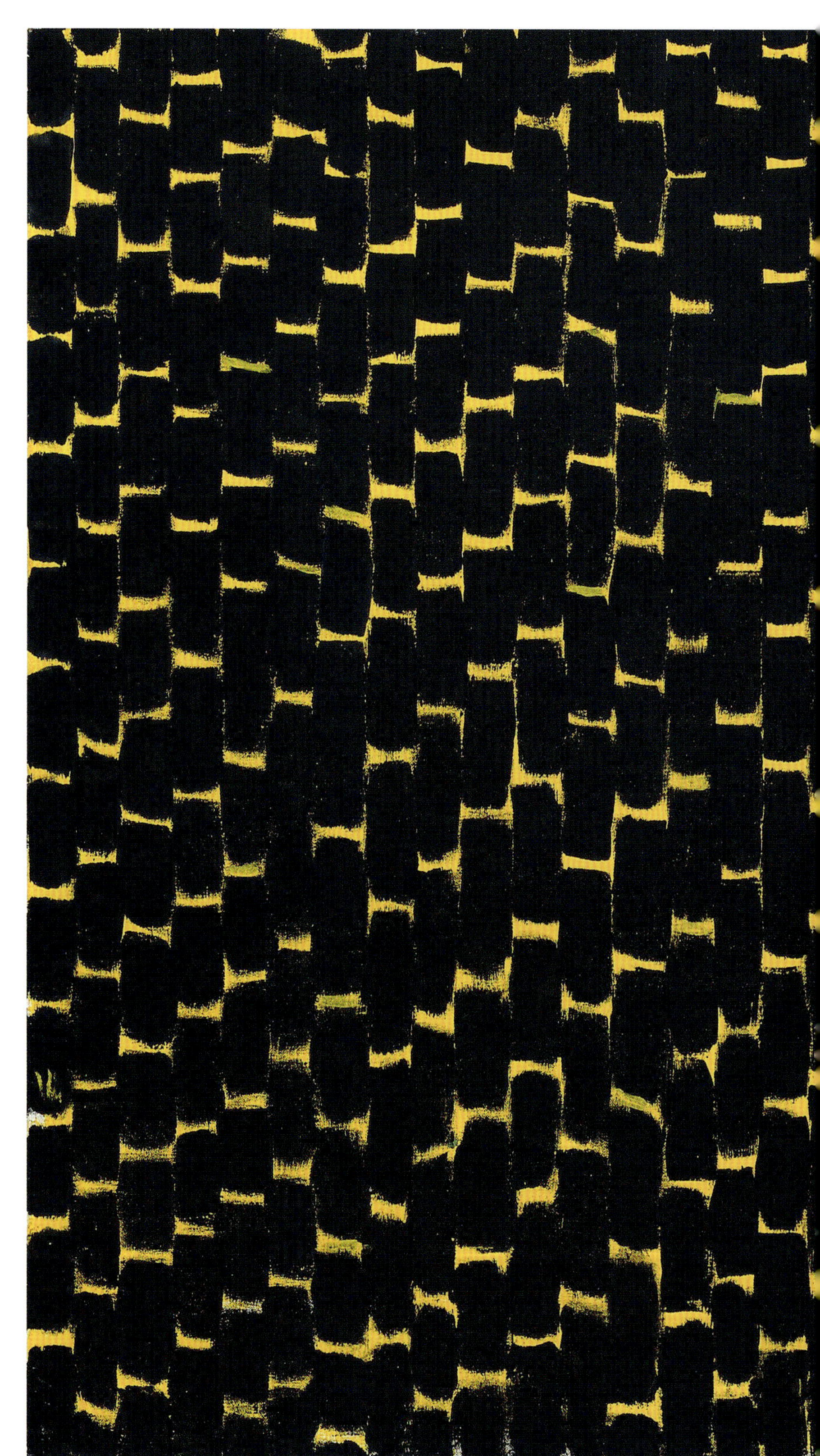

Alma Thomas
Late Night Reflections, 1972

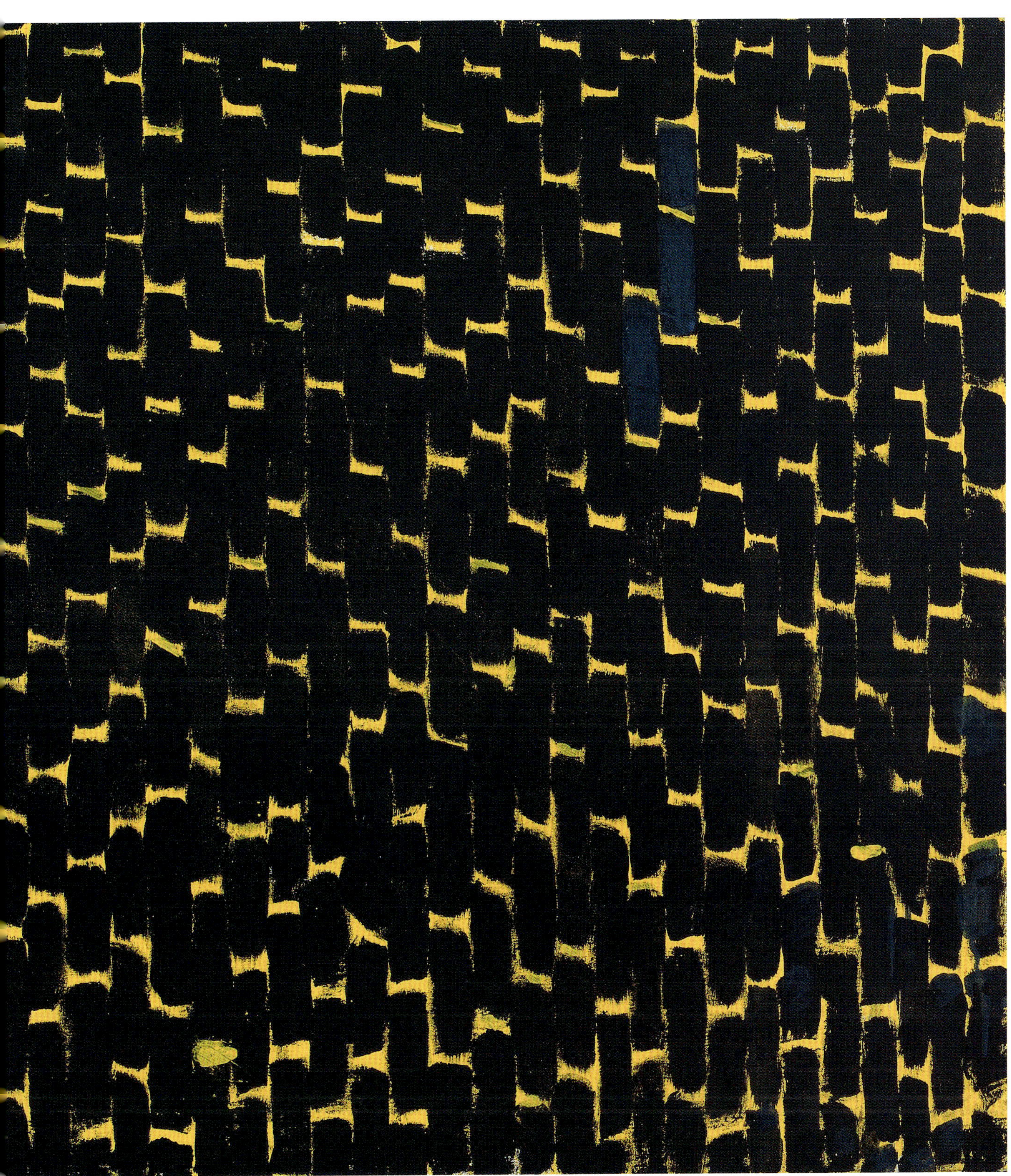

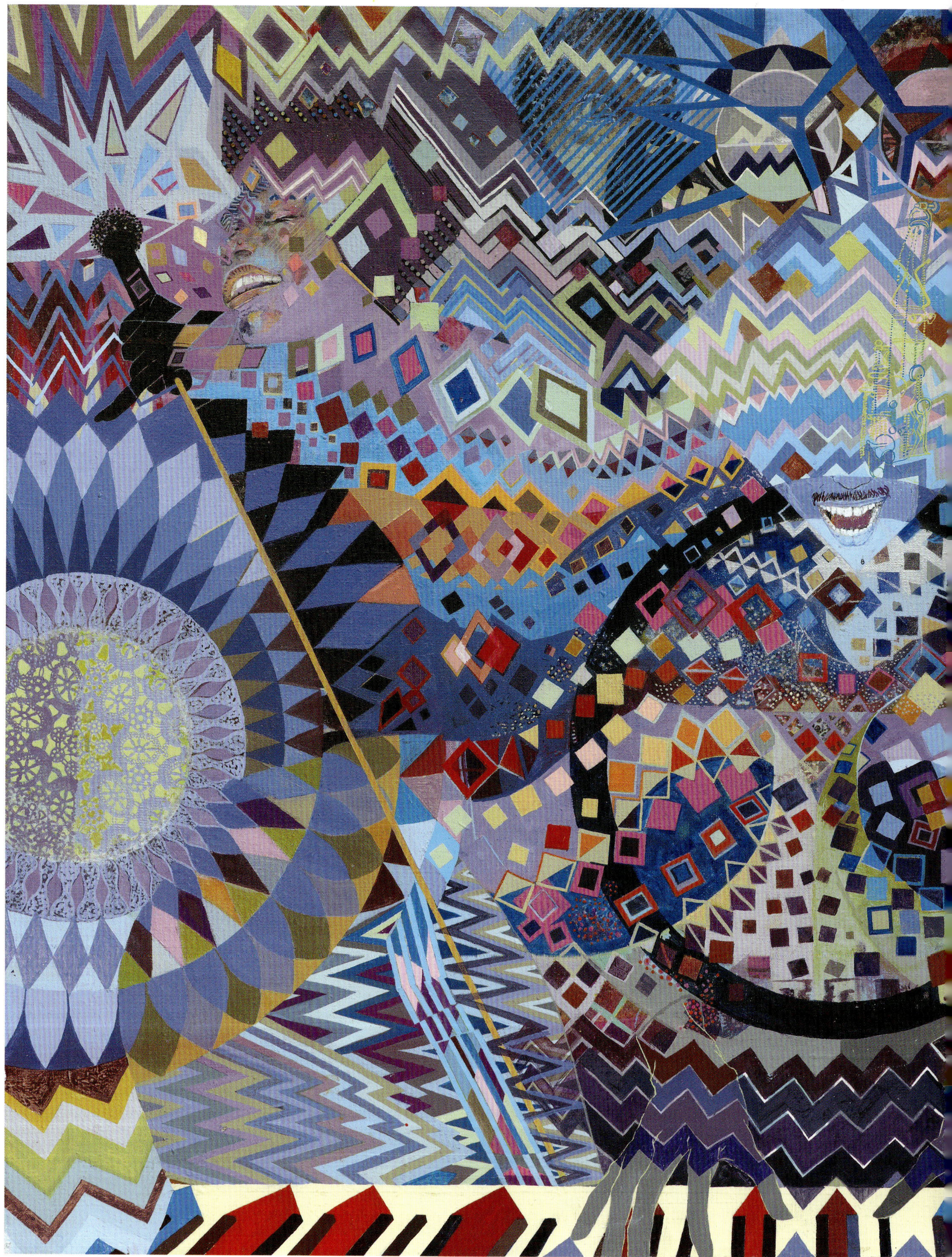

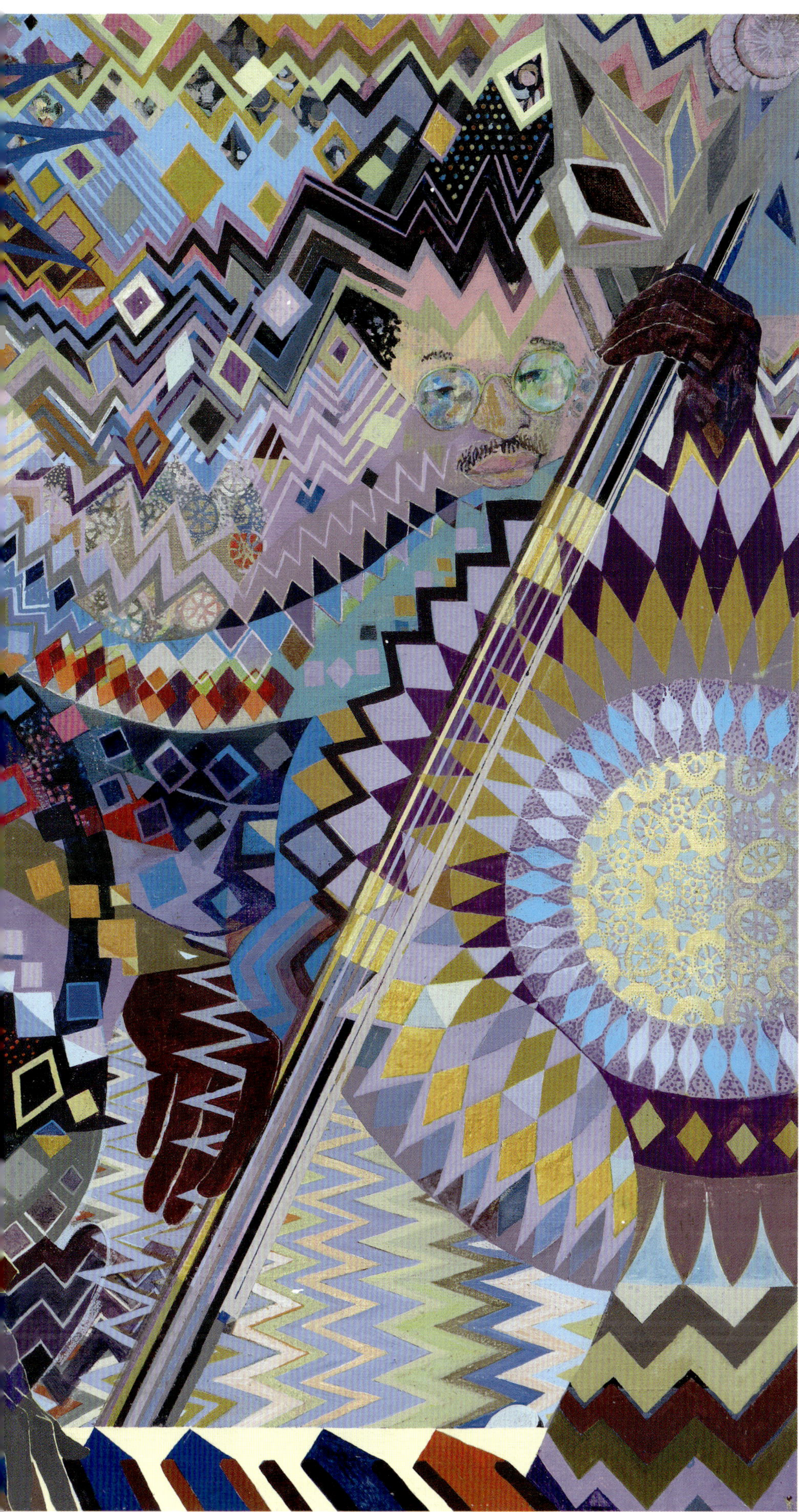

Jeff Donaldson
Jampact and Jelly Tite (for Jamila), 1988

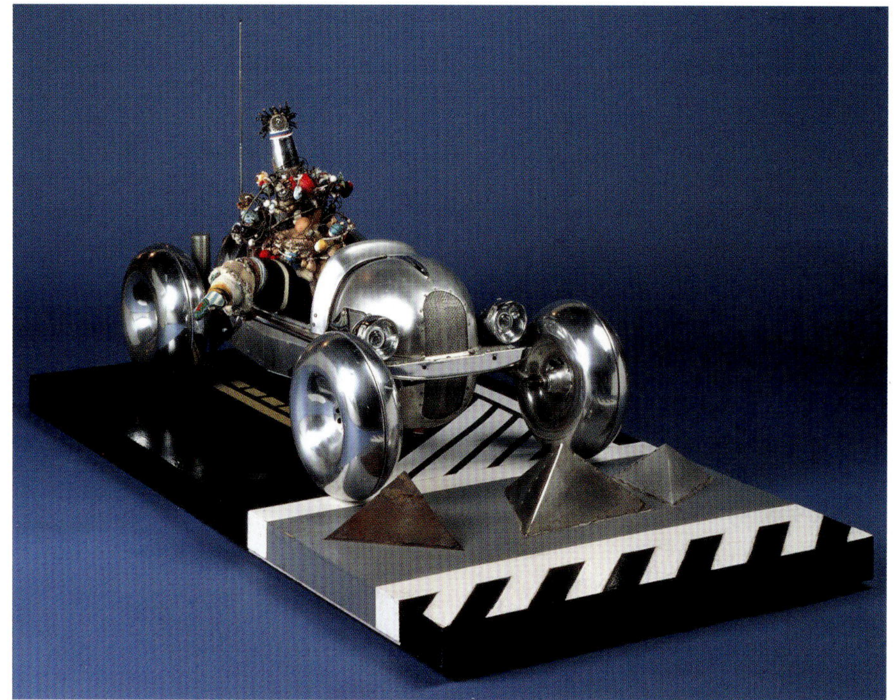

John Outterbridge
California Crosswalk, 1979

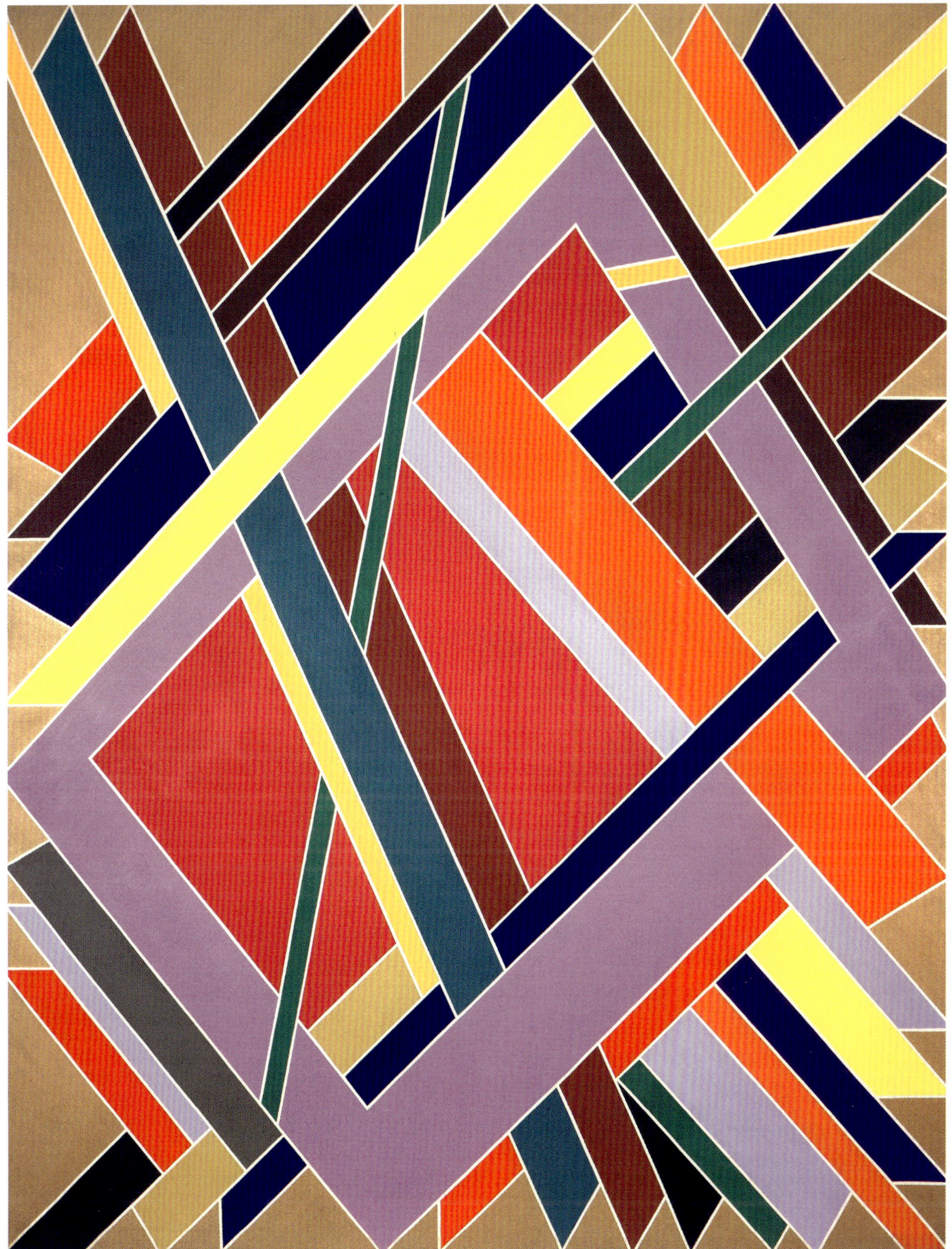

William T. Williams
Trane, 1969

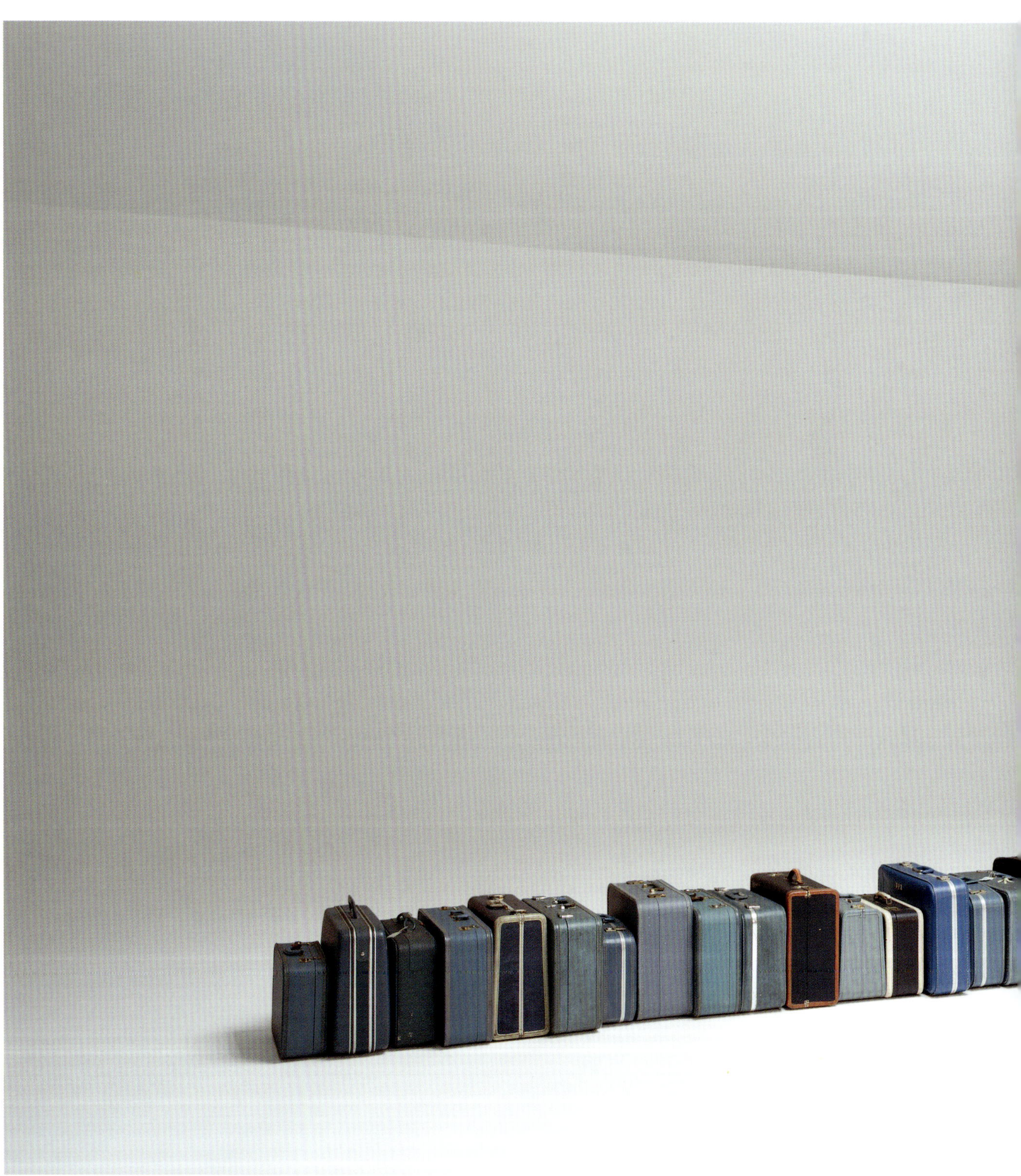

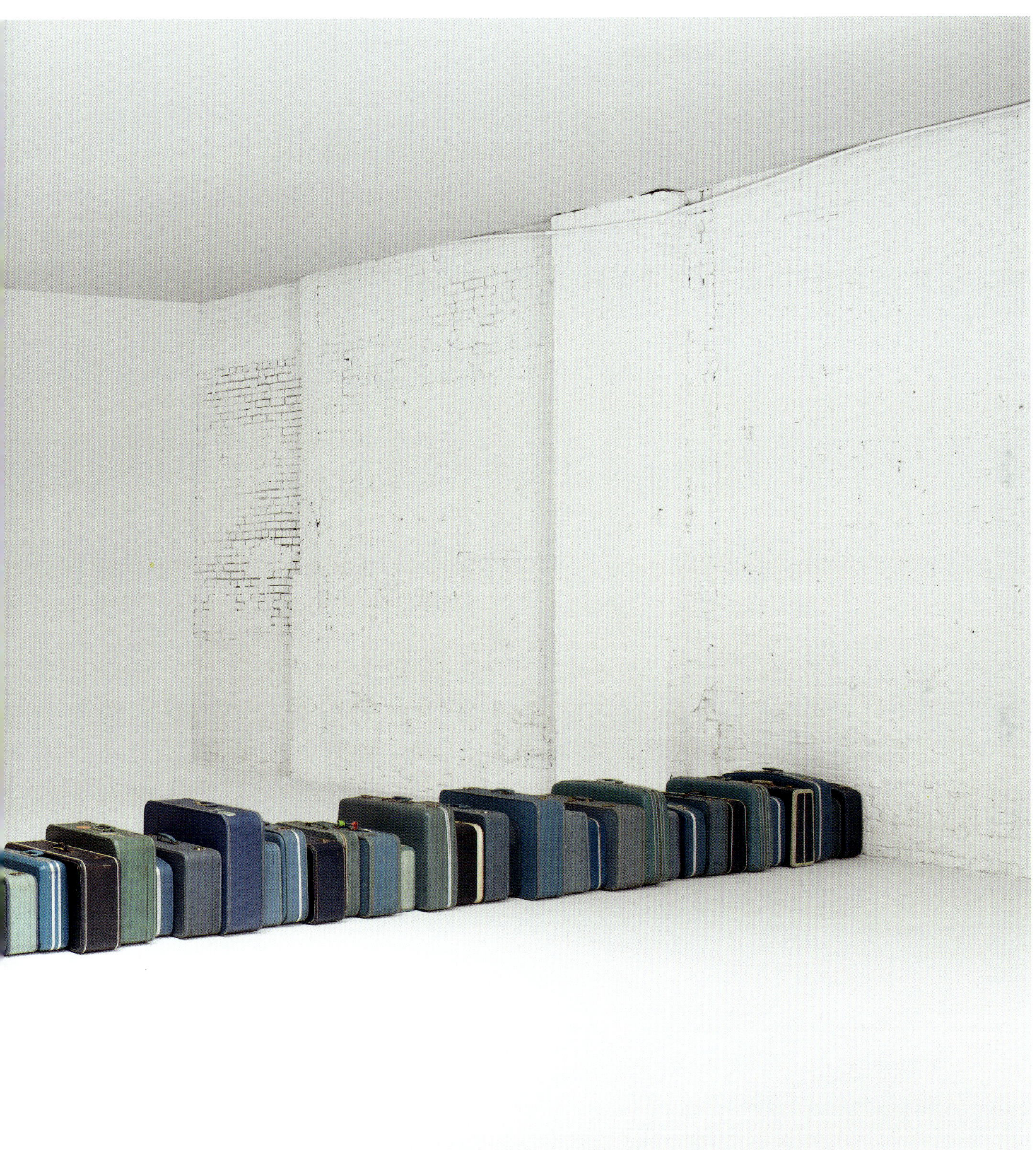

Zoe Leonard
1961, 2002–ongoing

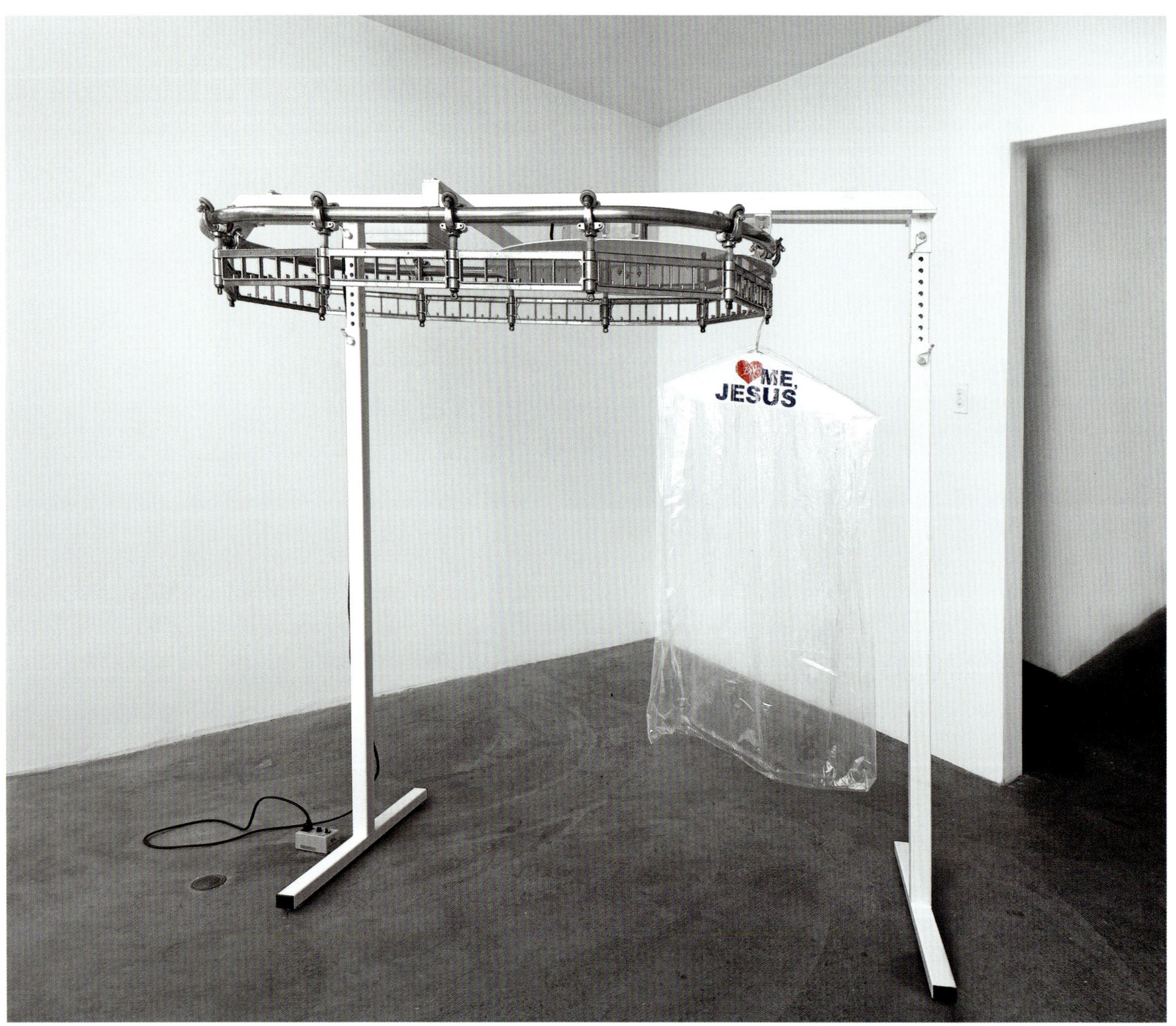

Dave McKenzie
Fear and Trembling, 2009

Charles Gaines
Detail from *Untitled (Regression Series: Group 3)*, 1973–74

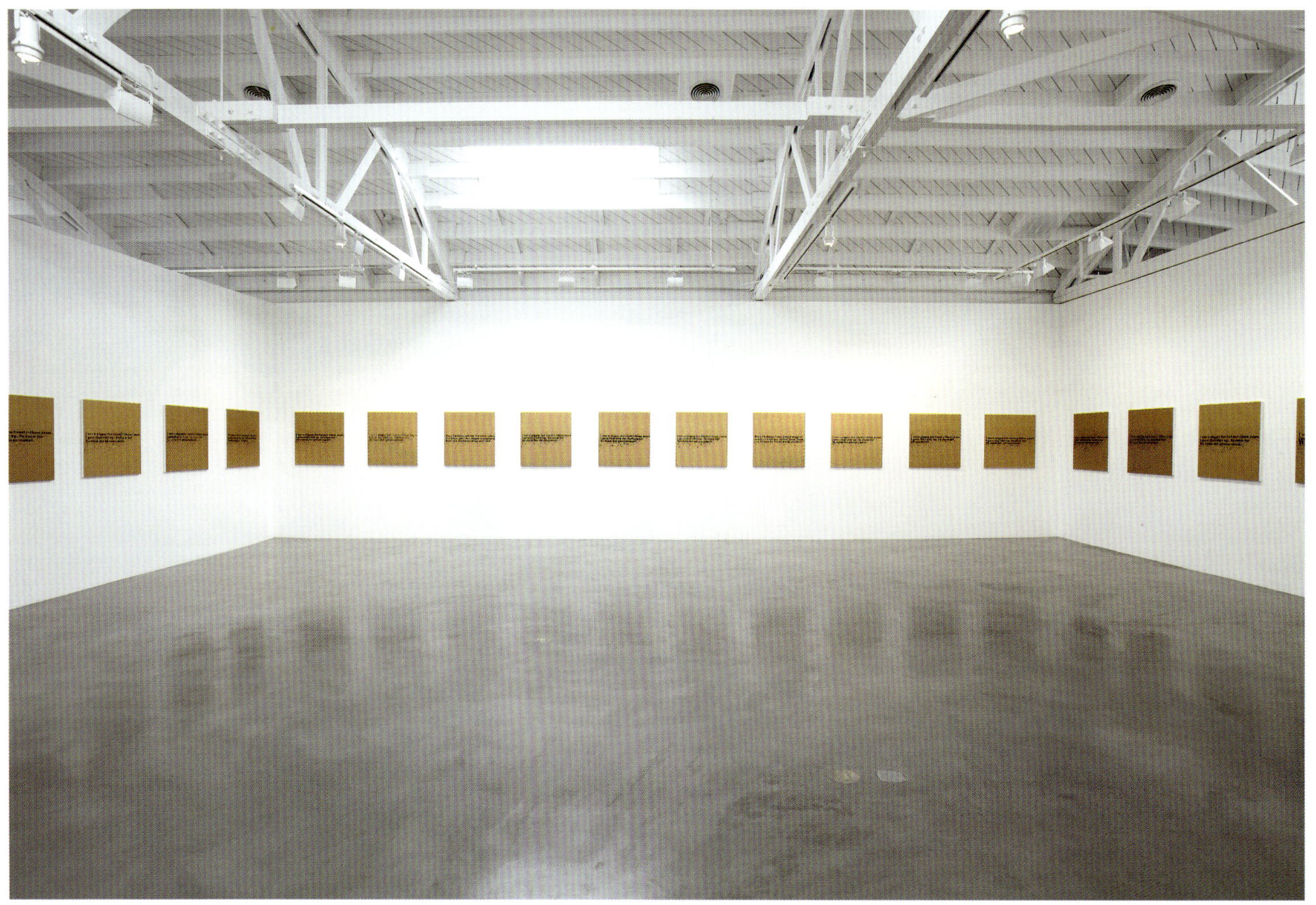

Glenn Ligon
Installation of *No Room (Gold)* paintings at Regen Projects, Los Angeles, 2007

I was a nigger for twenty-three years. I gave that shit up. No room for No room for advancement.

Glenn Ligon
No Room (Gold) #42, 2007

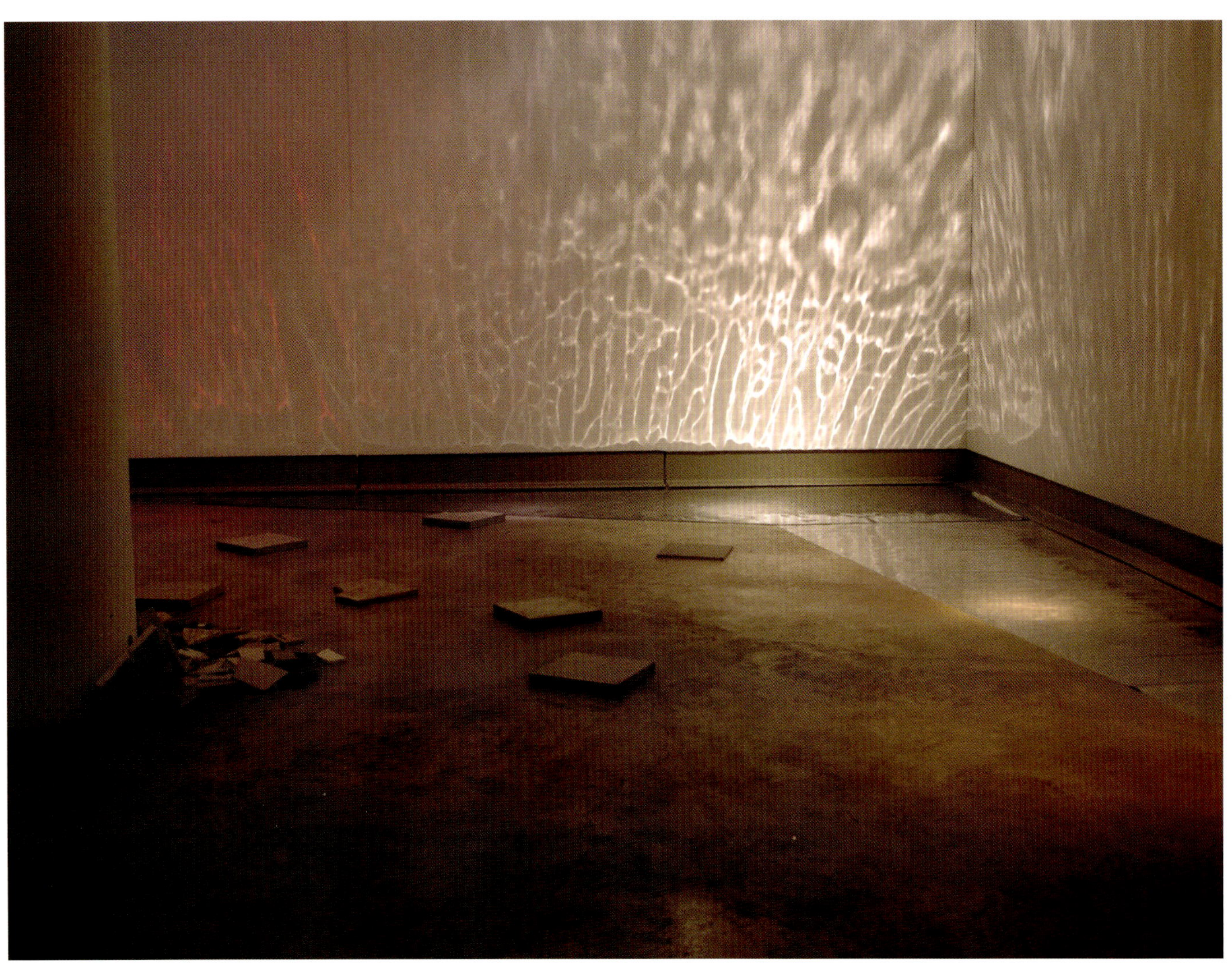

Kira Lynn Harris
Prism, Mirror, Lens, 2009
Silver Mylar, tiles, and lights
Dimensions variable
Courtesy of the artist
Installation at the CUE Art Foundation, New York, 2009

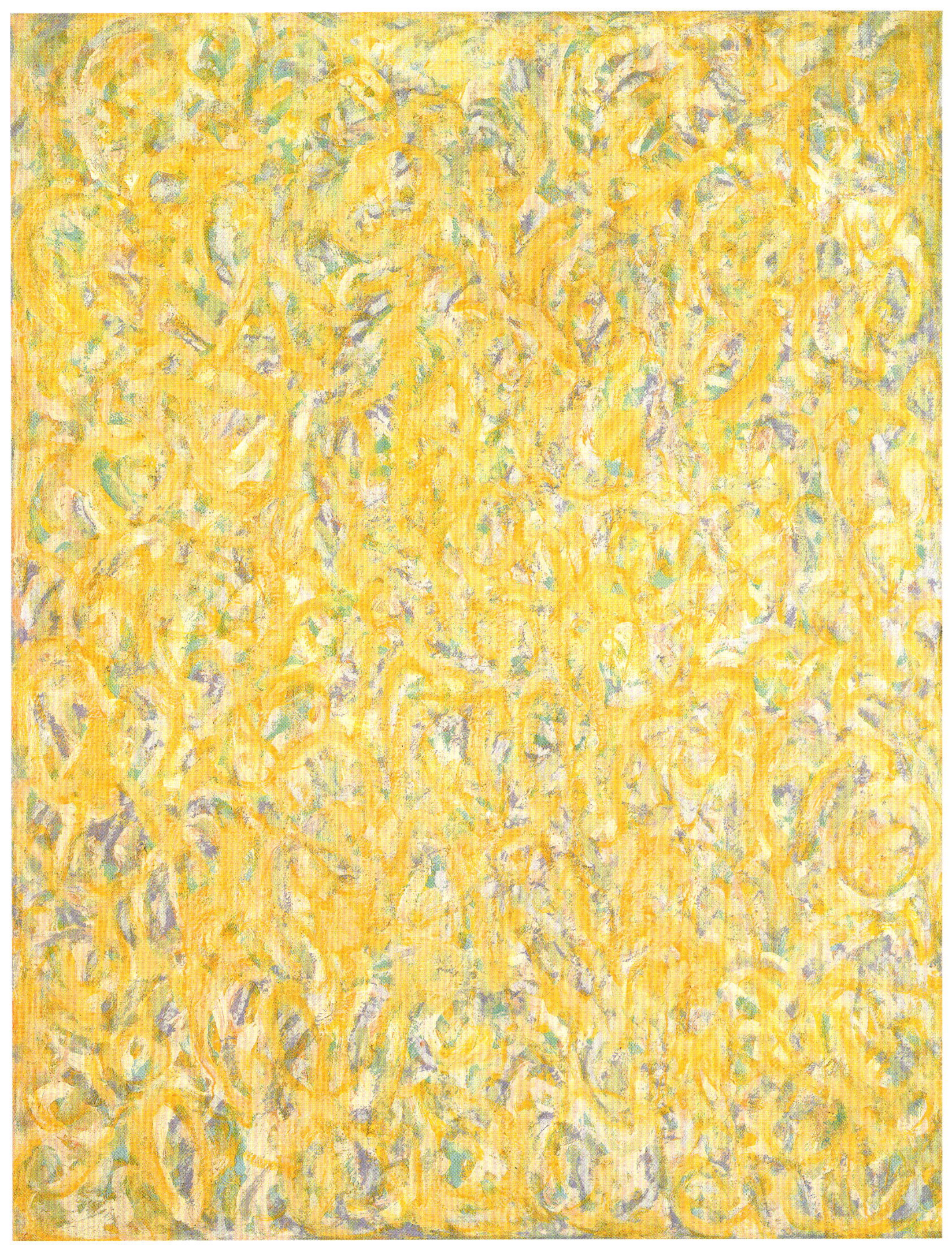

Beauford Delaney
Untitled, c. 1958

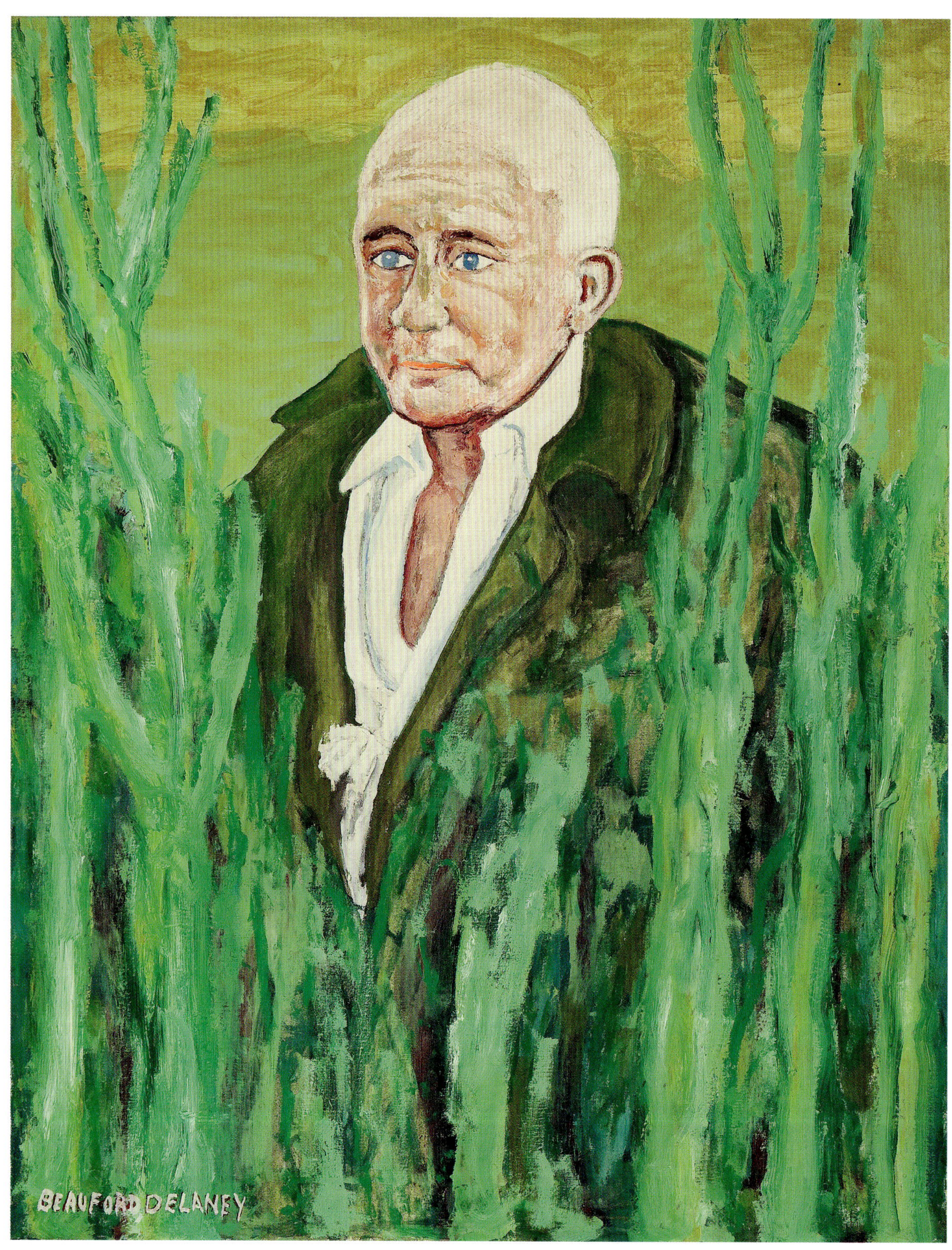

Beauford Delaney
Portrait of Jean Genet, 1972

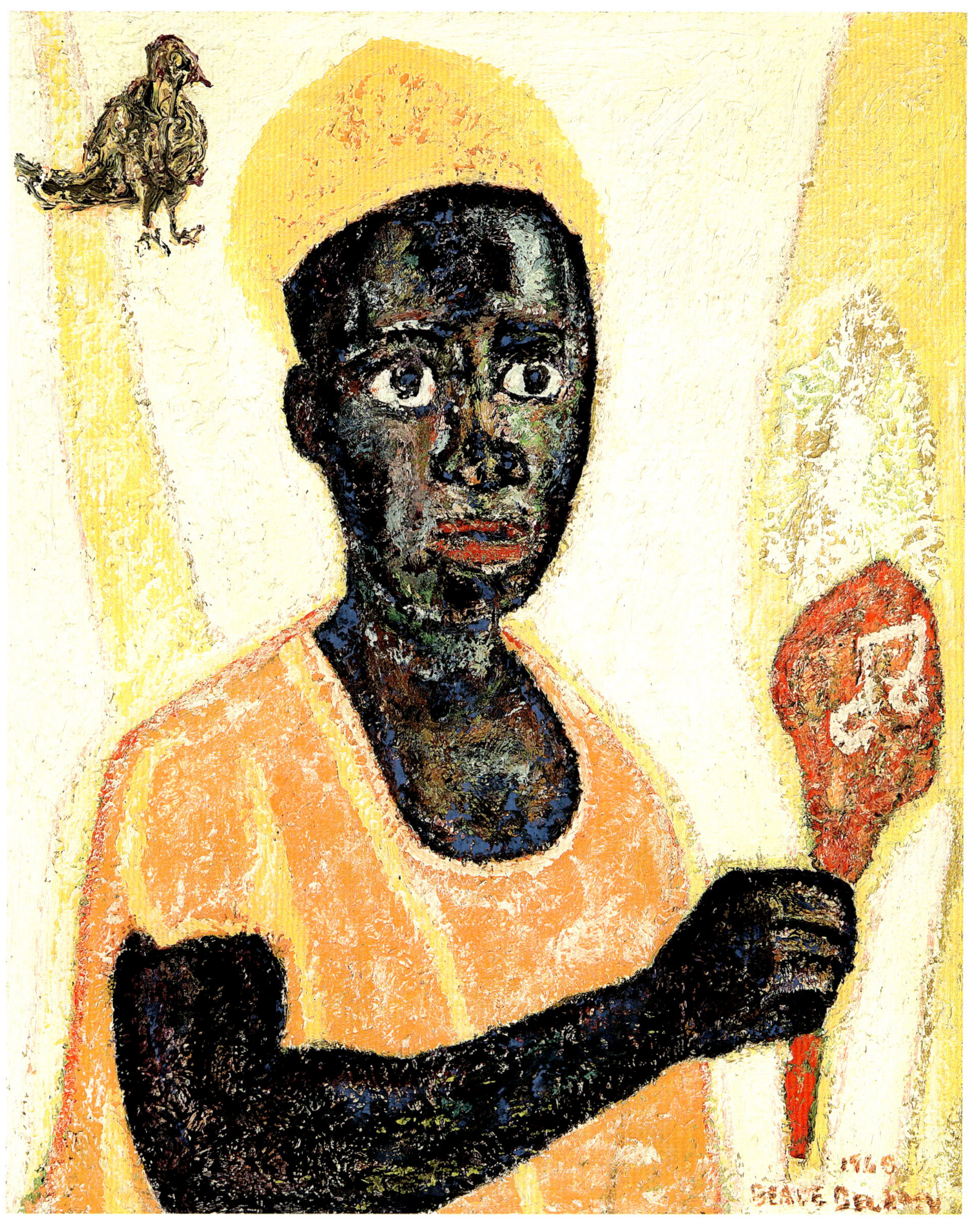

Beauford Delaney
Portrait of Charlie Parker, 1968

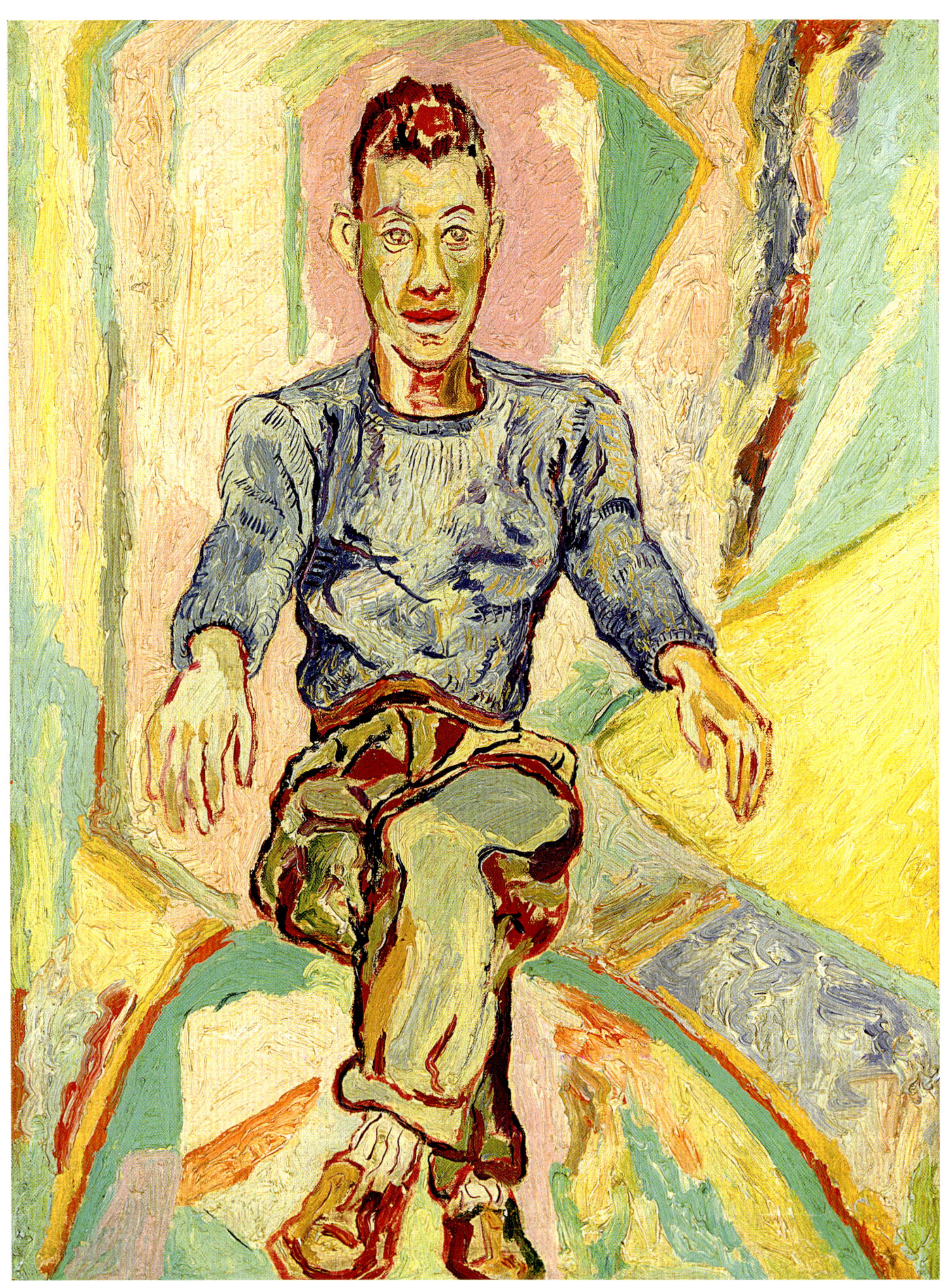

Beauford Delaney
James Baldwin, c. 1955

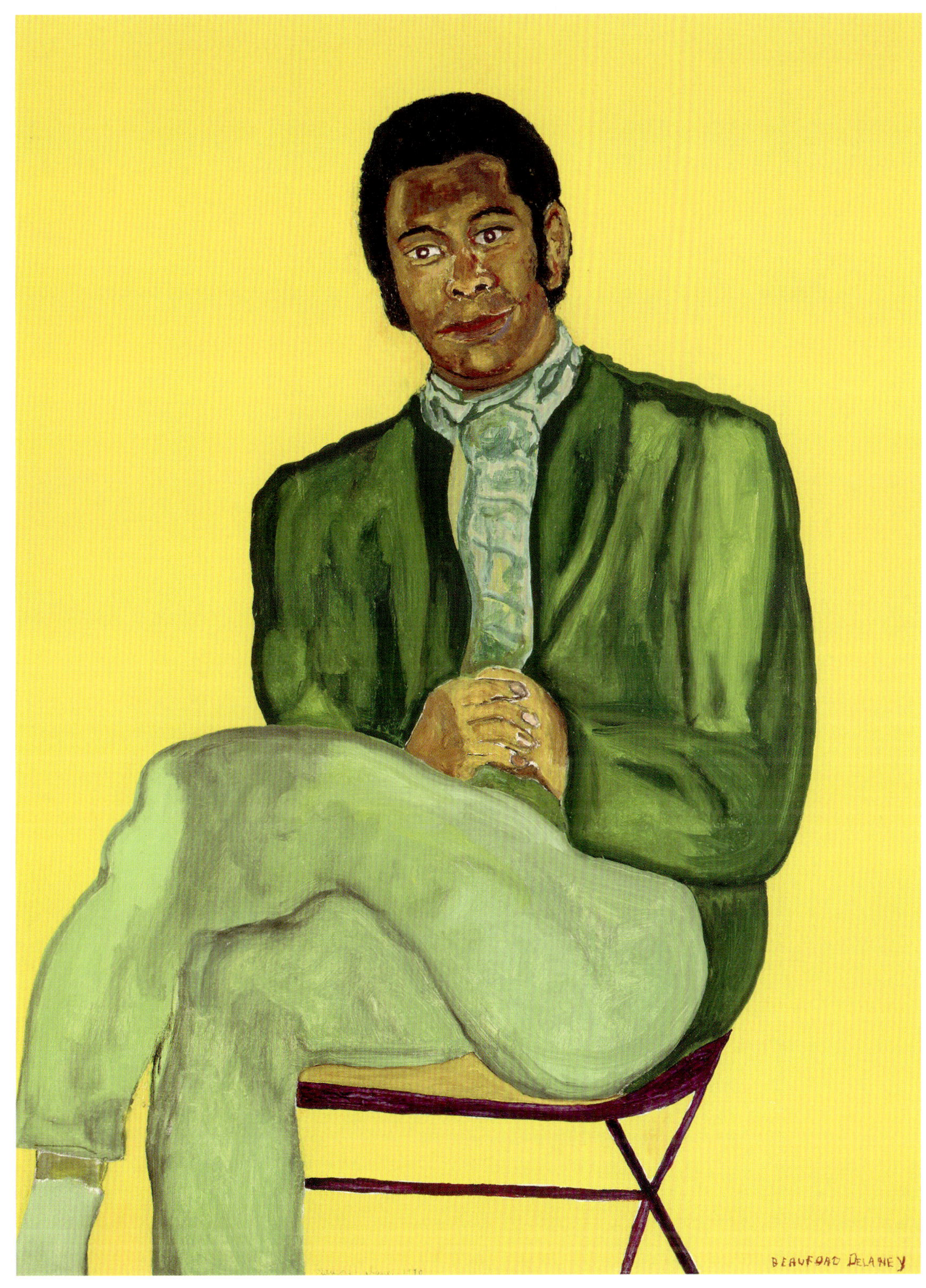

Beauford Delaney
Portrait of a Young Musician, n.d.

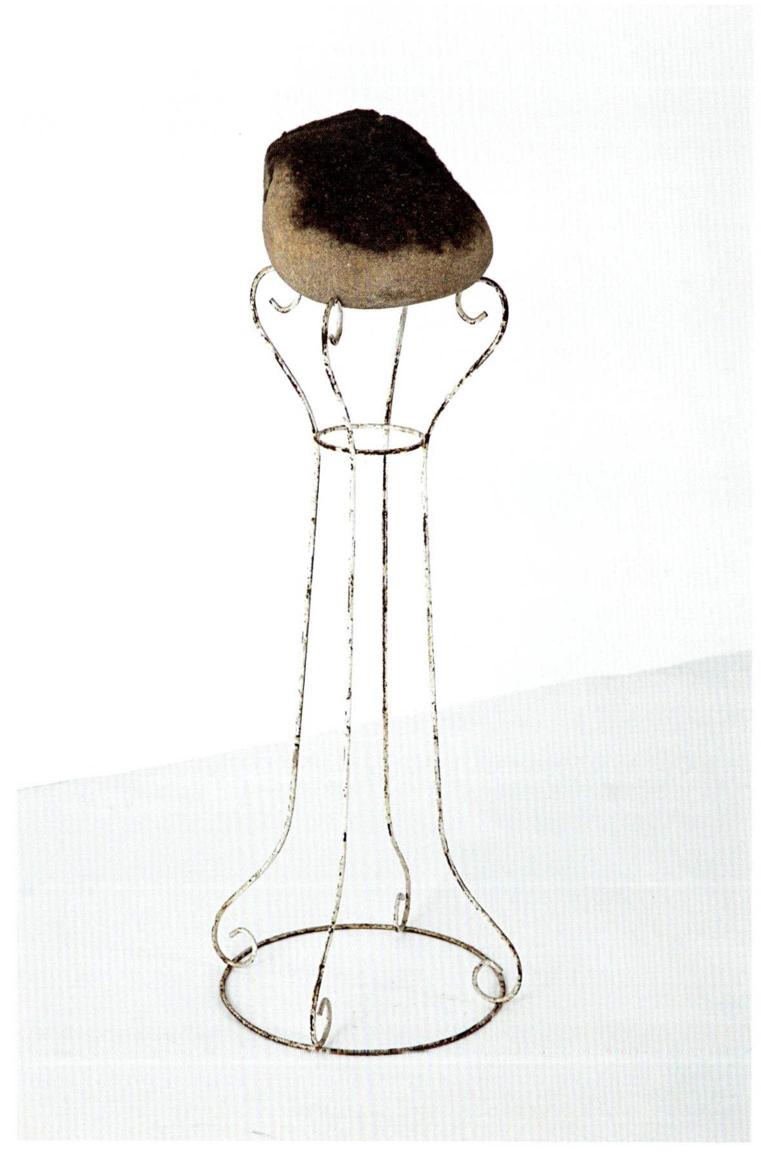

David Hammons
Rocky, 1990

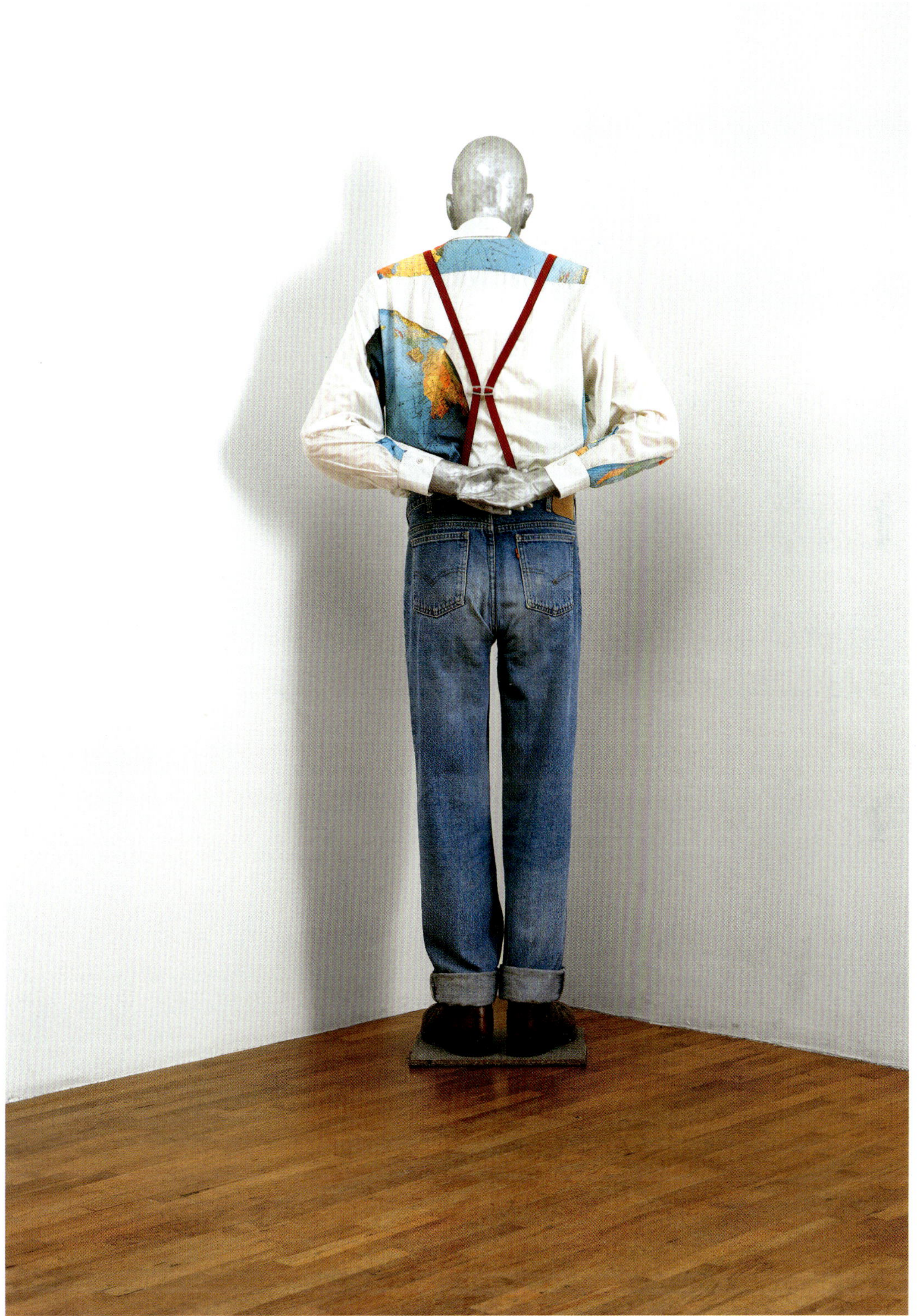

Martin Kippenberger
Martin, ab in die Ecke und schäm dich (Martin, Into the Corner, You Should Be Ashamed of Yourself), 1992

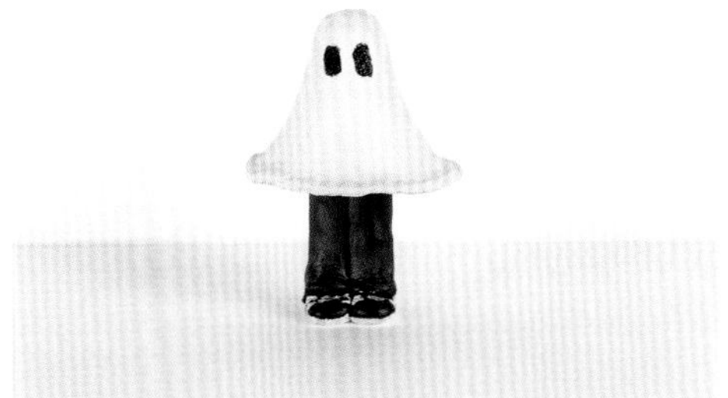

Dave McKenzie
Portrait as a Ghost, 2004

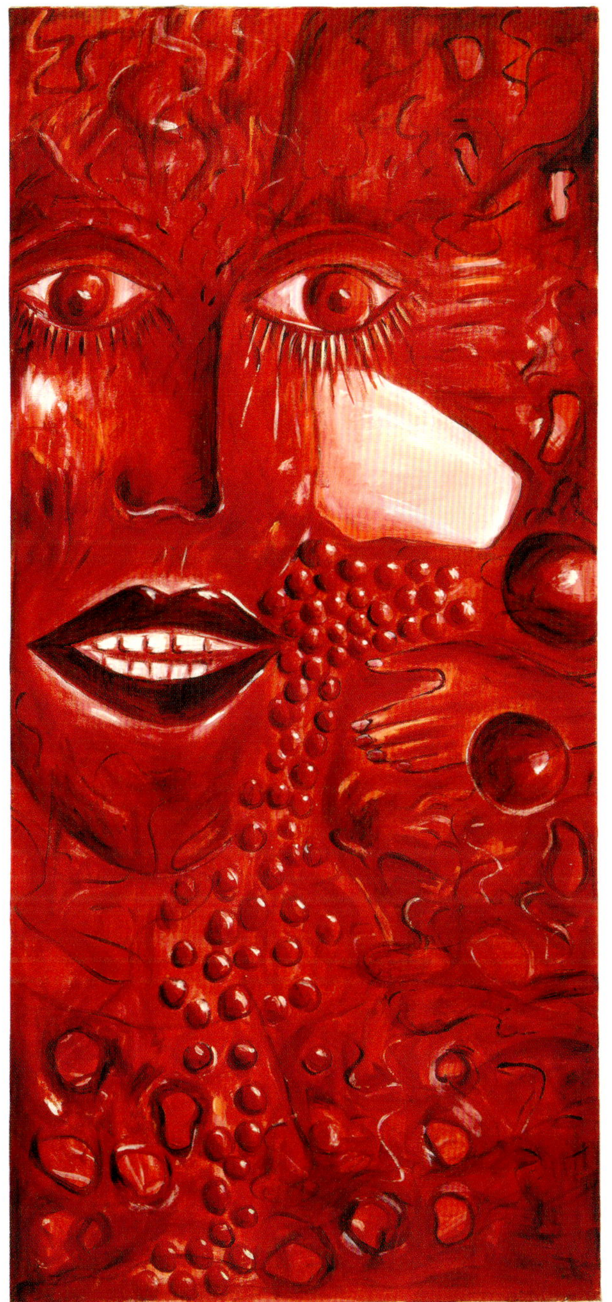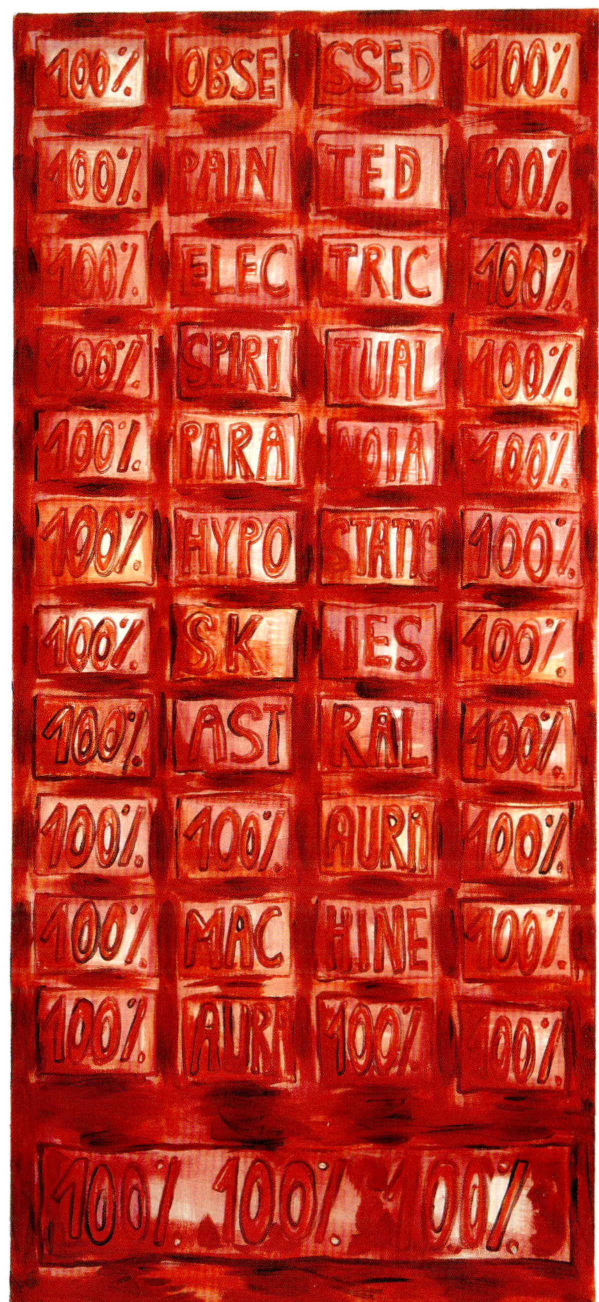

Jutta Koether
100% (Portrait Robert Johnson), 1990

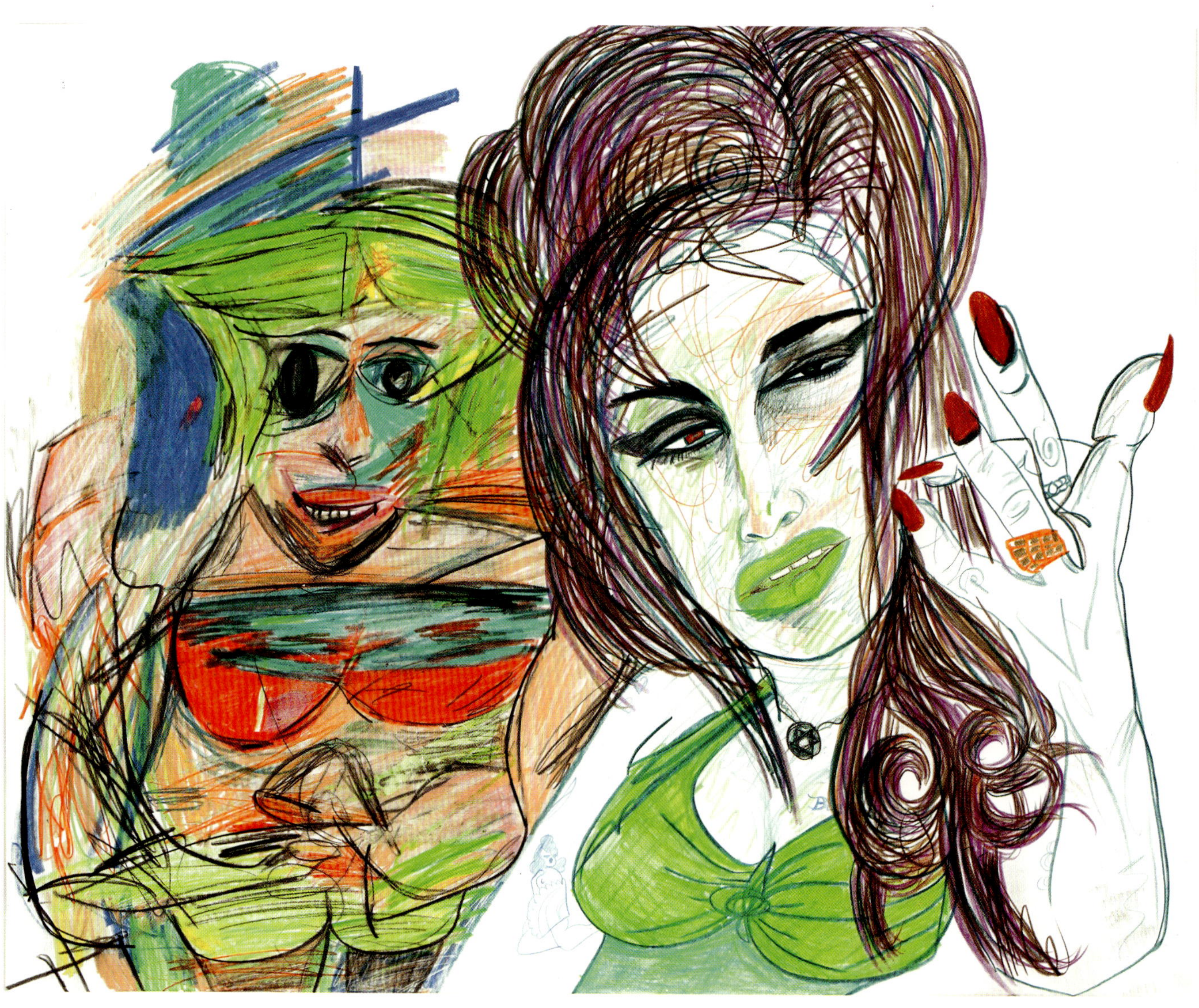

Rachel Harrison
Untitled, 2012

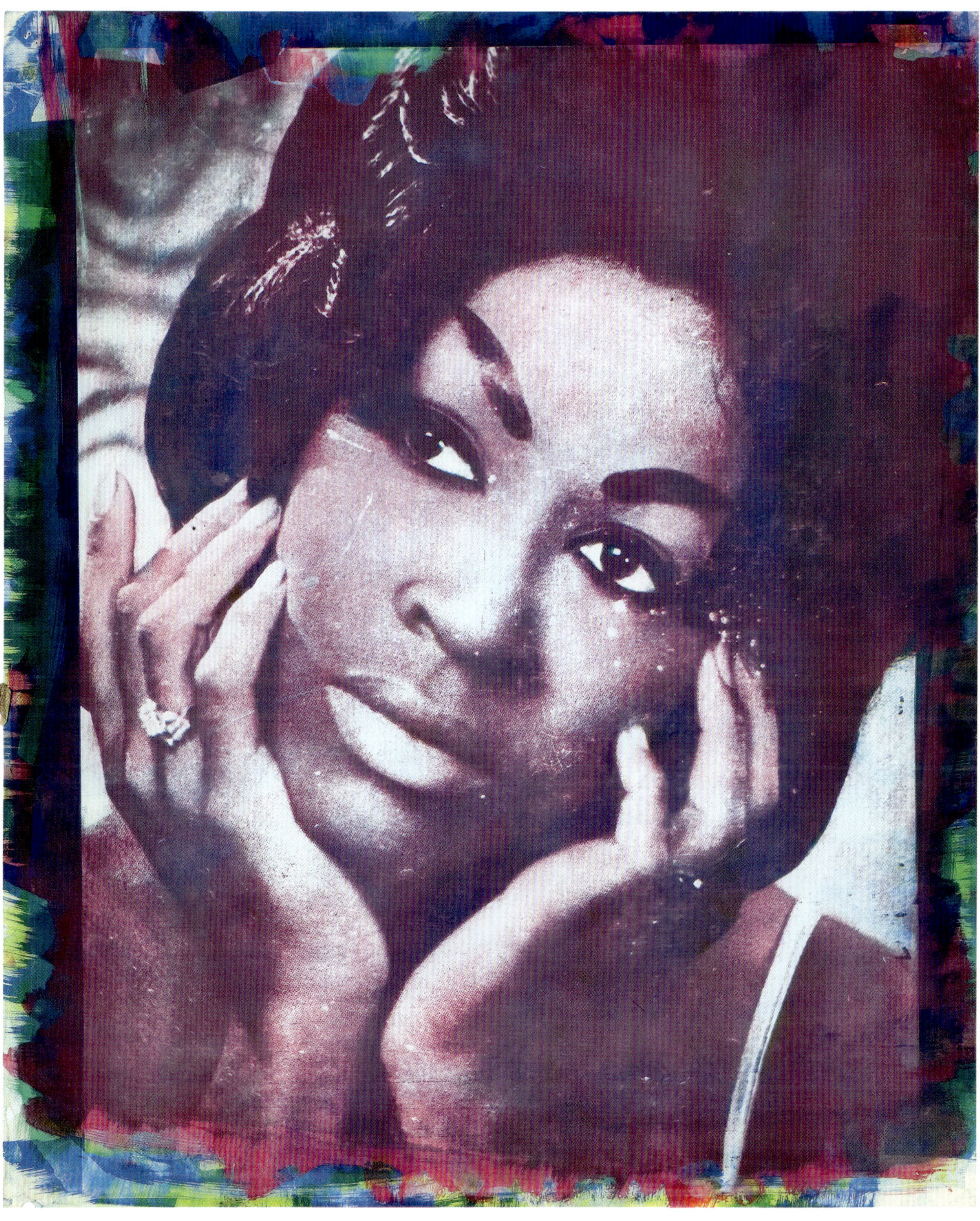

Mark Morrisroe
Untitled, c. 1981

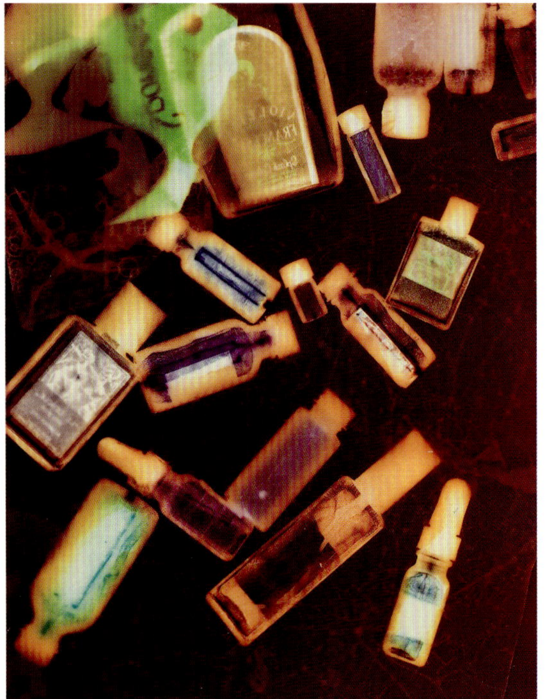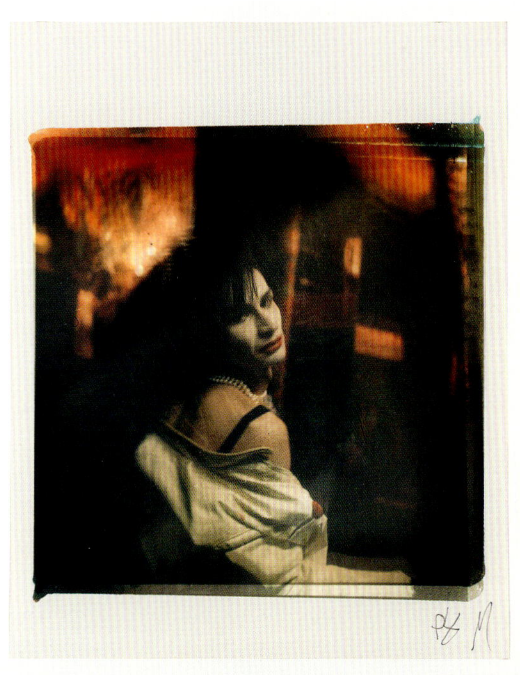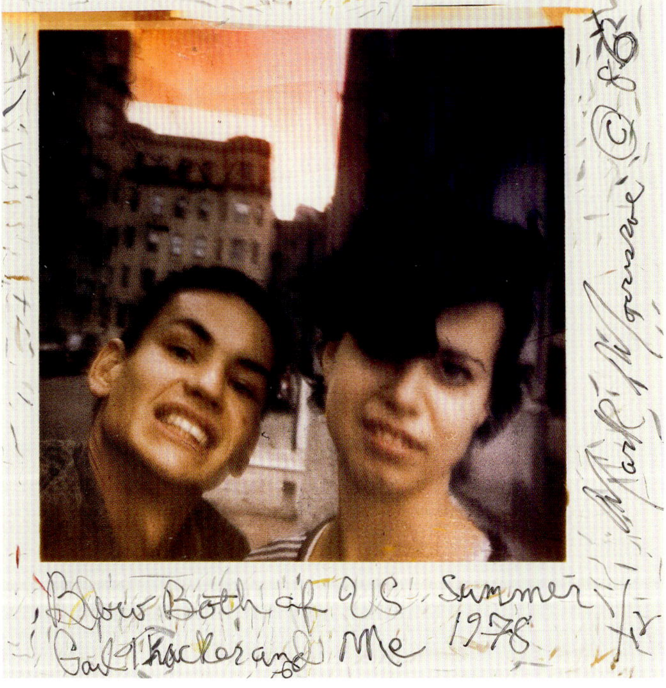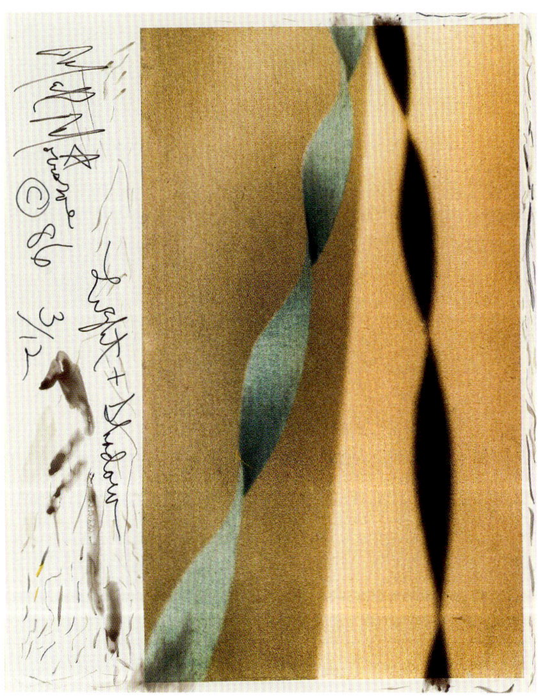

CLOCKWISE FROM TOP LEFT
Mark Morrisroe
Untitled, c. 1987
Sweet Raspberry, Spanish Madonna, 1986
Light and Shadow, 1986
Blow Both of Us, Gail Thacker and Me, Summer 1978, 1986

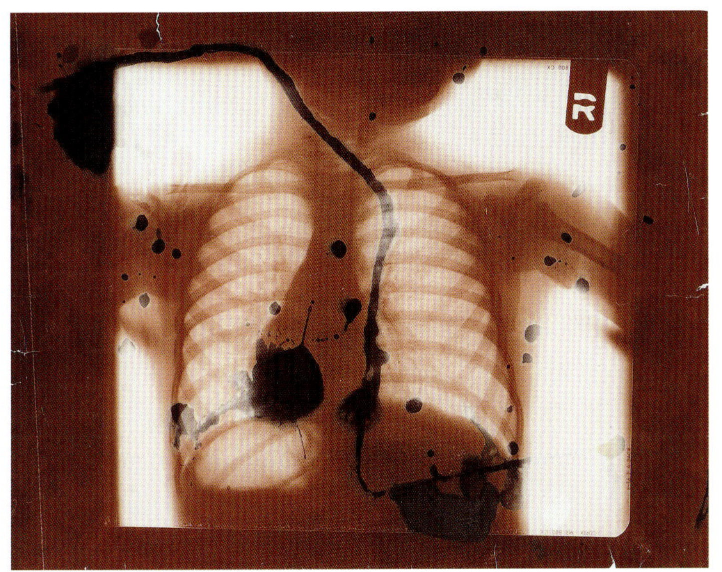
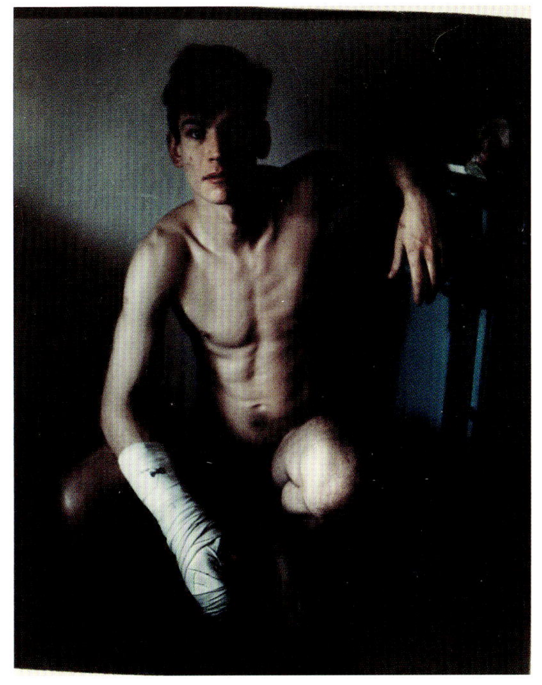
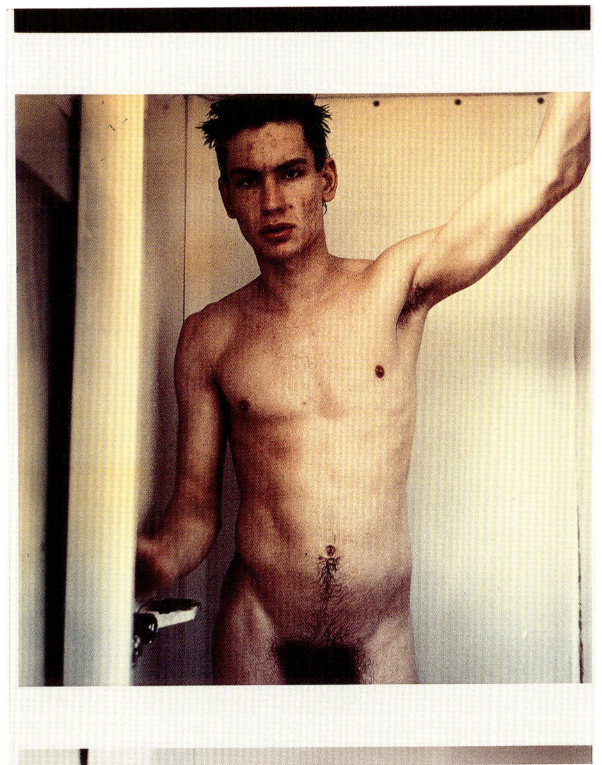

CLOCKWISE FROM TOP LEFT
Mark Morrisroe
Untitled, c. 1987
Untitled, 1985
Dismal Boston Skyline, 1986
Untitled, 1981/84

極度乾燥(しなさい) Superdry.
exclusively available at
LIVE! ON SUNSET
the interactive entertainment shopping experience
8801 sunset blvd., west hollywood, 90069
www.liveonsunset.com
FUCK STR

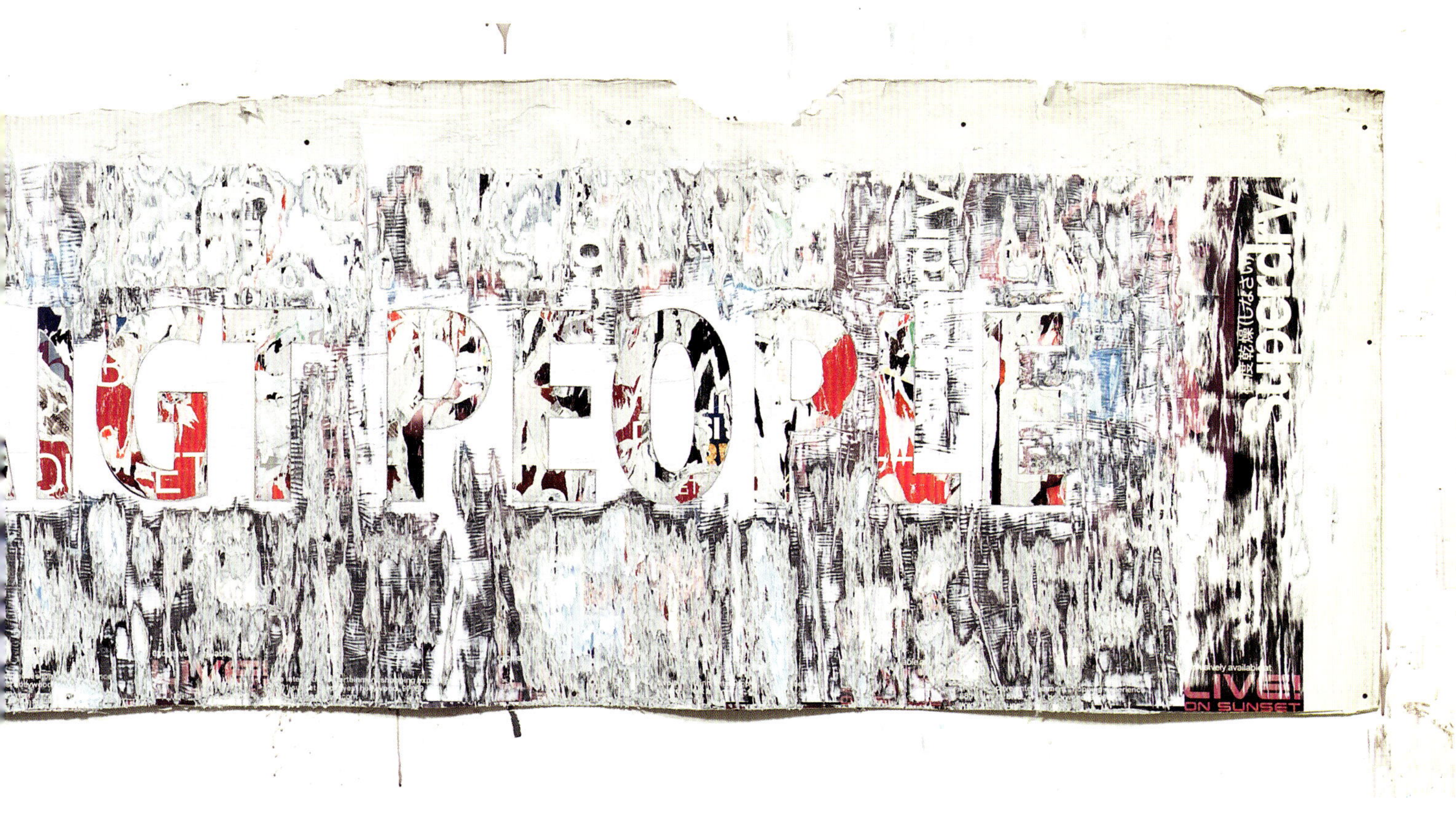

Mark Bradford
Paris Is Burning, 2010

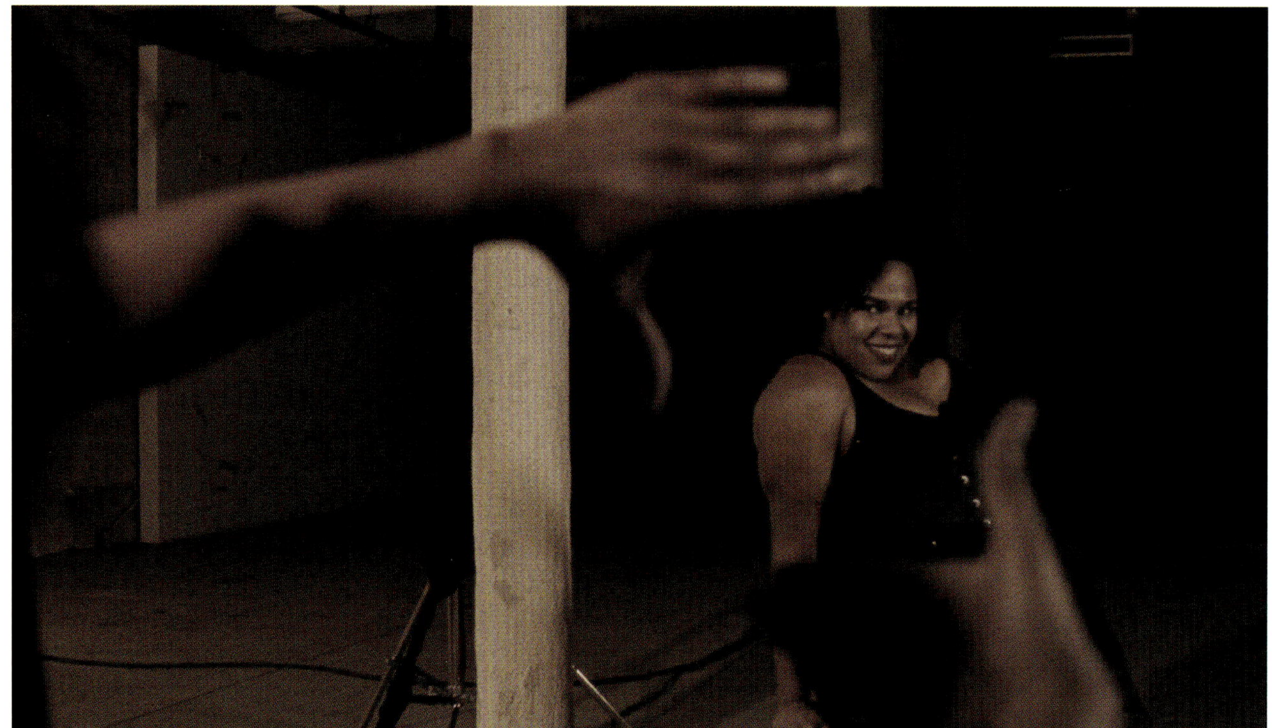

Wu Tsang
Still from *For how we perceived a life (Take 3)*, 2012

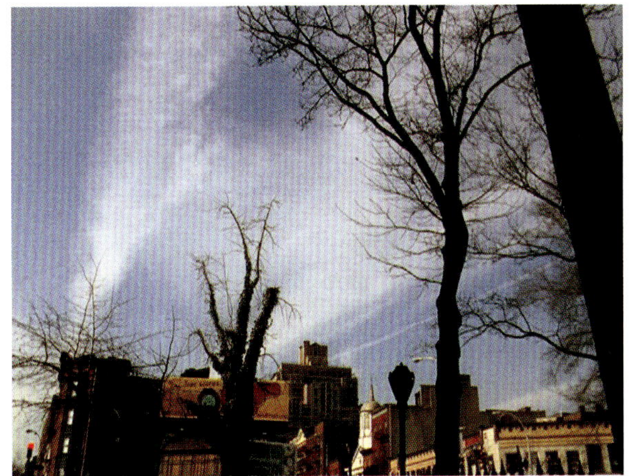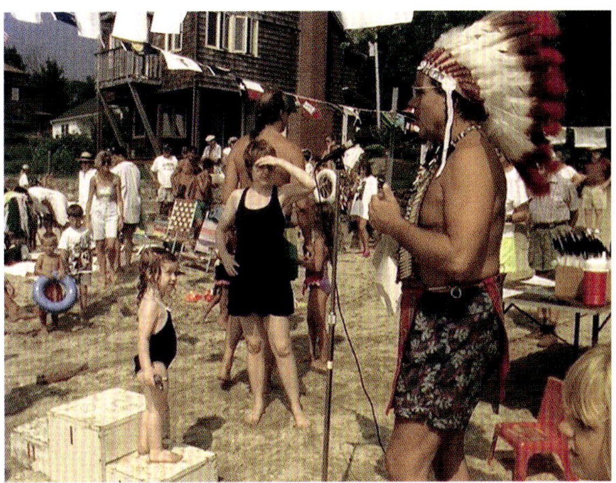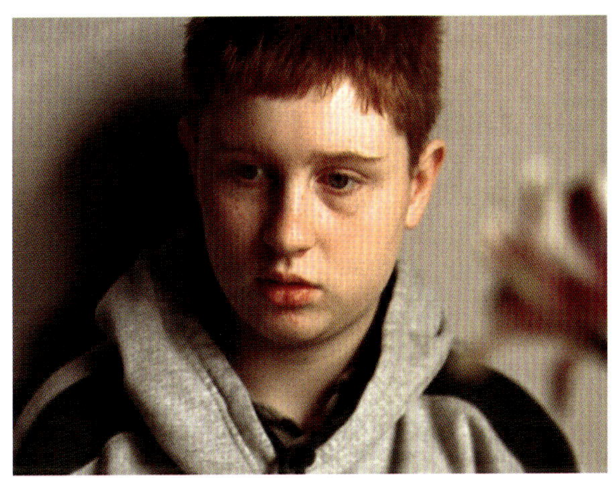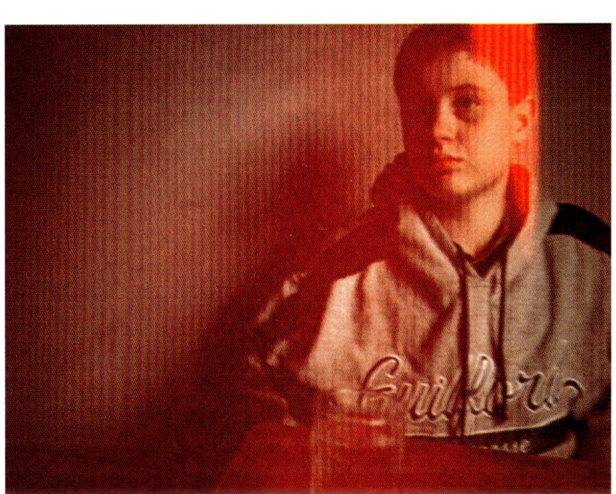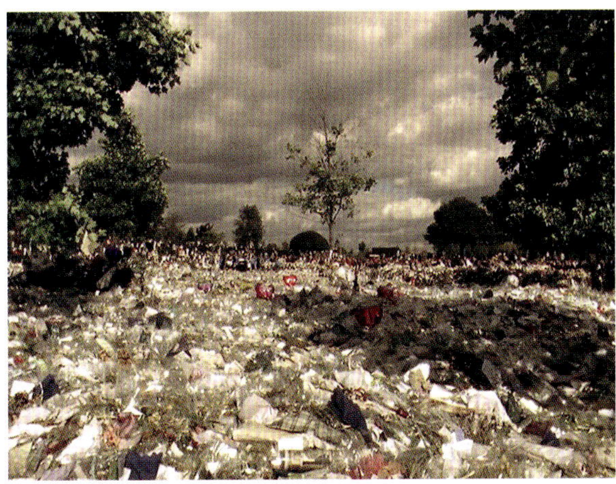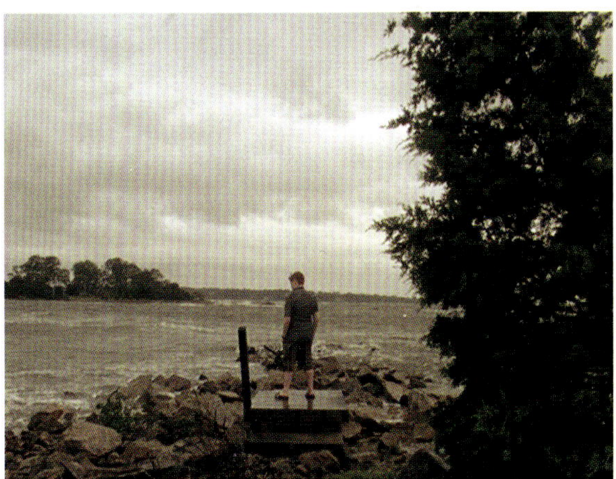

Jeff Preiss
Stills from *STOP*, 1995–2012

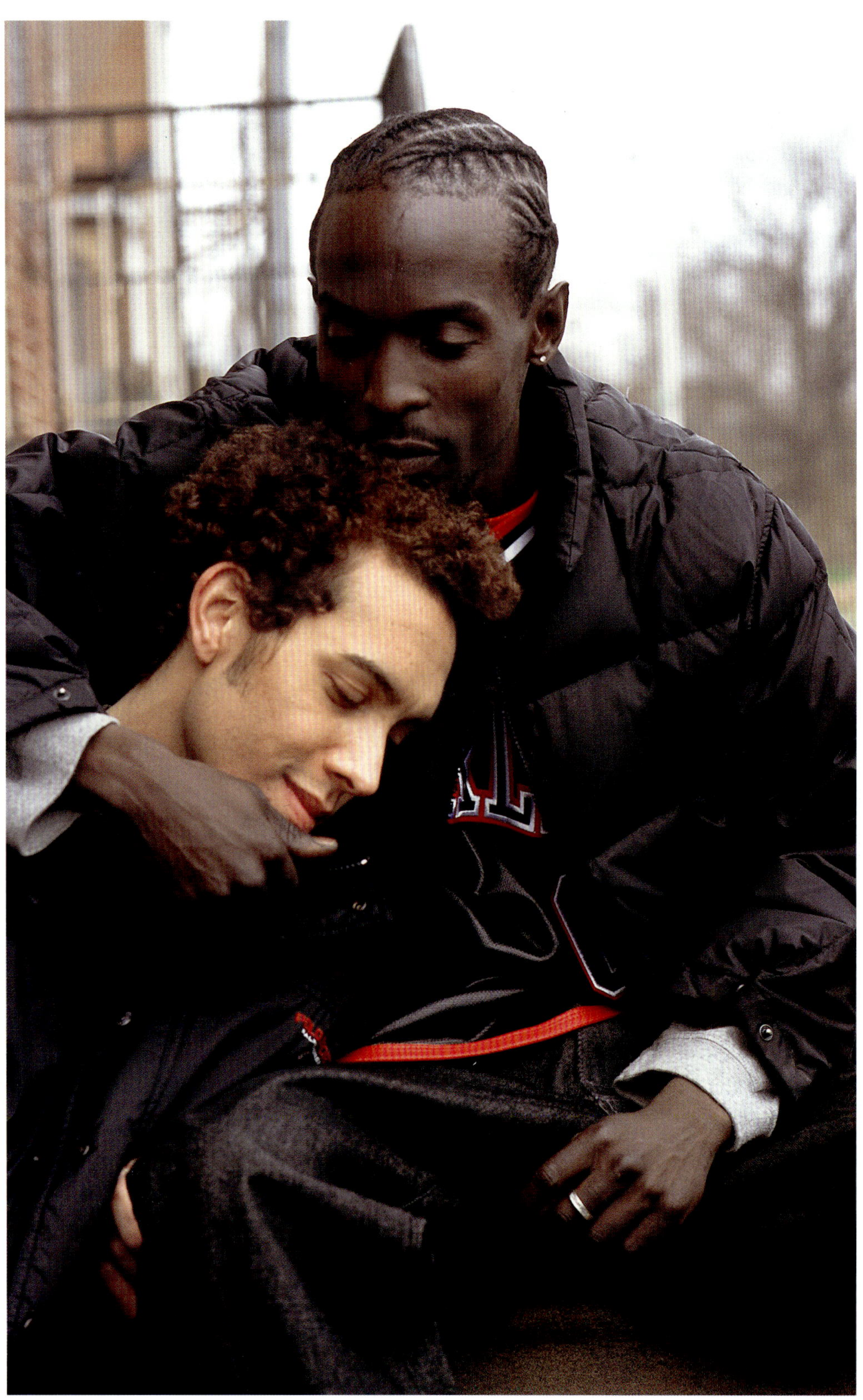

Omar (right) and Brandon, *The Wire*, season 1, 2002
Courtesy and © HBO

The Wire and the Blues

Glenn Ligon

During the opening of the first episode of the hit television series *The Wire*, Officer James McNulty (Dominic West) questions a witness to the killing of Snot Boogie, a low-level hustler from the streets of West Baltimore where the drama is set. It seems that every Friday night Snot Boogie made a habit of snatching the pot of the neighborhood crap game, after which he would run away, get caught, and get a beating. No big thing. But one Friday, Snot got shot. "Kill a man over some bullshit," the witness says, disgust in his voice. McNulty, incredulous, asks the witness why they would continue to play with a man who always took the money and ran. "Got to," the witness responds, as if the truth of his answer were self-evident, "this America, man."

In America, one has rights. On the impoverished and crime-ridden streets of West Baltimore, one has the right to remain silent and the right to play. Despite overwhelming evidence to the contrary, the myth of America as a place where a person's race, creed, color, religion, or national origin do not determine his or her success in the game still has a powerful grip on the imagination. Even for the drug runners, corner boys, and working girls on *The Wire*, this myth persists. If you just play the game right, the thinking goes, you will win, but regardless of the outcome, everyone has a right to play. This is the source of the witness's incomprehension at McNulty's question: of course Snot will snatch the money and get beat, and of course they will let him play. The repetition of his failure has no bearing on his future actions, just as homicide rates and incarceration statistics in the inner city do not deter players from joining what is ultimately a losing game.

To play the game you have to study it, and those positioned on the margins of society are often its most perceptive analysts. Take, for instance, the elegant observations on the game in Jennie Livingston's *Paris Is Burning* (1990), a documentary on New York City's voguing subculture of the 1980s. "This is white America," one of the queens opines. "And when it comes to the minorities, especially black, we as a people for the past four hundred years is the greatest example of behavior modification in the history of civilization. We have had everything taken away from us and yet we have all learned how to survive." Survival, in part, turns on learning the game and, as the queens say, learning it well. To be sure, one can argue that the election of the current president speaks to the advantages of a well-studied game. Yet, for the queens in *Paris Is Burning* and the characters on *The Wire*, victories are fleeting. The playing field is not level, and, black president or not, the game remains fixed. Indeed, a course at Harvard's Institute of Politics in the fall of 2010 was titled "Obama in the Age of *The Wire*," not "*The Wire* in the Age of Obama," suggesting that even the biggest game-changers can't really change the game.

2.

Question: Why are characters on *The Wire* like blues musicians?
Answer: Because they all playas.

In Elijah Wald's 2004 book *Escaping the Delta: Robert Johnson and the Invention of the Blues*, a bold claim is made for the connection between musical practices of the early twentieth century and the present: "We could easily think of Louis Jordan, Chuck Berry, Aretha Franklin, James Brown, George Clinton, Dr. Dre, and Missy Elliott as blues artists," Wald writes, "since there is an easily traceable continuity linking them to each other and to all the blues artists who preceded them."[1] And this continuity could be extended to include *The Wire*'s Snot Boogie, Omar Little, Stringer Bell, Snoop, Bodie, and Bubs. What connects them to the blues artists is the game, and to be in the game you have to play, and to play is to hustle. And when one is hustling, it makes little difference whether you are strumming a guitar in a juke joint on the Mississippi Delta or selling crack in a housing project in West Baltimore. Take, for instance, musician Johnny Shines's comments about fellow blues guitarist Robert Johnson: "Robert'd be standing up playing someplace, playing like nobody's business. At that time it was a hustle with him as well as a pleasure. And money'd be coming from all directions."[2] Although Johnson loved to play, playing was inextricably linked to getting women (Shines says he treated women like motel rooms) or money or liquor or clothes. New Orleans jazz pianist Jelly Roll Morton was even more explicit about the relationship between being a "player" and a "playa" when he boasted that music was just a sideline for him to the real business of pimping and gambling. All of which is not to diminish the genius of these musicians, but to acknowledge the economic and social realities of life in pre–civil rights era America, when ladders to the middle class were few and far between, and to acknowledge the allure of a lifestyle that seemingly freed musicians from rigid societal and legal boundaries.

3.

State's Attorney Ilene Nathan: State your name for the record.
Omar: Omar Devone Little.
Nathan: Mr. Little, how old are you?
Omar: About 29, thereabout.
Nathan: And where do you live?
Omar: No place in particular, ma'am.
Nathan: You're homeless?
Omar: In the wind, so to speak.
                   —*The Wire*, season 2, episode 6

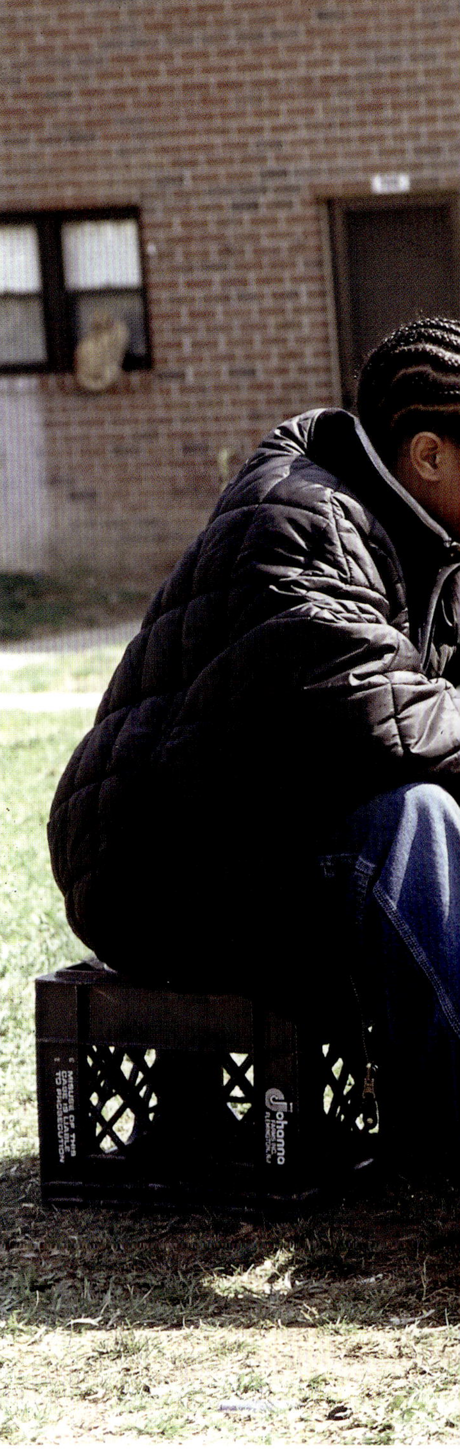

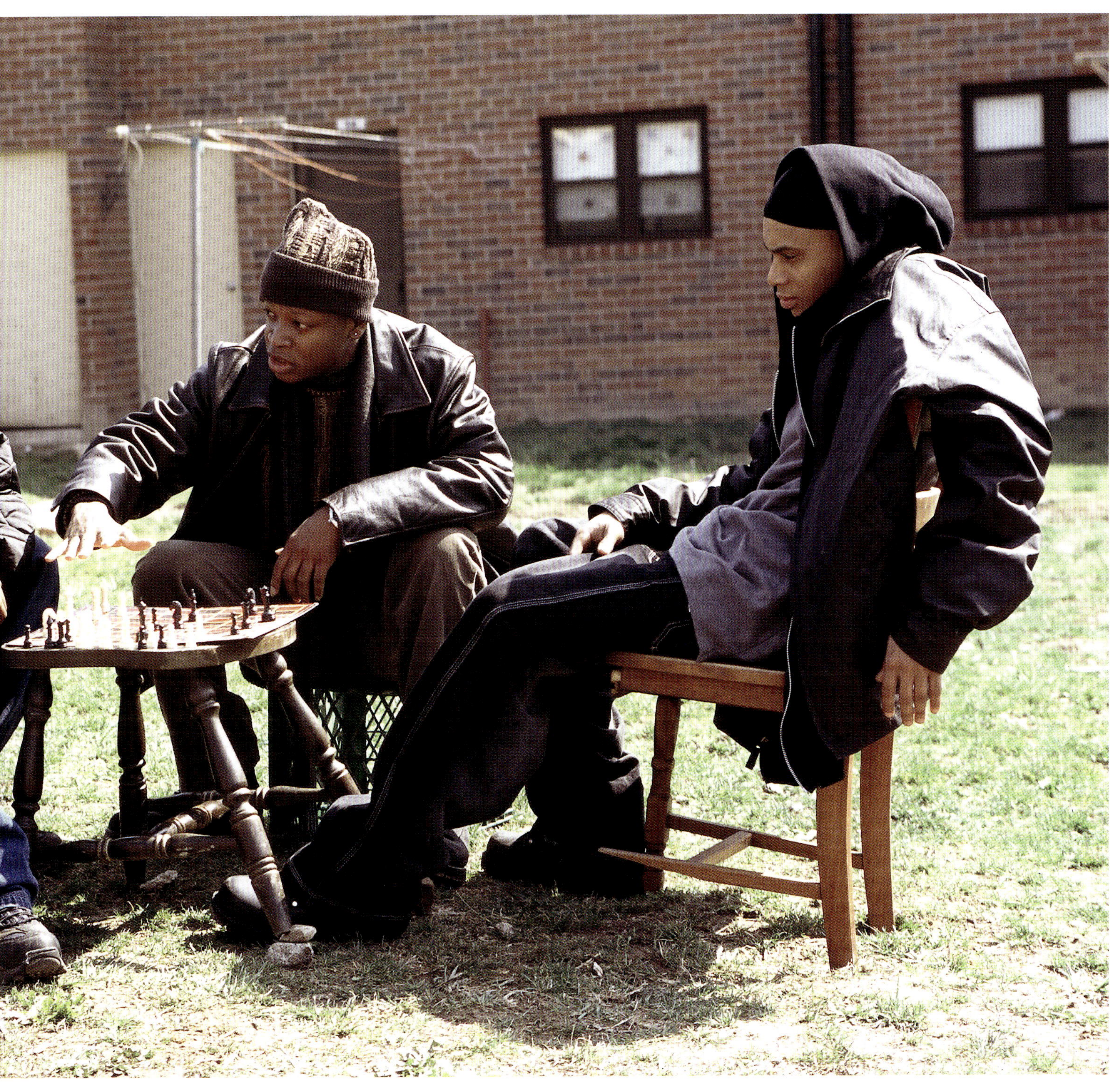

**From left to right: Wallace, D'Angelo, and Bodie playing chess, *The Wire*, season 1, 2002
Courtesy and © HBO**

Omar Little, the gay, scar-faced, drug-dealer-robbing protagonist on *The Wire* is hungry for some Honey Nut Cheerios. He pulls on a pair of teal pajama bottoms and a matching robe, but finding no convenient place to stash his .45, he walks down to the corner store from his safe house without it. The moment they spot him, kids playing in the alley and dope boys perched on the corners call out his name and run. On the way home he pauses in front of an abandoned house to light a cigarette and a bag of crack vials is tossed down from a window above, the drug dealers saving him the trouble of robbing them by handing over their stash. Omar Little iz tha rong nigga to fuck wit.

Yet despite his hypervisibility Omar remains elusive, fugitive, "in the wind." Although his safe house is located within the tight confines of West Baltimore, its whereabouts remain unknown both to the police and to the drug dealers he robs. When he sticks up Marlo Stanfield's drug crew and Stanfield vows revenge, Omar retorts, "I can find your peoples a whole lot easier than they can find me." Even his name speaks to a simultaneous presence and absence. While many of the characters on the show are known by their nicknames (Stringer, Poot, Wee-Bey, Cutty, Bunk, Prop Joe), Omar is just Omar. In a world where nicknames are a sign of belonging—proper names are most often spoken only in the presence of close family or the law—the most elusive figure on the show has the most straightforward and widely known moniker. Taken as a whole, Omar is the most blues-inflected character on *The Wire*, a solitary, almost mythic figure journeying within constricted social and economic spaces in much the same way that Robert Johnson and Jelly Roll Morton did.

From the lyrics of their songs it would seem that blues musicians were constantly "in the wind" too. They hopped freight trains, rode Greyhound buses, hitchhiked to hell and back. One reason for this was economic: to make money they had to follow the money, playing in speakeasies and taverns, at house parties, or on street corners across the country. Another reason was existential: mobility was a way to confront psychic demons, assert agency, or escape the strictures of segregated black Southern life. To be "in the wind" was a way not to live a life of dreams deferred. Johnny Shines recalls traveling with Robert Johnson to Illinois, Texas, New York, Kentucky, Indiana, and Canada, Johnson seemingly ready to hit the road at a moment's notice. Although they frequently journeyed together, Shines characterizes Johnson as "long-armed," meaning he kept most people at arms-length. He also recalls Johnson often leaving his fellow musicians mid-concert, walking off the stage and inexplicably disappearing for weeks at a time. This behavior, along with the oft-repeated myth that he sold his soul to the Devil in exchange for virtuosity on the guitar, cemented Johnson's reputation among a later generation of musicians such as Keith Richards and Eric Clapton, who were attracted as much to his persona as to his playing. His early death by poisoning at the age of twenty-seven posthumously catapulted Johnson into the realm of the legendary, paving the way for the likes of Brian Jones, Jimi Hendrix, Janis Joplin, Jim Morrison, Kurt Cobain, and Amy Winehouse.

4.

"I don't mess with what he do. I don't like that gay shit. I don't know about all that but that's my dude outside of that."
—Michael K. Williams in a radio interview, recalling a fan's response to his character Omar

Michael K. Williams has said that *The Wire* expanded the repertoire of available representations of black masculinity by presenting characters with complexity, nuance, and contradictions. A homothug like Omar becoming one of the most popular figures on *The Wire*, even earning a shout-out from President Obama, would seem to represent a seismic shift in the history of pop culture. To paraphrase the queens in *Paris Is Burning*, when characters on *The Wire* call Omar a "faggot" it's not a "read," it's a "fact." The writers of the series focused more on the content of his character than on his sexual preferences. But if this is a new representation of black masculinity, what about "Sissy Man Blues"? Recorded in 1935 by Kokomo Arnold and covered by Pinewood Tom (Josh White), George Noble, and Connie McLean's Rhythm Boys, "Sissy Man Blues" brought to vinyl the now infamous line "Lord, if you can't send me no woman, please send me some sissy man." That musicians covered a song privileging the urgency of desire over the gender of the partner is an indication of its popularity with black blues consumers, who were apparently not put off by the raunchy sentiments it contained. Expressions of sexuality were nothing new in the blues, as many songs contained double entendres that alluded to sexual acts between men and women. But in its expression of same-sex contact "Sissy Man Blues"—decades before the appearance of Omar on *The Wire*—explored territory that would seem radical for pop culture even today. And the song was by no means an anomaly. Throughout the height of the blues era, widely popular musicians such as Bessie Smith, Alberta Hunter, Ma Rainey, Frankie "Half-Pint" Jaxon, and others recorded songs with explicit or thinly veiled gay references. For example, Ma Rainey's "Prove It on Me" contains the lyrics:

> I went out last night with a crowd of my friends,
> It must've been women, 'cause I don't like no men.
> Wear my clothes just like a fan
> Talk to the gals just like any old man.

Rainey's song, coupled with songs like "B.D. Women's Blues," "Boy in the Boat," "Ain't That a Mess," and "Freakish Man Blues," speaks to a moment when artists and audiences were comfortable with the open expression of a range of sexual desires. The black community, it has been said, is more homophobic than other communities. Blackness cannot, it is imagined, tolerate any heterogeneity, or deviation, or play. While black popular music today scarcely accommodates expressions of same-sex desire, the embrace of Omar Little, Detective Kima Greggs, and Snoop as openly queer characters on *The Wire* does signal a crack in some monolithic notion of the black community and its mores. Like the blues before it, *The Wire* suggests a range of humanity that is often missing in popular accounts of black American life.

5.

Brother Mouzone: I want to ask you something ..."brother."
Omar: Omar listening.
       — ***The Wire**, season 3, episode 11*

In an article in *Ebony* magazine, Williams revealed that he was addicted to crack and other drugs while filming *The Wire*. Although his habit never prevented him from showing up for the day's call, it did collapse the distance between Omar the character and Williams the man. For Williams, the play became more attractive than the reality. "I was first addicted to the fantasy, wanting to be outside myself—anything but Mike," Williams remarks. "I never liked Mike: Mike was black. Mike was nappy-headed. Mike was bucktoothed, big eared, skinny, soft—everything unattractive, undesirable." Playing allowed Williams a momentary escape from the reality of addiction, but Omar was more than just a character for Williams. Omar became an alter ego, another side of Williams's personality. "Omar Little was my Spider-Man suit," Williams says. "He was everything I couldn't be in life—fearless, outspoken and honest about who he was." Indeed, when the character was killed off in season five, Williams says he went through a mourning period. "I felt like a part of me died. And [confronted] with the reality of who was left, I didn't know who the fuck that was."[3]

Another actor in *The Wire*, Felicia Pearson (Snoop), had a similar experience of the blurred line between fiction and reality. Pearson had served six and a half years in prison for second-degree murder and was working as a drug runner when Williams discovered her in a bar and persuaded the producers of *The Wire* to cast her as the androgynous, baby-faced lesbian enforcer for the Stanfield drug crew. Using her real nickname, Snoop, she played herself even more clearly than Williams did. In her autobiography *Grace after Midnight* she wrote that she would "wake up in the morning, get dressed, leave my work on the block to walk into a world about make-believe work on the block." As they say in Baltimore, "Real recognize real." Before appearing in *The Wire* Pearson was, she says, already "a little star in the hood," but *The Wire* changed the game. "When I dealt dope, no one came up and said, 'I love your work.' No one looked at me with eyes of appreciation."[4] It was *The Wire* that allowed her (at least temporarily) to leave the corners behind, landing her roles on other television shows. Ironically, her work brought a different kind of attention, attention from the family of Okia Toomer, the woman Pearson was convicted of murdering. Sylvia Williams, Toomer's grandmother, recalled receiving a

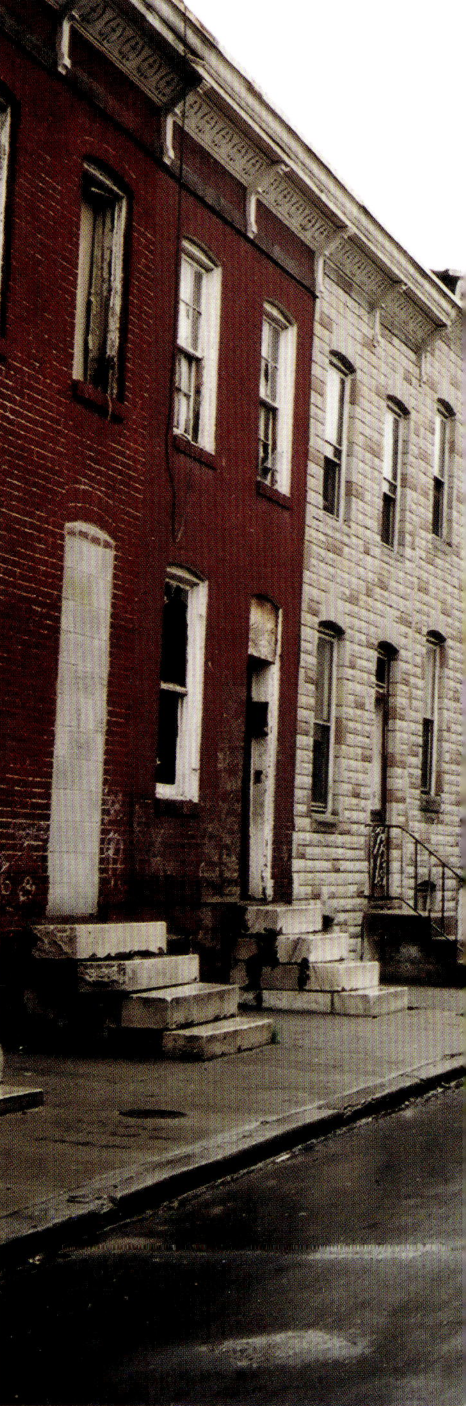

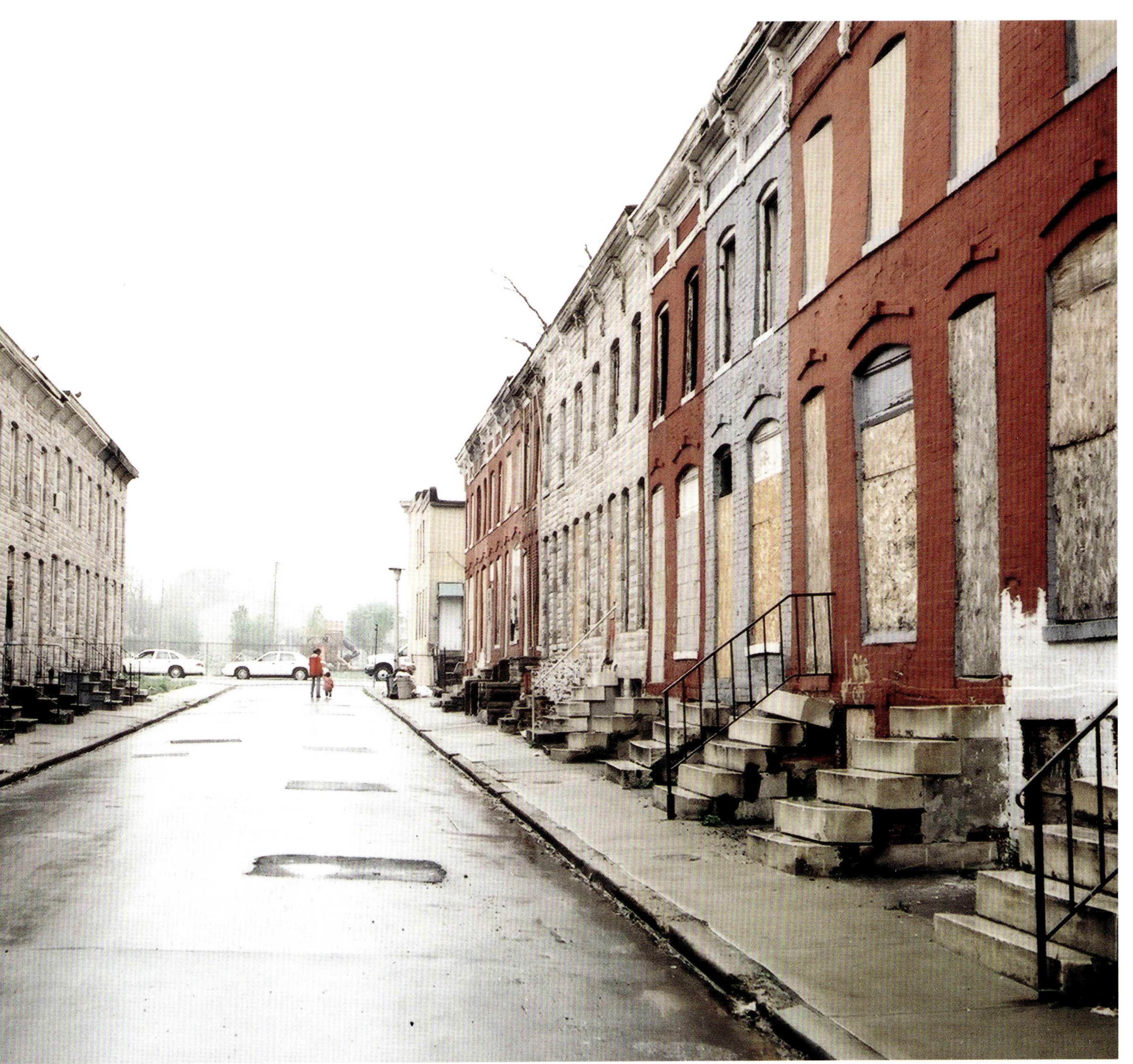

Baltimore row houses, *The Wire*, season 1, 2002
Courtesy and © HBO

phone call from one of her daughters when *The Wire* was broadcast. Crying, her daughter said, "That girl that killed Kia is on *The Wire*. She's still acting violent."[5] For the family of Okia Toomer the line between playing and being a playa was thin indeed.

To play yourself is to become another, a self-performance that slips between person and persona, often confusing the two. In fact, it is to create a third person, a hybrid that is both inside and outside the self. Both Omar and Williams constantly refer to themselves in the third person, a self-othering that speaks of the contradictions of their fictional and real lives. Whole passages in Pearson's autobiography are written in the third person, including those documenting a moment when she felt profound grief at the murder of a drug-dealing mentor. For Williams and Pearson *The Wire* presented a way out. By playing versions of themselves they altered their realities. "Acting," Pearson says, "by showing me how to feel, also showed me I hadn't been feeling at all."[6]

Similarly, blues musicians played themselves, creating personas that boosted record sales and increased their desirability. On a practical level, blues musicians played "blues musicians" by suppressing their range of influences and styles. Johnson's running buddy Shines claimed that Johnson could play "anything that he heard over the radio…. When I say anything, I mean *anything*—popular songs, ballads, blues, anything."[7] But Johnson, like many blues musicians, had to curtail these heterogeneous tastes to satisfy the producers of "race records" who held narrow notions of "authentic" style and audience appetite. More important, however, were the outsize, mythic versions of themselves that blues musicians played. The story of Johnson's bargain with the Devil was part of a mythology that he traded on, an image of a musician taken to the brink in service of his instrument—and his game.

When asked by McNulty to inform on a suspect Omar says, "I don't think that is how the game is played." Although violent, zero-sum, cadaverous, and inescapable, the game has rules and games of its own, codes that mirror the codes by which the society as a whole is structured. To play is to participate in the culture; it is as American as cherry pie. And you gotta let a man play. As the witness to Snot's murder said, "This America, man."

Notes

1. Elijah Wald, *Escaping the Delta: Robert Johnson and the Invention of the Blues* (New York: Amistad, 2004), 194.
2. Ibid., 113.
3. Michael K. Williams quoted in Timothy A. Ivy, "Sober Circumstances," *Ebony* 67, nos. 2/3 (December 2011/January 2012): 120–23.
4. Felicia "Snoop" Pearson and David Ritz, *Grace after Midnight: A Memoir* (New York: Grand Central, 2007), iPad e-book, locations 2845, 2921.
5. Sylvia Williams quoted in Oliver Burkeman, "When Pretend Is Real," *The Guardian*, May 23, 2008, W30.
6. Pearson and Ritz, *Grace after Midnight*, location 2937.
7. Wald, *Escaping the Delta*, 118.

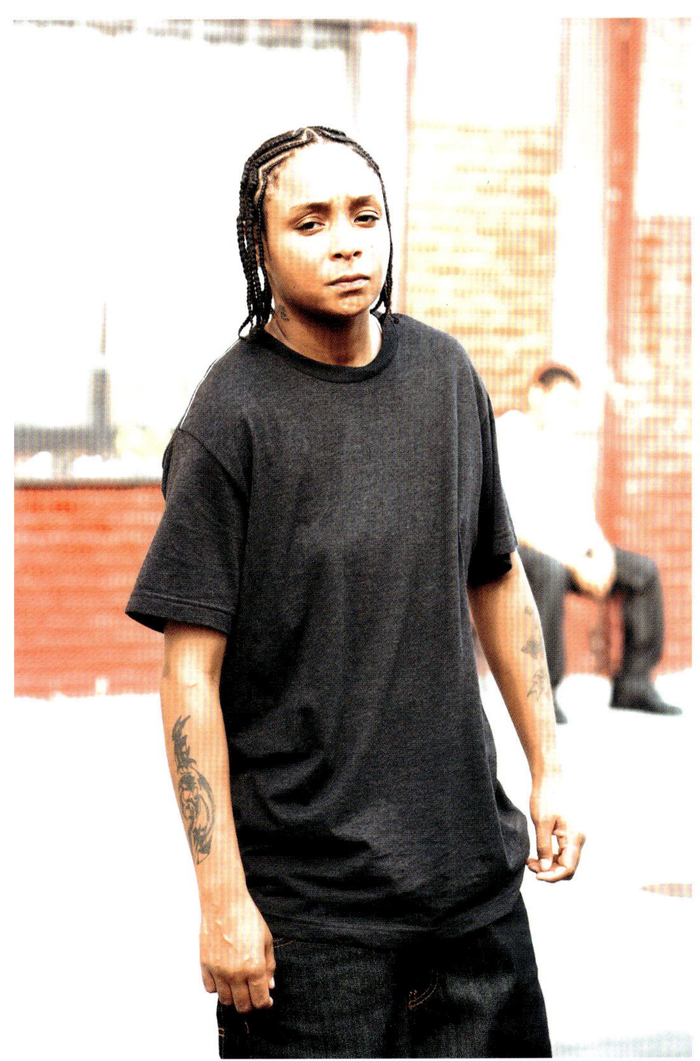

Snoop, *The Wire,* **season 3, 2005**
Courtesy and © HBO

The Timeless Blues

George E. Lewis

The writer and cultural critic Albert Murray viewed art as "a process by which raw experience is stylized into aesthetic statement."[1] In that spirit, this essay's performative, Gatesian Signifying will exercise the function of, in the words of John Cage, "making something out of a store of raw materials."[2] Or, as musician and composer Muhal Richard Abrams observed of his pedagogical process for teaching composition at the Association for the Advancement of Creative Musicians (AACM) School: "We learn how to develop things from the raw materials."[3] Nominally, both Cage and Abrams were speaking of experimental music, but, in the end, that is what the blues becomes when musicians, audiences, and whole societies invest their futures in it.

The development of the blues was contemporaneous with the Great Migration, the largest and longest internal migration in U.S. history, an Occupy-the-North-style improvisation of distributed intelligence pursued over half a century by ordinary working-class African Americans. The blues formed a large part of the soundtrack for that grand social experiment, chronicling its joys, hopes, fears, pains, successes, and failures—all alongside the risks of real-time actions that exemplified Cage's definition of experiment: "An experimental action is one the outcome of which is not foreseen."[4]

In Murray's view, African American culture's most enduring aesthetic statements have been centrally animated by what he calls the "blues idiom," and in the light of Migration history, it was hardly a stretch for him to comment

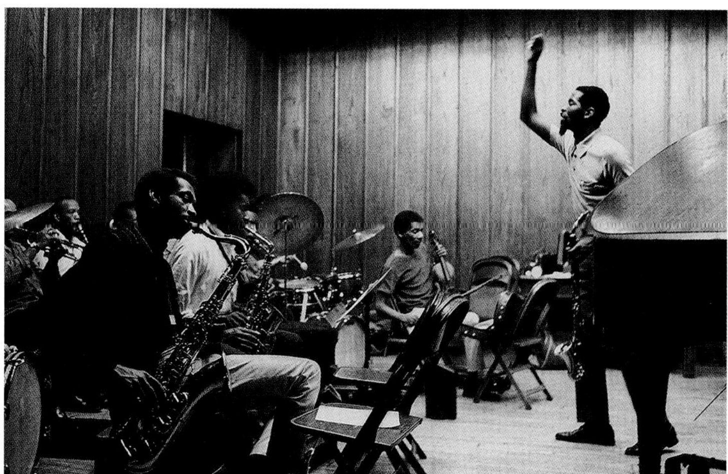

Musician and composer Muhal Richard Abrams conducts the Experimental Band, Association for the Advancement of Creative Musicians, Chicago, c. 1965

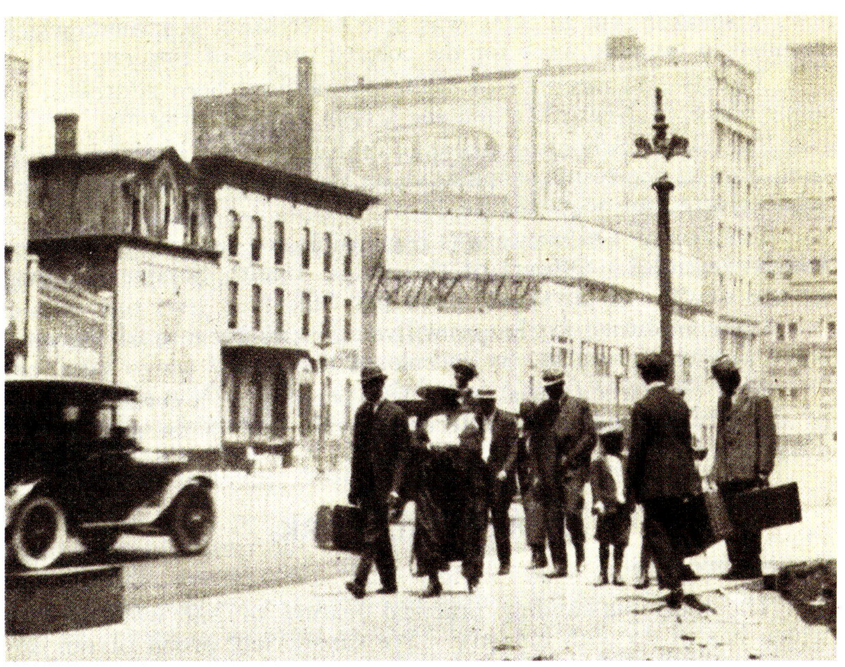

Photograph accompanying the Chicago Urban League's report on the Great Migration, 1928

on "the ease with which the blues idiom soundtrack can be extended from the cotton fields and the railroad through megalopolis and into outer space."[5] But Murray went further than this. His essay "The Blues Idiom and the Mainstream of Contemporary Life" declared that "the creation of an art style … is perhaps the highest as well as the most comprehensive fulfillment of culture … the ultimate synthesis and refinement of a life style."[6] Thus, his crucial turn was to associate the blues with high art:

> Most Americans know very well that the blues genre, which in its most elaborate extensions includes elements of the spirituals, gospel music, folk songs, chants, hollers, popular ditties, plus much of what goes into symphonic and even operatic composition, is the basic and definitive musical idiom of native-born U.S. Negroes. But few if any students of America … consider the blues idiom a major cultural achievement.[7]

That statement was reflective of its time; Murray's theories of art and blues were clearly crafted as a counterforce to a white supremacy that demeaned and denied any attempt at congruence between cultural-historical blackness and humanism—not to mention "great" art. But few would deny the achievement of the blues today, even as many would resist classifying the blues as high art or deploying it in a quixotic reinvigoration of a now-fading distinction between high and popular culture—or both.

A *Los Angeles Times* review of "The Blues Aesthetic: Black Culture and Modernism," a 1990 exhibition at the California Afro-American Museum curated by art historian Richard J. Powell, gives us a sense of the issues at stake.[8] By this time, books such as LeRoi Jones's *Blues People: Negro Music in White America* (1963), Charles Keil's *Urban Blues* (1966), and Eileen Southern's *The Music of Black Americans: A History* (1971) were becoming required reading in college music courses, and the *Times* reviewer recounts what had become a more or less standard celebratory narrative of blues origins:

> The African-based work songs of the blacks' slavery days blossomed into songs of protest, lamentation and solace, and thus was born America's greatest original musical form. A working man's music combining joy, sorrow and simple observations on human nature, blues is freighted with specific attitudes about history, race and politics, and it's had an enormous impact on American life. Styles of dress, dance and food have been shaped by it, gospel music, rhythm & blues, rap and jazz are rooted in it, and literature has borrowed freely from it (the '50s Beat poets and the New Journalism of the '70s clearly owe it a debt).[9]

However, according to the article, the blues engine loses steam as it approaches the visual arts:

> One thing the blues hasn't done, however, is spawn a visual arts movement. Countless white artists have looked to African and African-American culture for inspiration—Picasso was profoundly effected [*sic*] by African art, the Surrealists claimed jazz as part of their subconscious heritage, and graffiti art has obvious connections with black music—yet, blacks have played a minor role in the avant-garde art movements of the 20th century.

Indeed, what relationships obtain between the historical and neo-avant-gardes and the blues? How have historians of the avant-garde treated the blues and its influence, not only on American, but on global culture? As it happens, one searches the major literature in vain for anything more than cursory references, but the insouciance of the *Times* reporter's gaze notwithstanding, there is smoke and possibly fire here: The blues has essentially *not* been received as part of the set of historiographical questions on the avant-garde that have come down to us. Rather, at least in the most commonly asserted historical narratives, any possible influence of a blues idiom, blues culture, or a blues aesthetic has been relegated to carefully defined margins, its dominant tropes denied, excluded, ignored.

Fast forward two decades, and we find in the present exhibition an expression of blues consciousness that standard art histories have somehow missed. "Blues for Smoke" functions not as vindication, recovery, or redress, but as both a critical intervention in an earlier history of exclusion and a critical

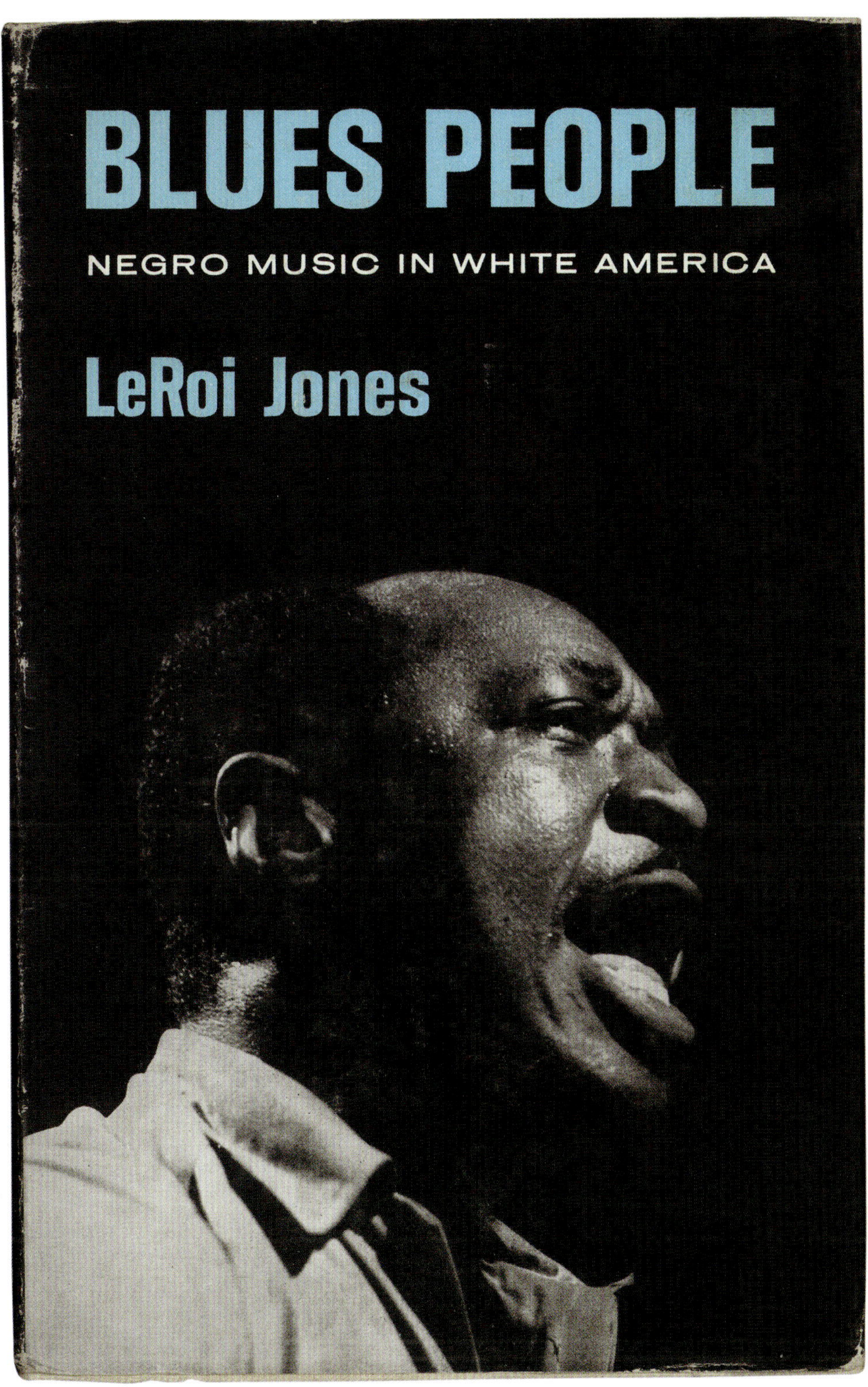

Cover of LeRoi Jones, *Blues People: Negro Music in White America* (New York: William Morrow, 1963)

interruption of an anxiety that marks the stereotype of disconnection between the blues and experimental art-making, or what Homi K. Bhabha described as the stereotype's vacillation "between what is always 'in place,' already known, and something that must be anxiously repeated."[10]

In fact, criticality is what the blues is all about. Murray tells us that the bearers of the blues idiom—"Ma Rainey, Bessie, Clara, Mamie, and Trixie Smith, to name a few"[11]—were certainly not averse to burlesque, mockery, derision, and ridicule. This criticality continued with the infinite set of possibilities navigated by the five members of the classic Art Ensemble of Chicago (Joseph Jarman, Roscoe Mitchell, Lester Bowie, Malachi Favors Maghostout, and Famoudou Don Moye), whose visual iconography symbolized the diversity of viewpoints that characterizes the black diaspora. Art Ensemble humor was certainly not above self-parody and burlesque, and those five different articulations of male Afrologic presented a multivoiced, internationalist vision of blackness that made common cause with Romare Bearden's 1964 painting *Train Whistle Blues: II*.

If Cubism showed us multiple perspectives, with Bearden and the Art Ensemble we traverse various instantiations of the quantum multiverse. More generally, the criticality embodied in the works in the present exhibition asserts trenchant alternative standpoints to standard notions of the historical avant-garde—not by setting out received relationships between the blues and the avant-garde, but by identifying possible new worlds and relationships.

The Devil's Music

African American literary theorist Houston A. Baker's 1984 book *Blues, Ideology, and Afro-American Literature* celebrated the music's vernacular provenance as a key to its power. Going further even than Ralph Ellison's observations on the subject, Baker maintained that "the vernacular (in its expressive adequacy and adept critical facility) always *absorbs* 'classical' elements of American life and art."[12] Baker's view of the blues declined to utilize its aesthetic, affective, and political achievements as tools for social uplift; a bit more than a decade earlier, historian and social activist Ron Karenga, who as Maulana Karenga later conceived the now-canonical African American holiday of Kwanzaa, denied the very possibility of using the blues in this way. His ringing demand in 1971 for what he called "social criteria for judging art" declared that "all art must reflect and support the Black Revolution, and any art that does not discuss and contribute to the revolution is invalid, no matter how many lines and spaces are produced in proportion and symmetry and no matter how many sounds are boxed in or blown out and called music…. Therefore, we say the blues are invalid; for they teach resignation, in a word acceptance of reality—and we have come to change reality."[13]

The Art Ensemble of Chicago, S.O.B.'s, New York, 1996
From left to right: Famoudou Don Moye, Roscoe Mitchell, Lester Bowie, Joseph Jarman, and Malachi Favors Maghostout

Indeed, a traditional blues lyric cited in Baker's book seems to support
Karenga's charge:

> Standing at the crossroads, tried to flag a ride,
> Standing at the crossroads, tried to flag a ride,
> Ain't nobody seem to know me, everybody passed me by.[14]

At first glance, the lyric seems resigned to the non-agency of the blues subject:
no progress, no resolution—only literal stasis. But here, Friedrich Nietzsche's
classic thought experiment on "eternal recurrence" in *The Gay Science* reso-
nates with this discussion in surprising ways:

> What if some day or night a demon were to steal into your loneliest
> loneliness and say to you: "This life as you now live it and have lived
> it you will have to live once again and innumerable times again; and
> there will be nothing new in it, but every pain and every joy and every
> thought and sigh and everything unspeakably small or great in your
> life must return to you, all in the same succession and sequence...."
> Would you not throw yourself down and gnash your teeth and curse
> the demon who spoke thus?[15]

In one view, the demon's visit exemplifies one of European history's most terrifying myths: the fate of King Sisyphus, whom the gods punish by compelling him to push an enormous boulder up a hill, only to see it roll down again—a task he was doomed to repeat endlessly, throughout eternity. In James Snead's essay "On Repetition in Black Culture," an against-the-grain reading of Hegel's severely negative view of African culture, Hegel's "African" is "terrifyingly close to the cycles and rhythms of nature," with "no idea of history or progress"—a direct mapping of the Sisyphean fate to this "alien" culture that "overturns all European categories of logic."[16] But Snead's methodology allows him to highlight Hegel's inadvertent identification of one of the African's great strengths:

> Having no self-consciousness, he is "immediate"—i.e., *always there*— in any given moment. Here we can see that, being there, the African is also *always already there*, or perhaps *always there before*, whereas the European is *headed there* or, better, *not yet there*.[17]

Here, we can turn to the affirmative side of the gift offered by Nietzsche's demon: "Or have you once experienced a tremendous moment when you would have answered him: 'You are a god, and never have I heard anything more divine.'"[18]

Karenga's analysis interests us with its inability to distinguish between tropes of resignation and despair and what amounts to a blues critique of progress, embedded in the music's assertion of a necessary absence of final resolution. One suspects, indeed, that for both Hegel and Karenga, the sentence of Sisyphus is the ultimate expression of hell. But in the condition of eternal recurrence, Hegel's notion of African "historylessness" leads us forward to Nietzsche's demon, who in turn is found looking over Ludwig Wittgenstein's shoulder when the latter defined eternity in his *Tractatus* as timelessness rather than infinite temporal duration. In this discussion, Wittgenstein went even further, telling us that "[e]ternal life belongs to those who live in the present."[19]

Where Nietzsche and Wittgenstein see timelessness, Baker tells us that "the blues singer's signatory coda is always *atopic*, placeless: 'If anybody ask you who sang this song / Tell 'em X done been here and gone.'"[20] Thus, in Snead's formulation, "in black culture, the thing (the ritual, the dance, the beat) is 'there for you to pick it up when you come back to get it.' If there is a goal (*Zweck*) in such a culture, it is always deferred; it continually 'cuts' back to the start … this magic of the 'cut' attempts to confront accident and rupture not by covering them over, but by making room for them inside the system itself."[21] The implication of "Crossroad Blues," then, is of an existential, *recursive* condition of eternal recurrence that gives us another view of why the blues was called "the devil's music."

Inside the Matrix

The Wachowski Brothers' turn-of-the-millennium film trilogy *The Matrix* (1999–2003) portrays a society in which the protagonists come to realize that they are ensnared in a virtual world in which they are doomed to repeat the same events *ad infinitum*—another formulation of Sisyphean destiny against which the protagonists struggle in each of the films.[22] Houston Baker provides a different take on the matrix in describing African American culture as "a complex, reflexive enterprise which finds its proper figuration in blues conceived as a matrix … a point of ceaseless input and output, a web of intersecting, crisscrossing impulses always in productive transit. Afro-American blues constitute such a vibrant network." He further observes of the "blues matrix" that "discrete blues instances are always intertextually related by the blues code as a whole. Moreover, they are involved in the code's manifold interconnections with other codes of Afro-American culture."[23]

Compare this poststructuralist understanding of the context of the blues with Pierre Bourdieu's notion of the *habitus*, developed in his 1972 *Outline of a Theory of Practice*, in which the sociologist ascribed the combination of large-scale stasis and short-term, indeterminate difference he observed in rural Berber kinship and gift-exchange practices to the working out of a "durably installed generative principle of regulated improvisations." An individual agent, acting without objectively structured correlation, "wittingly or unwittingly, willy nilly, is a producer and reproducer of objective meaning," in the fashion of a computer program's background "demon" subroutine. Those who produce these actions unwittingly, without "conscious mastery," manifest a kind of "*intentionless invention* of regulated improvisation."[24] New structures appear to be found (the *trouvaille*) but in fact are always and already present, recalling Baker's observation that the blues "are what Jacques Derrida might describe as the 'always already' of Afro-American culture."[25]

Thus, the blues matrix as Baker defined it functions as a habitus, meaning that it exists within a recursive, rather than a simply circular logic, being at the same time both generative and analytic. For Bourdieu, the habitus "produces practices which tend to reproduce the regularities immanent in the objective conditions of the production of their generative principle, while adjusting to the demands inscribed as objective potentialities in the situation, as defined by the cognitive and motivating structures making up the habitus … [T]he habitus is an endless capacity to engender products—thoughts, perceptions, expressions, actions—whose limits are set by the historically and socially situated conditions of its production."[26] At the same time, "giving, giving in return, offering one's services, paying a visit, etc.—can have completely different meanings at different times."[27] Thus, the habitus embodies indeterminacy and uncertainty as the ground for collective human action. The indeterminacy of memory and history prepares the ground for the improvisations that animate the habitus, and so it is with the blues matrix; as Fats Waller observed: "One never knows … do one?"

The blues habitus/matrix provides the background within which blues utterance can be understood, presented, and represented. In the end, however, the habitus is performed—achieved—and, as Bourdieu realized, we can call this animating performativity "improvisation," the ubiquitous practice of everyday life where meaning is developed and exchanged in real time, fundamental to the existence and survival of every human formation and as close to universal as contemporary critical method could responsibly entertain. The notion of the habitus is invoked when philosopher J. David Velleman likens humanity to "an improvisational theater troupe that, over many years of performing together, has developed an extensive repertoire of scenes that any member of the troupe can initiate in the expectation that the others will follow suit…. The totality of the repertoire shared among us is what might be called our way of life."[28]

Within the blues habitus/matrix, as with other matrices, both our musical and our everyday-life improvisations deal with a version of Booker T. Washington's admonition in his 1895 "Atlanta Exposition Address" to "cast down your bucket where you are." In this way, improvisation becomes a mode of analysis of where you are, a set of considered responses to your condition—or, as Max Roach told an interviewer in 1971, a music that compels you to say, "Listen, I'd better start thinking about our situation."[29] Improvisation as a practice develops ways to imagine the future and connect lives in real time while emphasizing the quotidian rather than the heroic: just "passing thru," as saxophonist Oliver Lake put it.

The Grid, the Train, and the Blues

Houston Baker's sensitivity to sound led to his blues-drenched theoretical observation that "the dominant blues syntagm in America is an instrumental imitation of *train-wheels-over-track-junctures*. This sound is the 'sign,' as it were, of the blues, and it combines an intriguing melange of phonics: rattling gondolas, clattering flatbeds, quilling whistles, clanging bells, rumbling boxcars, and other railroad sounds."[30] Indeed, the train is an enduring American metaphor. Quoting James Alan McPherson, Baker noted that

> Afro-Americans—at the bottom even of the vernacular ladder in America—responded to the railroad as a "meaningful symbol offering both economic progress and the possibility of aesthetic expression." This possibility came from the locomotive's drive and thrust, its promise of unrestrained mobility and unlimited freedom. The blues musician at the crossing, as I have already suggested, became an expert at reproducing or translating these locomotive energies.[31]

The artist Johnny Coleman once approached an arts commission in San Diego with a proposed project in tribute to Martin Luther King Jr. in which Dr. King was to be symbolized by an enormous black steam locomotive placed in a central plaza.[32] Perhaps Coleman had grown up with such children's books as *The Little Train That Could*, *The Little Red Caboose*, or other stories in which the "big black engine, puffing and chuffing" symbolized mythical, racial (and presexual) intimations of power while, at the same time, unrelenting determination—"We Shall Overcome" combined with "Keep on Pushin'."[33] The Coleman image, even unrealized as it ultimately was, functioned as a conceptual space embodying multiple resonances with the history of the blues and the history of African America.

The sound of the train is the sound of repetition, and in three signal works of the twentieth century—Duke Ellington's 1933 *Daybreak Express*, Pierre Schaeffer's 1948 *musique concrète* experiment *Étude aux chemins de fer*, and Steve Reich's 1988 *Different Trains*—we hear three different evocations of repetition that recall Rosalind Krauss's influential 1978 theory of the grid's emergence as a master trope of modernist art. The grid served as a particularly powerful explanatory metaphor for Minimalist art. Indeed, the grids of Sol LeWitt and Agnes Martin are repetition in visual form. But, as Krauss wrote, "as we have a more and more extended experience of the grid, we have discovered that one of the most modernist things about it is its capacity to serve as a paradigm or model for the antidevelopmental, the antinarrative, the antihistorical."[34] We can walk a few feet farther with Krauss, in a passage where she maintained that "As the experience of Mondrian amply demonstrates, development is precisely what the grid resists."[35] But if we modulate the grid's oscillations by the blues, we wind up with a matrix of sidebands that encompass Robert Farris Thompson's histories of the rhythmized textiles of Mande culture[36] and two signifying riffs on Mondrian's 1942–43 *Broadway Boogie Woogie*: Martin Wong's double signifying on Mondrian and Frank Lloyd Wright in *Flagstone Boogie Woogie* (1984), and an even more playful animated video versioning, *Mondrian Variations* (1992/2011), by California-based composer and media artist Jaroslaw Kapuscinski.[37]

Jack Whitten's 1974 painting *Black Table Setting (Homage to Duke Ellington)* seems to whizz past, after the fashion of the Duke's *Daybreak Express*. In composer Gunther Schuller's analysis of Ellington's piece,

> You'll hear in musical terms the whole sound picture of a train—at first gathering tempo, eventually coming up to full speed, racing through the countryside—complete with the train's whistle and the clickety-clack of the wheels on the track … eventually you hear the train pulling into the next station—slowing down, with the locomotive bell ringing, and then sort of settling down at the station, hissing and wheezing as locomotives used to do in those days.[38]

Schuller's description strongly recalls the sounds of Schaeffer's *musique concrète* étude, and given French culture's enduring encounter with African

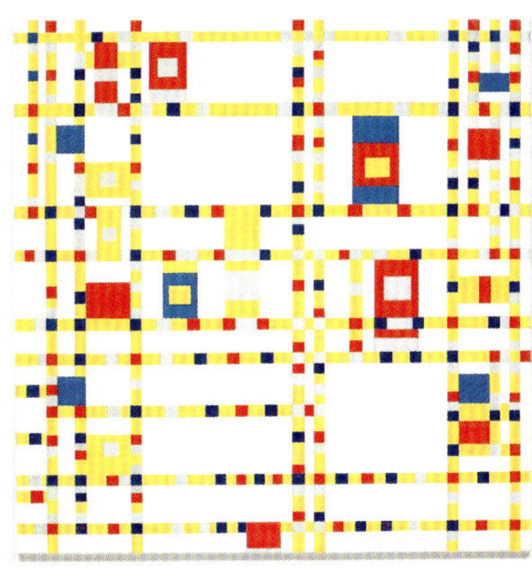

Piet Mondrian
Broadway Boogie Woogie, 1942–43
Oil on canvas
50 x 50 inches
The Museum of Modern Art, New York, given anonymously

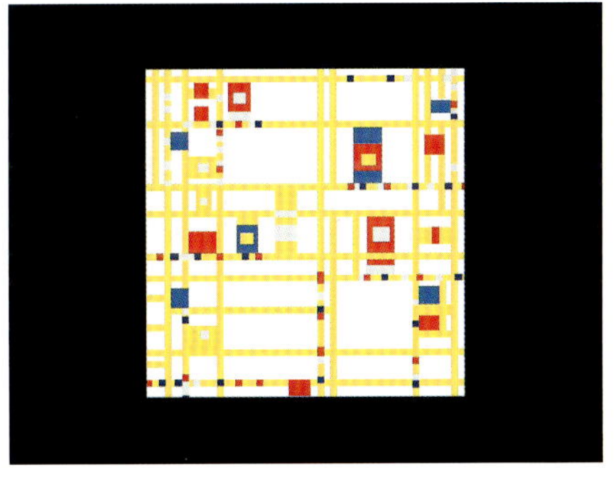

Jaroslaw Kapuscinski
Still from *Mondrian Variations*, 1992/2011
Video; color and sound
9 minutes
Courtesy of the artist

American music, it is doubtful that any French composer or intellectual of the 1940s and 50s would be unfamiliar with Ellington's work. For Schuller, *Daybreak Express* is "a remarkable musical evocation of a ride on an express train in the early 1930s—a train with a steam engine, of course, not even a diesel."[39] But the cover for a 1972 Columbia Records 33 1/3 vinyl reissue of Count Basie's 1942 *Super Chief* featured a color image of Basie's face adorning the pride of the now-defunct Santa Fe Railroad in a pun on the honorific "The Chief" that Basie's band members accorded him.[40] So diesels *can* be bluesy, if not the Orient Express, the Shinkansen, the TGV (Train à Grande Vitesse), or its still faster Japanese maglev descendent—trains that, however marvelous, are not generally seen as funky or bluesy.

The cover to Jaki Byard's *Blues for Smoke*,[41] with its old-style "big black engine, puffing and chuffing" against a blue background, deliberately takes us back to the sounds of *Daybreak Express* and so many other railroad-evoking works. A similar musical onomatopoeia, albeit in a very different register, animates the work of former jazz drummer Reich's *Different Trains*. Even if, as we've already noted, the neo-avant-garde tended to distance itself from the blues, American minimalist music wouldn't have emerged without it—the lack of interest on this point by virtually all the most important scholarly treatments notwithstanding. Thoroughly imbued from the outset with Afrodiasporicisms, what makes American minimalist composers American is what Henry Louis Gates Jr. called "repetition with a signal difference,"[42] the very essence of Reich's theory of "Music as a Gradual Process,"[43] a structure that the blues taught Reich, Philip Glass, and us. In this context, it seems fitting that Reich's 1966 tape-delay-based work *Come Out*, composed in the wake of John Coltrane's modal protominimalism (and just one year after saxophonist Eddie Harris's recorded experiments with Echoplex-based electronic repetition music), featured as the central sonic presence the recorded voice of an Afrodiasporic resident of Spanish Harlem, just then attacked by the police, repeating over and over the phrase, "I had to, like, open the bruise up and let some of the blues [*sic*] blood come out to show them."[44]

Different Trains transposes the imagery of the train to satisfy what Ralph Ellison called "an impulse to keep the painful details and episodes of a brutal experience alive in one's aching consciousness."[45] The work's three movements extract rhythm from samples of spoken phrases. Here, Reich revisits the use of African American voices; in the first movement, "America: Before the War," we hear the voices-as-characters "Virginia" (actually Reich's childhood nanny) and "Mr. Davis" (Lawrence Davis), a retired African American Pullman porter whose recollections and personal effects later became the subject of oral histories and an exhibition at the National Museum of American History.[46]

Reich's piece explores the genocidal side of modernism and technocultural fascism, facing squarely Theodor Adorno's ongoing negative dialectic

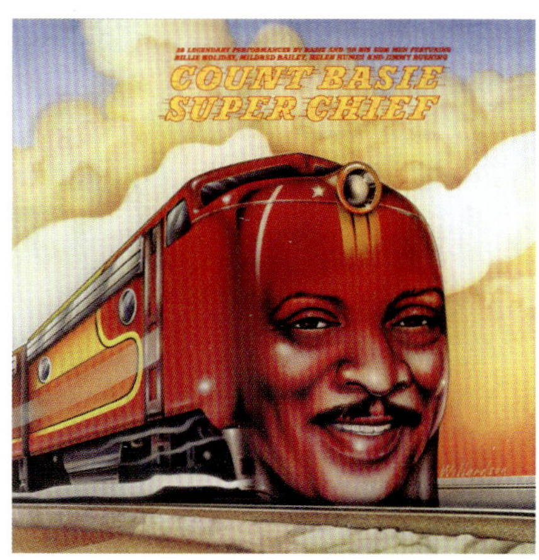

Cover of the reissue of Count Basie's 1942 album *Super Chief* (Columbia, 1972)

confrontation, throughout his life, with how one could create art after Auschwitz, although the philosopher would never quite understand how the sensibility that produced Ellington's compositions *Daybreak Express* and *Black, Brown, and Beige* could also embody these deeper issues in ways specific to the post-slavery histories of the bearers of blues idiom. Ultimately, what Reich and other minimalist composers such as Terry Riley and La Monte Young discovered was how to overcome the Sisyphean horror of which Hegel lived in mortal dread, simply by signifying on the recursive blues versioning of Nietzsche's eternal recurrence to reveal that the practice of freedom draws its main power from freedom itself.

Blues Colors

Updating Fats Waller's mock-plaintive lament of 1929, a number of artists today seem to be asking not "What Did I Do," but "What *Can* I Do to Be So Black and Blue." Joni Mitchell has asked this same question; sometimes she was said to feel "like a black man in a white woman's body," as a 1998 *New York Times Magazine* article told it,[47] and the African American contemporary composer Alvin Singleton tells us why in his 1988 composition for string quartet "Secret Desire to Be Black."

"Black and Blue," of course, refers to bruises and pain—the cicatrices that often attend "an autobiographical chronicle of personal catastrophe."[48] But black and blue are also colors, and for many of the artists in this collection, they are blues colors—Edward Clark's *The Stove* from 1952; Kerry James Marshall's *Blue Water Silver Moon (Mermaid)* from 1991, recalling the paintings of Oliver Jackson; or the blue(s) covers to both Byard's album and the 1995 edition of Kamau Brathwaite's book *Black + Blues*. And like the deep blues, blues colors are often deeply saturated, a dynamic recognized by Muhal Richard Abrams, himself a painter, in his 1986 work for full orchestra *Saturation Blue*.

But there are more blues colors. Listen to King Pleasure singing "Red Top" while having a look at the deeply red (not Simply Red) Jimmie Durham assemblage *Pocahontas' Underwear* from 1985. Put on some of that scary devil blues (sorry, there is no such thing as angel blues) while you confront the supersaturated red/black palette of Jutta Koether's *100% (Portrait Robert Johnson)*, a work from 1990 that reminded me of my encounter with some sculptures in a folk art museum in a small Polish town; a poet friend later informed me that black and red were commonly used to depict Jews as the Devil.

The filmmaker Thomas Allen Harris once told me that he saw African skin not as black, but as gold. Remembering that, suddenly I saw blues gold

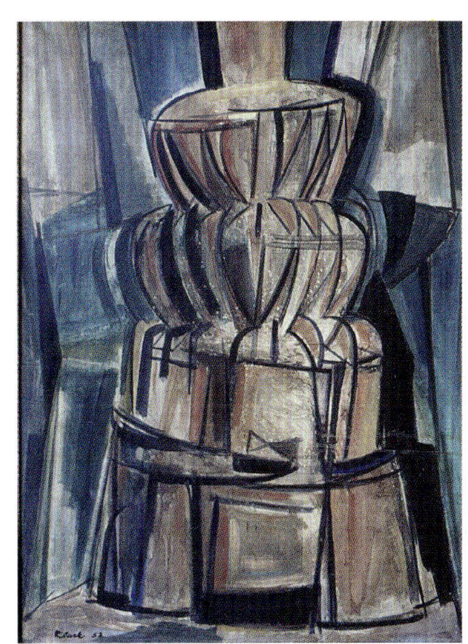

Edward Clark
The Stove, 1952

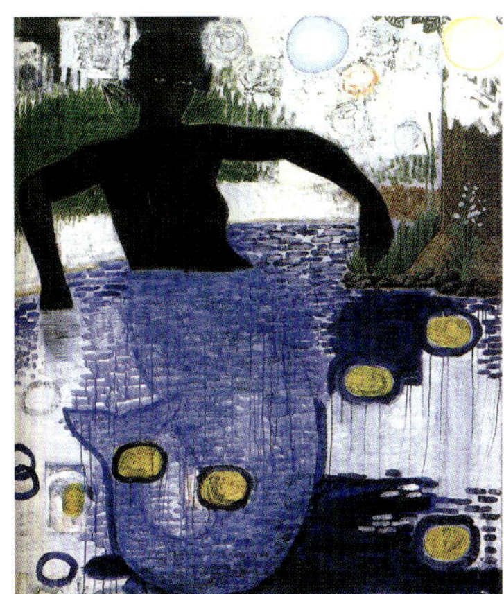

Kerry James Marshall
Blue Water Silver Moon (Mermaid), 1991

everywhere in the current exhibition. Glenn Ligon uses the blues colors black and gold in a large collection of canvases that declare to the world that there is no room for advancement in what my father used to call "niggerology." Wadada Leo Smith's synesthetically imbued, saturated black-red-gold-blue score to *The Dream*, a composition written in his Ankhrasmation system of musical notation, is the product of a son of the Mississippi Delta who began composing at the age of eight and whose father was himself a bluesman.

Jeff Donaldson's large-scale 1988 painting *Jampact/Jelly Tite (for Jamila)* radically exemplifies his ecstatic determination, first articulated in 1970, to deploy "*Color* color Color color that shines, color that is free of rules and regulations…. color that is expressively awesome…. Superreal color…. Color as bright and as real as the color dealing on the streets of Watts and the Southside … in Roxbury and in Harlem, in Abidjan … Bahia … Dakar."[49] *Too many colors, too many notes*, went the Africobra challenge to the aesthetics of the hegemon—a way to achieve what virtual-reality artists would call immersion, or even saturation, a theme taken up by the free-jazz-influenced French composer Franck Bedrossian in works such as *Charleston* (2005/2007).

Blues for…

As Houston Baker tells us, "The blues are a synthesis … always becoming, shaping, transforming, displacing the peculiar experiences of Africans in the New World."[50] Well, yes, but not just New World Africans anymore. For Albert Murray, in *Stomping the Blues*,

> the blues idiom, whatever the source or sources of its components, is native to the United States. It is a synthesis of African and European elements, the product of an Afro-American sensibility in an American mainland situation. There is no evidence, for example, that an African musical sensibility interacting with an Italian, German, French, British, or Hungarian musical sensibility results in anything like blues music.[51]

The genetic metaphor is plain, and is as plainly contradicted by at least one very important recording, Miles Davis's *Sketches of Spain* (1960), arranged by my former bandmaster Gil Evans, in which the "cry of jazz" forms common ground with the Andalusian gypsy's flamenco lament.[52] Later, the 1993 film *Latcho Drom* traced the Romany flamenco cry from dual Egyptian and Indian origins through Turkey, France, and Hungary to its present location in Spain. Whereas Murray extended American exceptionalism to re-create the blues and its progenitors as "Omni-American,"[53] Davis invokes intercultural, even global commonality, as with Dr. King's opening speech at the 1964 Berlin Jazz Festival. "And now, Jazz is exported to the world," King intoned. "For in the particular struggle of the Negro in America there is something akin to the universal struggle of modern man. Everybody has the blues."[54] If we want to explore structure in a more subliminal way, we could think about why the number twelve bears significance across three musical cultures of storytelling, praise-singing, lament, and social commentary: the blues, the twelve-beat structures of Korean *p'ansori*, and flamenco's *bulería*. If you've been there, as I have, the shouts of encouragement from both audience and drummer at a *p'ansori* performance recall nothing so much as black Baptist and Pentecostal witnessing.

On some level, like *p'ansori* or flamenco, the blues is most always for or about something. I realize now that simply naming a work *Blues* (as I did in 1978) isn't enough; writing a blues is, often enough, either a commentary or a form of homage.[55] That's what makes Kerry James Marshall's 1998 painting *Souvenir IV* a blues painting, just as Quincy Troupe's "Following the North Star Boogaloo," a text I incorporated in a 1995 composition for percussion and computer, is a blues poem:

> word, when we knew ourselves through songs
> through what we saw alive in homeboys eyes
> through love, through what it was we were before
> commercials told us how to move & groove, who to love
> when we did it all & had fun & knew the heroes
> new & old & never confused dope for the bomb.[56]

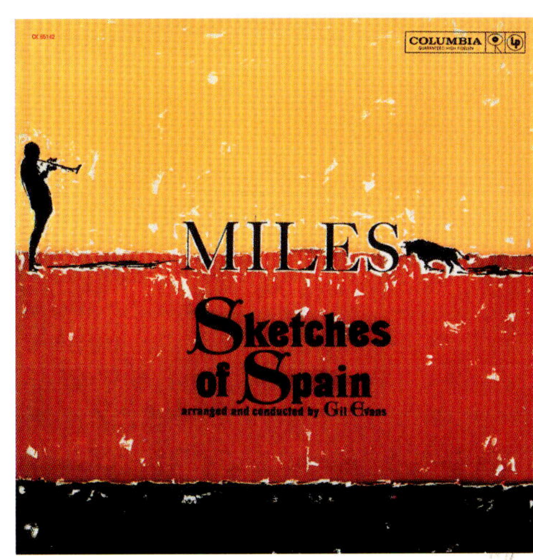

Cover of Miles Davis's album *Sketches of Spain* (Columbia, 1960)

Marshall's painting knows the heroes, and like Troupe's poem, mourns their passing. But what about old William Grant Still, the father of the Western classical blues, who dared in 1930 to create an *Afro-American Symphony* that broke with the ultramodernism of his teacher Edgard Varèse? Still's symphony used the blues as a form of New Negro–sympathetic political intervention to decisively mark the heretofore unmarked whiteness at the core of American classical music, at the very historical moment that it was being decided that blackness would have no purchase on it. But to paraphrase Winston Rodney's plea for Marcus Garvey, "No one remembah him, no one…."[57] Judging from the grudging treatment Still receives to this day by critics in U.S. newspapers of record, the establishment never forgave him this simple yet audacious transgression of marrying the blues with sonata form—miscegenation then, hybridity now. George Gershwin, another father of American blues hybridity and a student of the experimental Schillinger System of Musical Composition, also paid dearly for his sins by the studied refusal of the musicology of the day to recognize his work as "serious music."

In fact, like Gershwin, black classical composers active from 1930 to the present have never been as dismissive of popular music as their white colleagues have been. While one should feel slightly embarrassed by attempts to draw arbitrary homologies between musical structures and cultural and political forms, composers from Still to Florence Price to Tania Léon to Anthony Davis continue to reference elements of the blues, black folk culture, vernacular black life, and pan-African imaginings. In pursuing dialogue with the hegemon, the European tradition, these composers and others showed American musical culture how classical music could be viably connected with an African diasporic sonic culture whose worldwide influence throughout the twentieth century and into the twenty-first can hardly be overstated. If we've learned anything from Amiri Baraka, Nathaniel Mackey, or Ellington, for that matter, it's that if the blues is a structure, it is along the lines of the "structure of feeling" indicated by cultural critic Raymond Williams.

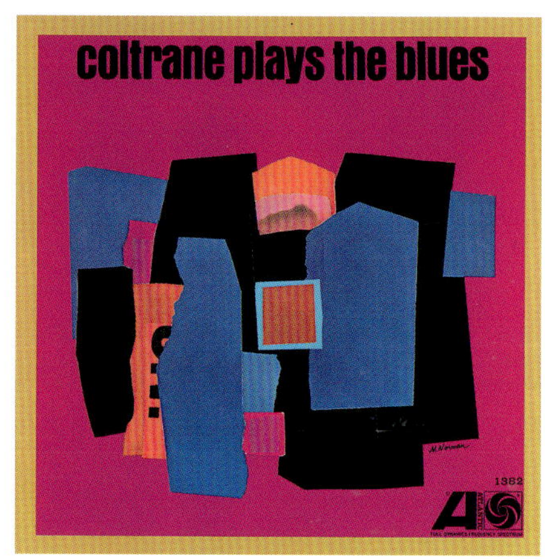

Cover of John Coltrane's album
Coltrane Plays the Blues (Atlantic, 1962)

Often enough, a blues song had a premise built into its title—"Dippermouth Blues," "Lonesome Lover Blues," or whatever. Then there were the dedications, as with John Coltrane's 1962 album *Coltrane Plays the Blues*, with work titles in the form "Blues to [entity]": "Blues to Bechet," "Blues to Elvin," and, anticipating *Time* magazine's 2006 Person of the Year by decades, "Blues to You."[58] Another form of dedication, even more prevalent than the "Blues to ___" syntax, is the "Blues for ___" form. Riffing on this venerable tradition, James Baldwin gave us the play *Blues for Mister Charlie* in 1964, and in 1971 I played in an AACM ensemble led by guitarist Pete Cosey, with Malachi Favors Maghostout, Kalaparusha Maurice McIntyre, and Famoudou Don Moye, playing Cosey's syntactically open, repetition-based composition "Blues For."

But what do you think the record producers said when Byard told them that his solo record album, brand new for 1960, would be titled *Blues for Smoke*? History appears not to record the title's provenance, so just as John Cage would have it, that information, by not being given, is indeterminate. After glossing the obvious—the ephemeral, the immaterial, and the cryptic (was "smoke" already a code word for marijuana in 1960?)—I had to admit that decoding this title was beyond my hermeneutic capabilities. Listening to this record, though, you quickly discover that the potent blues lessons the young Byard was handing out were already established within a traditional mission in blues history: reasserting the blues idiom by critically boxing with it and evading attempts at formal standardization, as the old blues people and their jazz descendents and contemporaries had done. Utterly secure in its blues skin, with no need for anxious harangues about "the fundamentals," Byard's music tells us that maybe, just maybe, if you listened to everything and everyone, you'd hear a lot of things you could use—if your *ear* was on the sparrow.

But I bet that those record company guys didn't get that far. I think that what they said was this: "Blues for Smoke? Who's 'Smoke'?"

Notes

1. Roberta S. Maguire, ed., *Conversations with Albert Murray* (Jackson: University of Mississippi Press, 1997), 92.

2. John Cage, "Composition as Process: Indeterminacy," in *Silence: Lectures and Writings by John Cage* (Middletown, Conn.: Wesleyan University Press, 1973), 39.

3. Quoted in George E. Lewis, *A Power Stronger Than Itself: The AACM and American Experimental Music* (Chicago: University of Chicago Press, 2008), 177.

4. Cage, "Composition as Process: Indeterminacy," 38.

5. Albert Murray, *The Omni-Americans: Black Experience and American Culture* (New York: Da Capo Press, 1990), 60.

6. Ibid., 54.

7. Ibid., 56.

8. The Washington, D.C., version of the exhibition formed the basis for its catalogue. See Richard J. Powell, ed., *The Blues Aesthetic: Black Culture and Modernism* (Washington, D.C.: Washington Project for the Arts, 1989).

9. Kristine McKenna, "The Blues and Visual Arts: It's a Gray Picture," *Los Angeles Times*, January 20, 1990.

10. This discussion of stereotype is found in Homi K. Bhabha, *The Location of Culture* (New York: Routledge, 1994), 66.

11. Murray, *Stomping the Blues* (New York: Da Capo Press, 2000), 70.

12. Houston A. Baker Jr., *Blues, Ideology, and Afro-American Literature: A Vernacular Theory* (Chicago: University of Chicago Press, 1984), 12–13.

13. Ron Karenga, "Black Cultural Nationalism," in *The Black Aesthetic*, ed. Addison Gayle Jr. (New York: Doubleday, 1971), 33.

14. Baker, *Blues*, 1.

15. Friedrich Nietzsche, *The Gay Science*, ed. Bernard Williams with a prelude in German rhymes and an appendix of songs (Cambridge, England: Cambridge University Press, 2001), 194.

16. James Snead, "On Repetition in Black Culture," *Black American Literature Forum* 15, no. 4 (Winter 1981): 148.

17. Ibid.

18. Nietzsche, *The Gay Science*, 194.

19. Ludwig Wittgenstein, *Tractatus Logico-Philosophicus*, trans. D. F. Pears and B. F. McGuinness (New York: Routledge, 2001), 87. In the original: "Wenn man unter Ewigkeit nicht unendliche Zeitdauer, sondern Unzeitlichkeit versteht, dann lebt er ewig, der in der Gegenwart lebt."

20. Baker, *Blues*, 5.

21. Snead, "On Repetition," 149–50.

22. *The Matrix* (1999); *The Matrix Reloaded* (2003); and *The Matrix Revolutions* (2003), dir. Andy and Larry Wachowski (Warner Bros. Pictures).

23. Baker, *Blues*, 3–4, 6.

24. Pierre Bourdieu, *Outline of a Theory of Practice*, trans. Richard Nice, *Cambridge Studies in Social Anthropology*, no. 16. (Cambridge, England: Cambridge University Press, 1977), 78–79.

25. Baker, *Blues*, 4.

26. Bourdieu, *Outline*, 78, 95.

27. Ibid., 6.

28. J. David Velleman, *How We Get Along* (Cambridge, England: Cambridge University Press, 2009), 76.

29. "Self-Determination and the Black Aesthetic: An Interview with Max Roach," *Black World* (November 1973): 68.

30. Baker, *Blues*, 8.

31. Ibid., 11.

32. Robert L. Pincus, "Fruitful Yet Flawed Year Left Impression," *San Diego Union-Tribune*, December 26, 1993.

33. Marian Potter, *The Little Red Caboose* (Racine: Western Publishing Company, 1953). See also Watty Piper, *The Little Engine That Could* (New York: Platt and Munk, 1992), first published in 1930.

34. Rosalind Krauss, "Grids," *October* 9 (Summer 1979): 64.

35. Ibid., 51.

36. See Robert Farris Thompson, *Flash of the Spirit: African and Afro-American Art and Philosophy* (New York: Vintage, 1984).

37. See http://jaroslawkapuscinski.com/work-mondrianvariations.html, accessed February 6, 2012.

38. Gunther Schuller, "Stated Meeting Report, Jazz and Composition: The Many Sides of Duke Ellington, the Music's Greatest Composer," *Bulletin of the American Academy of Arts and Sciences* 46, no. 1 (October 1992): 45.

39. Ibid.

40. Count Basie, *Super Chief*, Wounded Bird Records, 2007 (Columbia Records, 1972). In my personal experience playing in the Basie band in 1976, Basie was called "The Chief." See "Interview with Bill Hughes," *Cadence* 23, no. 11 (November 1997).

41. Jaki Byard, *Blues for Smoke*, Candid, 1960.

42. Henry Louis Gates Jr., *The Signifying Monkey: A Theory of African-American Literary Criticism* (Oxford: Oxford University Press, 1988), 51.

43. Steve Reich, "Music as a Gradual Process" (1968), in *Writings on Music, 1965–2000*, ed. Paul Hillier (Oxford: Oxford University Press, 2002), 34–36.

44. Reich, "Come Out" (1966), on *Steve Reich: Early Works*, Nonesuch, 1992. For a reference to the *Come Out* speaker's malapropism (the speaker clearly meant to say "bruise blood"), see Sumanth Gopinath, "The Problem of the Political in Steve Reich's *Come Out*," in Robert Adlington, ed., *Sound Commitments: Avant-Garde Music and the Sixties* (New York: Oxford University Press, 2009), 121–44.

45. Ralph Ellison, "Richard Wright's Blues," in *The Jazz Cadence of American Culture*, ed. Robert G. O'Meally (New York: Columbia University Press, 1998), 553.

46. See Amy Lynn Wlodarski, "The Testimonial Aesthetics of *Different Trains*," *Journal of the American Musicological Society* 63, no. 1 (Spring 2010): 99–142. Also hear Steve Reich, *Different Trains (Kronos Quartet)*, Nonesuch, 1990.

47. Neil Strauss, "The Hissing of a Living Legend," *New York Times Magazine*, October 4, 1998, available at http://www.nytimes.com/1998/10/04/magazine/the-hissing-of-a-living-legend.html.

48. Ellison, "Richard Wright's Blues," 553.

49. Jeff Donaldson, "Africobra—African Commune of Bad Relevant Artists: Ten in Search of a Nation," *Black World* (October 1970): 85–86. For a discussion of the relationships between black musicians and black visual artists in 1960s Chicago, see Lewis, "Purposive Patterning: Jeff Donaldson, Muhal Richard Abrams, and the Multidominance of Consciousness," *Lenox Avenue: A Journal of Interarts Inquiry* 5 (1999): 63–69.

50. Baker, *Blues*, 5.

51. Murray, *Stomping the Blues*, 63.

52. Miles Davis, *Sketches of Spain* (1960), arranged and conducted by Gil Evans, Sony, 1997.

53. Murray, *The Omni-Americans*.

54. Katherine McKittrick and Clyde Adrian Woods, eds., *Black Geographies and the Politics of Place* (Toronto: Between the Lines; Cambridge, Mass.: South End Press, 2007), 70.

55. Lewis, *Homage to Charles Parker*, Black Saint, 1979.

56. Quincy Troupe, "Following the North Star Boogaloo," in *Transcircularities: New and Selected Poems* (Minneapolis: Coffee House Press, 2002), 199–200.

57. Burning Spear (b. Winston Rodney), "Old Marcus Garvey," on *Marcus Garvey*, Island Records, 1975.

58. John Coltrane, *Coltrane Plays the Blues*, Atlantic, 1962.

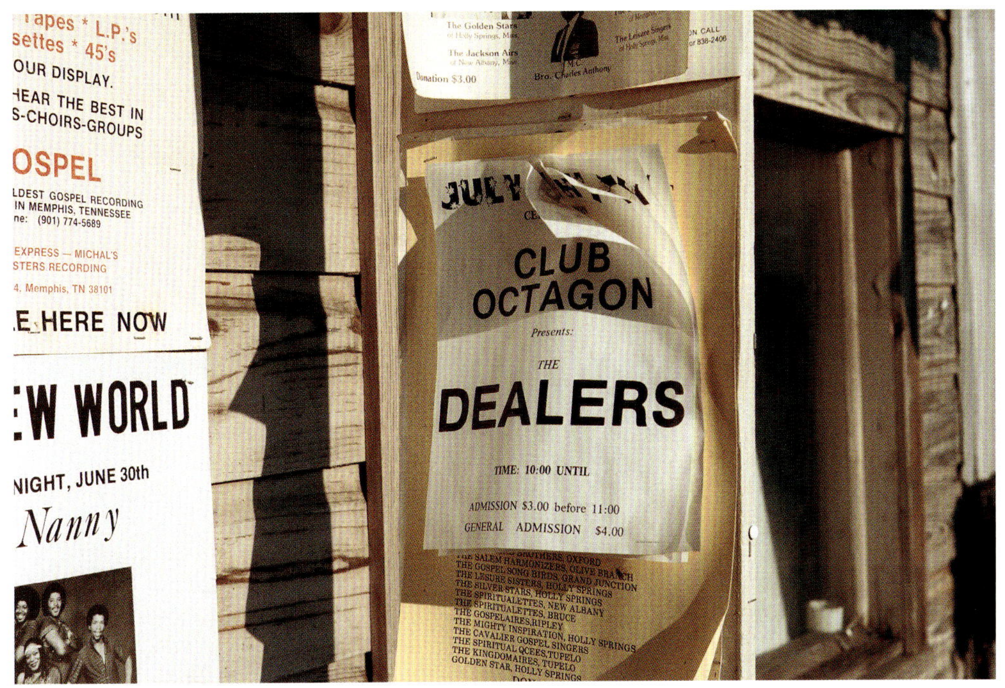

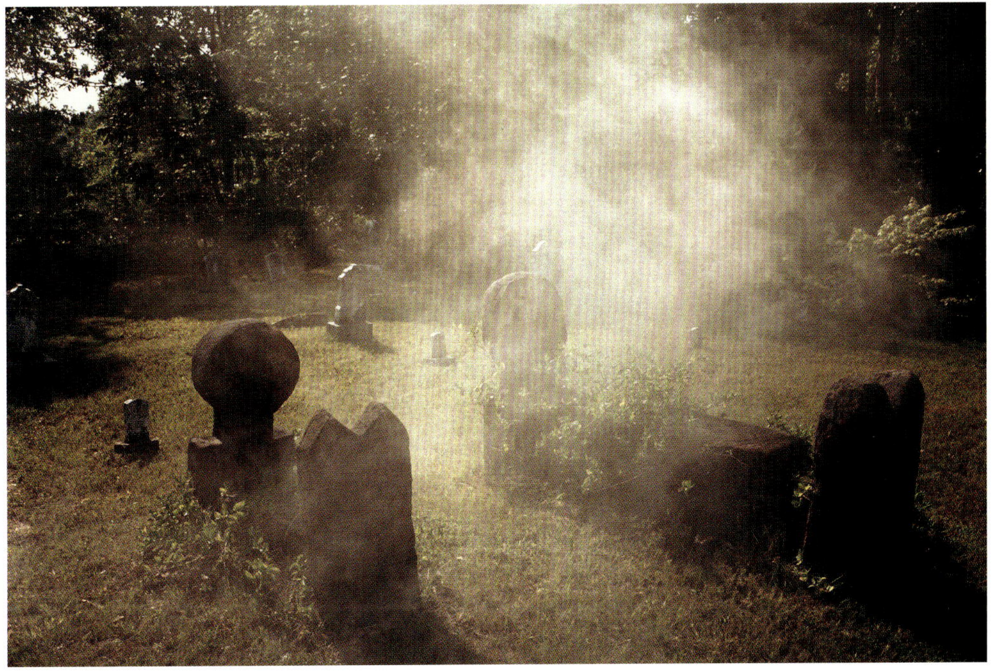

TOP AND BOTTOM
William Eggleston
Untitled (Gathering Place at Holly Springs, Mississippi), c. 1982–85
Untitled (Near Oxford, Mississippi), c. 1982–85

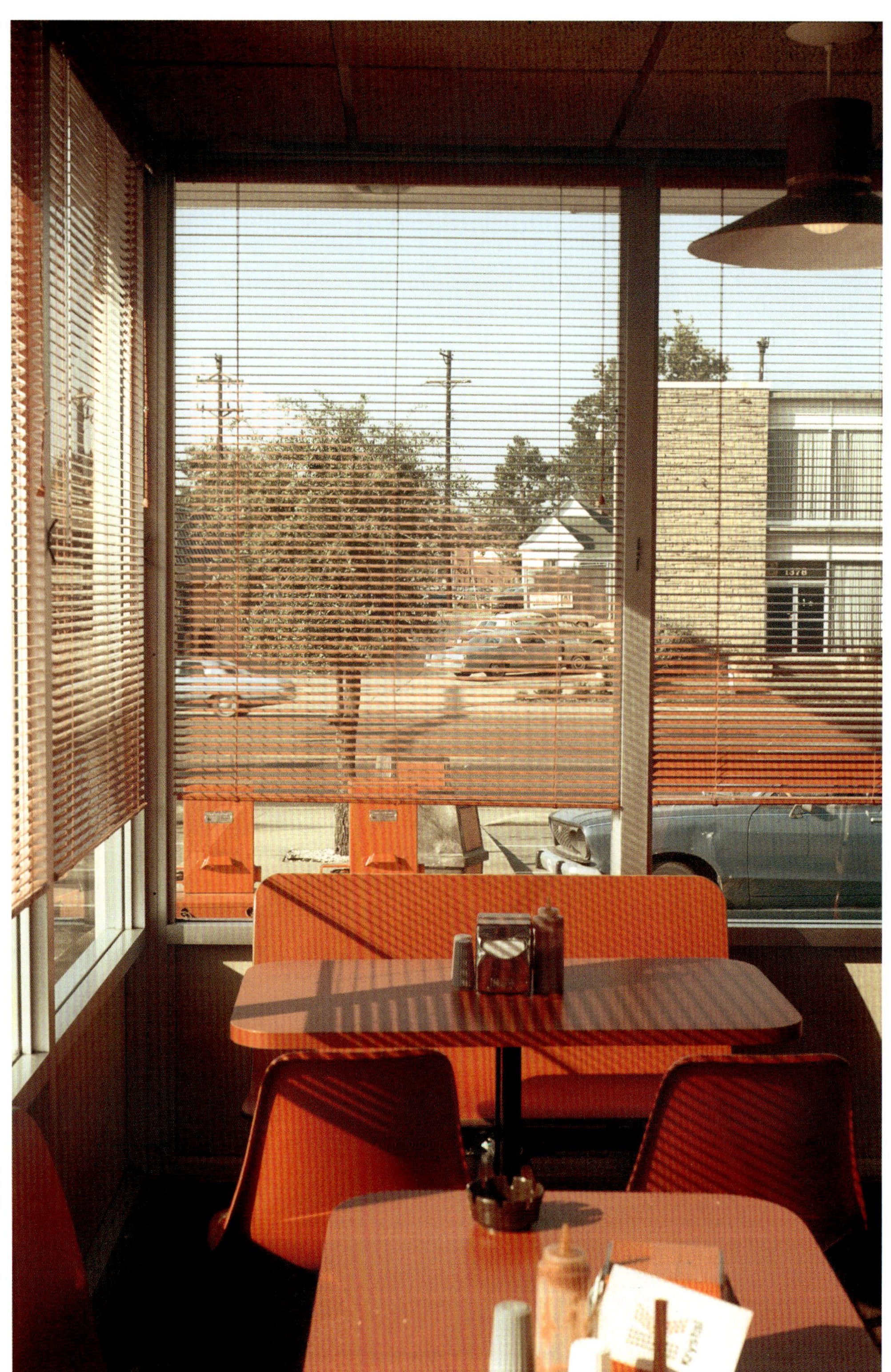

William Eggleston
Untitled (Memphis, Krystal), c. 1982–85

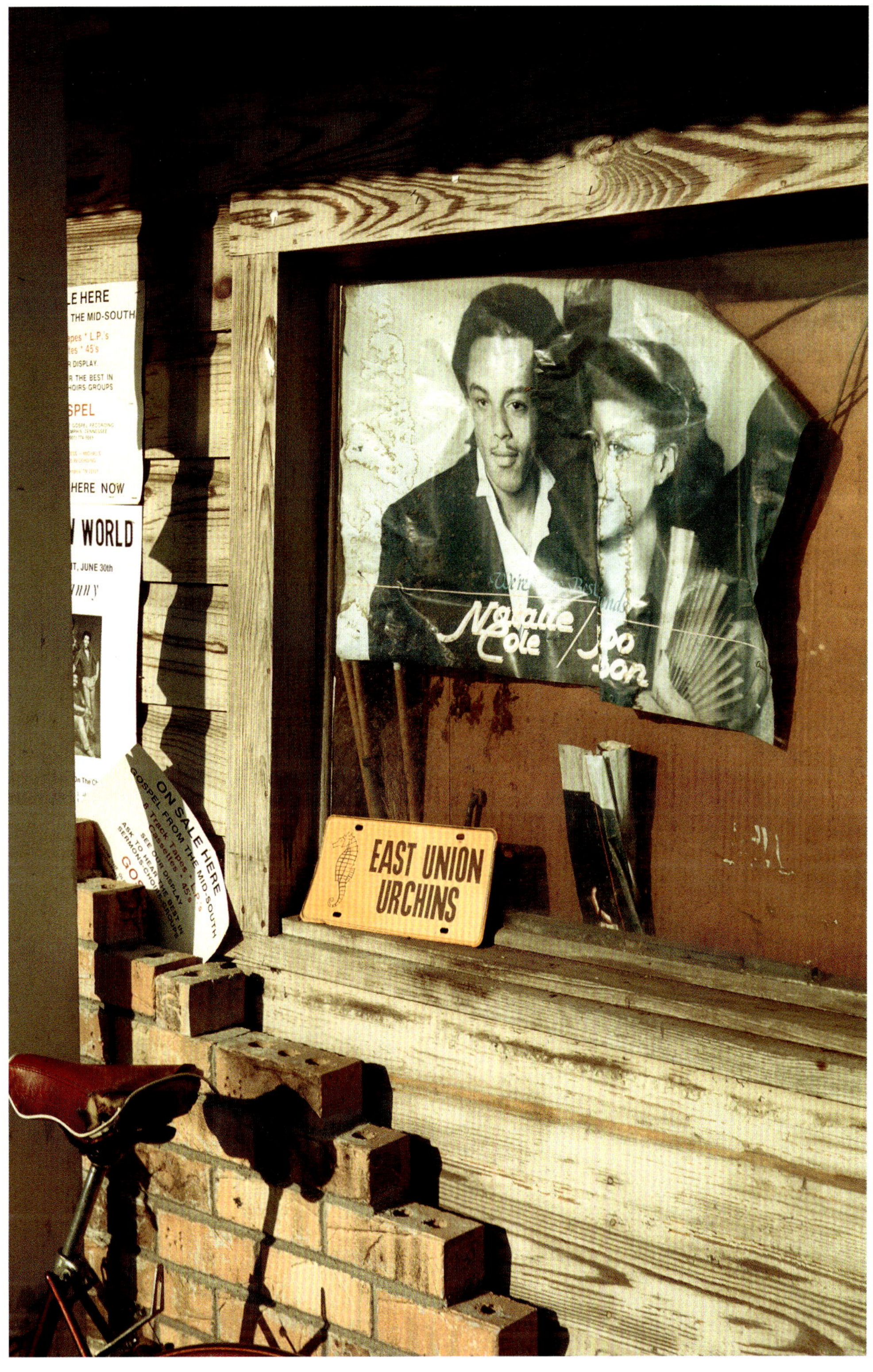

William Eggleston
Untitled (Holly Springs, Mississippi), c. 1982–85

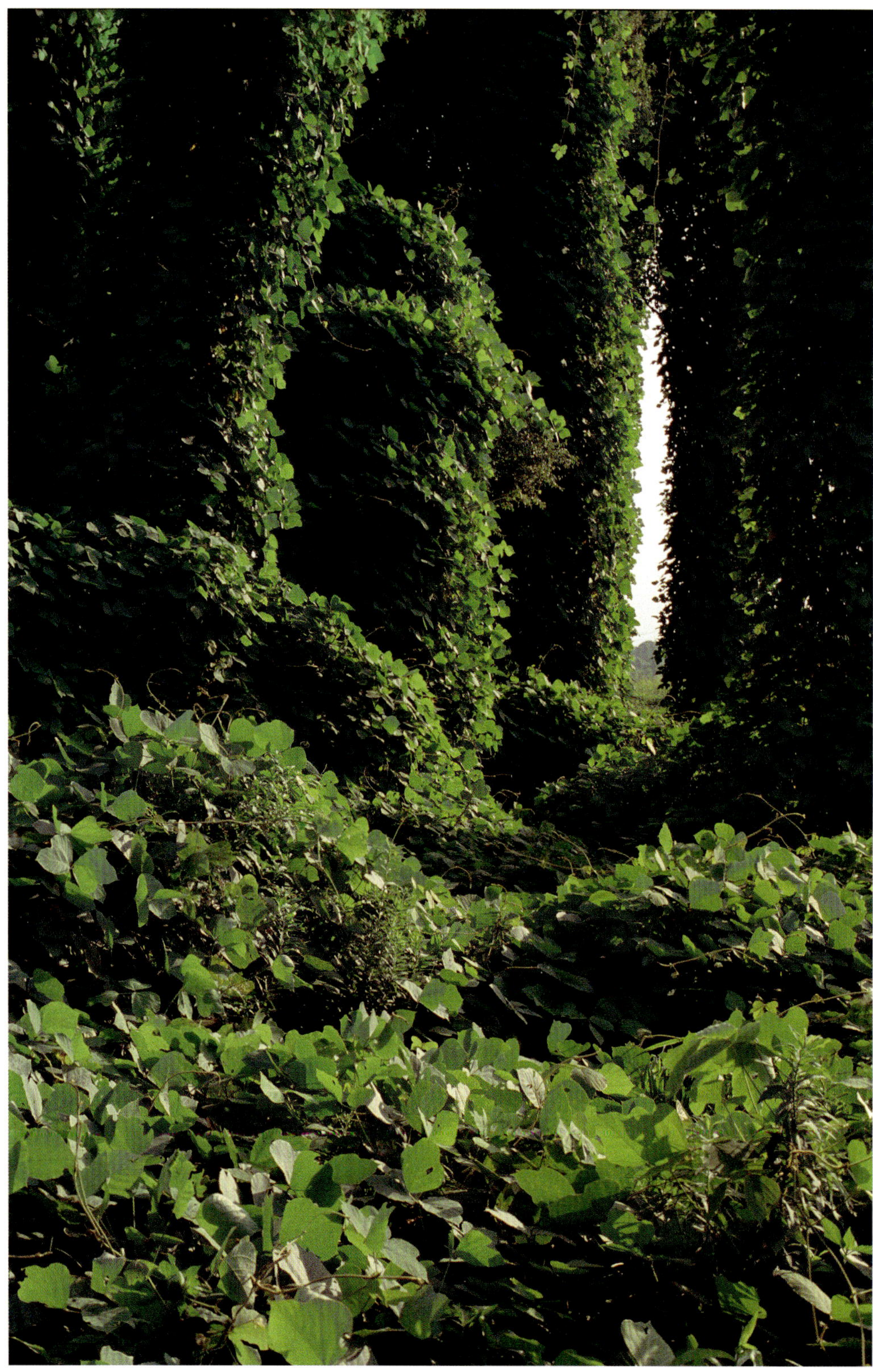

William Eggleston
Untitled (Mississippi), 1992

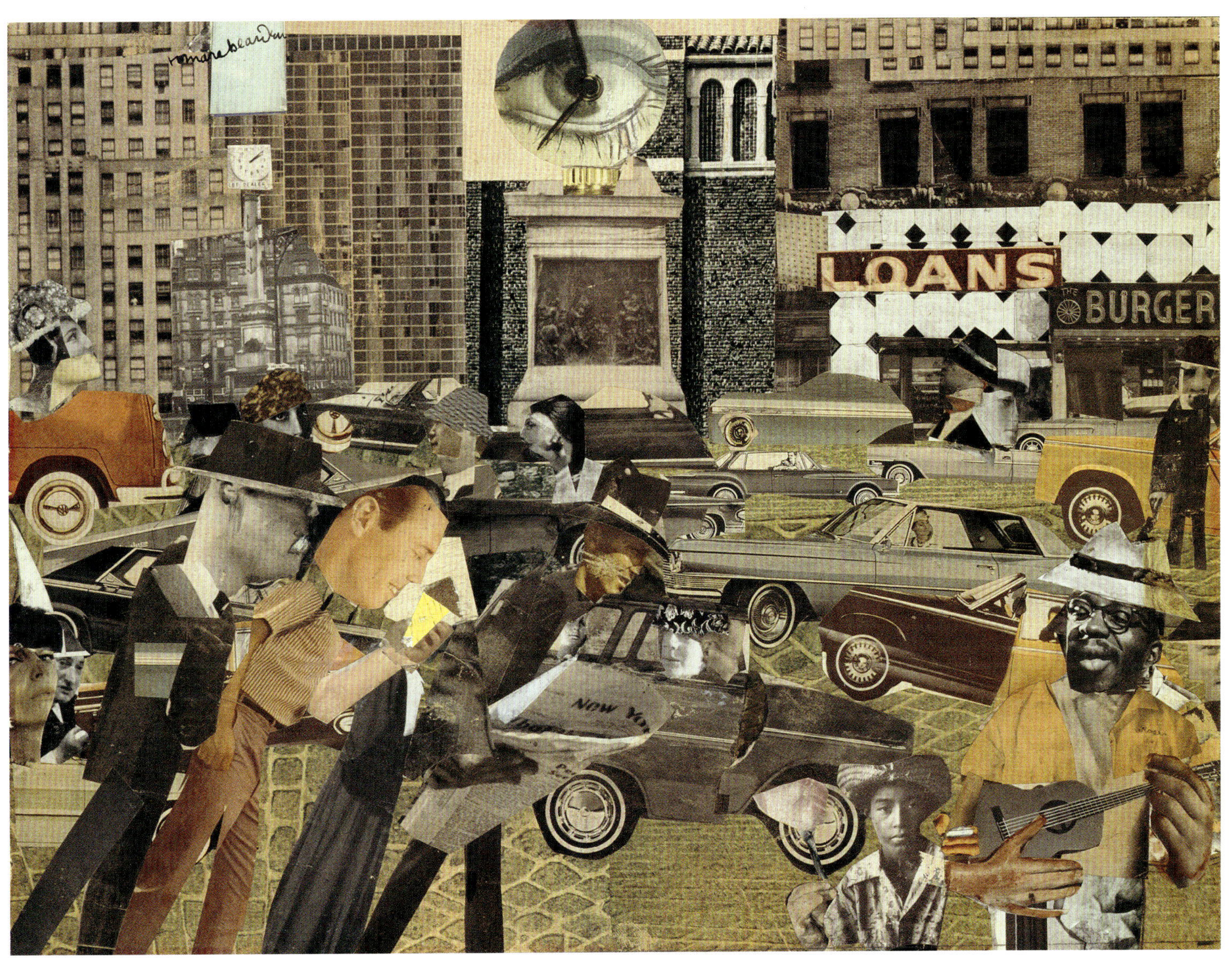

Romare Bearden
Uptown Looking Downtown, 1965

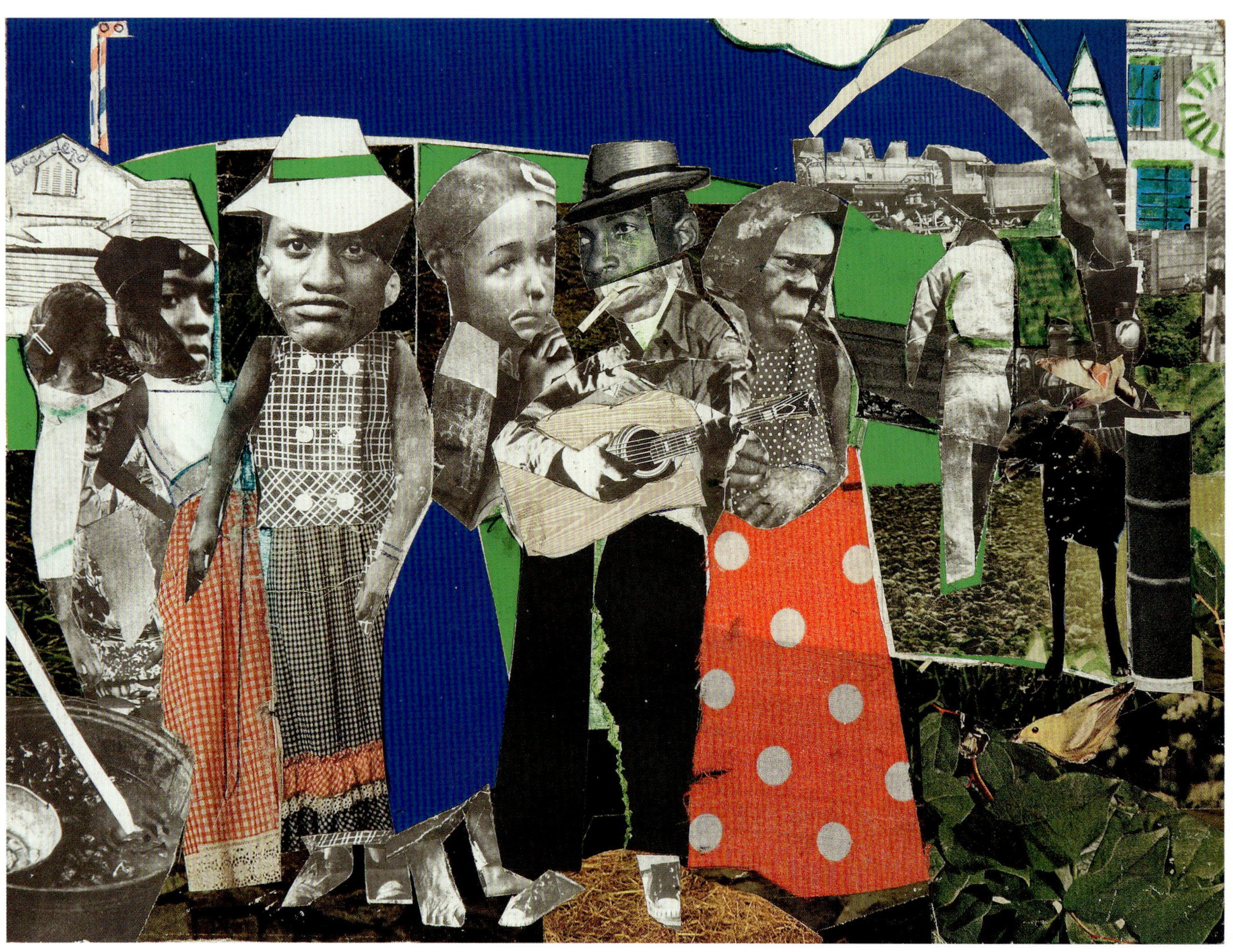

Romare Bearden
Watching the Trains Go By, c. 1969

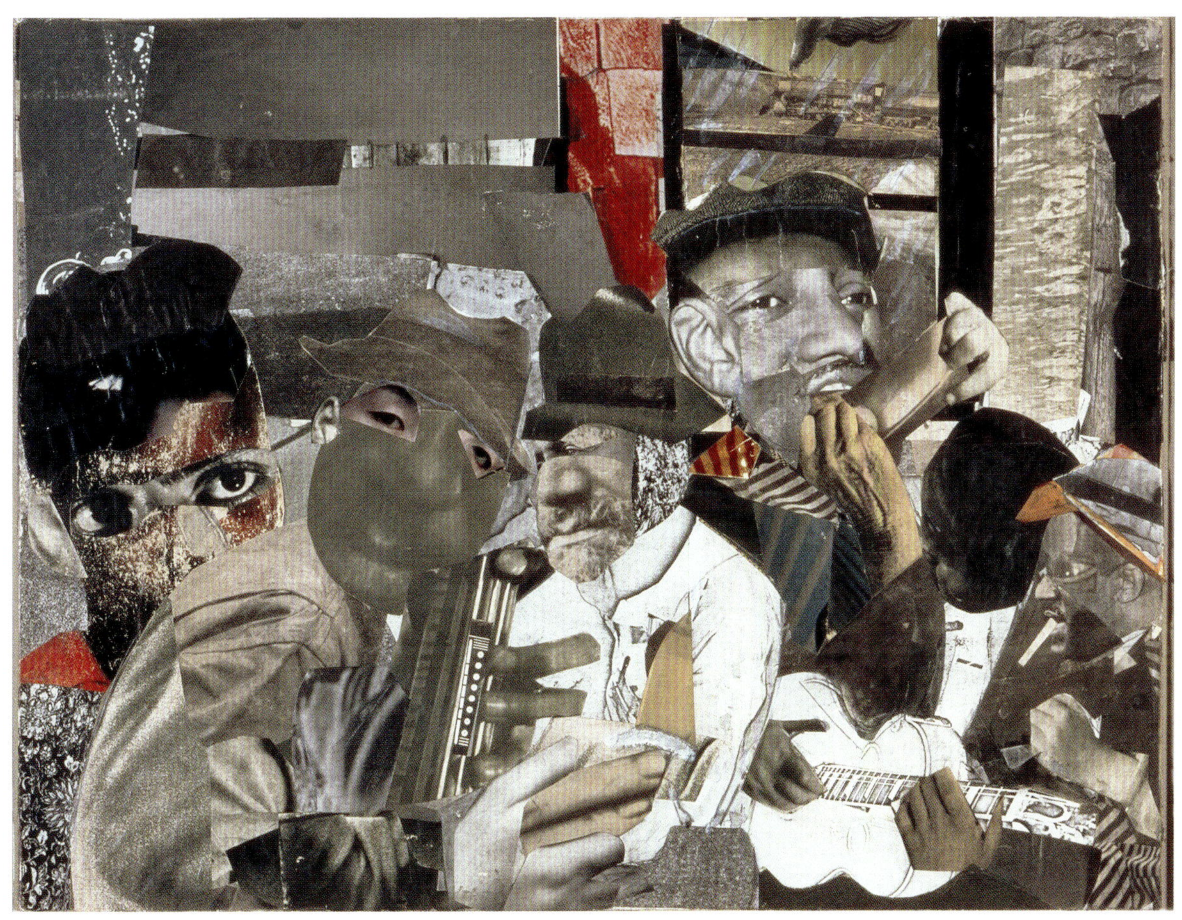

Romare Bearden
Train Whistle Blues: II, 1964

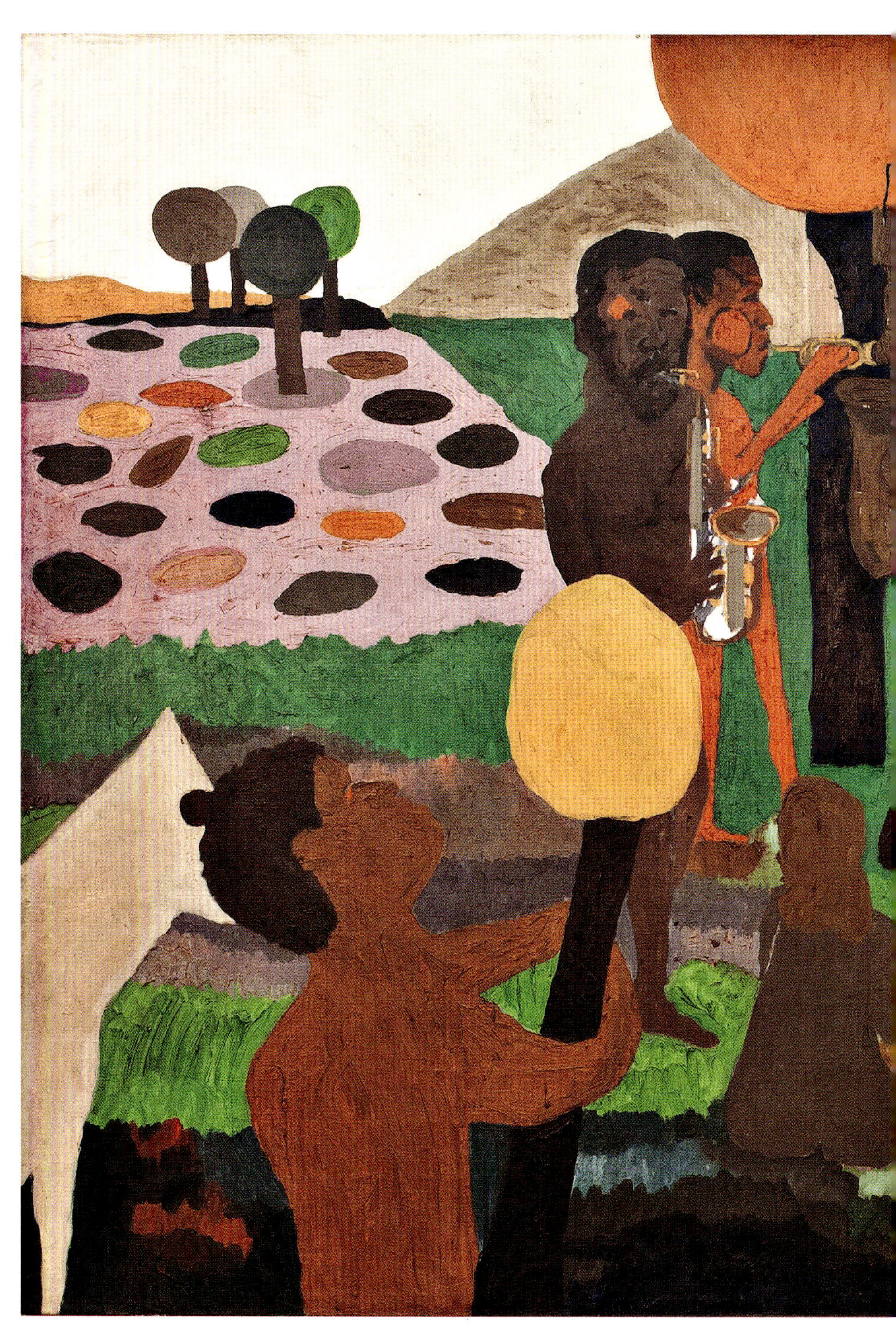

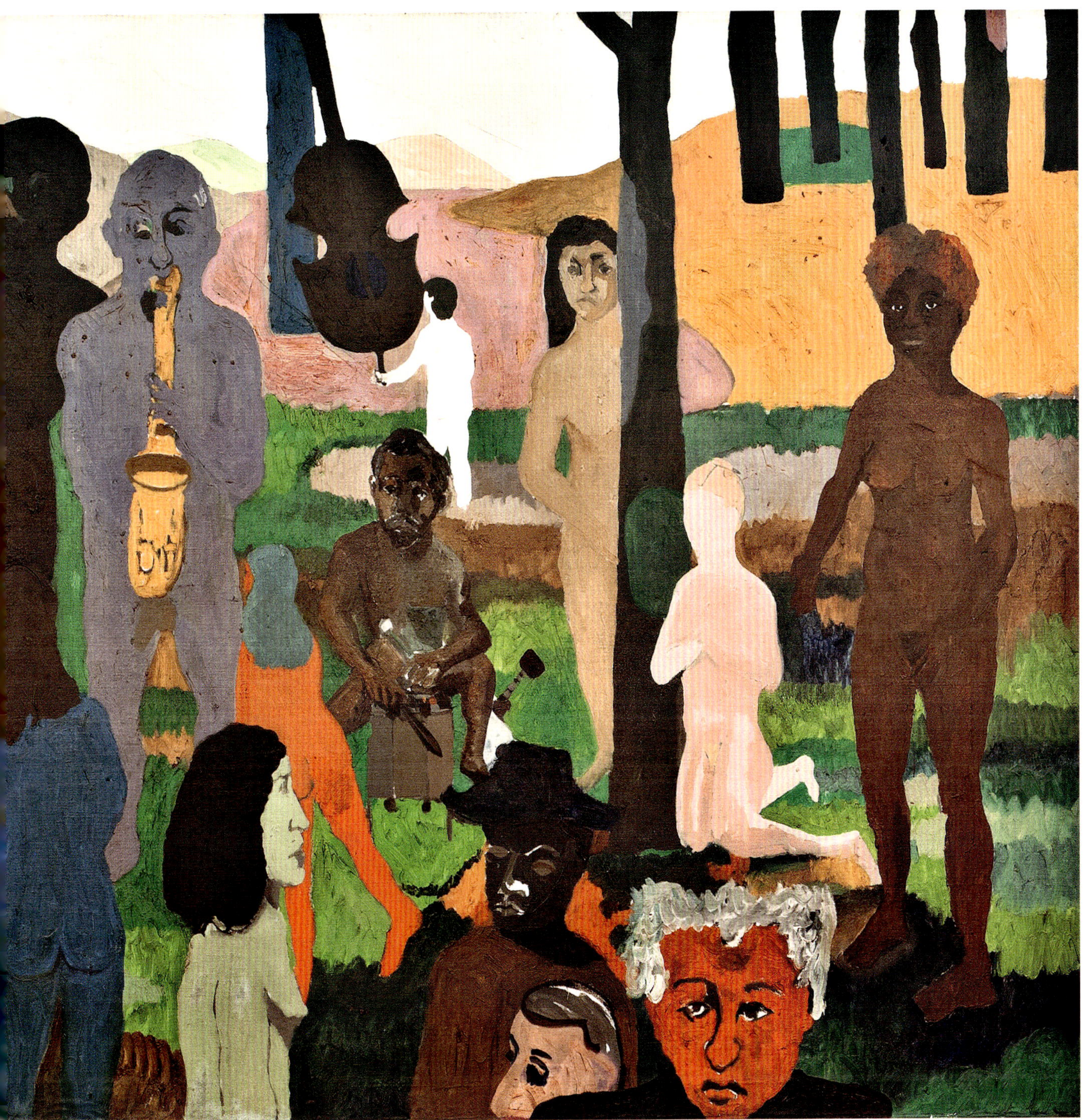

Bob Thompson
Garden of Music, 1960

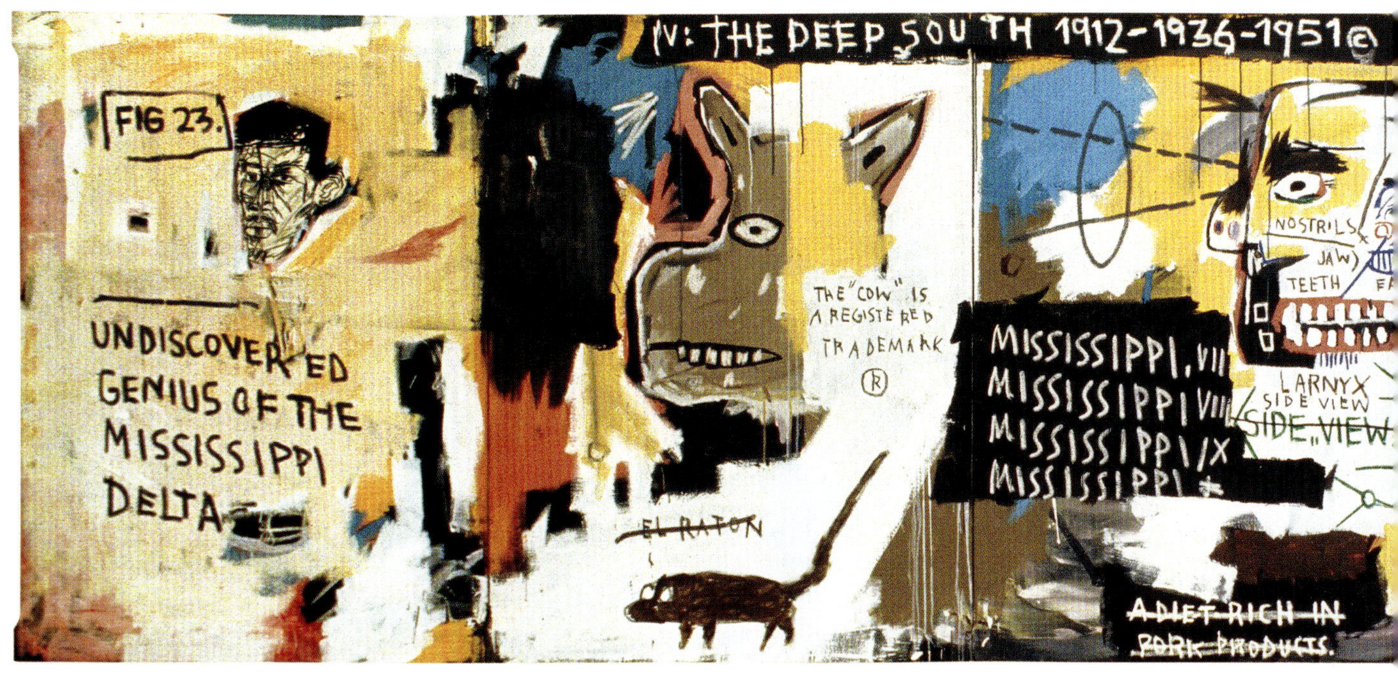
IV: THE DEEP SOUTH 1912-1936-1951 ©
FIG 23.
UNDISCOVERED
GENIUS OF THE
MISSISSIPPI
DELTA
THE "COW" IS
A REGISTERED
TRADEMARK
®
EL RATON
MISSISSIPPI. VII
MISSISSIPPI VIII
MISSISSIPPI IX
MISSISSIPPI X
NOSTRILS
JAW
TEETH
LARNYX
SIDE VIEW
"SIDE VIEW
A DIET RICH IN
PORK PRODUCTS.

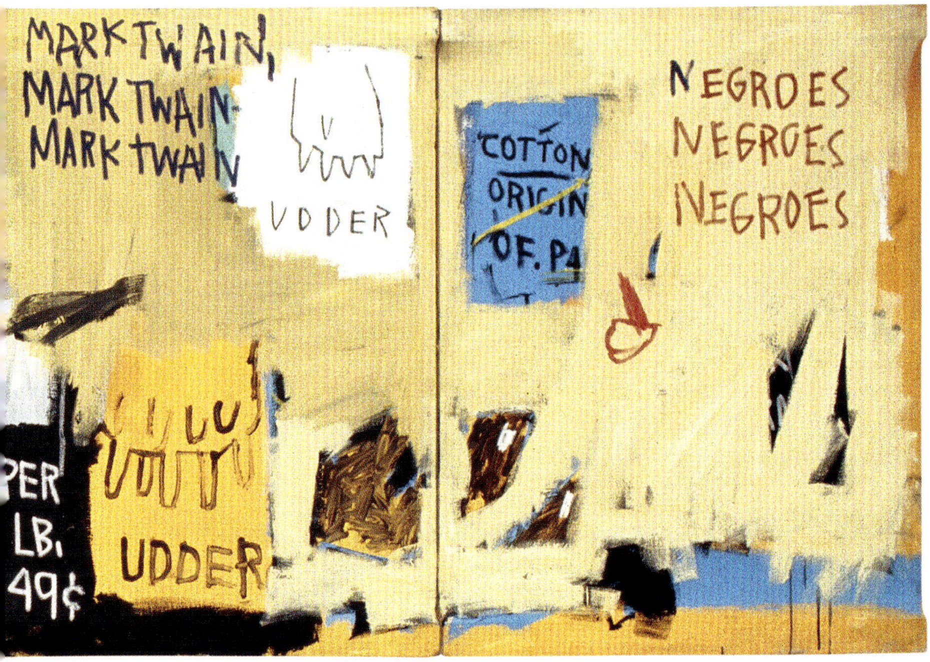

Jean-Michel Basquiat
Undiscovered Genius of the Mississippi Delta, 1983

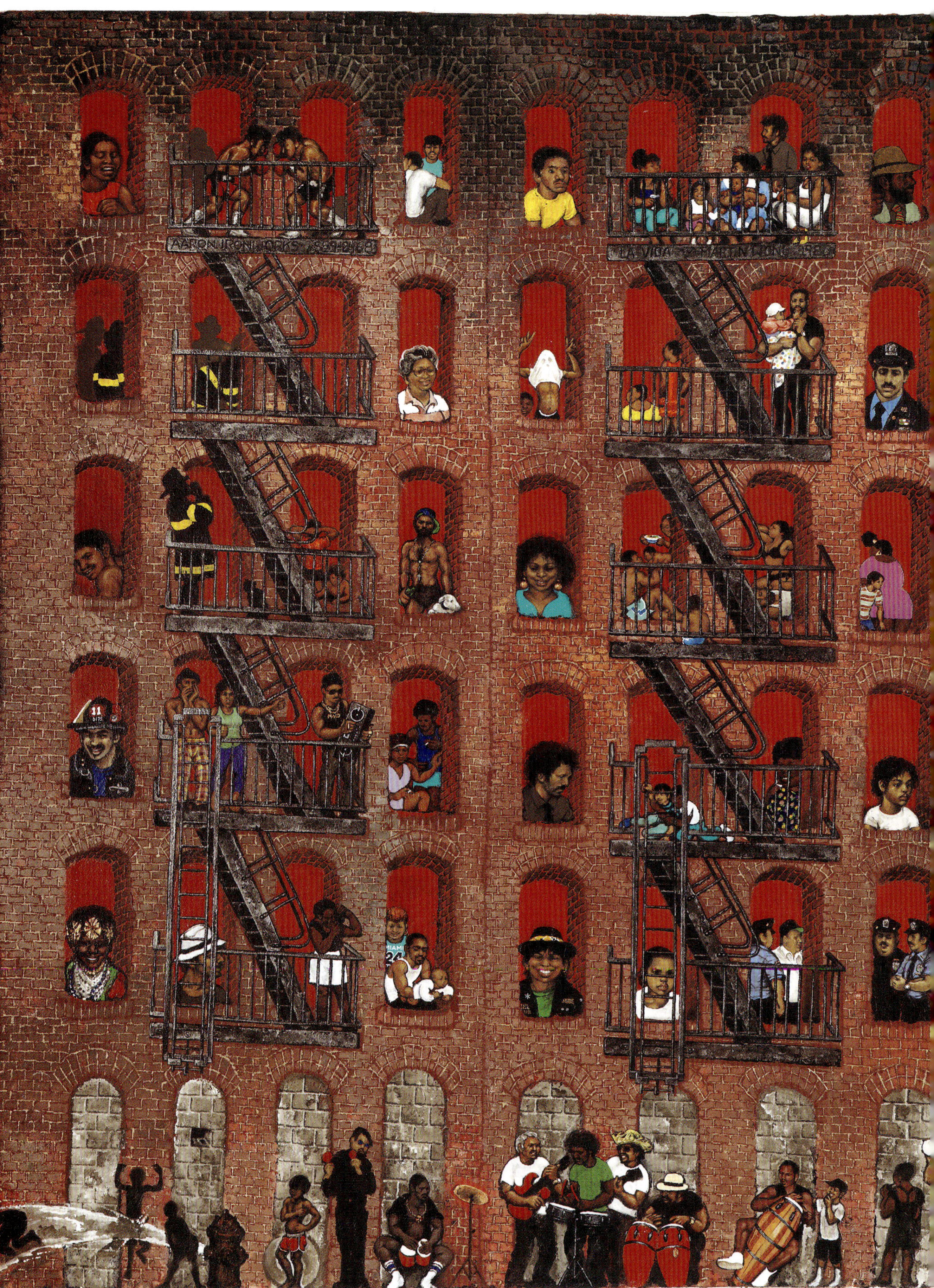

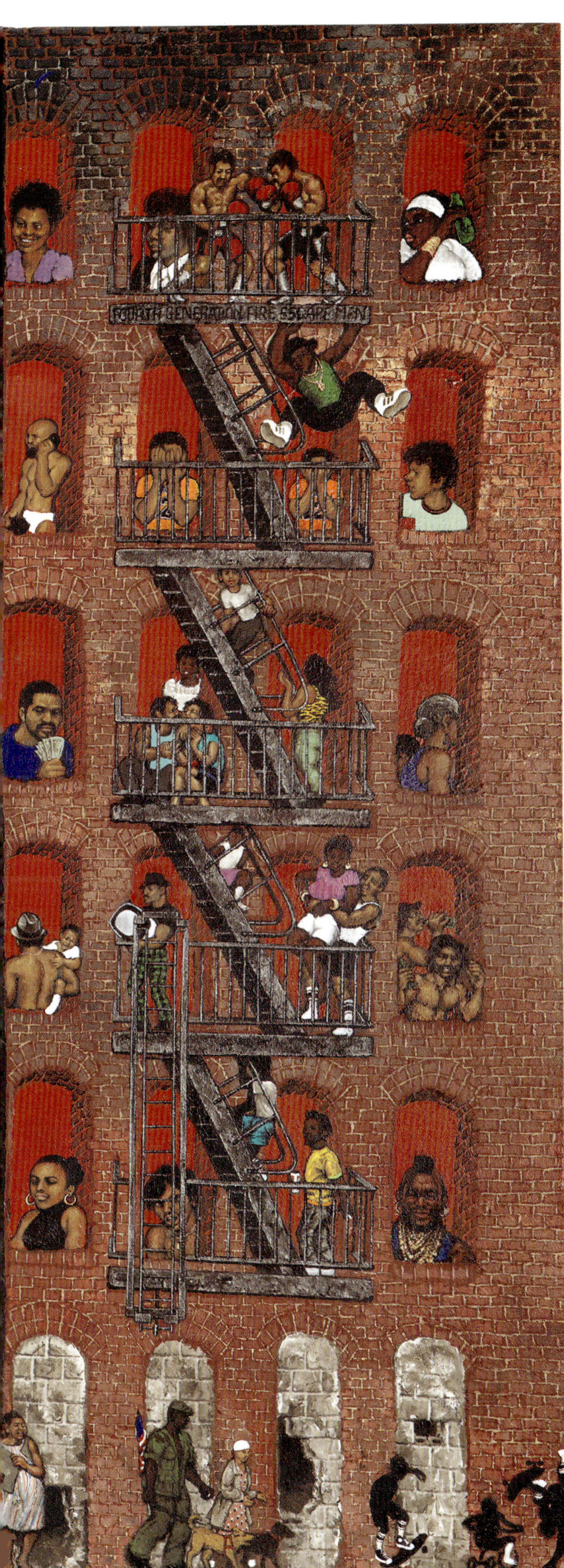

Martin Wong
La Vida, 1988

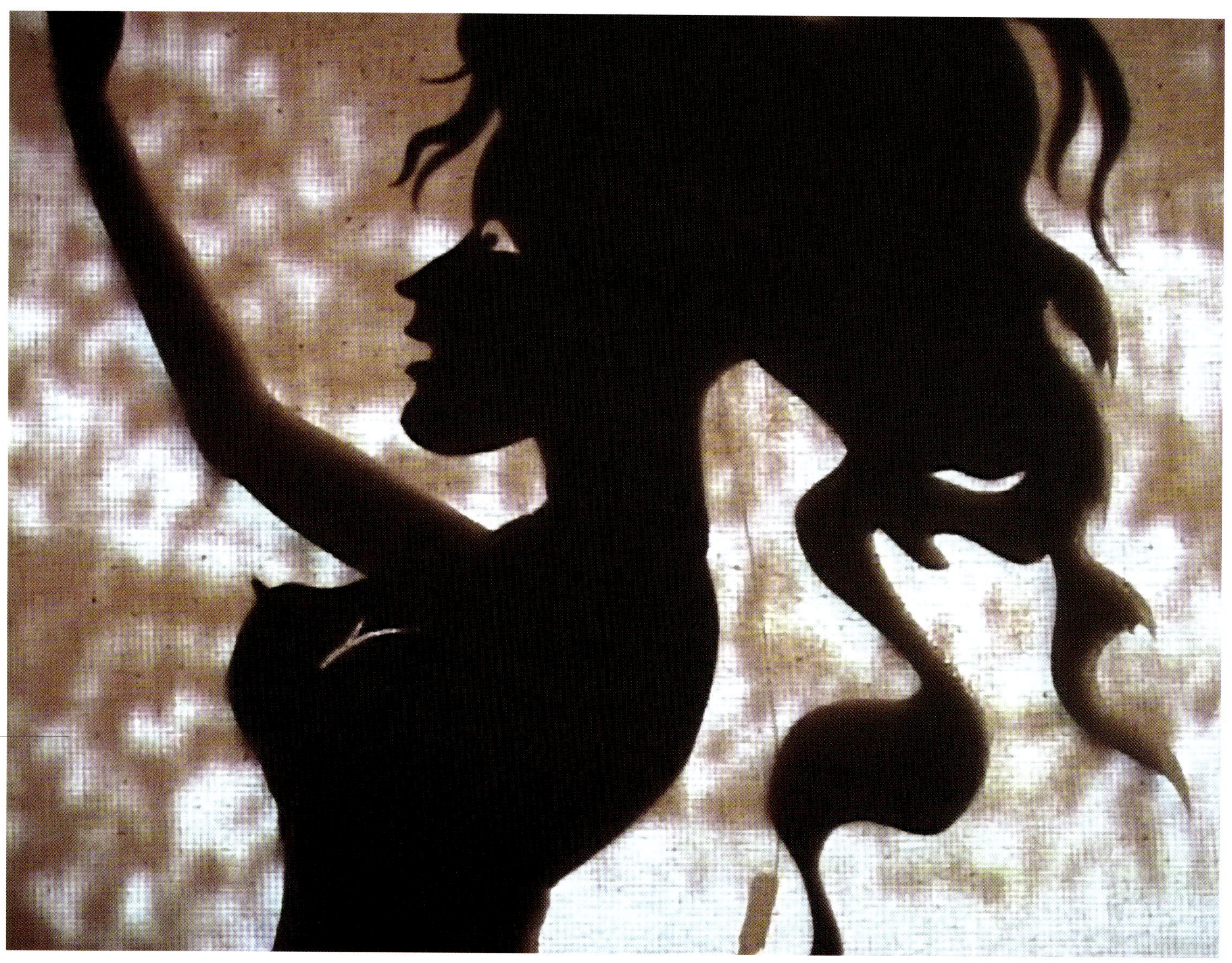

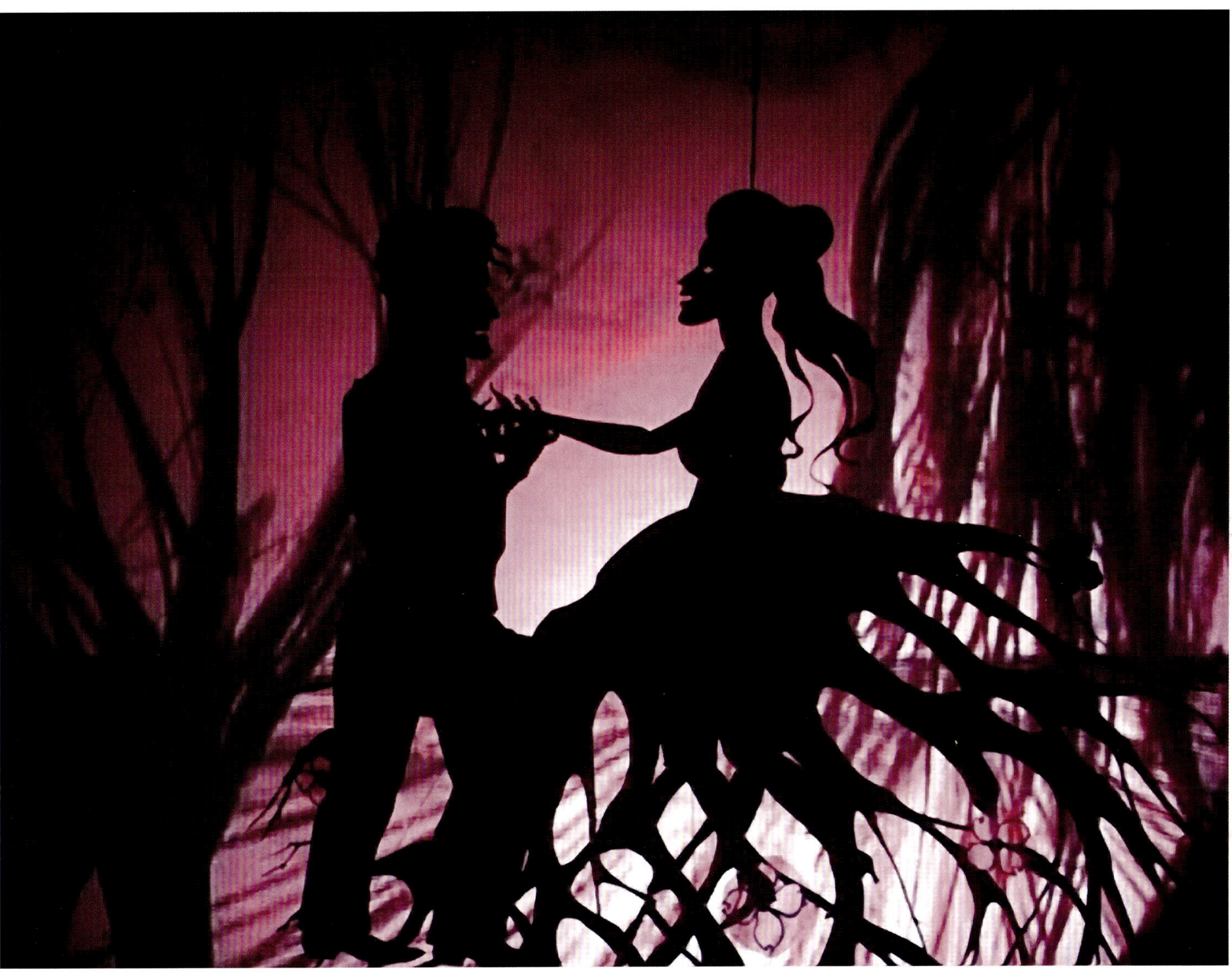

Kara Walker
Stills from *Fall Frum Grace: Miss Pipi's Blue Tale*, 2011

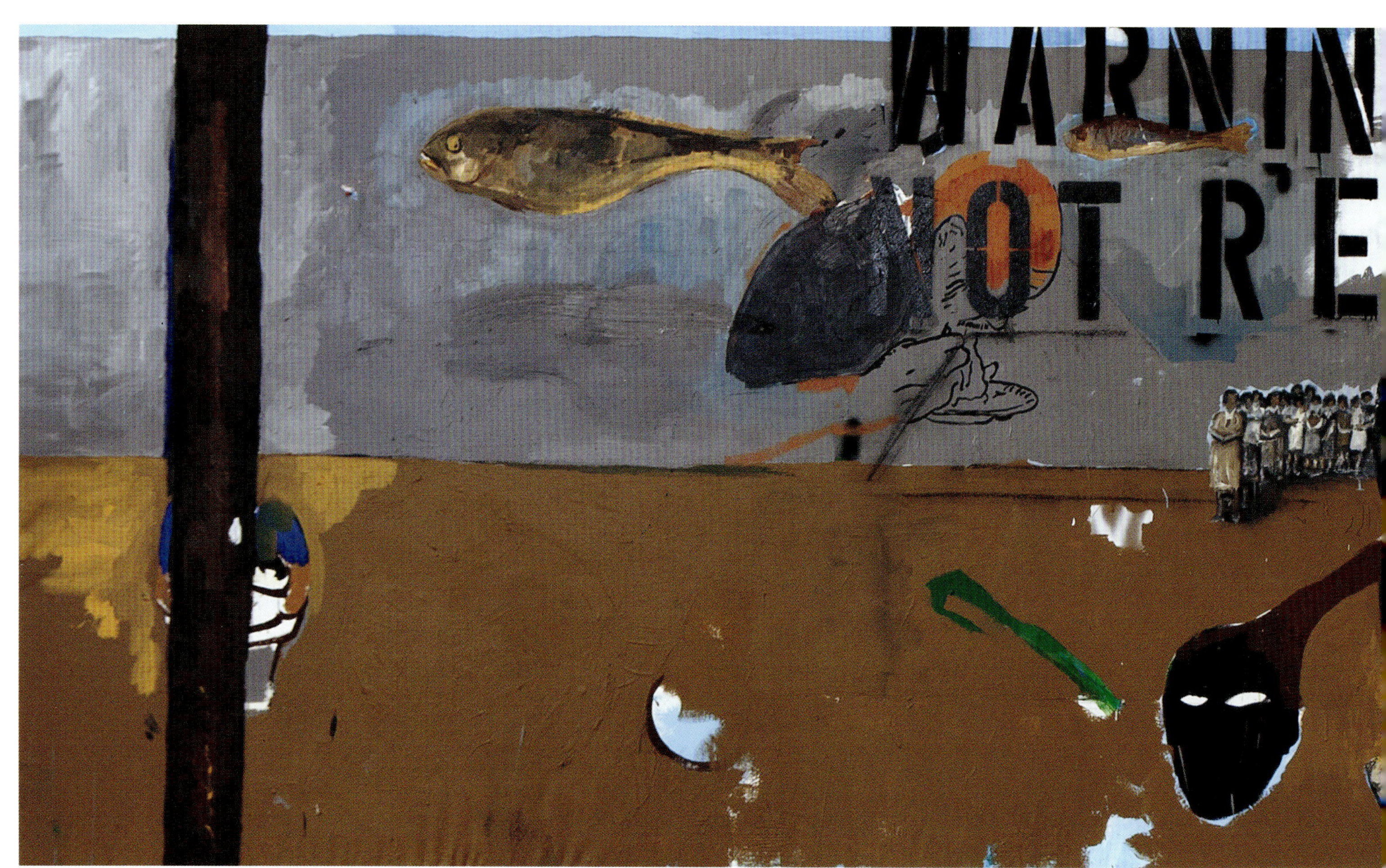
WARNIN
OT RE

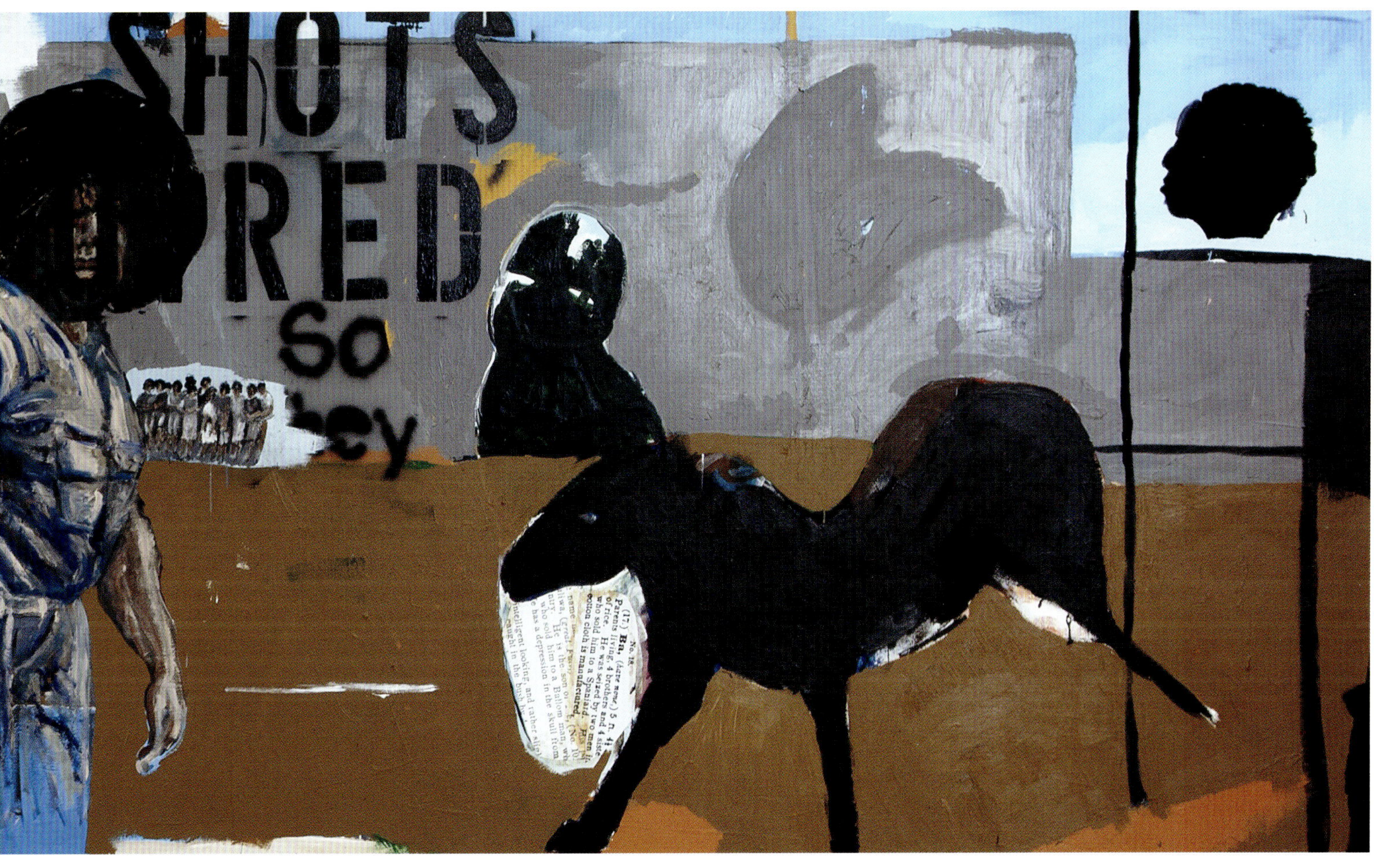

Henry Taylor
Warning Shots Not Required, 2011

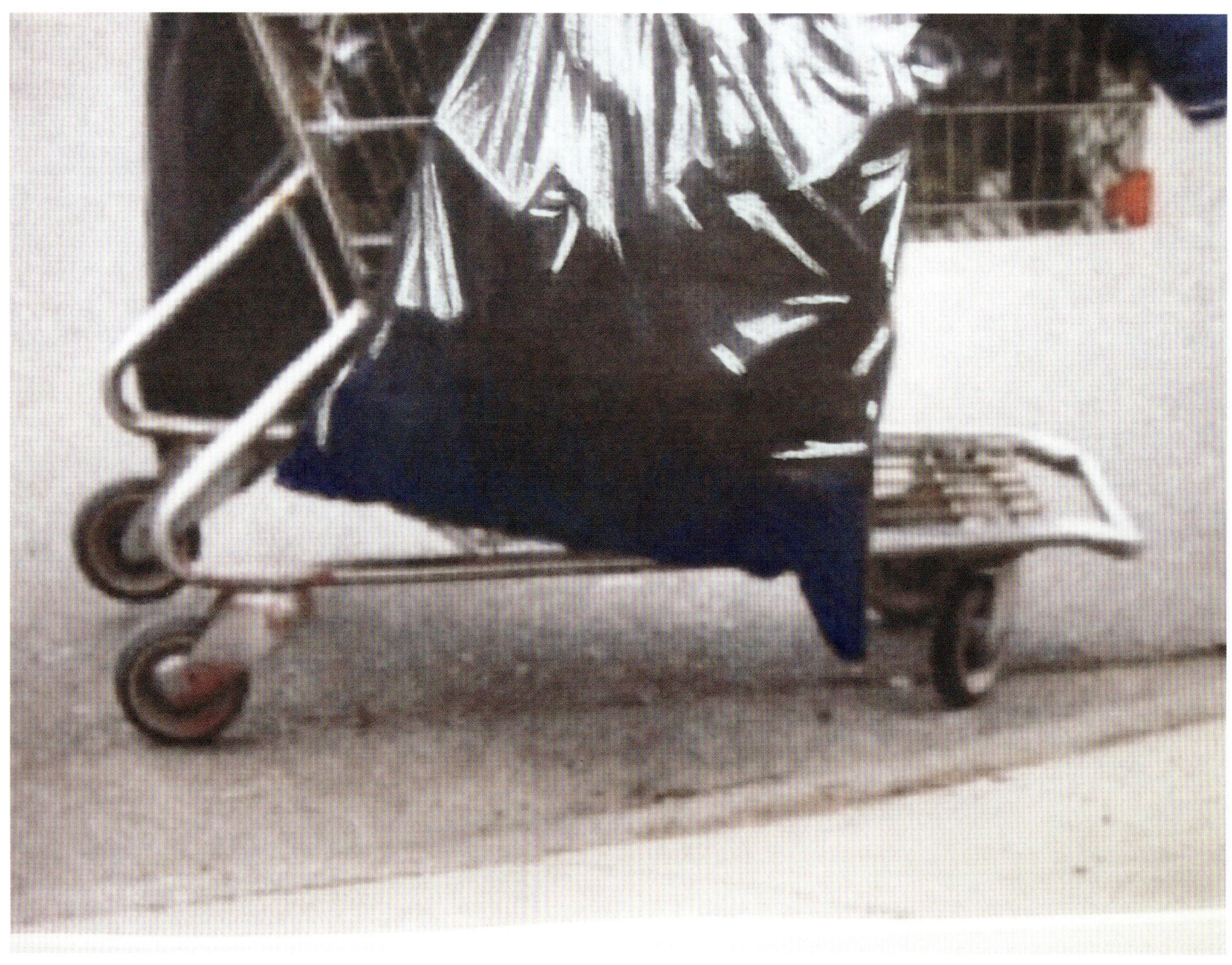

Kori Newkirk
Yall, 2012

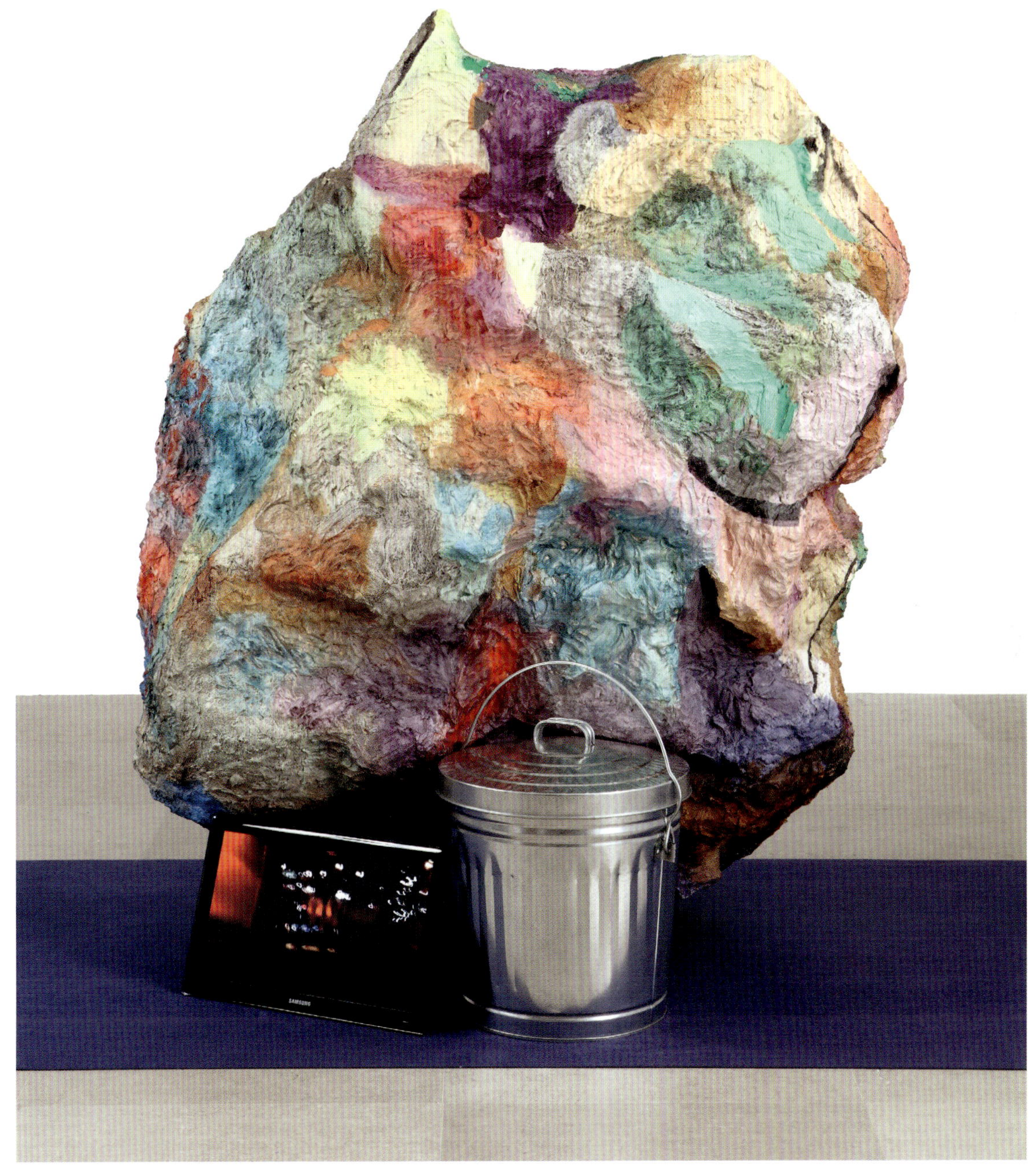

Rachel Harrison
Hoarders, 2012

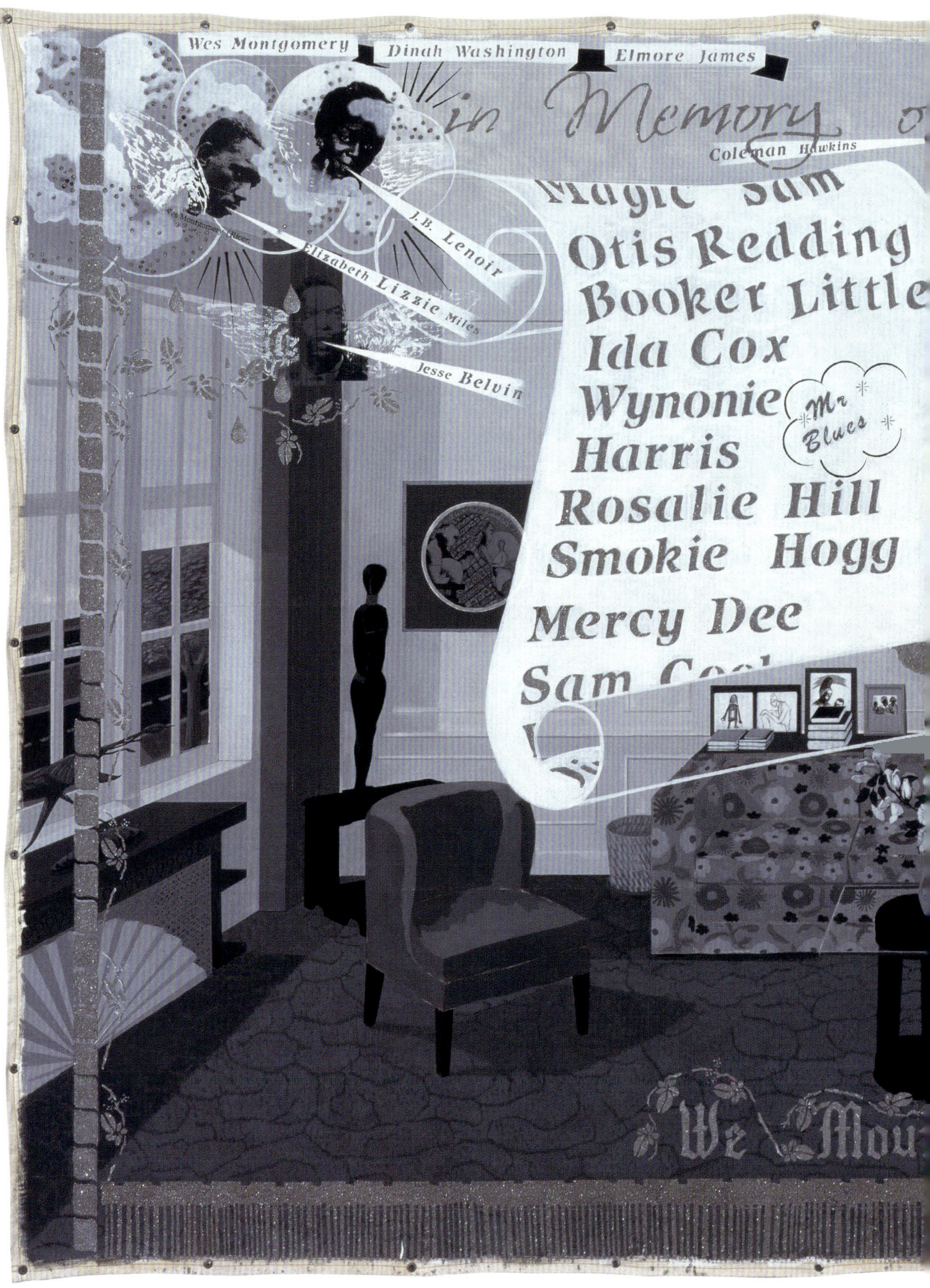

Wes Montgomery
Dinah Washington
Elmore James
in Memory of
Coleman Hawkins
Magic Sam
Otis Redding
Booker Little
Ida Cox
Wynonie
Mr. Blues
Harris
Rosalie Hill
Smokie Hogg
Mercy Dee
Sam Cooke
J.B. Lenoir
Wes Montgomery Nixon
Elizabeth Lizzie Miles
Jesse Belvin
We Mou

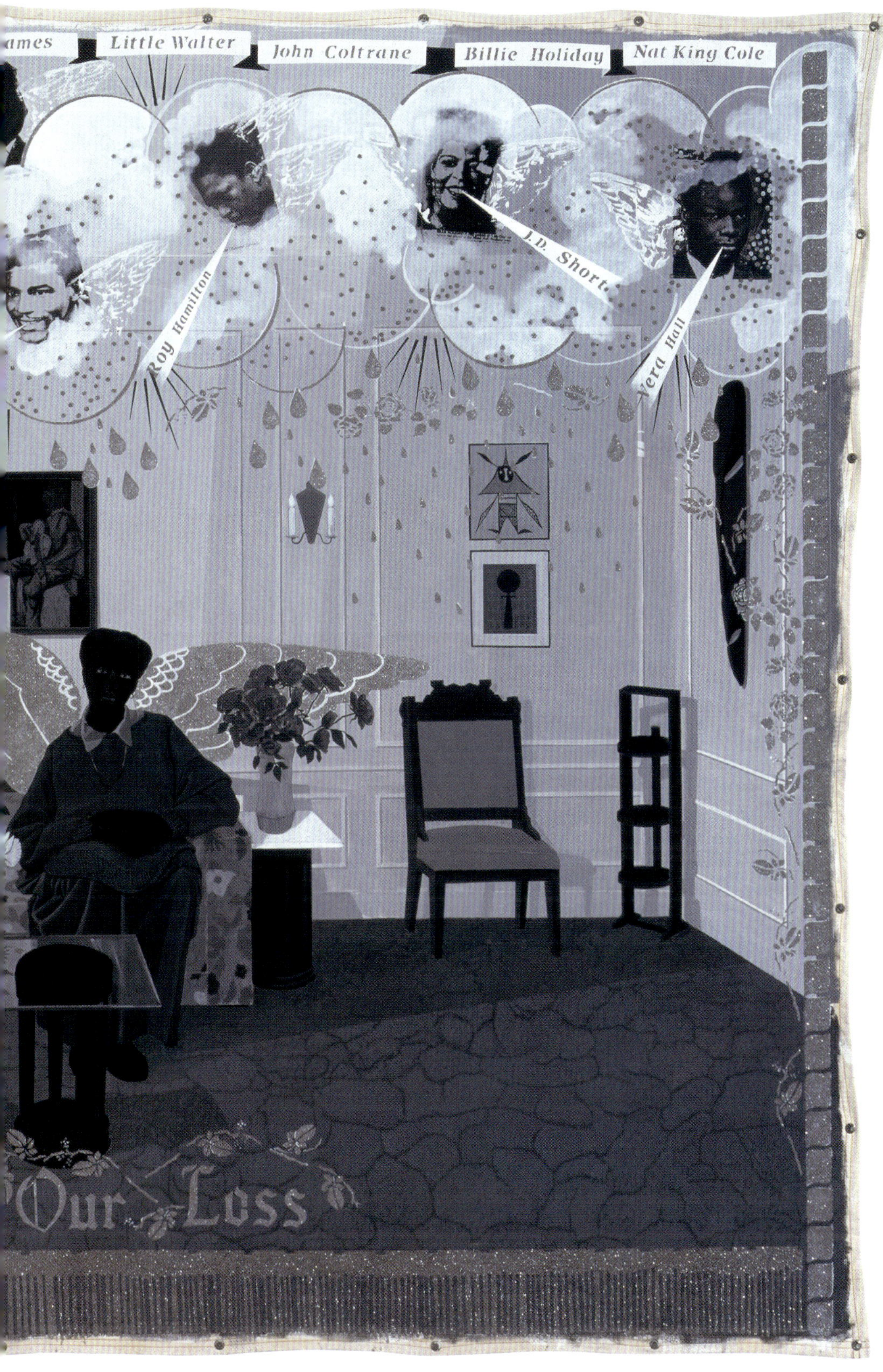

Kerry James Marshall
Souvenir IV, 1998

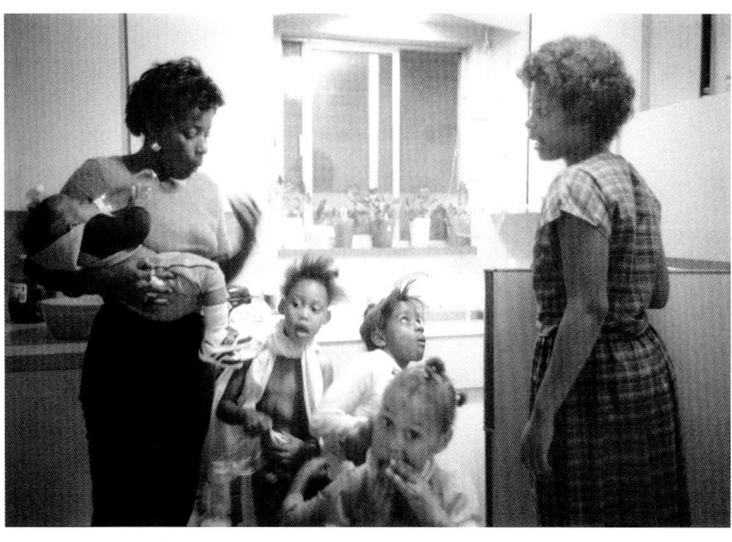

It Amazes me that even in the midst of a bunch of crazy wild kids, my sisters still manage to carry on a half-way decent conversation. I'm really impressed.

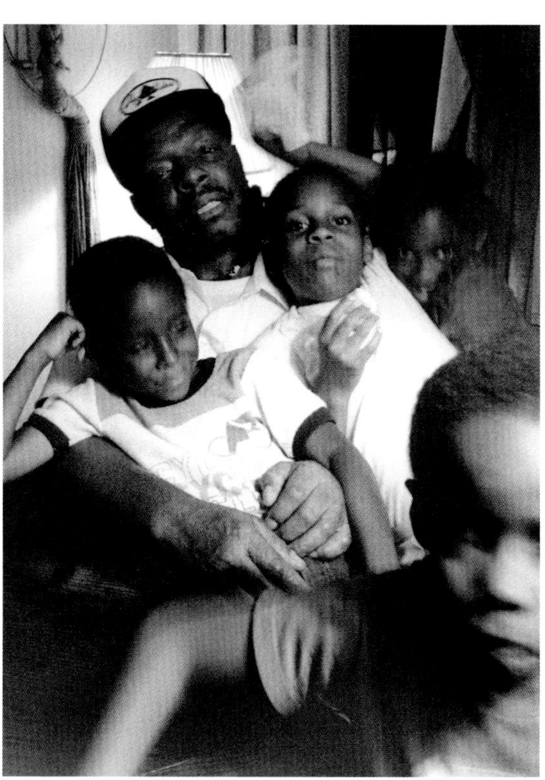

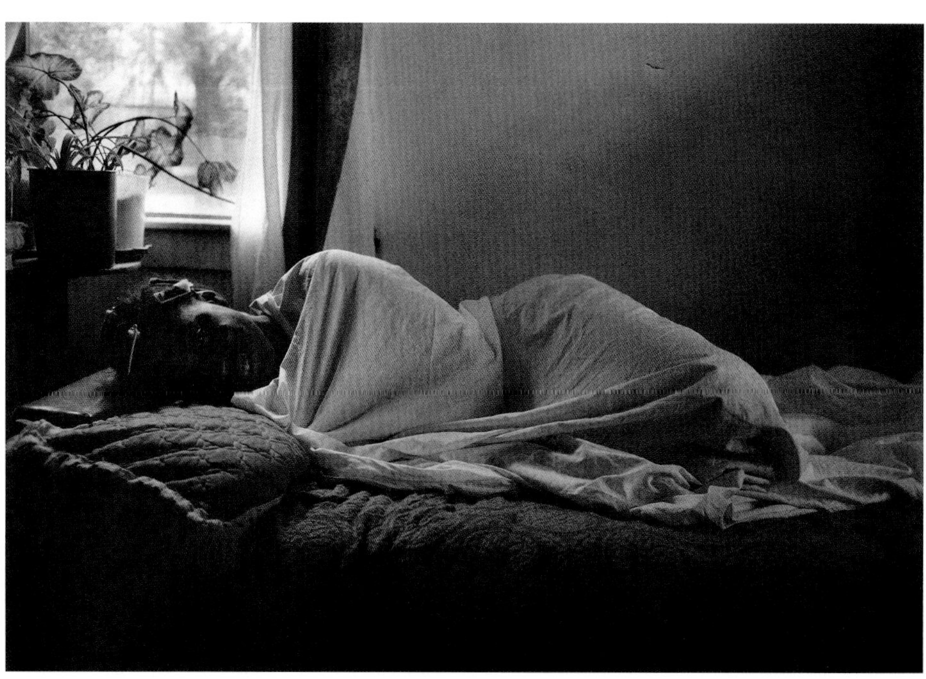

Alice is the oldest and as the oldest—when momma wasn't home—cooked our food, washed our clothes and us, cleaned the house, when necessary even whipped our behinds. She's a no jive kinda woman, taking no slack from nobody for no reason. And the thing I like about her is her profound commitment to family. Girl will do whatever to hold it together. Tough cookie.

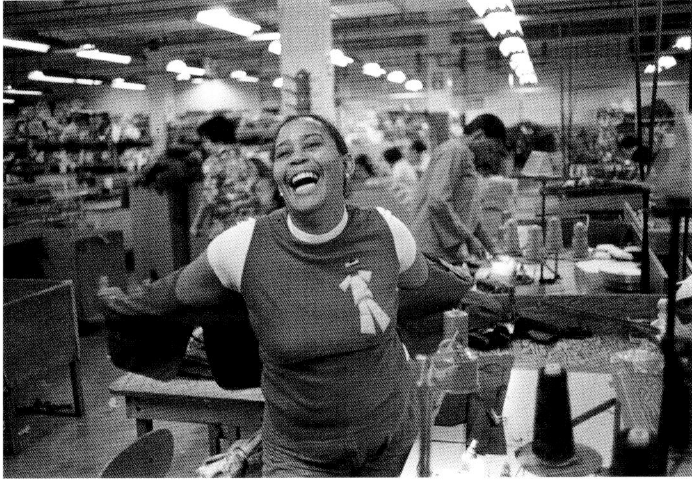

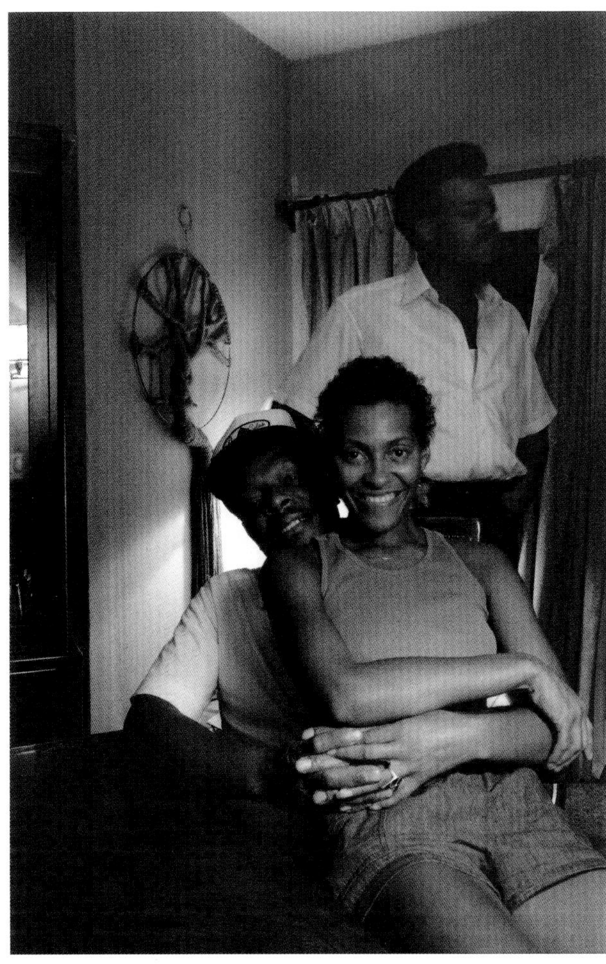

Daddy and I have a special thing going, and to this day I use his lap as my private domain.
He says, "See Carrie Mae, what I like about you is you can talk that talk to them white folks, and
you's smart too, just like your daddy."

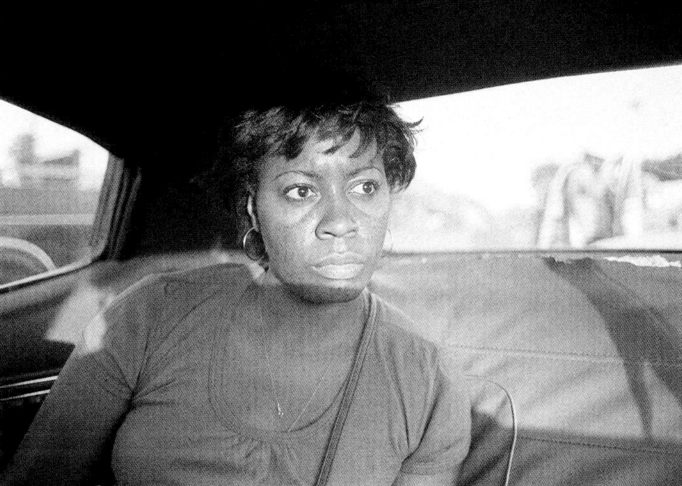

Carrie Mae Weems
Details from *Family Pictures and Stories*, 1982–84

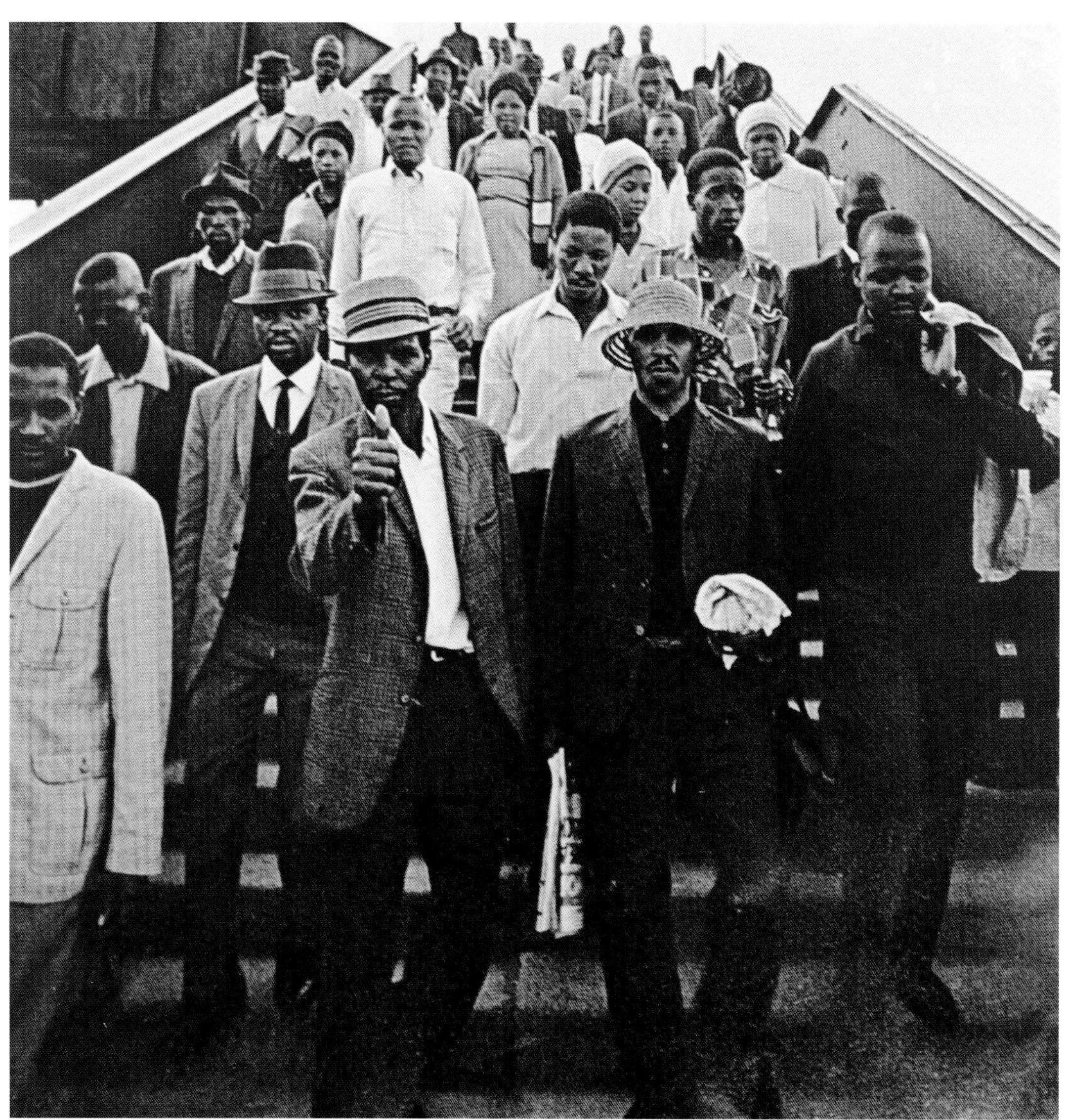

Adrian Piper
Detail from *Aspects of the Liberal Dilemma*, 1978

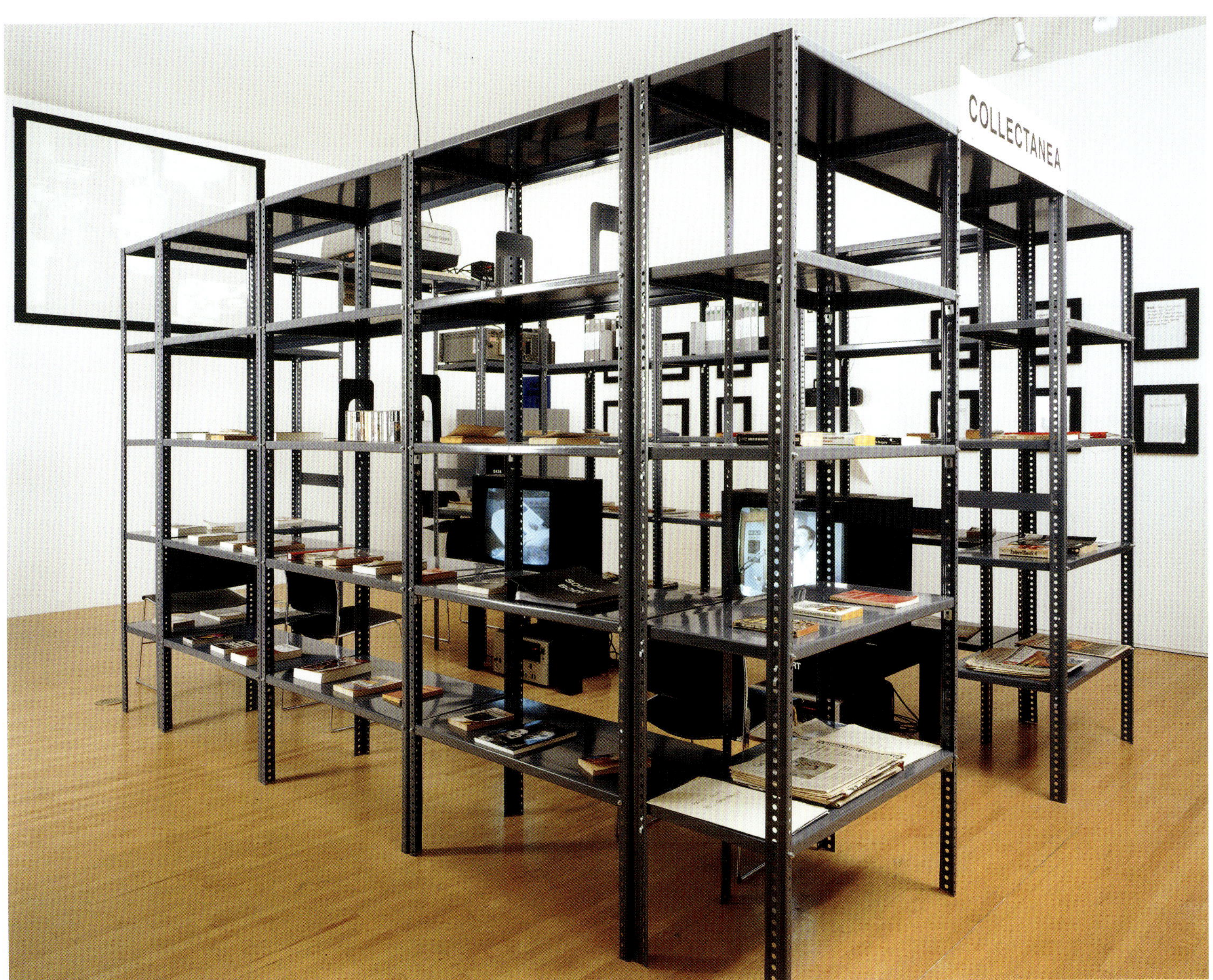

Renée Green
Import/Export Funk Office, 1992–93

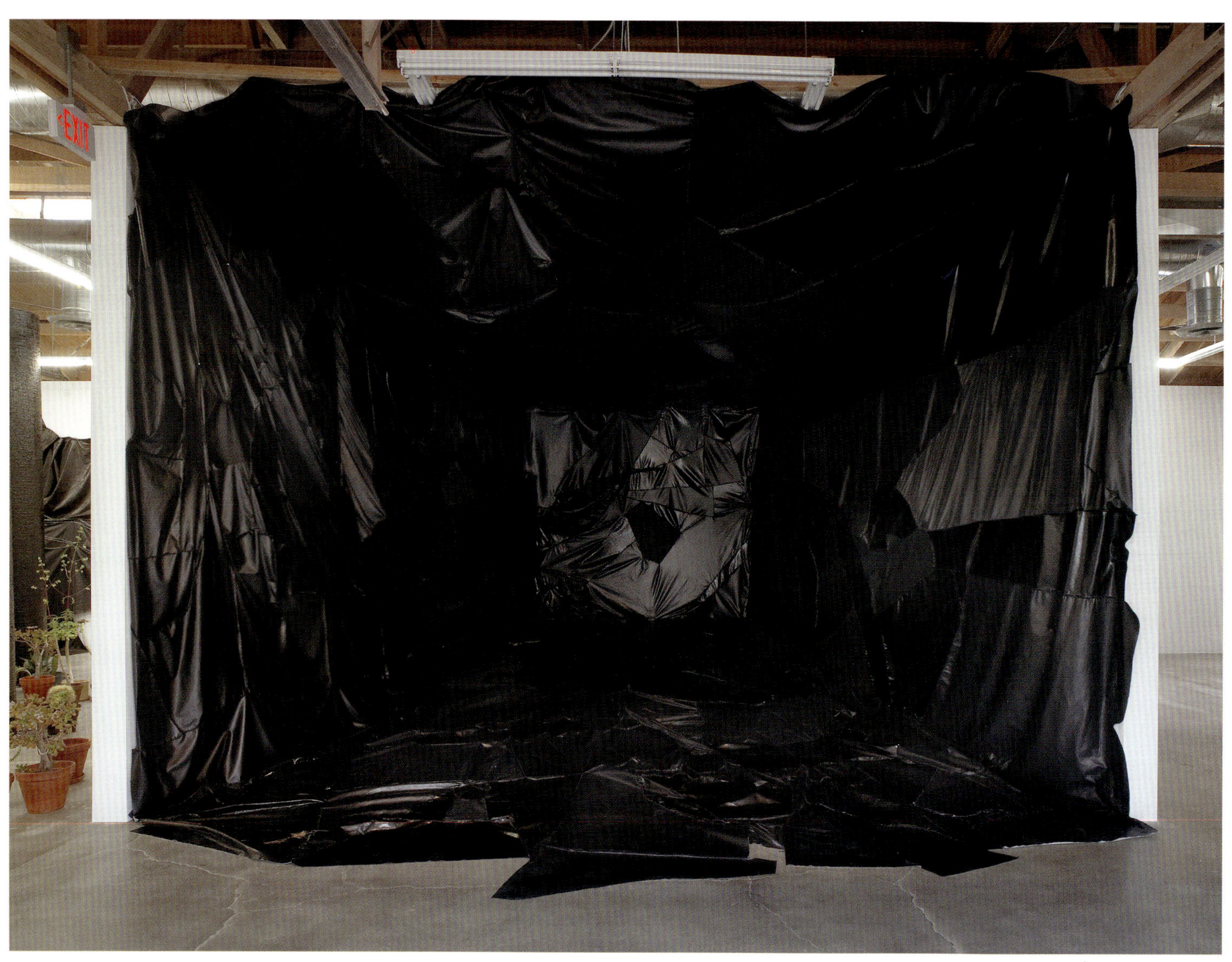

Rodney McMillian
Untitled, 2010
Vinyl and thread
Dimensions variable
Courtesy of the artist

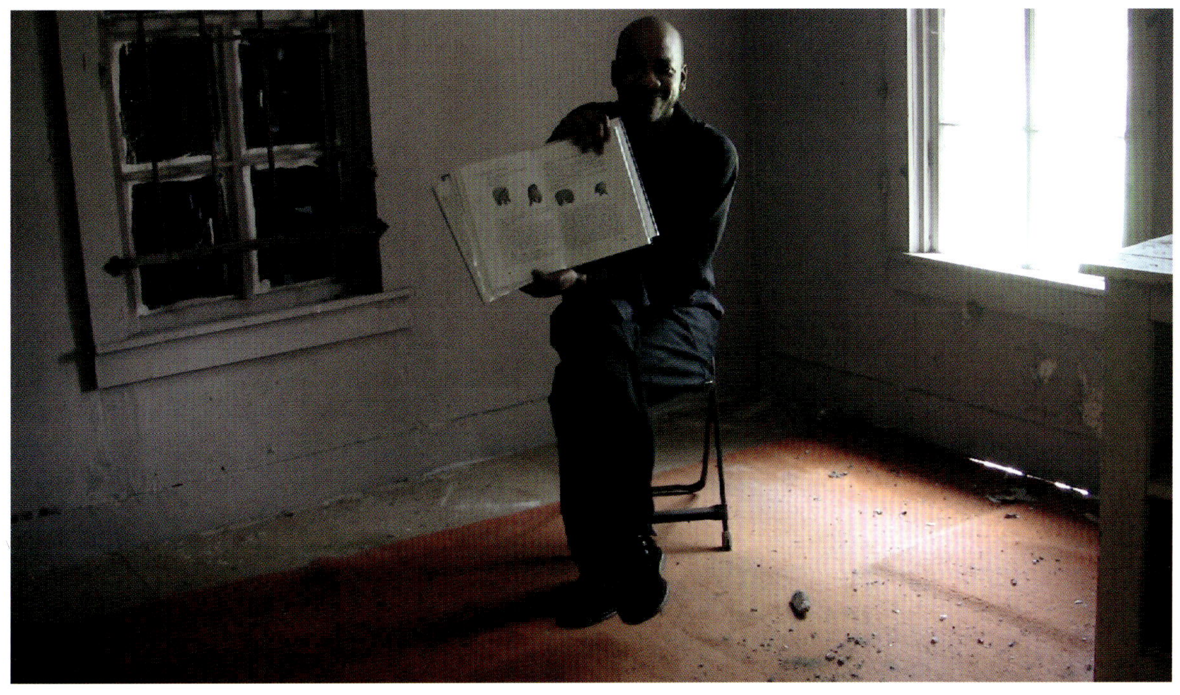

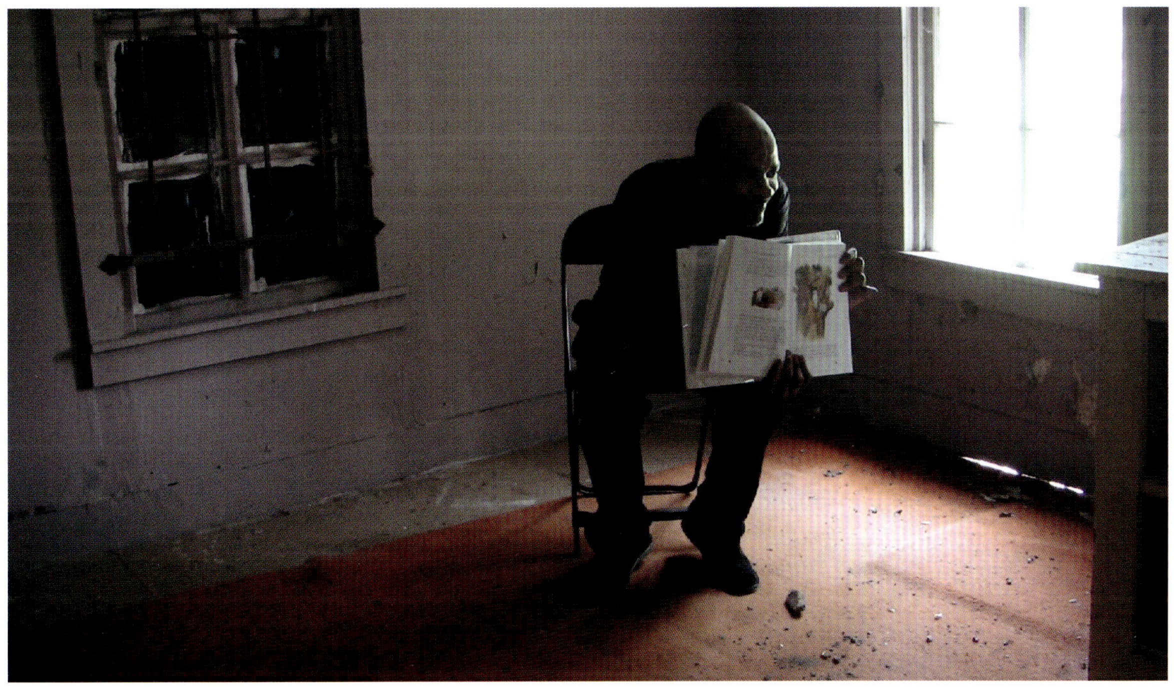

Rodney McMillian
Stills from *From Asterisks in Dockery*, 2012

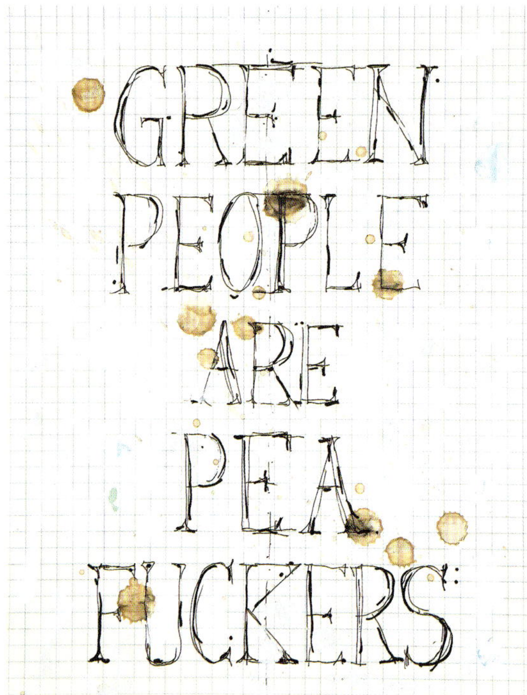

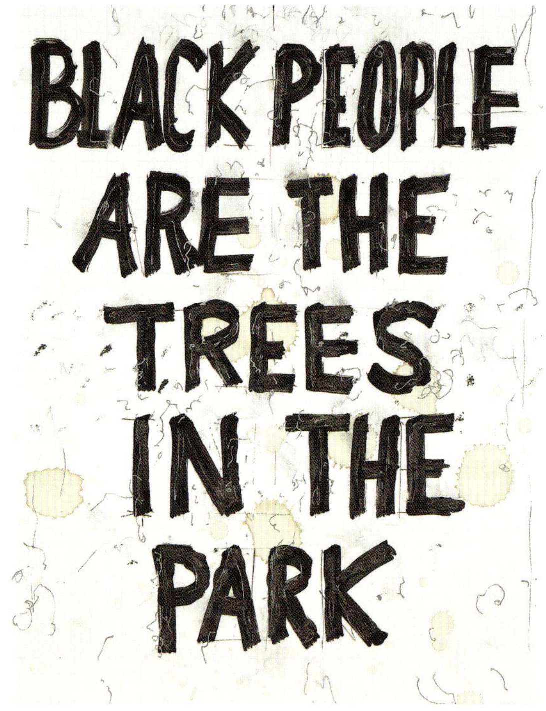

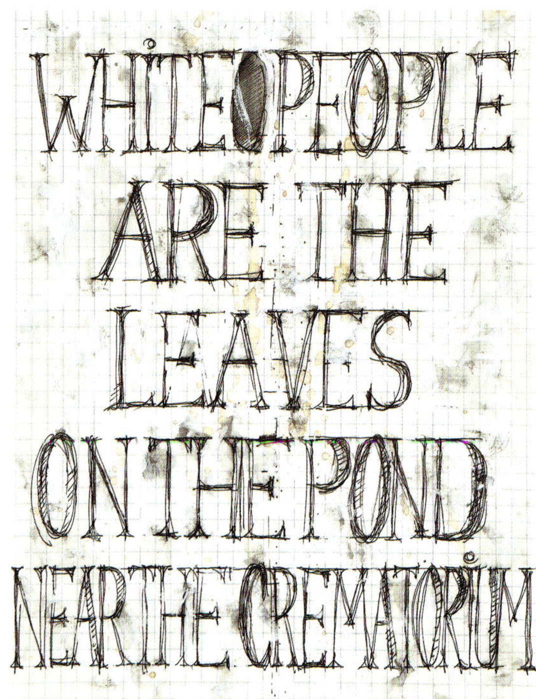

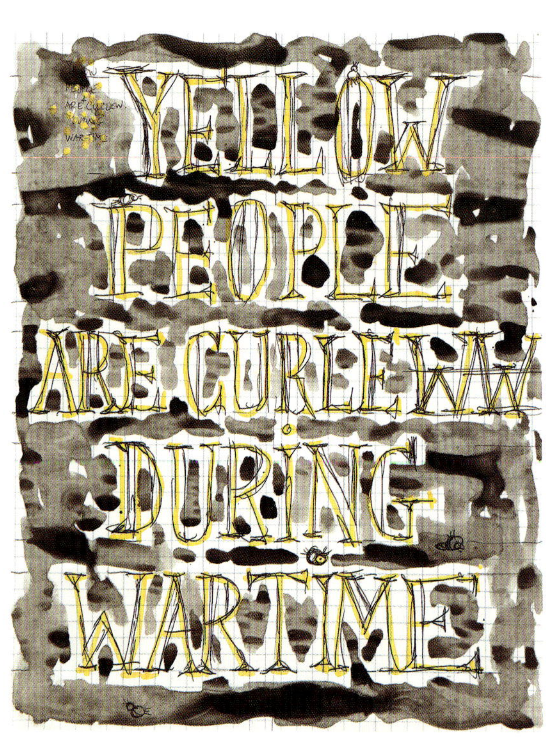

William Pope.L
Details from *Skin Set Drawings*, 2001–5

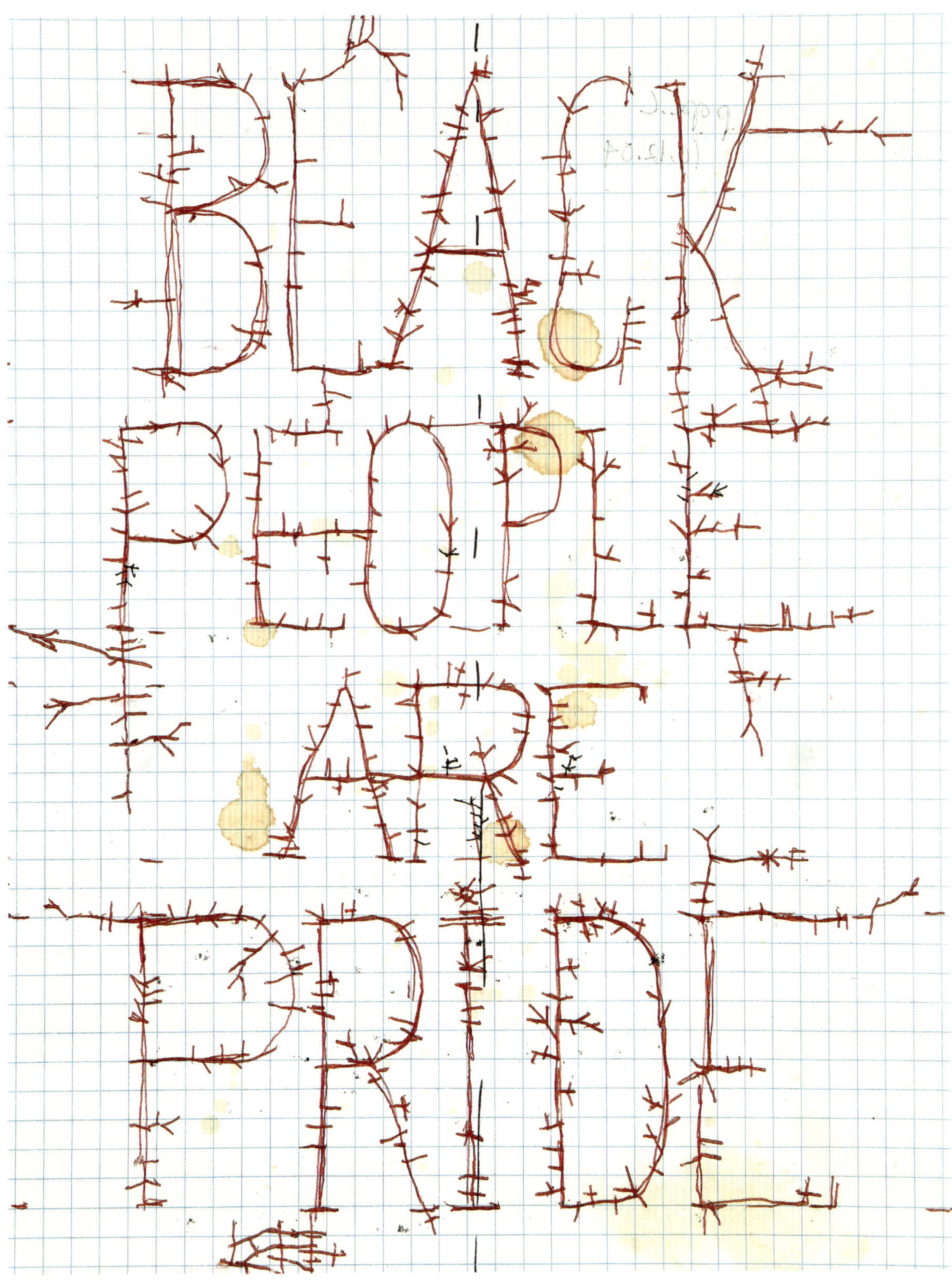
BLACK
PEOPLE
ARE
PRIDE

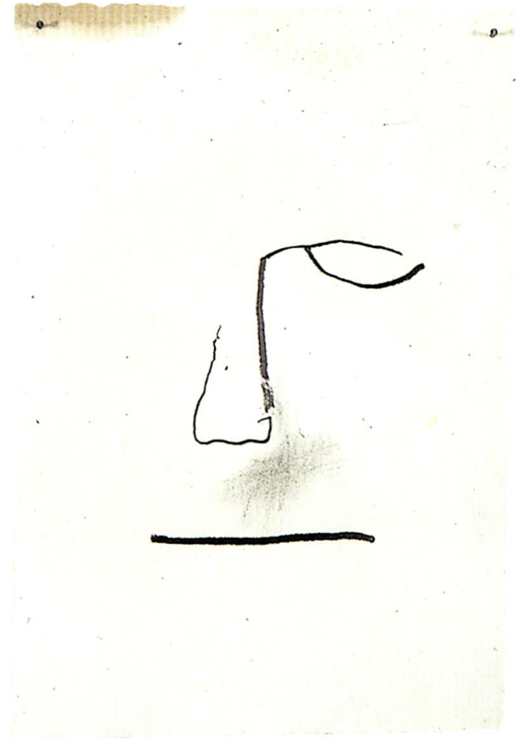

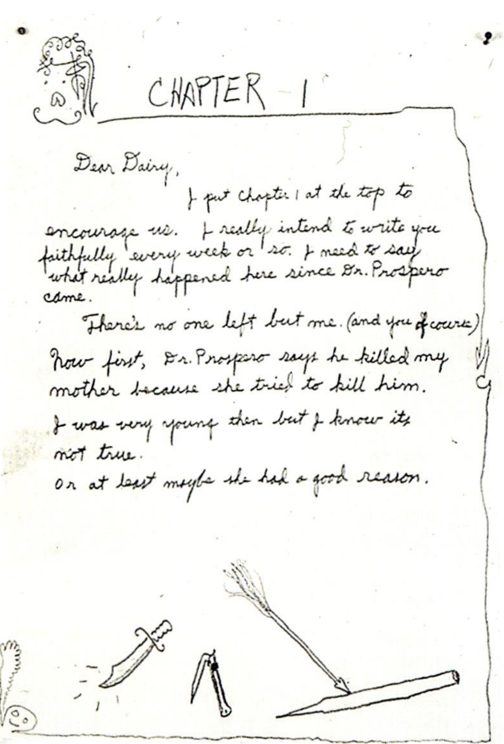

Jimmie Durham
Details from *Caliban Codex*, 1992

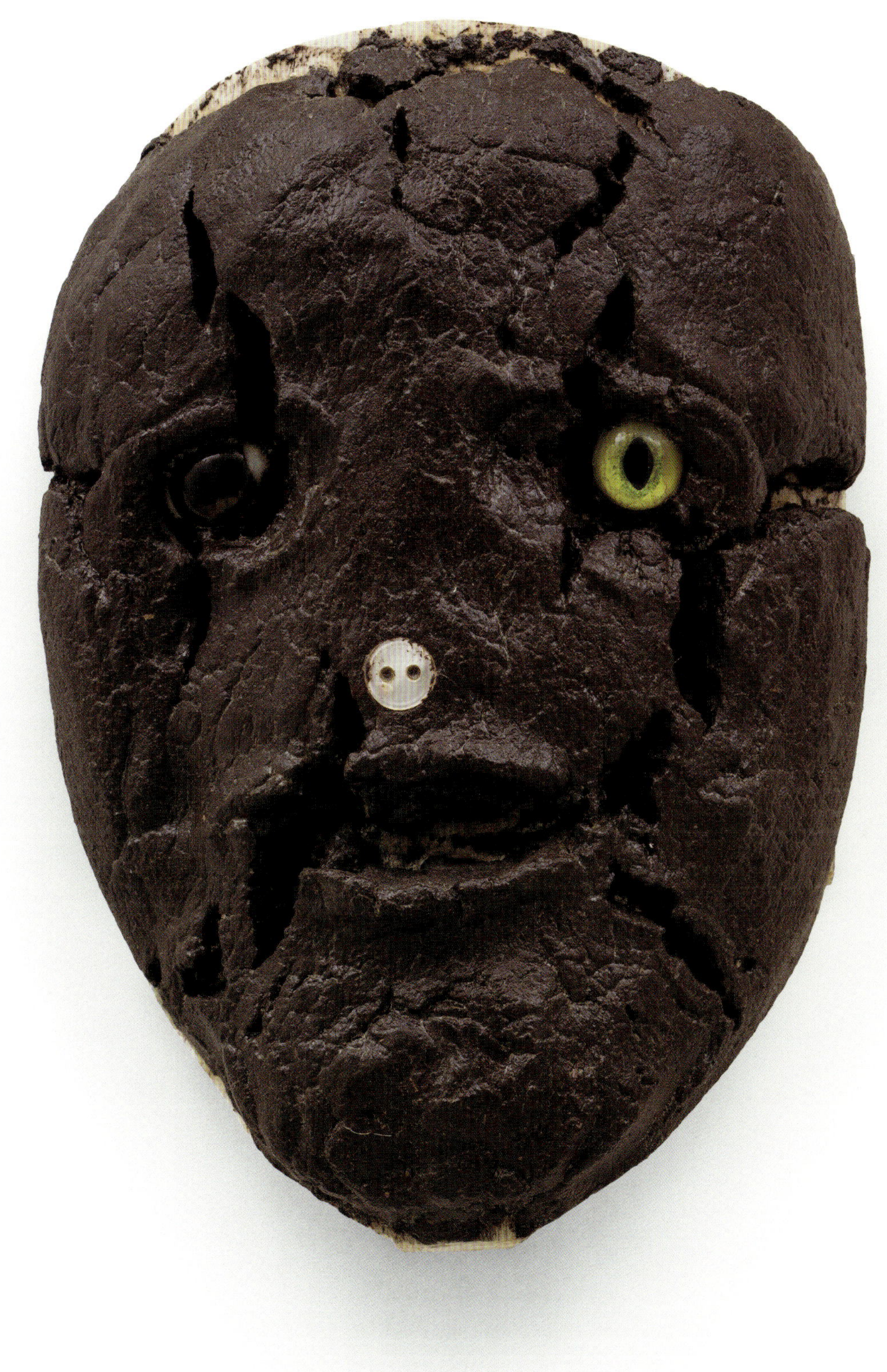

Jimmie Durham
Untitled (Caliban Mask), 1992

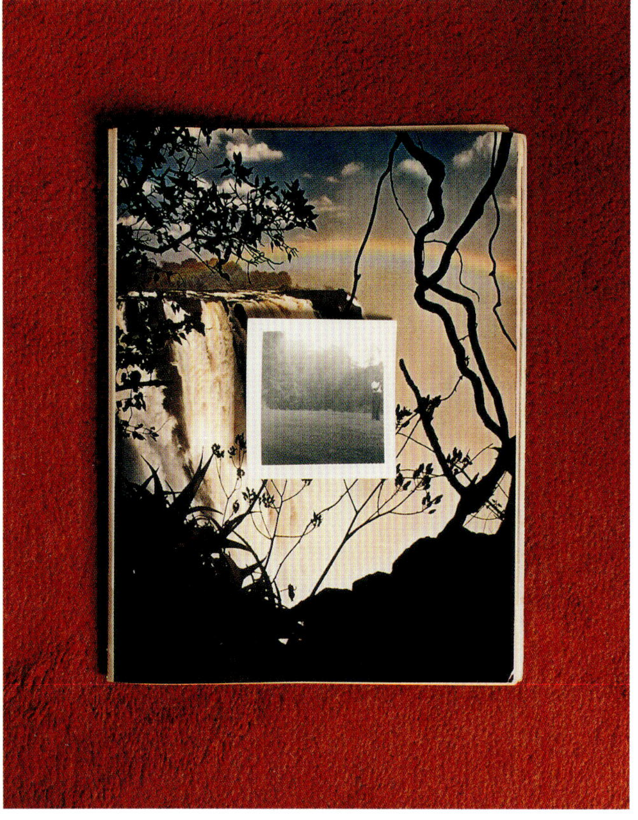

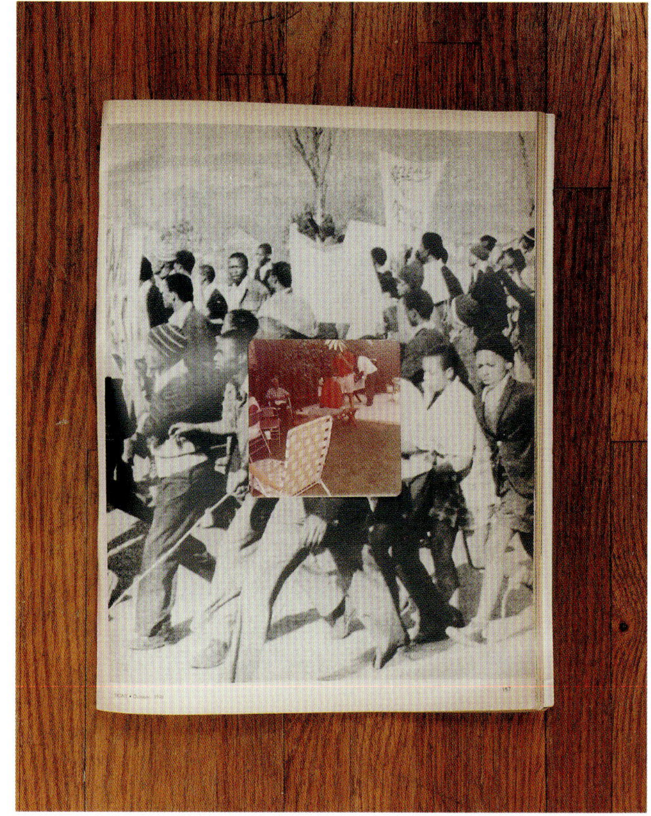

Leslie Hewitt
Riffs on Real Time (4 of 10), 2006–9

Riffs on Real Time (7 of 10), 2006–9

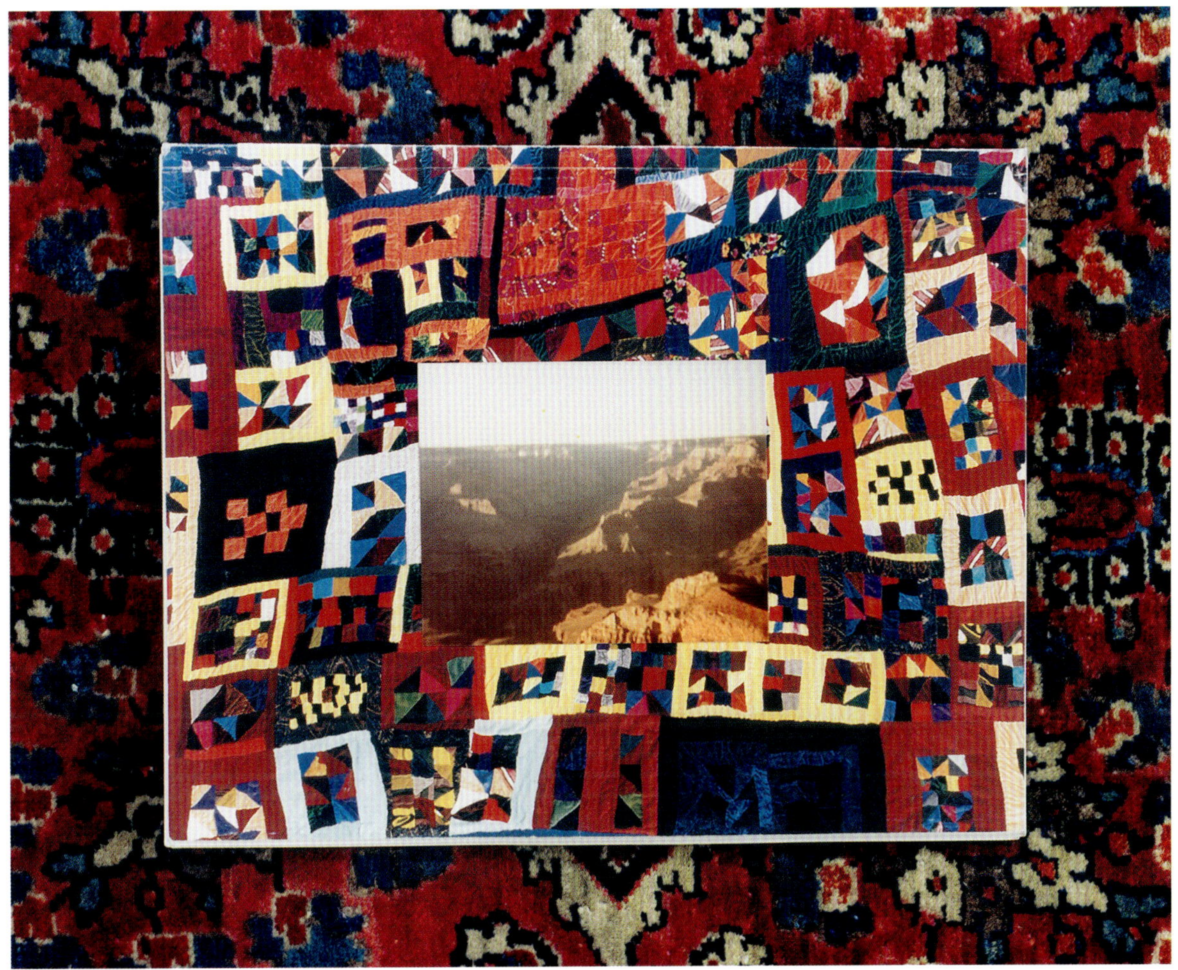

Leslie Hewitt
Riffs on Real Time (5 of 10), 2006–9

Muse & Drudge

Harryette Mullen

---

go ahead and sing the blues
then ask for forgiveness
you can't do everything
and still be saved

update old records
tune around the verses
fast time and swing out
head set in a groove

felt some good sounds
but didn't have the time
sing it in my voice
put words in like I want them

noise in the market
my mustang done slowed down
tore up bad now
put a ruination on it

bring money bring love
lucky floorwash seven
powers of Africa la mano
ponderosa ayudame numerous sueños

restore lost nature
with hoodoo paraphernalia
get cured in Cuban by a charming
shaman in an urban turban

forgotten formula cures
endemic mnemonic plague
statisticians were sure
the figures were vague

sister mystery listens
helps souls in misery
get to the square root
of evil and render it moot

wine's wicked wine's divine
pickled drunk down to the rind
depression ham ain't got no bone
watermelons rampant emblazoned

island named Dawta
Gullah backwater
she swim she fish
here it be fresh

cassava yucca taro dasheen
spicy yam okra vinegary greens
guava salt cod catfish ackee
fatmeat's greasy that's too easy

not to be outdone she put
the big pot in the little pot
when you get food this good
you know the cook stuck her foot in it

they pass their good air
mixed with fresh air
complex ions somewhere
frimpted frone she's stand alone

female of the specifically
human woman not called
by dog or dug by some tool—no fool who
takes stray pets or rakes implements for compliments

what I do with my hats
they make their own parade
of float and glitter like the birds
adorn the open umbrella

my dreams could take
advantage of me and no
one would tell me because
they don't know where to reach me

mothers have spawned
what warriors now own
cruel emblems and secrets
divulged only to the adept

signs in the heavens
graphemes leave the trees
turning over fresh pages
of notation: a choreography for bees

cooter got her back scratched
with spirit scribble
sent down under water
with some letters for the ancestors

the folks shuffle off
this mortal coffle and
bamboula back to
the motherland

why these blues come from us
threadbare material soils
the original colored
pregnant with heavenly spirit

stop running from the gift
slow down to catch up with it
knots mend the string quilt
of kente stripped when kin split

white covers of black material
dense fabric that obeys its own logic
shadows pieced together tears and all
unfurling sheets of bluish music

burning cloth in a public place
a crime against the state
raised the cost of free expression
smoke rose to offer a blessing

with all that rope they gave us
we pulled a mule out of the mud
dragging backwoods along
in our strong blackward progress

she just laughs
at weak-kneed scarecrow
as rainbow crow flies
over those ornery cornrows

everlasting arms
too short for boxers
leaning meaning
signifying say what

Ethiopian breakdown
underbelly tussle
lose the facts just keep the hustle
leave your fine-tooth comb at home

if your complexion is a mess
our elixir spells skin success
you'll have appeal bewitch be adored
hechizando con crema dermoblanqueadora

what we sell is enlightenment
nothing less than beauty itself
since when can be seen in the dark
what shines hidden in dirt

double dutch darky
take kisses back to Africa
they dipped you in a vat
at the wacky chocolate factory

color we've got in spades
melanin gives perpetual shade
though rhythm's no answer to cancer
pancakes pale and butter can get rancid

the essence lady
wears her irregular uniform
a pinstripe kente
syncopation suit

she dreads her hair
sprung from lock down
under steel teeth press gang
galleys upstart crow's nest

eyes lashed half open
look of lust bitten
lips licked the dusky
wicked tongued huzzy

am I your type
that latest lurid blurb
was all she wrote her
highbrow pencil broke

self-made woman gets
the hang—it's a stretch
she's overextended weaving
many spindly strands on her hair loom

walking through the alley
all night alone
stalked by a shadow
throw the black cat a bone

step off bottom woman
when the joint gets jinky
come blazing the moment
the hens get hincty

raw souls get ready
people rock steady
the brown gals in this town
know how to roll the woodpile down

dry bones in the valley
turn over with wonder
was it to die for our piece
of buy 'n' buy pie chart

hot water cornbread
fresh water trout
God's plenty the preacher shouts
while the congregation's eating out

women of honey harmonies offer
alfalfa wild flower buckwheat and clover
to feed Oshun who has sweet teeth
and is pleased to accept their gift

these mounts that heaven touched
saints sleep in their beds
distress is hushed by dream when
they allow the bird to lift their heads

ain't your fancy
handsome gal
feets too big
my hair don't twirl

from hunger call
on the telephone
asking my oven for
some warm jellyroll

if I can't have love
I'll take sunshine
if I'm too plain for champagne
I'll go float on red wine

what you can do
is what women do
I know you know
what I mean, don't you

Excerpted and reprinted from Harryette Mullen, *Muse & Drudge* (Philadelphia: Singing Horse Press, 1995), 27–38.

My Blues Love Affair

Wanda Coleman

Ol' blues gonna get me
Ol' blues gonna get me high

I grew up in the Southern California of the late 1940s through '50s listening primarily to country-and-western, gospel, and popular music. My mother's relationship to my father, ethnically speaking, was ambivalent—though they both identified as colored. She did not seem to understand or care for the "race music" of the day made by Black folk, or the attendant fashions. I recall one incident where Father brought home a gift for himself, new duds in a large pretty department-store box. He folded back the tissues and lifted out a zoot suit. He even had the wide-brimmed hat and a pair of those exaggerated nines, or kicks (shoes). Mother told him in choice icy terms that she wouldn't be seen with him on the streets "in that silly getup." He closed the box and took the threads back to the store. Her ears were as critical as her eyes when it came to his record collection.

Pop sounds around our household were as diverse as Hoagy Carmichael (*Stardust*), Fats Domino (*Honey Chile*), Peggy Lee (*Mañana*), and Liberace (*September Song*). Al Jarvis's *Make Believe Ballroom* (on KFWB) was one of Mother's radio favorites. Above all, my mother preferred music with a twang: Edd[y] Arnold, Johnny Cash, Patsy Cline, Tennessee Ernie Ford (on Cliffie Stone's *Hometown Jamboree*, featuring Molly Bee), George Jones, Tex Ritter, The Sons of the Pioneers, Conway Twitty, and Kitty Wells. Mother sang a beautiful soprano along with Patti Page on *Tennessee Waltz*, while *Jezebel* and the wild goose cried regularly through our afternoons on the lips of Frankie Laine.

When we got television in 1951, *Cavalcade of Bands*, *Perry Como*, *Name That Tune*, *It's Polka Time*, *The Frank Sinatra Show*, *The Kate Smith Evening Hour*, Arthur Murray's *Dance Party*, *Stop the Music*, Paul Whiteman's *Goodyear Review*, and *Your Hit Parade* were among the programs that brought the remnants of Tin Pan Alley (1890s to 1950s) and vaudeville (1870s to 1930s) into our living room—the variety shows too numerous to mention except for *The Grand Ole Opry*, *The Hoffman Hayride* (Spade Cooley), and *The Lawrence Welk Show*. Like much of the rest of the nation, no New Year's celebration was complete without Guy Lombardo and His Royal Canadians.

Together with art, literature, and dance, classical music was foremost in my at-home education, echoed in public-school musical appreciation classes where kids were taught to ritually worship the three Bs—Bach, Beethoven, and Brahms. (To them I added a fourth, Max Bruch.) In her efforts to transform me into the debutante I would never become, my mother spent her scrimpings on private piano, violin, and voice lessons. She prepared me for the world as she dreamed it rather than as it existed and would remain, for the working-class poor anyway: a world hostile to the notion of full and complete social parity for those trapped in (and at the bottom of) its African American subculture. In the post–WWII Southern California in which I was raised, there were no traditions, only the growth-industry consumerism that predicted we need only push a button to bring the future (free of racism?) into our homes. Underscoring (undermining?) my mother's Oklahoman colored-lady notions of high society were my father's pugilistic Arkansas pragmatism and love of a music that fascinated me in its aural contradictions. The music my father loved was simple yet complex. I instinctively recognized the difference between eight and twelve notes per bar. The lyrics of Dad's favorite songs seemed unusual, particularly Southern, and used expressions not always easily deciphered by my child's ear.

It did something to you.

Even when I appreciated the double entendres, my knowledge was minus the knowing. My sojourn into the sexual was still more than a decade away. I was also intrigued by the often gender-defying qualities of the voices of various singers beyond the phenomena of Little Willie John (*Fever*), Little Jimmy Scott (*All the Way*), and Ray Charles (particularly his androgynous rendition of *I Didn't Know What Time It Was*). While I could usually tell the difference between Black and White voices, I could not readily distinguish between the male or female voice of Negro singers. This ambiguity seemed, to my ears, deliciously rich. There was something else, profound and magnificent, going on under the surface of language in its marriage to sound. And often the language of the lyric was equally ambivalent words like "Baby" and "Honey" referring to either a male or female adult. A repressed dialogue!? I puzzled over this phenomenon throughout my childhood, spurred by the fact that my mother would not let my father's music into the house except one day of the year.

Father would frequently skirt Mother's commandment by singing loudly in the bathroom while he shaved or showered. I'm beset by the aromas of shaving cream and after-shave, along with images of him stropping his straight razor and mixing the suds with his shaving brush, whenever I hear *My Blue Heaven*, *St. Louis Blues*, or *Willow Weep for Me*. An admirer of Paul Robeson, he often sang solo at concerts on the then-glamorous stage of the auditorium at the Negro-owned Golden State Insurance Company. When egging his children out of recalcitrance, my father would warp a lyric of *Short'nin' Bread* or *Lazy Bones* … "sleepin' in da shade…." As the eldest, I was often privy to contentious moments between my parents while my siblings slept. On one such occasion I watched tearfully as Mother wielded a butcher's knife, ended when my father disarmed her in a manly fashion, without a single blow struck. I'll never forget the ways father would goad or tease her with blues lyrics. His favorite for this purpose was *The Blues in the Night*.

What, I wondered, did this "nigger music" *contain* that was so dangerous that Mother did not want it in our home?

> *When ol' man blues taps my shoulder*
> *I gets up to dance (don't matter what shoes I wear).*

When Father finally got the opportunity to play his music, we were treated to Johnny Ace, Hank Ballard, T-Bone Walker, and the like. Among his favorite songs, repeatedly played, were *Baby Don't You Tear My Clothes*, *The Hucklebuck*, *I Believe I'll Dust My Broom*, *Rag Mop*, and *T-99*. Curiously, that solitary day on which Mother allowed him to play his music uncensored, parties excepted, was Christmas Day.

Our home had no chimney, but for years we had a fake log fireplace that nested in the hollow base of the mantelpiece. Its yellow electric bulb flickered behind a plastic façade tinted to create the illusion of flames. Nevertheless, it threw a romantic cast across our living room into which Mother enjoyed snuggling on the couch, in Father's arms, before our glittering Christmas tree, as Bing Crosby crooned "I'm dreaming of a white Christmas, just like the ones I used to know," or Nat "King" Cole lilted "Chestnuts roasting on an open fire, Jack Frost nipping at your nose." But Charles Brown's *Merry Christmas, Baby*—"May Christmas bring you happiness"—was Father's blues noël of choice.

Mother's censorship piqued my curiosity to such an extent that Christmas became as memorable for the opportunity it afforded me to hear Dad's race music—boogie-woogie, jazz and bebop, but especially the blues—as for anything else. Our Christmas Day pleasures included the opening of gifts and the fact that we children were allowed to eat as much of anything we wanted, any hour of that day. But watching the pleasure on my father's face as he cleaned then mounted a stack of 78- or 33 1/3-RPM black vinyl disks on the console turntable was the true meaning of "a joyful noise." (Later, I would wear the grooves off his copies of *Flamingo*, Herb Jeffries's signature song à la Ellington, 1941, and Roy Hamilton's *Unchained Melody*, 1954.) It was a double joy when Father broke through Mother's resistance, grabbed her arm, and showed us the dances of their youth and courtship.

When it came to jazz, Mother enjoyed Dixieland via radio, and never hesitated to pop her fingers to the big swinging '40s band sounds of Jimmy and Tommy Dorsey, Benny Goodman, and Glenn Miller. At the colored-folk end-of-the-war-years spectrum were Louis "Satchmo" Armstrong ("my only sin the skin I'm in," à la Andy Razaf's *Black and Blue*), Cab Calloway (*Minnie the Moocher*), Duke Ellington (*Prelude to a Kiss*), and Ella Fitzgerald (*A-Tisket, A-Tasket*). Unfortunately, hearing these songs today usually evokes the onerous racist atmosphere of the times in which they were recorded. To this day, Armstrong's voice instantly brings back memories of Black adults afraid to voice their anger and indignation over their shabby lots in life, even in their own living rooms.

By the mid-'50s we were watching the Nat "King" Cole and Dinah Shore shows regularly (the unfounded rumor that Shore was passing for White sparked speculation in our household too). But Mother did not like Billie Holiday. At one time Holiday was played so often on local radio broadcasts that Mother actually complained. I recall one instance when she turned the dial from one station to pick up another, and both were airing the same Holiday song as I listened, ear-stung in the back seat, hanging on to every incredibly haunting note. The other Negro musicians and singers who appeared on our radios and TV made a shortlist prestigious for the era: Marian Anderson, Harry Belafonte, Sammy Davis Jr., Erroll Garner, Earl "Fatha" Hines, Eartha Kitt, Mahalia Jackson, Sarah Vaugh[a]n (in her days as an aspiring journalist, Mother interviewed Vaugh[a]n), and the groups the Ink Spots and the Mills Brothers. Later, Ray Charles, Jackie Gleason, and Mitch Miller. While the whole family watched *The Johnny Otis Show* ("doin' that crazy hand jive") on Channel 13, I had pop-culture shows like Bill Horn's *Bandstand* (soon to become Dick Clark's *American Bandstand*) to myself after school or while finishing homework. As puberty deepened, the new musics took hold of my attention, hawked by regional DJs like Chuck "quiver mah liver" Dyer (victim of the payola scandal), Hunter Hancock (kingpin of the beauty parlors), Magnificent Montague (popularizer of the ghetto phrase "burn, baby, burn," a reference to the horizontal dance "the alligator crawl," which often gave young Black men rug burns), Tom "Master Blaster" Reed (still on local cable TV with *For Members Only*), and the legendary croak-throated Wolfman Jack. I was among the thousands watching *The Big Beat* when Frankie Lym[o]n stepped down from the stage in 1957 and took the hand of a young White teen queen, in a move that would knock rock impresario Alan Freed off ABC-TV and into alcoholism.

My grasp on racism in the entertainment world was a mere child's grasp, yet I wondered what my parents thought of the absence of Our People on these programs. Rarely did they complain, expressing gratitude and relief whenever "one of us" appeared. I usually felt embarrassed and angry at things I sensed but could not lend words to. My two brothers and baby sister seemed too young to notice. But thanks to Christmas, I was beginning to regard certain kinds of music as tepid if not torturous. Mother tried but could not keep out the world. On outings, she was unable to control what was accessible. The airways of Black Los Angeles left the country-and-western, border-Mexican, and gospel sounds she preferred out of range. Not to mention the afterschool sock-hops or dances staged for teenagers where the 45s were spun over the PA system. Transistor radios were introduced in 1959 and within a few years all the well-heeled teens were carrying the portables to and from school, annoying bus drivers and teachers alike.

(In my junior-high-school days, young ladies—a.k.a. bobbysoxers—were not yet allowed to wear nylons except for special events. The bobbysox fad was a holdover from the '40s when swooning over crooners was epidemic and the traditional Oxfords were in the process of displacement by plimsolls or sneakers. At the height of our local sock-hop era, two-toned socks—that is, differing pairs of socks cuffed to show two colors—were as big a fad as switchblades, tattoos, gang insignias, and smoking in the bathroom. The rebels wore nylons under their bobbysox.)

Rhythm and blues, rock 'n' roll, and the street-corner serenades of doo-wop (that splendid harmonic answer to barbershop-quartet a cappella) were soon dominating my listening hours, supplemented by the classical and popular tunes Mother allowed at home.

> *When ol' man blues taps me, darlin',*
> *I hit the floor (smelly bare feet will do).*

In the mid-to-late '60s, long gone from home, I would trail my first husband, an itinerant folksinger and civil rights worker, through the coffeehouses and music dens of Hollywood and Echo Park. Jazz, rhythm and blues (soul), and rock 'n' roll (psychedelic soul) were my musics of choice; nevertheless, he would introduce me to the world of folk and blues musicians, from Woody Guthrie and Hank Williams to Robert Johnson and Son House. I would learn the difference between playing with a pick, a slide, and fingernails—more about the dialogue that took place between the words, and workings of the music. Ed Pearl's Ash Grove, a club on Melrose Avenue in Hollywood, would be our main stomping ground. There I would witness the artistry of blues and folk men from Gatemouth Brown to John Lee Hooker, Lightnin' Hopkins to Pete Seeger and Josh White. I even saw the Ash Grove debut of Taj Mahal (and still have the LP). At another venue, we witnessed the dramatic reunion of Sonny Terry and Brownie McGhee, which brought everyone in the crowded room to their feet.

In 1969, I was reintroduced to Ma Rainey and Bessie Smith by a songwriter-musician friend. She also reminded me of how great Billie Holiday remained, whether singing jazz or blues, nearly a decade after death. Through her, I would rediscover the indisputable power of a cappella, hosted one night by Jimmy Witherspoon at Howard Rumsey's club, the Lighthouse, in Hermosa Beach. There I would witness the single most electrifying performance—of any kind outside the call to worship—I ever expect to see as the Persuasions proceeded to literally rock the rafters. Five Black men jumped up on the wooden tables and stomped. I sat wide-eyed and gasping throughout the entire splendid spectacle. What I felt for them was as powerful as it was nameless. I wondered at my luck that my friend had opened for them, as the only act in town unafraid of the group's monstrous performance style, and that I was her transportation for the night. I didn't even drink wine in those days, but I was so sound-drunk afterwards it was all I could do to drive her home safely, then get home alone, to tremble for hours as I relived their greatness. The recording device has not been invented that could capture what those five men gave to an audience.

Certainly, while the new blues was rooted in the going contemporary residuals of Slavery, it was, like jazz, finding mainstream acceptance as an original American art form. Others were adopting it, and I listened, intrigued by what those who did not necessarily identify as Black, did to our form. How the blues moved through the Allman Brothers Band, Big Brother & the Holding Company (Janis Joplin), Cream, the Rolling Stones, Stevie Ray Vaugh[a]n, and Led Zeppelin fascinated me. Acculturation on all sides of the racial/cultural divides was, I noted, an inevitable part of the blues tradition and—because of the constraints of the fad-driven music business—necessary for its survival. The blues was essentially Black, however. It stained anything it touched.

The Jimi Hendrix Experience claimed a musical realm of its own, it seemed to me, and its psychedelic blues-rock found a special chamber in my listening heart. (A blue on black velvet portrait of Jimi graces my office wall; I visited his grave the fall of Y2K.)

In the '70s, divorced and on my own, I danced at the discos, dug on Black Sabbath, David Bowie, and Alice Cooper; I interviewed Bob Marley (*Catch a Fire*) on three occasions, and made the St. Patrick's Day Riots at Elks Hall when New Wave stormed Los Angeles—the Plugz, Go-Gos, and X on stage; yet I began wearing the grooves off my Bobby "Blue" Bland, Taj Mahal, and Otis Redding LPs. On the jazz-hand side, I was a devotee of Herbie Hancock (*Hornets*), thrice catching him crosstown at Doug Weston's Troubadour. I was also rediscovering the merits of Little Esther (Phillips) and Nina Simone alongside Mingus and Monk. While listening, I am able to visualize fingering, particularly piano and guitar, instruments I've studied. Monk's keyboard style would eventually influence my poetic style once a critic pointed out to me that I was writing jazz poetry. (I would eventually discuss Monk's influence in two essays, "On Theloniousism," in *Caliban*, 1988, and "Avant-Garde with Mainstream Tendencies," in *Tripwire* 5, 2001.)

Nevertheless, when it came to private pleasures, the blues held its spot. Several live performances by Etta James in the better clubs across town would make me a forever fan. Yet, it is the unmitigated funk and grit of those ghetto nightspots that still makes my heart pound. That period of my nightlife would be highlighted by the Ike & Tina Turner Revue (featuring the Ikettes) at the California Club; I caught their dazzling act up-close twice. The Hide-Away, Jefty's, the Sportsman's Lounge (particularly open mike on Blue Mondays), the Parisian Room, and Memory Lane were among my haunts. Ironing Board Sam, Swamp Dogg (Little Jerry Williams), Big Mama Thornton, and Big Joe Turner were likewise becoming permanent parts of my (musical) vocabulary.

By the '80s a number of Black women writers emerged who laid claim to Holiday's heady influence (such as Alexis De Veaux, *Don't Explain*). I was doing likewise; but in recent years, upon looking back, I've come to acknowledge that, thanks to Mother, Patsy Cline is as much a part of my vocabulary as Lady Day. However, after catching Betty Carter twice at the Vine St. Bar & Grill in 1980s Hollywood, I determined that this incredibly gifted improvisator, like Monk, is much more my aesthetic kindred.

Roots *à la symphonie* had become the issue.

> Come on out here with me, lover. Let's
> make romance (do that hoochie-coo) . . .

As much as the rhythm and blues enjoyed by my friends and schoolmates, the rock 'n' roll of the '50s was a music rooted in the culture of Americans of Slave Origin. I found my evidence for this in the traditional place, the Negro church. Throughout childhood and into my teens, our family attended the African Methodist Episcopal churches my mother preferred, and often I sang in the youth choirs; but I was repeatedly shocked whenever we attended the Baptist churches my father favored, overwhelmed by the differences in how the music of worship was presented, often the same hymns with radically altered lyrics and arrangements. The third Sunday, during the call to worship, that ritualized form of mass hypnosis was particularly memorable, the minister and choir at its core. The trauma I experienced, centered in the stomach and lower intestinal tract, was akin to the blistering shock and confusion felt when watching James Brown's debut appearance on *The Ed Sullivan Show* (*Please, Please, Please*, in the early '60s). I was disturbed by all of that—a disturbance compounded when I asked Mother why people like the Baptists behaved as Brown did. "Because they are happy," came her answer, which puzzled me.

Happy?

Father's explanations of "speaking in tongues," "being touched," and "feeling The Spirit" were significantly better. Once my stomach settled, I decided that when it came to musical expression, I preferred the Baptists' way. (The Holy Rollers', too, tambourines included. What impressed me most about the music was its undeniable power to move.) But I dwelled on Mother's one-word expression for this phenomenon, eventually discovering others used that word as well. (Might it be akin to the bliss of Zen? I later wondered.) Within my limited knowledge and exposure, White entertainers of the period, with the exceptions of Johnnie Ray and Elvis Presley, simply did not behave in that manner, nor did those within my sphere of observation. The 1960 film *Elmer Gantry* would suggest otherwise, but I was still nearly a decade away from attending my first Pentecostal revival meeting—in a tent.

On weekend afternoons, while we listened to the radio as we did chores or played board games, there aired for too brief a period this magical vocal jazz composition that blitzed my nine-year-old ears, making me instantly happy, in the usual sense of the word. Enthralled, I could never grasp enough of its lyrics to fathom its title no matter how hard I listened. Perhaps it was being played too softly, I thought. My parents objected to loud music unless a party was in progress. Mother said turning up the volume wouldn't help me because they were singing in French and she couldn't understand it either. I would become an adult before I rediscovered *Lullaby of Birdland*, by George David Weiss, sung by the Blue Stars of France, 1955.

For a number of years, my father worked as a janitor for RCA Victor records (RCA developed the 45 in 1951), bringing home returns or the undistributed boxes of 78s, 33s, and 45s discarded by management, allowing us to have our pick of whatever we liked. One of my lucky picks was "Mambo King" Perez Prado's 45 of *Cherry Pink and Apple Blossom White* (1955). As the oldest of four children, left in charge whenever my parents were out of the house, I began going through Father's record collection, playing my favorites over and over to my ears' content. This was doubly forbidden, because my father, too, objected to his children playing his 78s, should we scratch, crack, chip, or break the heavy yet delicate disks. Eventually, Mother raised her restrictions and permitted Father to play his records any time he pleased, if he could get past me to get to the hi-fi. My hunger for the Black in music was insatiable. Circa 1960, Father would take me across town to purchase my first 45 singles, *Harlem Nocturne* by the Viscounts and Barrett Strong's *Money* (*That's What I Want*). Mother would soon buy me a portable record player to keep the peace.

Over time, with close observation and careful listening, drawing on my musical training, I began to patch together my version of a blues aesthetic, stitching what I had garnered into some semblance of understanding, with added bits and pieces from the friends and mentors to come, and from authors read. At the root of all of this cultural quilting, I surmised, lay the blues, which, like ragtime, was a fusion of the slave musics brought from Africa and the folk music of in-dentured Scotch-Irish servants. It had emerged after the end of the post–Civil War Reconstruction period before World War I, in the years between 1877 and 1910, and fused with the field hollers, spirituals, and work songs as it evolved.

> *Ol' man blues comin' ta get me,*
> *Gonna take me way up high*

In my mother's refusal to allow my father to play his music in our home, she was, in effect, keeping out of those "dirty low-down" places in Black culture, those that the White world defined (and was largely culpable for). In this music, natural rhythm was wedded to a forbidden and mythified sexuality, and to the notorious streets. Mother was, in her way, being a good Christian (like the reverend father in the movie *St. Louis Blues*, in which Nat "King" Cole plays W. C. Handy), keeping the music of the cotton fields, gin mills, bawdy houses, gut buckets, and various dives of iniquity away from her children.

Around fall of 1989, as one of my husband's poetry students left Los Angeles to return east, he left me a tape of blues songs featuring Otis Rush (*Right Place, Wrong Time*) and Larry Smith (*Funny Stuff*). I played that tape until its ruination by a faulty tape deck. Months later, on one of my first trips to Illinois, I chanced to catch Otis Rush during the Chicago Blues Festival. The remarkable thing about that night was that there were more African Americans on stage than were seated in the packed house. I was, uncomfortably, one of two. The blues, I was reminded, had long crossed over.

In today's Black urban subculture, few young people seem to care about the blues, if they are informed about it at all. It remains associated with the roots of racism, the rural (plantation), and the impoverished. On the flip side, jazz is considered demanding and elitist. The signifyings of Oscar Brown Jr. and Gil Scott-Heron, the scattings of King Pleasure, the autocratic hipness of Lord Buckley, the jazzifications of Jack Kerouac and Ken Nordine, the rhythm-rap of the Last Poets and the Watts Prophets, to name the few, have merged and caught fire as hiphop (diminutive of hippity-hoppity) and as rap in all its incarnations, especially the gangster rap inspired by the toasts of "mackdaddy" Robert Beck (a.k.a. Iceberg Slim) and his hustler's novel tour de force, *Pimp*, [established] a cultural dynamic that would bring forth the Sugar Hill Gang in 1977 and Grandmaster Flash & the Furious Five in the '80s—and eventually spawn such rhythm-rap extremes as Cameo (*Word Up*, 1996) and Niggaz With Attitude (NWA, *Straight Outta Compton*, 1988).

Yet, the blues persists despite fad and fashion.

Music folklorist Alan Lomax once described Negro music as having the greens, the reds, and the yellows as well as the blues, each color having a specific social context, lost to me as of this writing. However, it's my contention that those other kinds of Negro folk song have been recast or transmogrified into vaudeville/ musical theatre, like the cakewalks and minstrel shows, or else they have been absorbed into their sibling, the blues. Granted, during Slavery, as is now known, there were freed men and women, an infinitesimal landed Black gentry, and Blacks who, as some say "came over on the Mayflower." However, encapsulated in our blues is the path walked by that majority of us who were denigrated by involuntary servitude in America's past. Our blues also contains the bigger mechanism designed to set off the resulting bitternesses, hurts, rages, and sadnesses that must be suppressed by the individual in order to ensure collective day-to-day survival. Thus, the inherent danger of intraracial violence (or, rarer, violence outside the barrier of race) is the organic consequence of the oft ill-examined residuals of Slavery still manifest in present-day American society.

Them blues were also fight songs.

In this new millennium, my love affair with music continues—at this stage, oldies, retro, jazz (acid jazz), and new music. Also, listening to music remains a family affair. My son has become an authority on rock from the '70s forward, my daughter is a Golden Oldies maven, and I often enjoy discussing the merits of one classical composer over another with my husband of twenty-odd years. But when it comes to rhythm and blues, I'm usually on my own.

When I'm feeling down in those dumps, instead of seeking the head shrinker's couch or pharmaceuticals, I hit the stereo to get my music fix. There's an unobtrusive pasteboard box kept atop one bookshelf in the master bedroom where the scratchy 45s sleep. I recently purchased a teenager's old record player for three dollars at a yard sale, exclusively for those precious excursions into my youth. I might warm up with Muddy Waters's *Still a Fool*, or Funkadelic's equally turgid *Qualify & Satisfy*. Freddie King's *Going Down* or Fugi's *Mary Don't Take Me on No Bad Trip* will get into my hips. O. V. Wright's *Love the Way You Love* or Dyke and the Blazers' *Let a Woman Be a Woman—Let a Man Be a Man* usually brings on my feet. By the time I get to Syl Johnson's *I Only Have Love* and the Watts 103rd Street Band's *Your Love (Means Everything to Me)*, I'm full tilt in good motion and mood. Should I be in a dreamy, nostalgic state, I'm more apt to groove to Chairmen of the Board's *Try on My Love for Size*, Gene Chandler's *Rainbow*, the Delphonics' *Tell Me This Is a Dream*, Sam Russell's *Play It by Ear*, or the Soul Generation's cover of *Tell Me This Is a Dream*. By the end of each musical journey I'm myself again and feel like dealing with the world.

Or—while working about the house, doing chores, I'm apt to turn off the digital stuff, dust off the turntable, and start spinning those old LPs, from Boosty to Grover Washington. Between long spells at the computer I often jump up from the monitor, run into the playroom, and dance the Duck, Four Corners, or Pony to the likes of James Brown (*Baby Don't You Weep*), Al Green (*Drivin' Wheel*), and Curtis Mayfield (*Ain't Got Time*), or cry to Smokey Robinson & the Miracles (*When Sundown Comes*) or Otis Redding (*These Arms of Mine*). Without fail, whatever ails me passes almost instantly. It may not be what most call happiness, but it probably is as close as I will ever come.

> *When that ol' blues come to get you*
> *Ya bettah bolt the door 'n' run . . .*
> *When ol' man blues come to get you*
> *Ya bettah bolt that door 'n' join the fun*
> *When ol' blues done gone and got you*
> *Your soul be singing sun to sun.*

Reprinted from Wanda Coleman, *The Riot Inside Me: More Trials & Tremors* (Boston: Black Sparrow, 2005), 13–27.

Five Lines Four Spaces

Jack Whitten

Now is the time. When my white slave masters discovered that my drum was a subversive instrument they took it from me. My time was stolen. To steal a man's time is an attempt to steal his soul. The only instrument available was my body, so I used my skin: I clapped my hands, slapped my thighs, and stomped my feet in dynamic rhythms. I stretched my mouth wide open and allowed my vocal chords to strike a primal cry. I forced the world to listen. I discovered that my pain was a universal pain. Even those who could not understand my native language could understand my pain.

Born in the slave fields of the Deep South, call and refrain is the cornerstone of jazz and blues. Dialogue, however painful, starts between two or more people.... I call, you answer. How I feel is always about power: I, and only I, have control of my feelings. Empowerment serves identity and identity is an act of will. Beyond the political there is always the power of love. Whether in the guise of the divine or celebrated in the joy of sex, jazz and blues continue to inspire the power of love.

Time is a memory bank. The past, present, and future are encoded in time. Art can be used as a tool to decipher time. Break the code and consciousness will expand. When consciousness expands, freedom expands. The philosophical underpinning of jazz is the expansion of freedom. We have entered third-stage modernism, which is a global aesthetic based on otherness. Like jazz, third-stage modernism insists on the expansion of freedom. Experimentation is the key. I believe that there are sounds we have not heard. I believe that there are colors we have not seen. And I believe that there are feelings yet to be felt.

Postmodernism was a welcome intermission. It allowed an opening for all the various multicultural, disinherited, and fragmented sensibilities to make their voices heard. First- and second-stage modernism did not acknowledge any artistic contribution by African Americans; such inclusion was simply not an issue worthy of consideration. Third-stage modernism, with its emphasis on otherness and inclusion, offers the best scenario of hope for reconciliation. Without hope there is no reason for freedom. Anarchy is not a viable option, and romantic nihilism is only an immature, masturbatory response to the threat of total planetary chaos. We must learn to overcome our existentialist notion of being.

Abstract artists are attracted to jazz because of its expandable qualities. Jazz imposes no limit on feeling and its basic elements of spontaneity/improvisation preserve freshness of spirit. Spirit does not like stale air! Spontaneity/improvisation are necessary ingredients of art. The acceptance of spontaneity/improvisation does not reject the value of conceptual thought. Conceptualism is a tool in the service of spontaneity/improvisation. The multidimensional sheets of sound in John Coltrane's music could not reach cognition without the conceptual. As an abstract painter, I translate Coltrane's sheets of sound into sheets of light. Every emotion that ripples through my body is compressed into a plane of light.

My light is a physical fact: I freeze, boil, burn, hammer, saw, sand, grind, and glue sheets of acrylic paint with weights and clamps. The paint is the light. Being a physical fact, it is therefore concrete. The concrete must be transcended through sensibility in order to become abstract. For me, abstraction is a matter of choice, and transcendence is not attributed to any divine ordinance. I spoke of empowerment serving identity; likewise, transcendence empowers us to overcome. "We Shall Overcome" was not an arbitrary gesture of defiance. It was, and is, an act of identity.

Now is the time. Every day in the studio is an adventure. Formal materialism is only a means: it is not an end. Matter is dead meat without spirit. Spirit lives in sensibility. Sensibility, and only sensibility, makes art possible. Plasticity makes sensibility visual. My cosmic guides are: John Coltrane, Thelonius Monk, Charlie Parker, Miles Davis, Charles Mingus, Kenny Dorham, Bud Powell, Ron Carter, Fats Navarro, Dexter Gordon, Cecil Taylor, Ornette Coleman, Sonny Rollins, Coleman Hawkins, Eric Dolphy, Albert Ayler, Sun Ra, Clifford Brown … I am so blessed.

The historical continuity of jazz and blues is a valuable cultural asset. For the artist, especially the abstract artist, it is raw material, a resource of infinite possibilities available to anyone capable of deciphering its emotional codes. Good news, I found my stolen drum. I found it while experimenting with the formal element of space. Evidently, Rashied Ali, Alvin Jones, Philly Jo Jones, Art Blakey, Max Roach, Roy Haynes, Arthur Taylor, and others had retrieved it and stashed it in deep space.

Matt Mullican
Untitled (Birth to Death List), 1973

Her Birth
Her family
Her house, Home
learning to Crawl
The Heat from the kitchen stove
learning to walk
Hearing Her mother downstairs
learning to talk
learning to use her hands
Feeling Hungry after her nap.
her fourth birthday.
The salt on their dinning room table
Smelling the fresh autumn air
bleeding after skinning her knee
going to School, learning to make friends
the pillow on her parents bed.
traviling to the mountains
the sun seemed Ht. Her in the mountains
the people living down the street
learning to read and write
the Dinning room table
the sky was a light shade of Blue
learning mathimatics
Her best friends older brother
feeling Hungry after skipping lunch
learning to ride a bike
The full moon lit up the night sky
Learning about gravity in School
The light in the hallway
catching Her breath after running home
entering the 6th grade
their pet dog
the door between her and her older sisters room
Having to g. t. the bathroom
the tree growing in the backyard.
feeling the glair of the sun on her eyes.
they got 2 inches of rain that week
the street light
getting good grades in school
looking at her self in the mirror
playing in the backyard.
entering the 7th grade
going to her first dance
food cans in the kitchen cabinet
Tasting too much salt in the salad
wanting to have a boy friend
going throw puberty
they where so many stars she couldn't count them all
looking at her bed room window
going to partys
getting new friends
having a boy friend, going steady
as the year progressed the days got shorter
visiting her aunts house
her dog dies
When she touched the light socket she was shocked
entering the drama club.
her boyfriends little sister
riding the bus to school
entering the 10th grade, High School
after gym she worked out and was very tired
The Telephone ringing in the hallway
Spending the summer on a beach house
the ocean seemed endless
learning to drive a car
remembering the time she hurt her self skiing
Touching her right eye with her index finger
family moves to new neiborhood
the sound of an airplane flying overhead
fantisizing about getting married
Deciding to major in History
going to the movies
Hugging Her Father
Taking a bath
graduating from Highschool
entering college, moving away from Home
Her roomate
Her roomates Home town
Majoring in Hist in College
getting a boyfriend
The amount of time it takes to walk to school
The sound of the record player in the next room
watching the sunrise from her Bedroom
studying the Hist of her country
getting married in the afternoon
quiting school
moving to a large city with her husband.
The manhole in the street infront of their apt
getting herself a job
The Boiling water on the stove
looking at her self in the mirror
getting a letter from her parents
Having her wisdom teeth removed
wanting to have a baby
Cutting bread
noticing the light @ refract thru the kitchen window
getting Her hands wet
making new friends at work
having a baby
The baby crying early in the morning
the moving To a larger apt
burning her left hand while cooking
Her 25 Birthday
Her sons baby shoes
Feeling thirsty one Hot afternoon
Her Husbands Boss
Her Baby learning to walk and talk
Thinking about her mother and Home
the covers on their bed
she decided to have her hair trimmed
Her husband had a headache
Her sons going to School
going on a trip to south america for the summer
making love with her Husband
Her 29 birthday
feeling older, old almost 30
Having another child.
renewing an interest in Hist
looking at Her self in the mirror
feeling that Her son is in danger
Her baby is almost 5 years old
buying a day
One of the living room chairs
Her 35 birthday
The Days are going past much fast
an object in the backseat of their car
Moving to a house
the window facing the backyard in the kitchen
Her Husbands feeling tired after a hard day's work
Her son in highschool her daughter is of Highschool
watching the dish break, as she dropped it.
reading a book in the living room
making love with her husband
looking at herself in the mirror
feeling that she is getting older
their dog barking in the backyard
Her daughter breathing B her/around during the summer
Her Son graduating from Highschool
thinking about her sons a baby
her daughter graduating from Highschool
feeling bored with her life
thinking of Her childhood memorys.
taking a shower
Her sons liver
looking into the sun
Her daughter going to School in a foriegn country
spending Have the year in the city half on the beach.
looking at a photograph of Her self as a child
Having a grandchild
the years are going faster and faster
Her father dies, sudden grief
feeling like she's getting old
the people living down the street
Her sons first job
Her daughters marriage
moving past her self in the mirror
looking at her self in the mirror
Her husbands retirement
the move to the country Permits
spending a lot of time reading
looking at her white hair, complexion of a child
Her body feels weaker
looking at a photograph of her grandson
watching tv
the christmas tree
their car in the street
getting sick, going to a hospital
Thinking about her birth
a cloudy day
Her husband dies
Her world was changing, getting older
moving to a old peoples home
the door in between her and her sisters room
going for walks in the garden.
her of saying with her
not being able to do what she wants
thinking of her oncoming death
not being able to see clearly
looking at her feet
Her family
thinking of her parents
Thinking of husband
looking at her self in the mirror
Her thinking of her death
Her death

Matt Mullican
Untitled (Birth to Death List), 1973

Transcription

Her birth
Her family
Her house, home
Learning to crawl
The heat from the kitchen stove
Learning to walk
Hearing her mother upstairs
The street noises coming in the window
Learning to talk
The rug on the living room floor
The trees growing in the backyard
Learning to use her hands
Feeling hungry after her nap
The sunlight hurts her eyes
Her fourth birthday
The salt on the dining room table
Smelling the fresh autumn air
Bleeding after skinning her knee
Entering school
The pillow on her parents' bed
Making friends
Traveling to the mountains
Crying when feeling lost
The people living down the street
Learning to read words
The dining room table
The sky was a light shade of blue
Learning arithmetic
Her best friend's brother
Feeling hungry after skipping lunch
Learning to ride a bike
The full moon lights up the night sky
Learning about gravity in school
The light in the hallway
Catching her breath after running home
Entering the sixth grade—becoming older
Their pet dog
The door between her and her older sister's room
Having to go to the bathroom
Noticing that the tree in the backyard is changing color
Feeling the glare of the sun on her eyes
They got two inches of rain that week
Playing handball at school
The street light
Feeling proud of her schoolwork
Looking at herself in the mirror
Entering the seventh grade
Playing in the backyard
The food cans in the kitchen cabinet
Going to the school dance
Doing her homework
Tasting that there's too much salt in the salad
Thinking about going steady

Experiencing puberty
Scaring the dog by slamming the door
There were so many stars she couldn't count them all
Looking out of her bedroom window
Finding new friends in school
As the year progressed the days got shorter
Visiting her aunt's house
Getting a boyfriend and going steady
Brushing her teeth
Her dog dies
Getting an electric shock
Riding the bus to school
Entering the drama club
Her boyfriend's little sister
Going to camp over the summer
The sound of the record player in the living room
The air felt thick that morning
Becoming sick—not going to school
Making out
Hearing her parents argue
Getting a younger sister—thinking to herself
Getting scared
Going to parties often
Entering school
Hearing static while talking on the phone
Taking care of her little sister
After gym she was very tired
Burning herself while cooking
The telephone ringing in the hallway
Spending the summer at a beach house
The ocean seemed endless
A large man passing her on the sidewalk
Thinking about the people she has yet to meet
Learning to drive a car
Remembering the time she hurt herself skiing
Touching her right eye with her index finger
Family moves to a new neighborhood
The sound of an airplane flying overhead
Taking a bath
Becoming interested in history
Fantasizing about marriage
The dining room table set for eating
Going to the movies
Hugging her father
Entering college, moving away from home
Her roommate
Falling asleep while studying
Her roommate's home town
The amount of time it takes to walk to school
Majoring in history in college
Getting a boyfriend
The sound of the record player in the next room
Staying up, watching the sunrise from her rooftop
Cutting her hair
Studying the history of her country
Getting married in the afternoon
Their front door
Quitting school
Moving to a new house
Her husband's family

The manhole in the street
Thinking of her in-laws
Her husband's work
Boiling water while cooking
Getting a job for herself
Looking at herself in the mirror
Receiving a letter from her parents
Having her wisdom teeth removed
Watching the light retract through the kitchen window
Eating lunch
A pencil on her desk at work
Knowing she is going to have a baby
Thinking of her parents
Her baby is born
Moving to a larger house
There is lots of green around the new house
Her husband's mouth
Stubbing her toe while running
Her son's baby shoes
February twenty-sixth
Feeling thirsty one hot afternoon
Her husband's boss
Another birthday, she is getting older
Getting her hands wet
Thinking about her son's life
Making love with her husband
Smelling the fresh autumn air
Thinking of her childhood
The telephone wires
Her son's learning to walk
The people living next door
Trying to find her glasses
The covers on their bed
Having another baby, a girl
Not eating very much
She only had an hour to get home
Her son's school work
Visiting her husband's sister
The noise from a large truck
Her daughter's fourth birthday
Going shopping
Looking at herself in the mirror
Her thirty-fourth birthday
Sensing that her son is in danger
Renewing an interest in history
Her daughter's left hand
Taking a shower
Dreaming that she spoke a foreign language
Thinking of her husband's childhood
An object in the back seat of their car
The floor she stands on
October fifth
Her husband shaved regularly
Traveling to a large city
Her son's graduation
Taking a photograph
Reading a book in the study
Her husband's current income
Dropping a disk—watching a break
Kissing her husband

The days seemed to be going by faster
Having trouble breathing
The new living room furniture
The sidewalk around the corner
Touching the wall
Her father dies, sudden grief
The backyard flooded during a heavy rain
Looking at herself in the mirror
Her son's marriage
Brushing her teeth
Starting a garden
Her daughter's graduation
The broken glass in the basement door
Swimming
An itch in the lower part of her back
Her daughter's school in a foreign country
Spending half the year at the ocean
Looking at a photograph of herself as a child
Being scared to enter a dark room
Having a grandchild
Feeling older
Remembering schooldays
A glass of water
They have retired
Their son's independence
Touching herself
Cooking a "hearty meal"
Forgetting her age
Their house
Going for a trip around the world
Hair turning white
Her daughter's marriage
Working at her desk
Wondering where that person lives
Being visited by her daughter-in-law's parents
Noticing that the sky is a light shade of blue
The red car down the block
Catching her breath
Watching TV
Taking a nap in the hot sun
Her husband dies
Moving
Thinking about her eventual death
Scaring the dog by slamming the door
A family reunion during Christmas
Going for a walk in the garden
Feeling old, not caring
Looking at her feet
Not being able to see clearly
Bleeding after skinning her knee
Thinking of the faces of her parents
Cooking vegetables
The door between her and her sister's room
Looking at her eyes in the mirror
The floor she stands on
Thinking of her husband
Looking at herself in the mirror
Thinking of her death
Her death

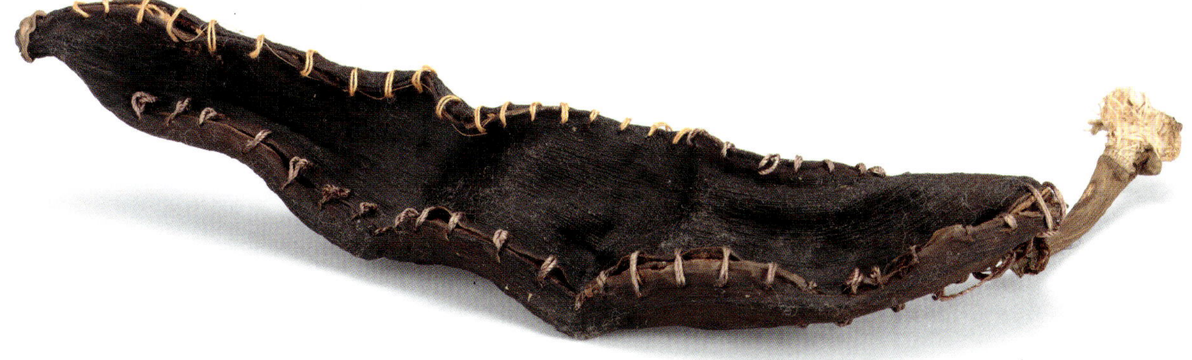

Zoe Leonard
Detail from *Untitled*, 1994–97

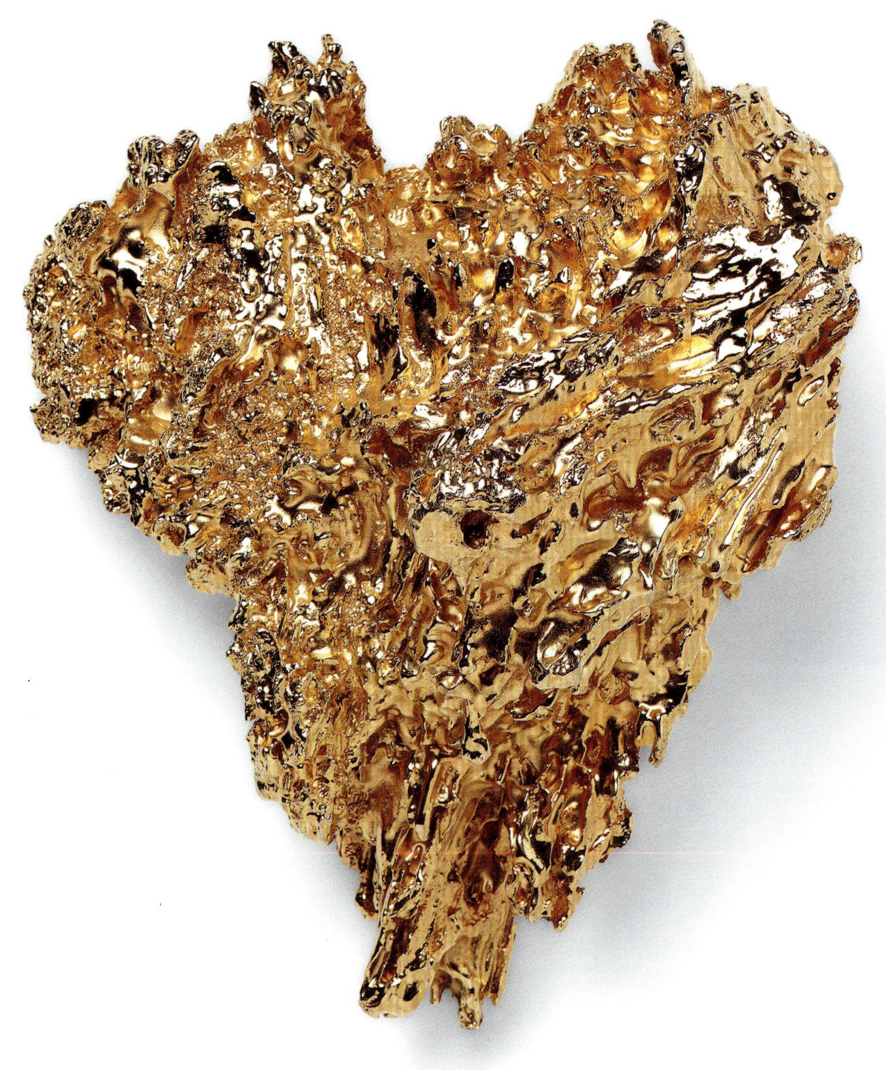

Liz Larner
Lux Interior (gold plated), 2010

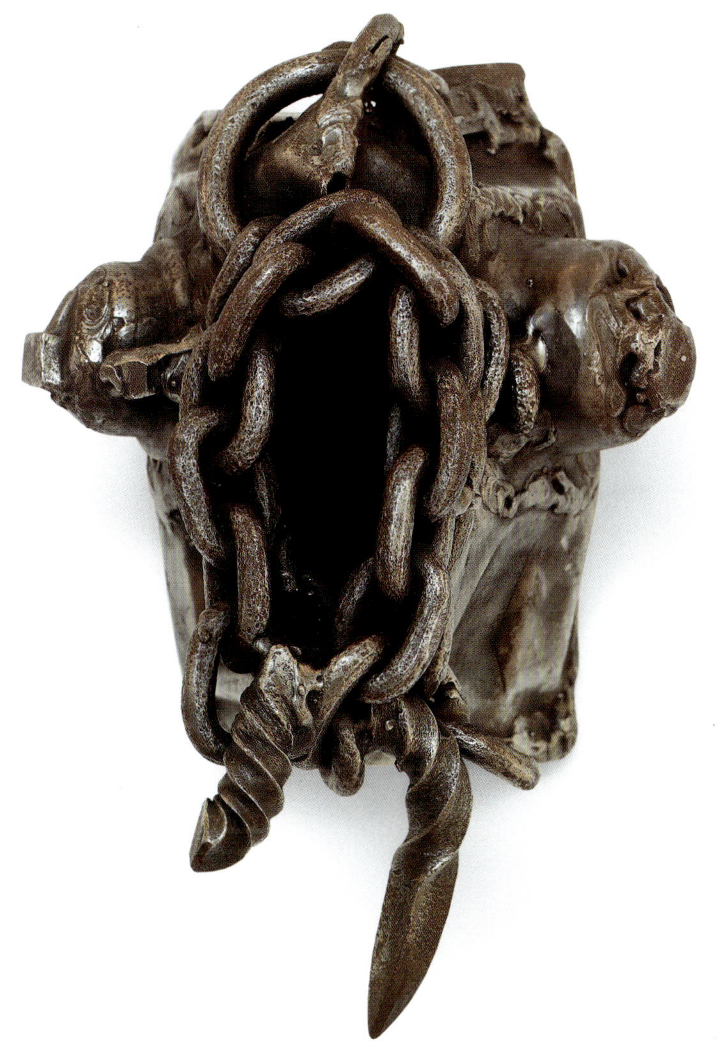

Melvin Edwards
Write When You Can, 1991

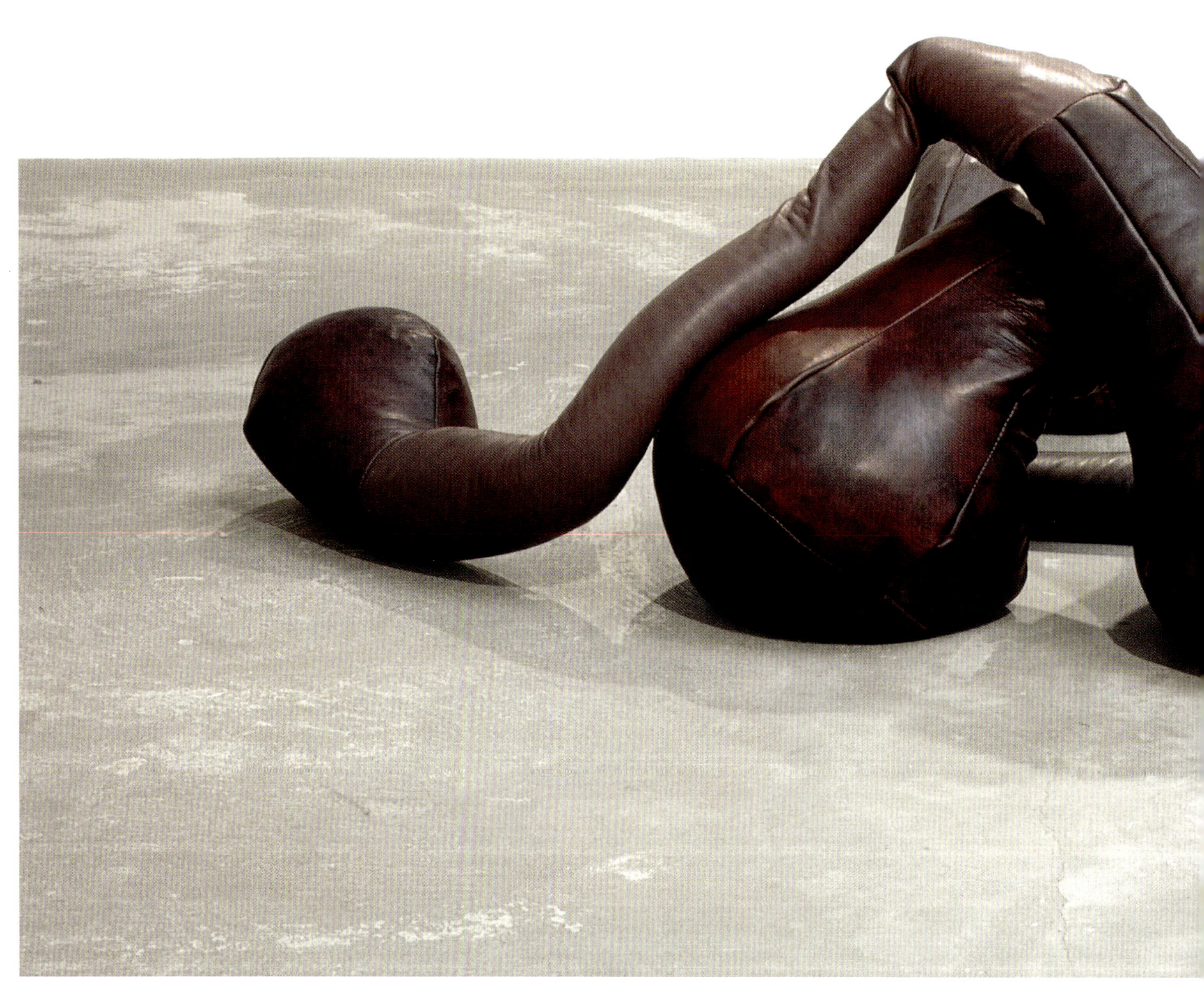

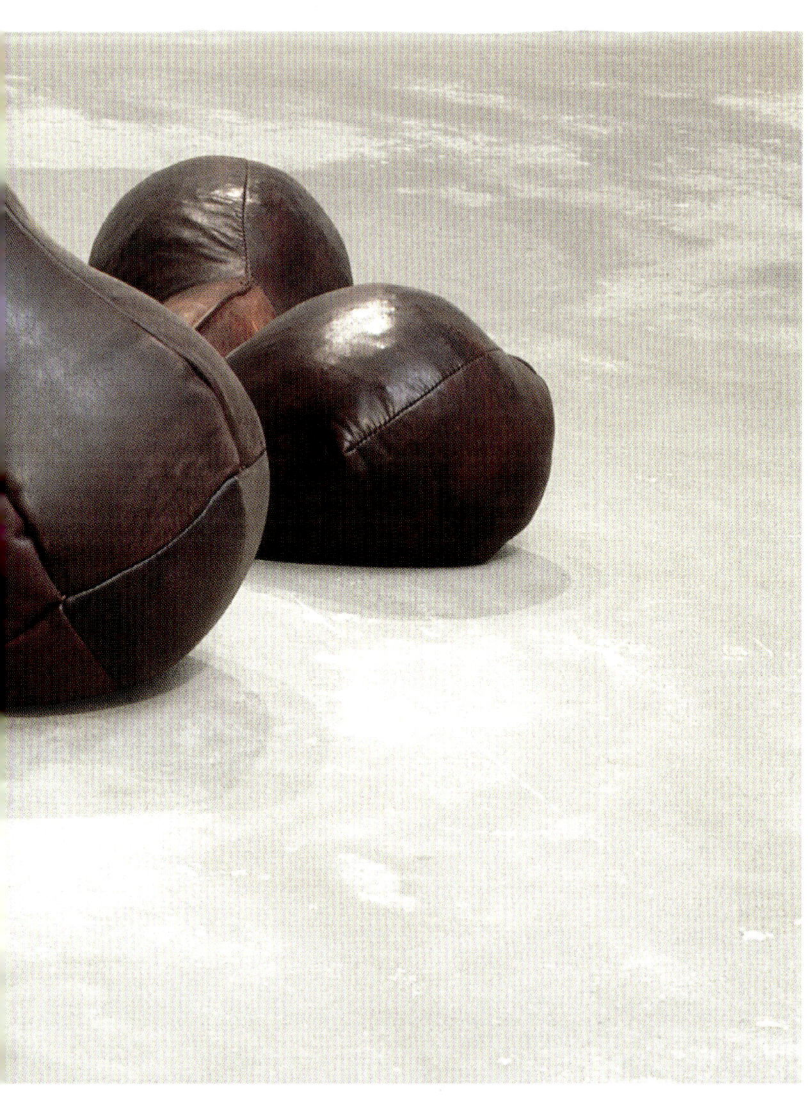

Liz Larner
No M, No D, Only S & B, 1990

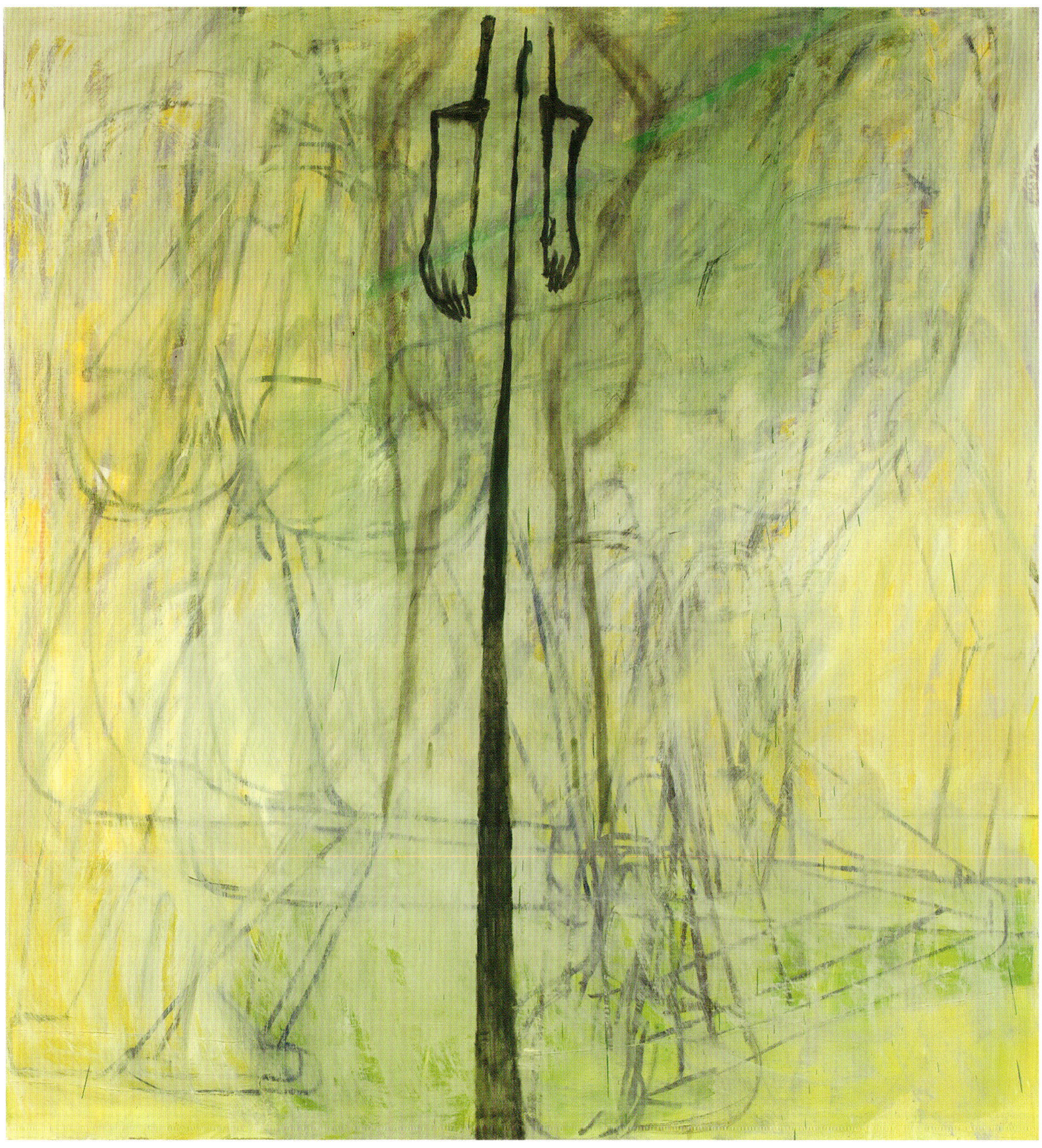

Amy Sillman
DUEL, 2011

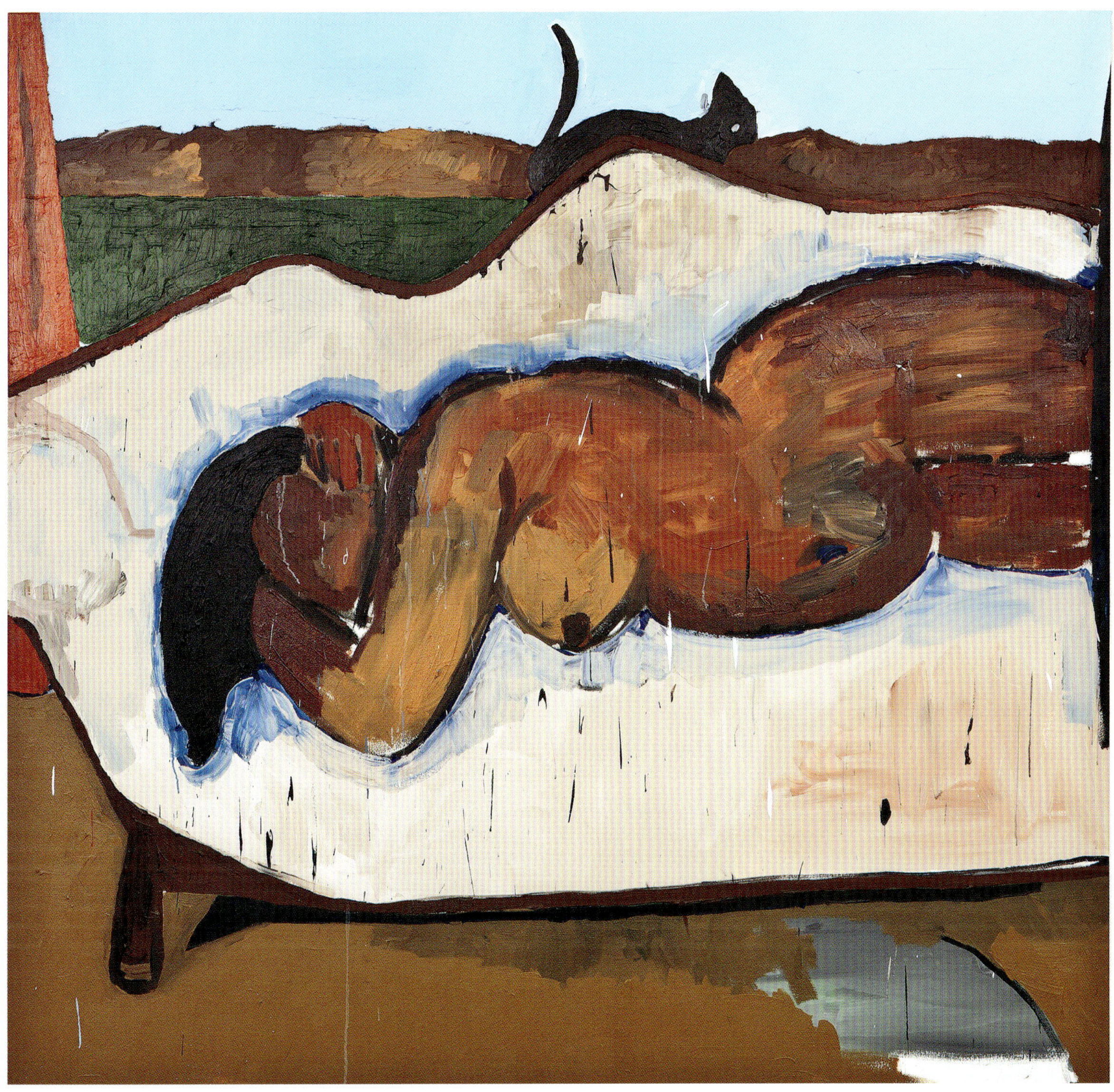

Henry Taylor
Emelda, 2011

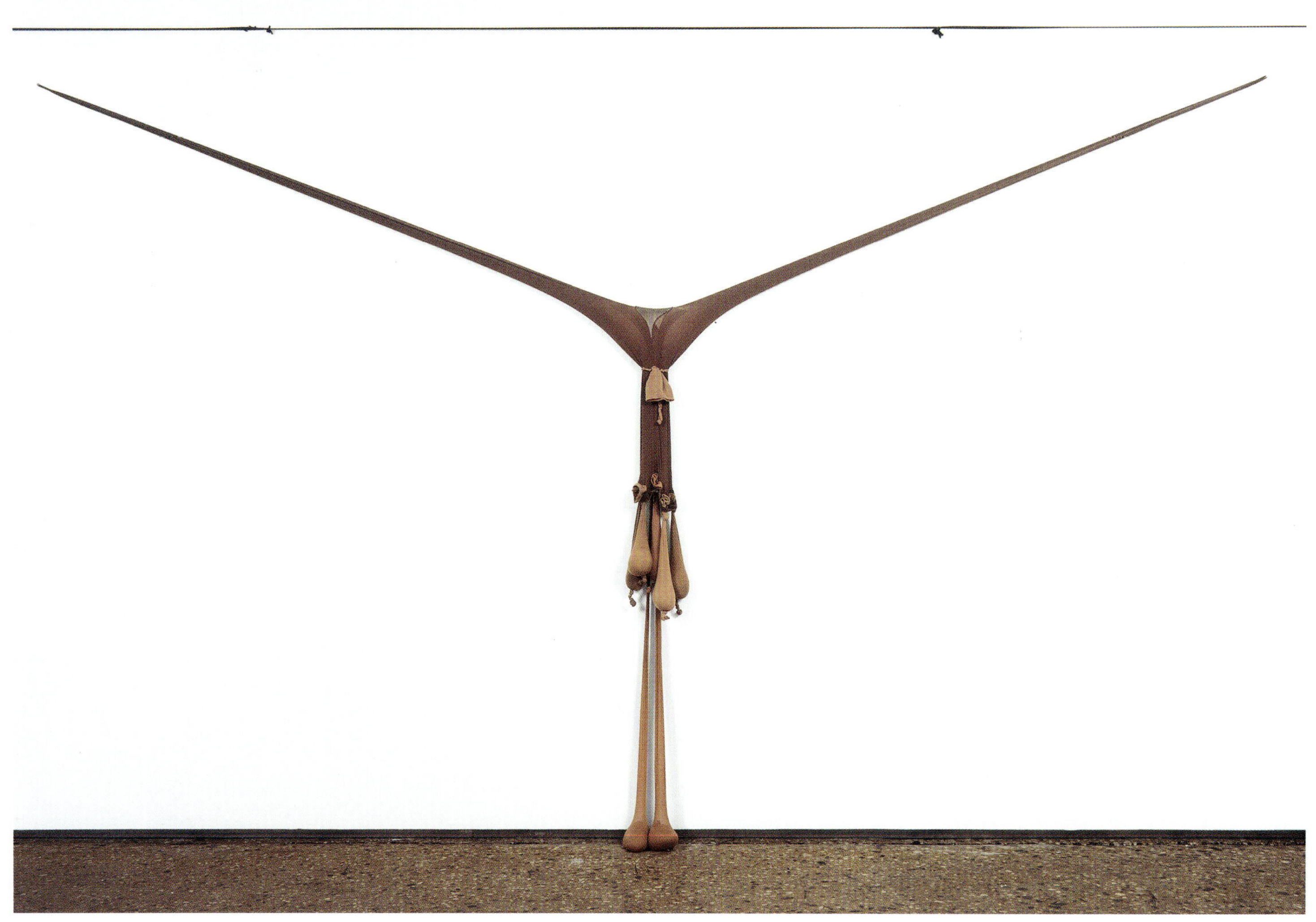

Senga Nengudi
R.S.V.P., 1975

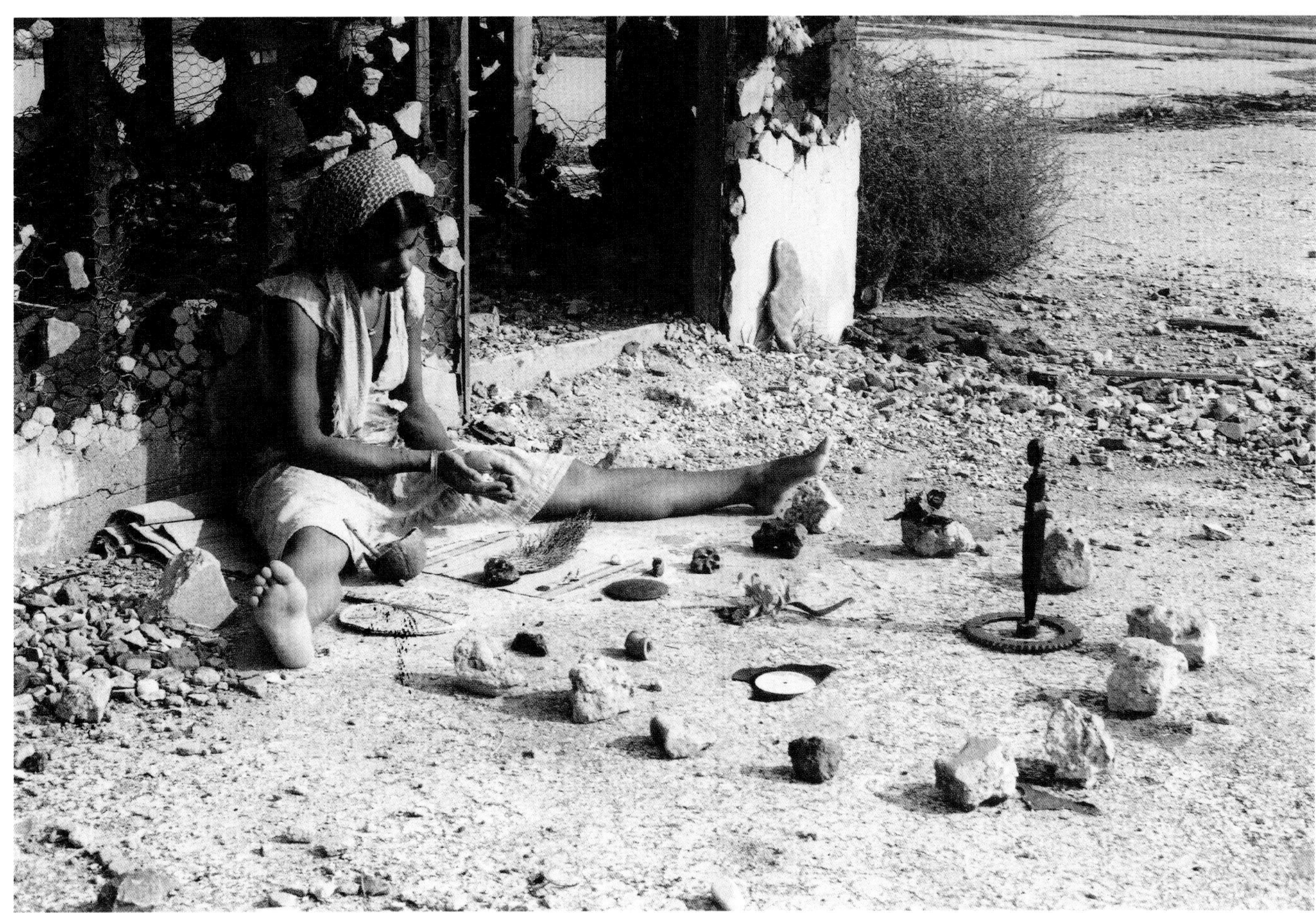

Barbara McCullough
Still from *Water Ritual #1: An Urban Rite of Purification*, 1979

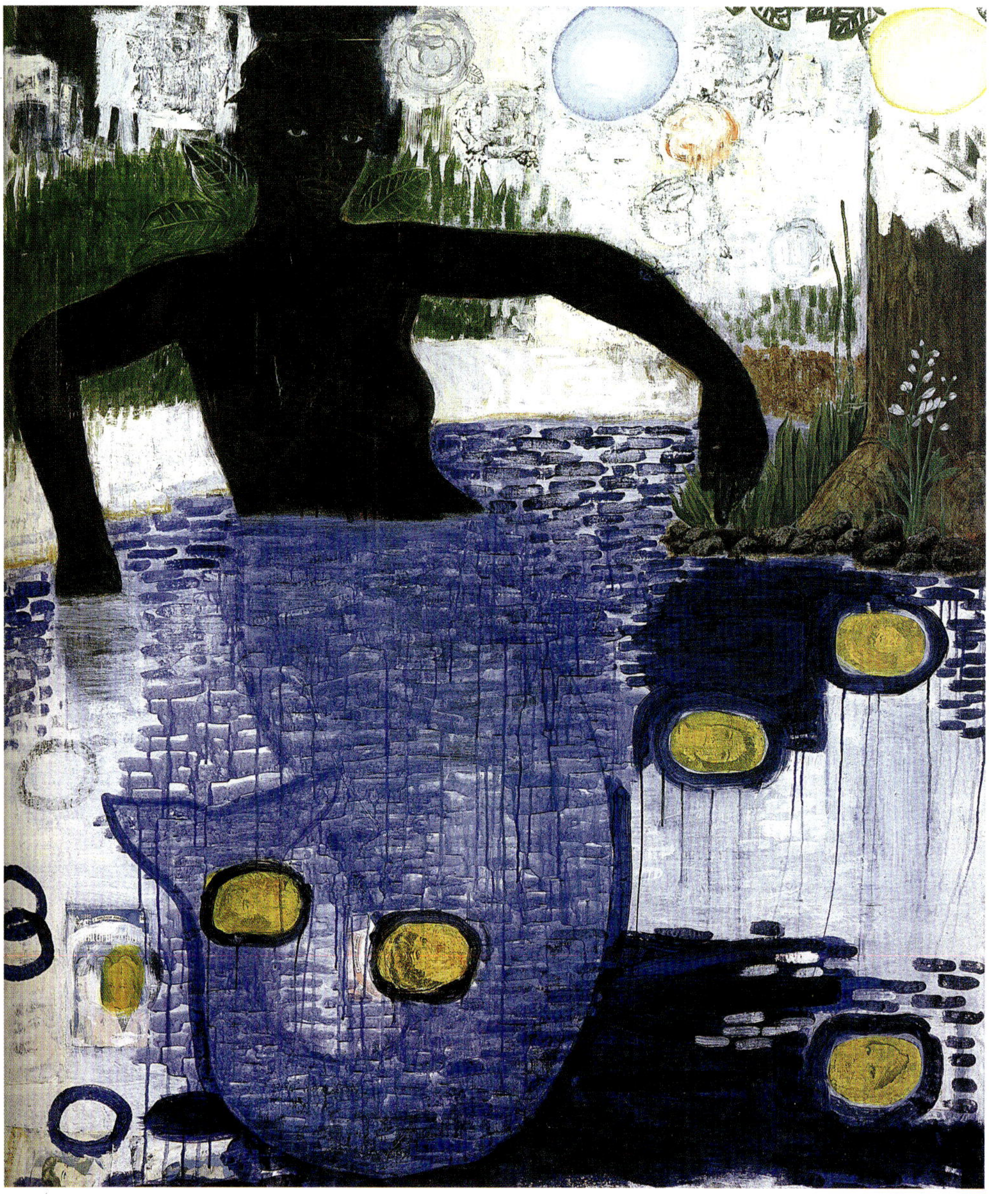

Kerry James Marshall
Blue Water Silver Moon (Mermaid), 1991

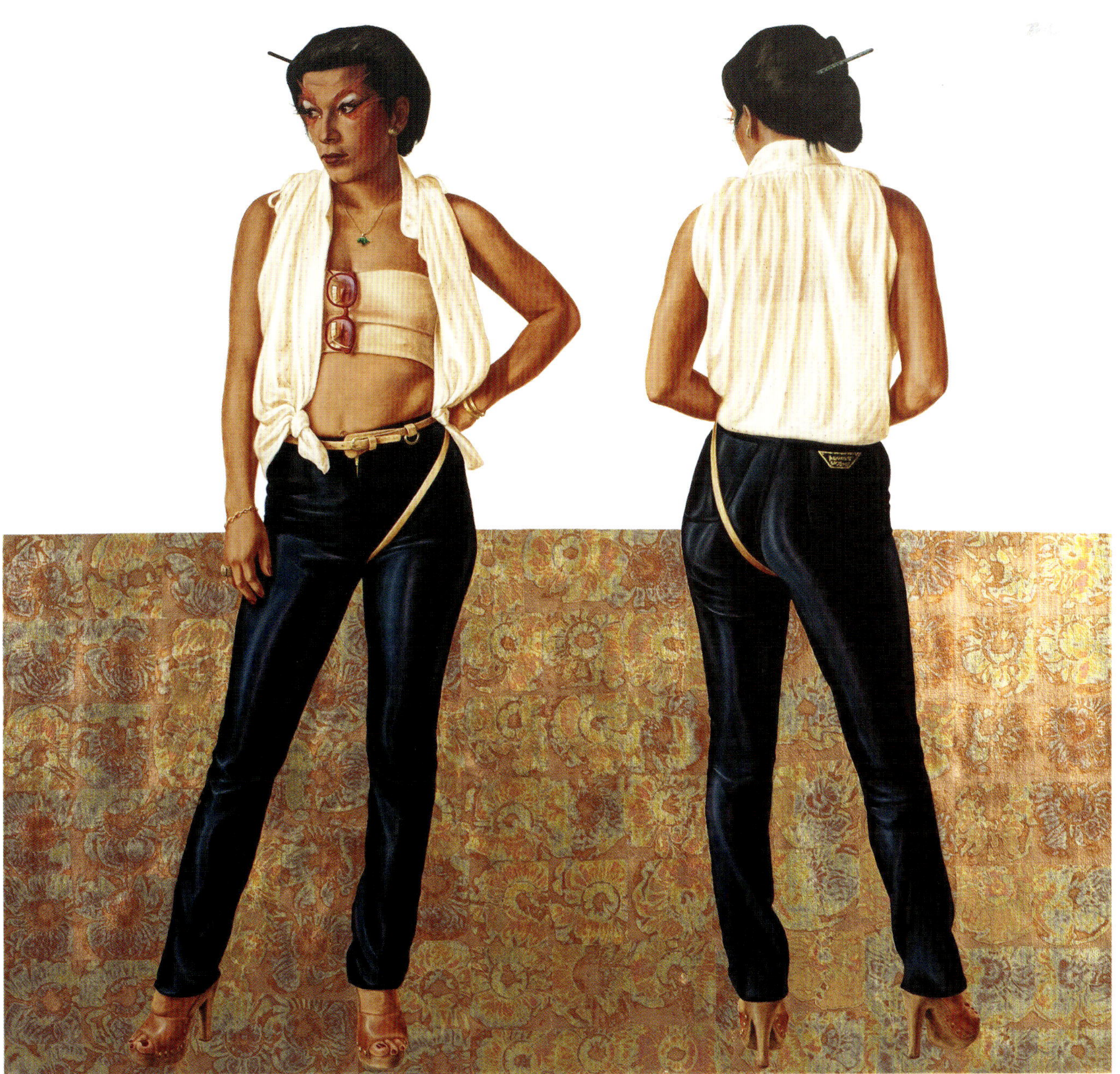

Barkley L. Hendricks
Something Like a Bird Double Barbara, 1982

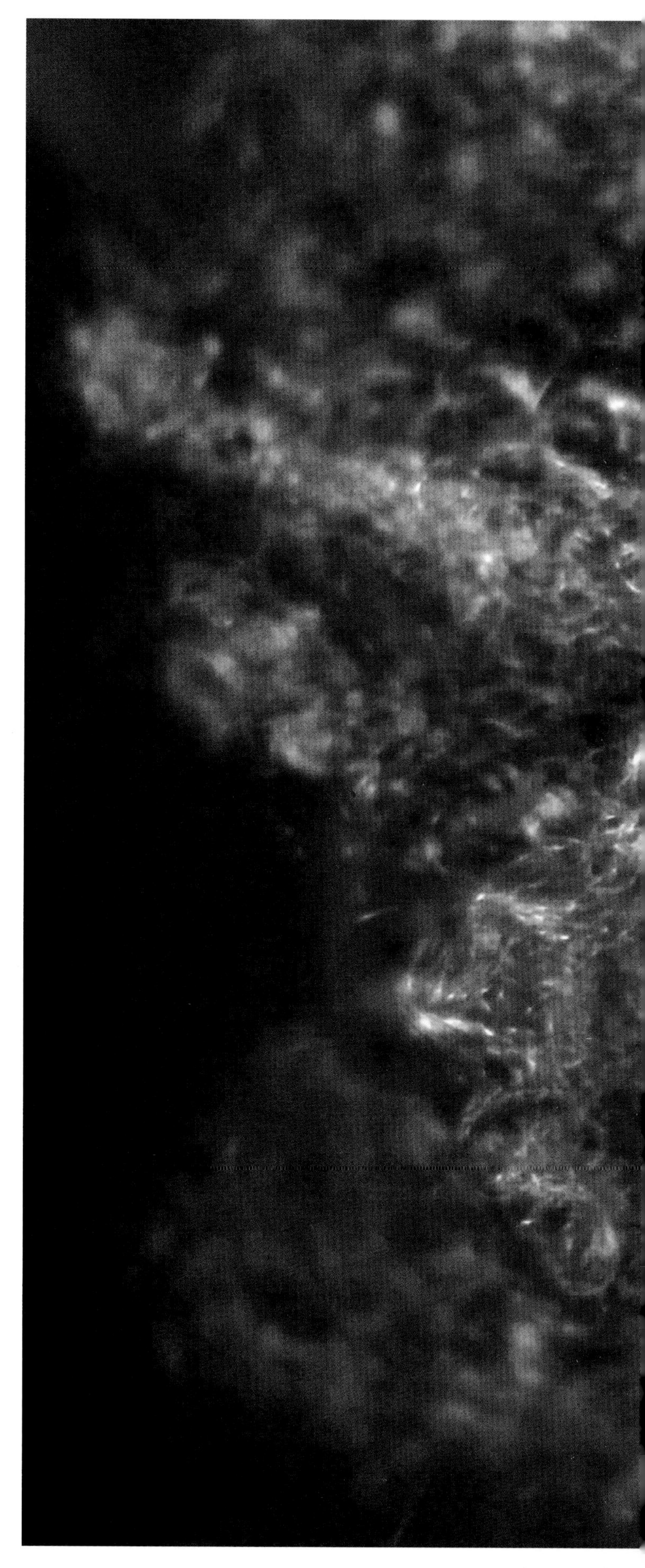

Lorraine O'Grady
Still from *Landscape (Western Hemisphere)*, 2010–11

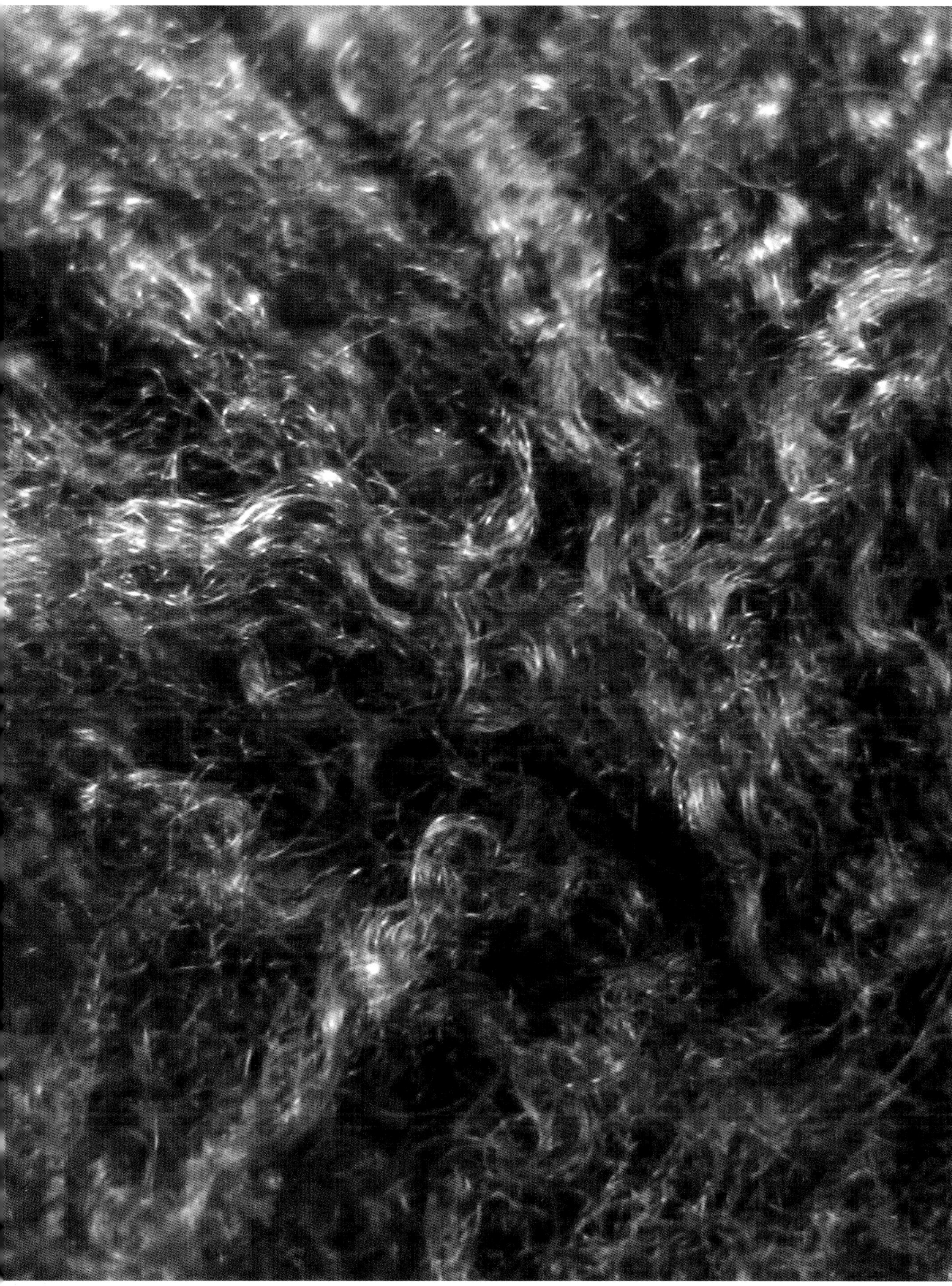

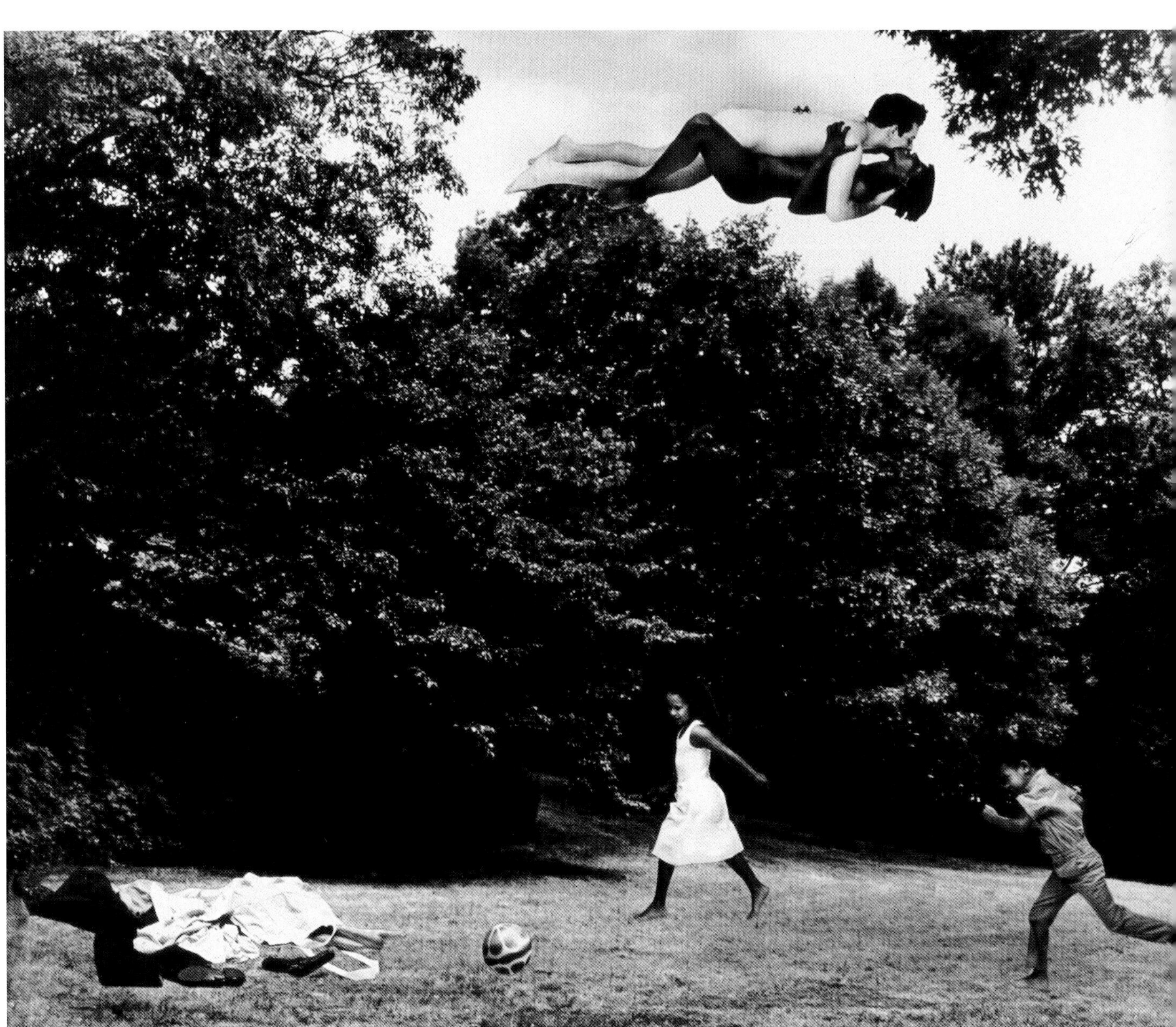

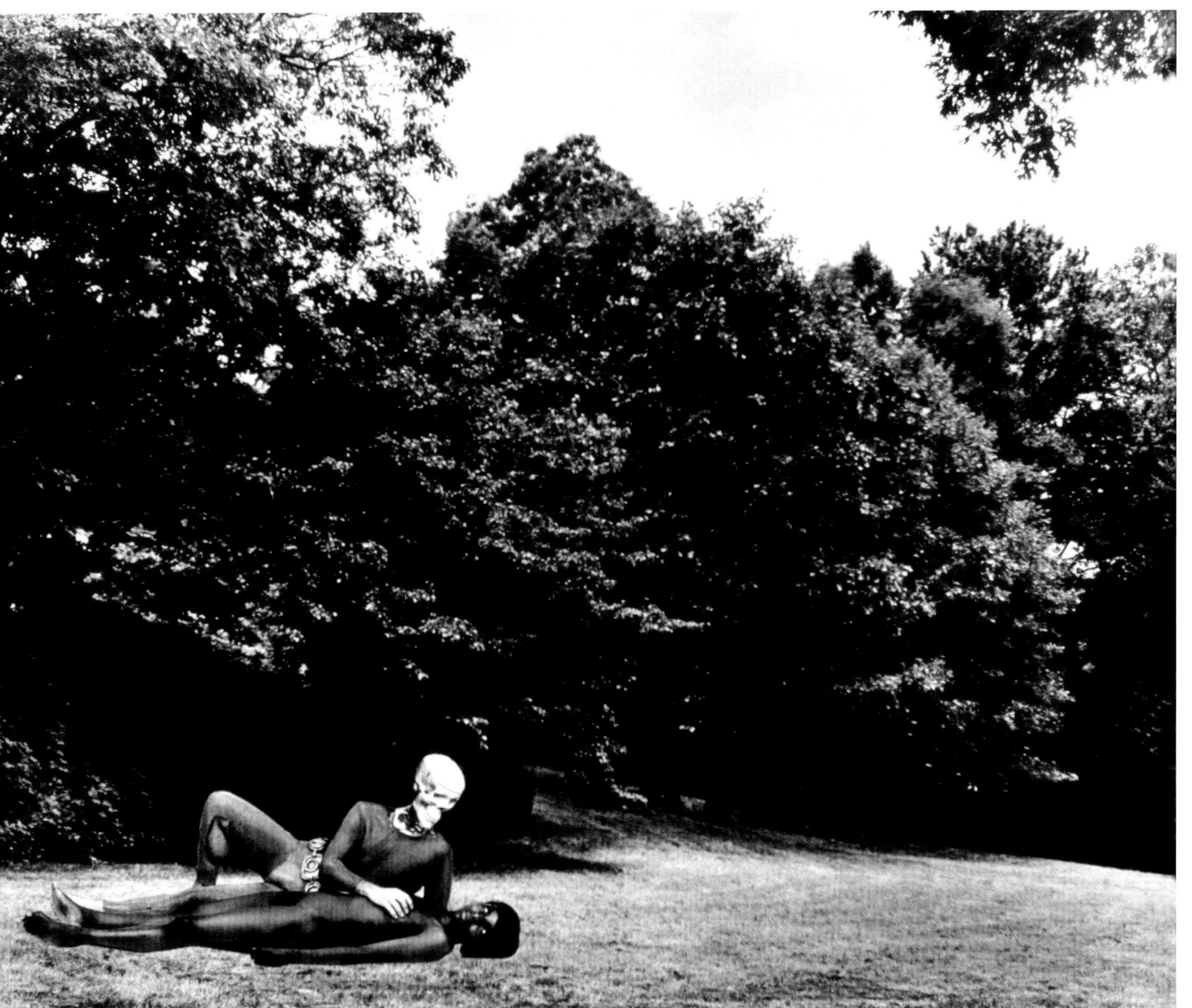

Lorraine O'Grady
*Body/Ground (The Clearing: Or Cortez and La Malinche, Thomas Jefferson
and Sally Hemings, N. and Me), 1991/2012*

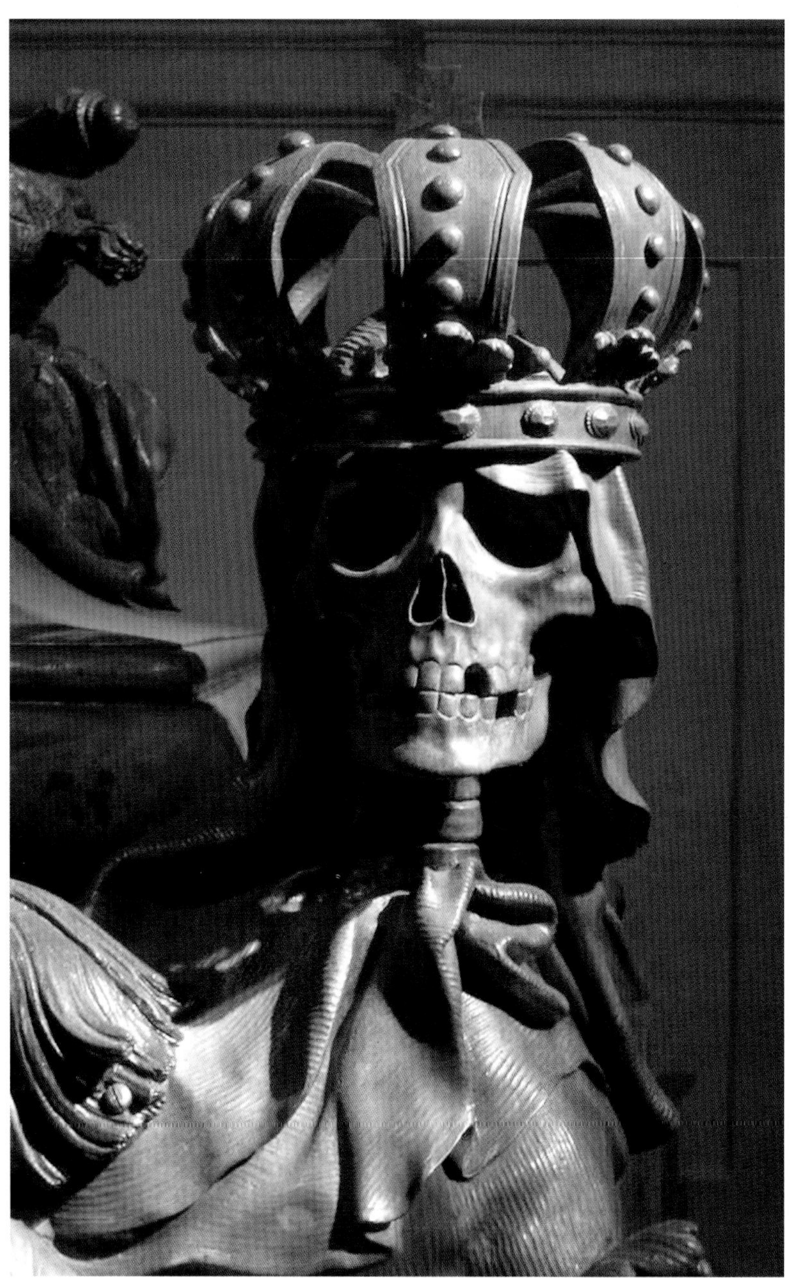

Die Kaisergruft, Wien, **2007**
Photograph by Gregg Bordowitz

There: A Feeling

Gregg Bordowitz

what is by now made here gone
gone now here by what is made
here made gone by what is now

where do you look?
and if you find
what you want
by sight
do you destroy it?

you walk into a room
you know she is angry
she doesn't say a word
her back is turned
you think
what have I done wrong?
you can't decide
but you know
she is angry
the room is dark
it's raining outside
the window
dull light
is it the weather?
grey

or
you walk into a room
and you know
he is gone
what is he's gone?
is absence the evidence?

I'm talking about our parents.
how our parents are appearances
how their volumes organize punctuations
here
there
gone
because spaces are edges
we end or extend
the meter
the measure of intent
a container for feelings
a mood
as people
like this one
him
her
him
yes
he is a girl

she is a fact
how
how is a fact
he is how
she is a fact
and she is how
how he is
she is
a fact
& its qualities
both
a fact & qualities
unique and curious and strange
as weird as art
which is matter

the substance
look
it
it is
what is it
look
how is it
how it is
how it is what
look
what is how it is
what is how it is it
is what how
is it how
is it
what
how
look

what's there
touch it
must we
do we
know
how it's done
done simply
as a practice
done as thinking
as words
as lectures
finished
is it done
as an end
as a terminus
as a theory
in itself
in
out
in & out

where it
arises
there
in the outside
it is
grief
when
ever
how
is the question
the answer

how
do we
attend
to words
each word
how is
belief tested
how
does
an order
disappear

it happens
messages fail
but
looks are different

they flicker
between he & she

he is handsome
without boundaries
he's an all-at-once
a form of traffic
his broken tooth smile is a street car
in a city where all tensions are spastic
look
how he holds my attention with guile
when he describes how bottles carried clink
when what we observe is what we think
we admire workers' style
though we're scared of them
when they speak
we know
we must ask
how the children
of the children
of the children
endure

now
he feels her anxiety
about being ignored
attention wanders
we oscillate
between

as a young boy she was tormented
she said
I don't need theory in order to exist
her difference didn't escape cruel eyes
she grew up with it
yet here she is
she is alive

never ask why
about gender
you're queer
it's not a form of resistance

thinking now
about how
repetition establishes space

what we can't wear
we sew

language is more or less
felt
the daily house shoes
what warms the feet
fibers held together under friction

home is the theme

what we can't hold
we hug
we hug
a single tree
among rows of trees
in a public garden
where little boys sing
listen
how
voices change
touch
what we lean upon between us
trust
what we can't know

what do you do
when the offer
of sex
turns
to fuck us?

we look
that is the drama of what comes next
we learn
to enjoy terror
to draw energy from random sensations

there is no necessity among connections that reason can
discern
all words are potential anagrams

things are parts
each is a piece
a remnant
of a unique order
and together
either more or less
is made

our feelings
you know
what we've chosen
but did not elect
the consequences
the backroom dealings

I am between the two arms of my own body
do I crush what I know in my palms?

she is right
he is left
pain pains
how I rush in
the flow of charms

look closely
at him to her
zig-zag
motions
confuse
words & things

is this it
have I found
what I do
what I need
when I need
this
is
it
choose a word
what eyes do
in each deed
what I read
what I see
there
I
fit
life is round
lies are true
I believe
what I cede
just to be
to
be

zero
both a quality & a quantity

nothing
nothing disrupts
whatever imagination condones
play is reality
arising
between mother & child
it belongs neither to me nor to her
&
father exists
alongside that between

I prefer solemn company
when windows darken
pitch
like a ball to a batter
the triangular arrangement of thought
captured
I wait
in the corner
a camera on a tripod
focus
stand secure
observe
what's figure
what's ground
how light passes through the lens
substance
vibrations
all that passes between

two speakers
left & right
stereo
cantatas fugues lieder variations
signals pulses recorded long ago
the crackling analog medium
where I sit to absorb the music's flow
I am
the center of attention
he is to she as I am to me
the third implied by a couplet
us
neither body nor name
their fictional unity
the stinking pile
the words
the mugs
an object's indifference to language
& that entity compelled to possess it
a thirdness

always standing apart
a reflection of a reflection

how
the nose shines
in the mirror
&

what stares out
from large pores
messy introspection
with its gooey revelations

he senses
the pain of separation
as both the glue & the glitter

she feels
how glamour withholds
to accrue power

on the surface of an oily residue
questions posing while answers lay to rest

boilers explode
heat costs
sinuses dry
a season
the most difficult to survive
between fall & spring
between sacred & profane
melodies rise then fall
coughing is a form of punctuation
it separates
the world's catastrophes

still
what exists outside the frame
is all
all of it
together
not one
though it is possible to conceive
there is no necessary meaning
only manifold embodiments
all multiplied by a factor of one
and then divided

matter occupies different states

boiler on
plumbing
preoccupations
sweat blood cum puss tears
along with their notions
their words

materials become properties by the way their sounds penetrate solid masses

she wakes from sleep in another room
the city where he lives remains secret
she stirs
he writes
utter anxiety
warming itself into paralysis
reflective self-describing piety

as if the words themselves constitute
the very meaning of society
glimpsed in solitude by analysis

meanwhile
food is broken down into sugar
& all theories become the embarrassing pleasure of gossip

excitations are drawn from analogies
ideas are both proximate & different
like
tea is gentle and coffee is harsh
look

I'm trying to show how conjunctions yield new substances
they release words from referents
they make distinctions
they are distinctions
in theory
cock pussy both adheres & sticks does pain
rough edges cut objects token actions
pussy cock lives alone lies down lays claim
steel fruit-bearing side-shoot tickles friction
pussy cock pussy cock pussy cock
embrace abandon predilections
cough
to whom from whom & when was I the first

consult bank calendars
enact festivities
bare trees
pine & cedar
burning logs
cough
each book is the same book
always red
cough cough
between the covers
conjugation wrestles zero tension

O eccentric motor of my desire
gyre shaped word sound exclamation
wood knot & would not scrawling civilize
mechanical hypnotic gyration
between whole & hole he lives he dies
he who's despondent seeks confusion

learn the ancient science
learn all the -ologies
drink more
shake loose from the vine
enlightenment

fine wine
divine
define
all rhymes

genesis Adam Eve knowledge fruit tree
tannenbaum candle lights ornaments
religion
seasons
& how they're changing
the worried look of a Christmas shopper

the theme here is panic

how the rooms of an apartment differ
silently
you find your way
to the bathroom at night

gyroscopes orientations night-lights
what governs bodies sets them in motion

messages go astray

I am the impersonal nature of a broadcast
I am back ache
carpal tunnel syndrome
eye strain
I am
what the closet is to the ensemble
a case for twisted fabrics &
abandoned single socks
I am
what leg wounds are to the furniture edges
the late night urination & constant thirst

cough

sometimes what's brought together won't rhyme

the theme is proportion of parts to whole

where labor compresses flour water & eggs
what's sustenance to the weary soul
her him whoever stands on two legs
is there more than breathing?
what's the goal?

I'm thankful for a thick slice of buttered bread

sigh

what lies beneath clumsy compliments
expectations
stolen glances
glimpsed peripheries
shadow figures vague threats arguments
repressed thoughts
too scary

what I thought
when I said it
we meant I

coincidences occur as a matter of pronouns
because
I & you don't always correspond
we combine words from limited supplies
consult PONS then press send
we are often surprised by others' replies

we try to bring old friendships to common ends
relations can without warning
like
two lines together sometimes accord
in space
though parallel lines never combine

asymmetry is the theme

among friends
do we require consensus for dinner?
do we all share the same portion?

each must be his or her own translator

where two men wearing ties can share jokes
mind mood murder sentiment sediment
violent combinations stirred cold
cereals serial predicament

violet morning mourning marigold
continuums temperaments senses
age wrinkles pillow creases fabric folds
how
people aggregate around feeding
words organize crowds into groups

farming & framing
slippers slippages
vegetations vivid variegations
alarmed & tamed flippant diligent
morel mushrooms
moral values
potions

the theme is distance
the theme is writing

a calm ocean

millions connect remotely

when words are the substance of attachments
where words & swear words incite excite I
sip wine eat melon with prosciutto
evening
window whining winding
finalizing

cello music
charm
chiaroscuro

varying shades of light & dark
form whole
Biblical stories
thinly painted
faces in Baroque pictures
drapery folds
suffering martyrs
& saints
cross-dressing models
swapping gender roles
where does the emotion reside?
in the painter
in the painting
in the viewer
staring holes
into the walls

you noticed red
in the shadows
feeling a
here
made now
by what's gone
there

what's here
made gone
now
by there
a
feeling

now
by
what's there
made here
a feeling
gone

where the sun
and the moon
both occupy the sky
a gardener kneels
to cultivate
a unique religion

The title of this poem is a line taken from "Homecoming," a poem by
Paul Celan, translated by Michael Hamburger.

Vienna, Berlin, Chicago, 2007–12

From a Broken Bottle Traces of Perfume Still Emanate, Volume Five

Nathaniel Mackey

24.IX.83

Dear Angel of Dust,

More balloons last night. It was during a Coltrane birthday concert we took part in at the Century City Playhouse. A number of bands played, the usual suspects from around town: Badi Taqsim's trio, the Boneyard Brass Octet, SunStick and the Chosen Few, etc. We played a couple of pieces, "Sun Ship" and "Sekhet Aaru Struff." It was our first public performance of "Sekhet Aaru Struff" and it was during this piece that the balloons emerged. It was actually, to be more precise, during a section toward the end of the piece that was a bit of a detour, a turn toward rumba initiated by Drennette.

We'd been talking about rumba earlier in the day, listening to and talking about an album by Totico y Sus Rumberos that came out a couple of years ago, so the turn Drennette initiated didn't entirely come as a surprise. Their rendition of "What's Your Name?," the old doo-wop hit by Don and Juan, had especially caught our attention, getting us going on the mesh between doo-wop's mellifluous come-on and rumba's courtship mimetics. Exactly how apt or effective a mesh it is was what we discussed, opinions ranging from endorsement, even outright rave, a claim that the merger isn't only beautiful but long overdue and that the piece is the best on the album by far (Penguin), to reservations regarding the advisedness of literalizing what's otherwise more subtle, productively so, otherwise more dynamically understated (Drennette).

It wasn't entirely a surprise, then, as I've said, when Penguin came to the end of his recitation and Drennette began to beat out a guaguancó rhythm on the conga, not only beating out the guaguancó but singing a lalaleo or diana, the introductory song-syllables "ana na na ana, ana na na ana," which in fact made the detour less jarring, contributing to and thereby continuing Lambert and Penguin's theme or thread of universal patois. Soon after finishing the lalaleo, however, she sped things up, switching from guaguancó to giribilla, a more strictly musical, non-mimetic form that has been called the bebop of rumba variations.

Aunt Nancy was the first to respond to Drennette's detour, letting the bounding figure go and imitating, in the bass's upper register, a segundo's giribilla pattern. Djamilaa's synthesizer turned its interred oratorio into a chorus answering Drennette's lalaleo, a bank of antiphonal echoes Djamilaa granted galactic reverb, intergalactic reach. I temporized for a few measures before letting my sputters give way to a golden run worthy of Chocolate Armenteros, but it was Lambert who most decisively responded to Drennette's detour. Removing the clothespins from his lips and putting them in his coat pocket (the clothespins, by the way, had drawn laughter from several people in the audience when the piece began but they'd gotten used to them and quieted down), he picked up his tenor, put it to his mouth, and motioned for me to pull back.

Lambert began by going back to the sputter my golden run had come out of, blowing a barrage of expectorant bleats and pops not unlike an attack of hiccups. Beginning there, he indeed never left, thriving on what sounded like obstruction even as he ran the gamut from belly laughs at the horn's low end to a wistful quizzicality in the upper register that at times took him to the spoons. More than Totico's "What's Your Name?" he appeared to have Frank Lowe's "Broadway Rhumba" in mind, rummaging around the horn as though it were a hot potato or a goose's neck or as though it were a clothespin pinching his tongue. He sustained a blustery tone, bursting, it seemed, with things to say, albeit more things than could be said, it seemed. It was during this solo that the balloons emerged, the first of them lifting heavily up out of the bell of the horn bearing these words: *An Egyptian rumba she said it would be, abstract, angular, undulant, pulse beaten out on a salted cod box, an Egyptian giribilla she said it would be. No BaKongo cloth kicked in a circle, no guaguancó, no lifted skirt edge, no not being caught by the vacunao. A giribilla, no euphemistic vaccine, she said it would be, an Egyptian rumba, ardent, austere.*

Following the first balloon's emergence Lambert took a more confidential tack, sputtering as before but as if under his breath, resorting to the sotto voce forage he pursues to such resounding effect. It was a more gauzy sound but one with which he parsed not a whit less, having no less recourse to angles, inversions, and reversals, breaking *rumba* apart, it seemed at points, and by turns putting *ba* before *rum* and putting *rum* before *ba*, an Egypto-Caribbean conjugation having to do with soul (spirits' bearing on soul, soul's bearing on spirits). It was at one such point that the second balloon came out of the horn bearing these words: *"Isis to his Osiris, I dreamt he stayed inside me all night, forever, stiff, unyielding," she said. "Damsel in distress, dread virgin, I lay scared stiff. Isisn't to my own Isis, stiff but not unyielding, I lay afraid, flat as a board beneath his weight."* The balloon disappeared when Lambert, put upon by a strain of quizzicality stronger than any that had come before, paused ever so slightly. When he resumed playing the third balloon floated up from the bell of the horn bearing these words: *"I lay afraid but unafraid, feigning frailty," she said, "stiffness answering stiffness, yielding even so, faux fragility stiffening him throughout all eternity. Stiff intruder I welcomed in and regaled with my own stiffness, he likes it when I start off stiff and begin to loosen."*

After the third balloon's emergence Lambert stepped back from the mike, let the balloon vanish, and put his tenor back in its stand, the audience applauding loudly. Drennette ever so subtly blushed, as though the balloons had peeped her heart of hearts, but she held her head higher than before, her back straighter than before. She let go of the giribilla pattern, Aunt Nancy returned to the bounding figure, I came back in on trumpet, and we took the piece out, the audience applauding loudly still.

As ever,

N.

4.X.83

Dear Angel of Dust,

I wouldn't say I'm taking a page out of the balloons' book, that I'm trying to beat them at their own game. Aunt Nancy suggested as much but I don't think that's it. No, this new thing I'm trying goes back to a story Yusef Lateef tells about the days when he was in Mingus's band, a story I was deeply struck by when I first heard it, a story I think about from time to time. Yusef says there was a composition on which he was to solo and that Mingus, rather than writing out chord symbols for him to improvise against, drew a picture of a coffin, that it was this that he was to base his improvisation on. A friend of mine once joked that Mingus simply meant that if Yusef messed up the solo he'd kill him, but I've long been intrigued by and attracted to the idea of getting musical information from a picture, and it's this that led me to a certain experiment with my latest composition. Braxton's diagrammatic, picto-grammic titles and the solo concert of his I caught a couple of years ago, the scores for which looked like pen-and-ink drawings, nonfigurative but drawings even so, had a role as well.

The new composition is called "Fossil Flow." I wrote it thinking about oil spills, the increasing number of them and the damage they do. Just this year there've been two massive ones: in February, the Nowruz Field platform in Iran spilled 80 million gallons of oil into the Persian Gulf; in August, a Spanish tanker, the *Castillo de Bellver*, caught fire and spilled 78 million gallons off the coast of Cape Town, South Africa. I was thinking about the distant past (prehistoric apocalypse, collapse, or catastrophe) achieving fluidity, the oxy-moronic play between fossil and flow of such dimension as to put the present at risk. It's as though it were the dinosaurs' and the mastodons' revenge, prehistory's grudge against what came after, a brief against preservation or containment, fossil solidity, an entropic brief against past and present keeping their places. It's as though, Dredj-like, I saw solidity's hand and solubility's hand, gripped though they were by each other, holding history's hand, leading the way as it broke. Or was it, oil and water notoriously not mixing, solidity's hand and insolubility's hand? I'm not sure it matters. Recalling the rationing and the long lines at gas stations a few years ago, I saw dependency's hand and depletion's hand take solidity's hand and (in)solubility's hand's places, presided over by an entropic sun.

Much of the piece is written out but I'm trying something new, something of a built-in improvisation approach, by leaving gaps at various points in everyone's parts, gaps of a certain number of measures (which varies) marked by the words "Wild Card." The latter refer to a drawing and text with which each musician is provided, a 9-by-12-inch posterboard "card" on which he or she is to base what he or she plays at that point. I'm enclosing a copy. As you can see, the "card" consists of a drawing, captioned "Molimo m'Atet's Figurehead Consoled on the Revival Bench," beneath which is a brief para-graph. I struggled over whether or not to include the latter, fearing it might be spelling things out too much, taking away from the suggestiveness of the

drawing. I decided in favor of keeping it, realizing that it adds a suggestiveness of its own, that words, regardless of how much they point or specify,
can't altogether escape indefiniteness or inference, that, indeed, specifica-
tion has a way of being shadowed by implication. What, for example, is to be
musically made of the fact that the figurehead's ribs show, simply enough, in
the drawing but also show, in an augmented, not so simple way, in the words
"visible, as were the planks of the ship's busted hull"?

 I'm also enclosing a tape. Let me know what you think.

 Yours,

 N.

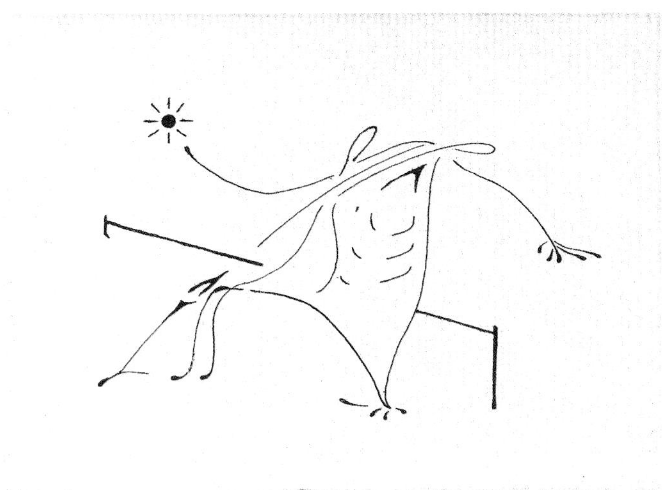

Molimo m'Atet's Figurehead Consoled on the Revival Bench

An oil tanker had run aground farther up the coast and broken apart. Brothers in black before
they knew it, B'Loon and Djbouche washed ashore with the news of the spill. People gathered
on the beach to help clean up and help rescue seabirds, oil and tar stuck to their feathers from
alighting on the water or, standing or prancing on the shore, being caught by the tide. Bright
sun and blue sky notwithstanding, the spill cast a pall over everything and everyone, not least of
all the members of Djband, who, likening themselves to a ship, the sun boat of Egyptian belief,
felt as though they too had run aground. Epitomizing the "boat-bodied lightness, light-bodied
bigness" one of them had once extolled, the female figure gracing the prow of the ship they
took themselves to be (the goddess Maat, some said) stepped away, walked ashore, and sat
down on a bench facing the sea, head down, dejected, ribs visible, as were the planks of the
ship's busted hull. Impromptu patron saint of shipwreck, ad hoc angel, Dredj immediately sat
down beside her and put his arm around her, offering comfort, consolation, recondite sun, as if
to look to and be lit by eclipse were the only amenity.

8.X.83

Dear Angel of Dust,

Many thanks for your letter. I appreciate your comments on "Fossil Flow," your reaction to which, I have to admit, I was nervous about. Yes, you heard it right. "Stratified extinction," as you say, does pervade the piece, a tributary distinction between extinction and exhaustion woven in. I'm impressed by your picking up on the "Wild Card" sections of each band member's playing and what about the drawing and/or text informs how he or she plays. Drennette says you're right that the abstract bench Dredj and the figurehead sit on (and, by implication, the abstract revival available to them) particularly caught her eye and especially spoke to her, giving rise to the stroked, retreating figure she has recourse to with brushes that you note a couple of minutes into the piece (not unlike, she agrees, sand pulled away from the shore by a receding wave). You're also right that the "welter of double-reed hustle" Penguin and Lambert get into on oboe and English horn, respectively, the outbreak of metaphysical sweat with its needling or drilling insistence as if to answer a spiritual-materialist clot begging to be cut thru, is one of the places where two players' "Wild Card" sections coincide. And your surmise that Penguin's choppy, shehnai-like drone has to do with a focus on the apparently oil-toed and oil-fingered extremities on the drawing's right side agrees with his account; a meditation, he calls it, upon those extremities' "tarpit premises." Likewise, Lambert's barking, dilated, alto-sounding complaints derived, Lambert says, from an impulse born of both pictorial and textual cues, an impulse to "occupy ribcage arena," as he puts it, those cues being exactly the depiction of and the reference to the figurehead's ribs that you suggest animated his playing at that point. Nothing much else to report. Just a quick thanks for your letter.

As ever,

N.

10.X.83

Dear Angel of Dust,

Penguin seems to have been heartened by the subtle blush the balloons brought to Drennette's face at the Century City Playhouse. It came up as he and I were talking today. "Lambert got it right," he said. "Or should I say the balloons got it right? They blew the whistle on Drennette's fake reticence, ripped away the blasé front she puts up. With all that stuff about the balloons following her home, all but about being stalked or maybe outright about being stalked, she got it right as well, auguring a muse of pursuit and pursuit's engine or draw, reluctance, a ruse of rebuff, a prude poetics." He paused a moment, savoring the thought. "There was more to that blush than met the eye," he resumed. "Her heart's blood flew to her head." It seemed it flew to his as well, for he paused again, subtly blushing at the conceit before going on. "The balloons not only blew the whistle," he then went on. "They let the air, so to speak, out of an inflated self-regard. They all but burst with Drennette's recondite desire to be found out, contested, caught by lordly science alone." He subtly blushed again, inwardly balked, twin to the balking inwardness that was more than met the eye, the prude interiority he took to heart and took heart from, the soul whose mating twin he'd be if he could.

"Just like Lambert likes to say about the griot," Penguin said when he took up speaking again, gazing into the distance as if what he was going to say came from afar, "the balloons, bless their hearts, have a big mouth." He no longer subtly blushed but again he paused. "Drennette's a little bit off," he said when he spoke again. I took him to mean more than he said. I took him to mean the balloons call interiority out, their mouths, insofar as they can be said to have them, open in awe at Drennette's abscondity, her becoming all the more an object of pursuit by not being all there. He sought leverage it struck me. He'd have made B'Loon's wan smile a satchel mouth. He'd have pried B'Loon's wan smile open, ransacked it, anything to get next to Drennette. Confirmation came at once. Penguin repeated, "Drennette's a little bit off," adding, "but the balloons would have none of her not-nearness. They would abide by nothing short of not-nearness beginning to see its end, not-nearness beginning to be sashay."

I could not have seen Penguin more clearly. I saw him in nothing if not namesake light, hallowed by eponymous aura: ripped, wingless bird, wind-afflicted, flightless, devout. "The balloons would know Drennette otherwise," he said, "knowing her by her being a little bit off no longer enough. They would have her no more than two bows' lengths away, no more than an atom's breadth away. The balloons would be her throne and her footstool." He was quietly raving, caught in a low-key agitation, a game of hide-and-seek (hers with him, the balloons' with the band), agnostic stranger, grounded bird.

Still, he would aver what was yet to be seen, given heart by the balloons' intimations. He now spoke explicitly of himself, changing the course it had seemed he was on, contrasting himself with the balloons. "I, however, would know her by her distant footfall, footsteps down a dark hallway, a rustle outside my door." I'd all along taken the balloons to be a stand-in for himself and I continued to see them that way though he now employed them as a foil. He fell silent and I remained silent.

I had said nothing all the while Penguin spoke, and it seemed he expected as much. It was a run of pure devotion, a poem, a paean, an oath.

Yours,

N.

30.X.83

Dear Angel of Dust,

No, it's not that the balloons have gotten into our heads. We're not Maxine Brown, we're not singing "All in My Mind." The problem is that it's not that. It's that the balloons are actually out there and evidently they have a mind of their own. They dwell, as I've said before, in a deep-seated impulse toward caption, a deep-seated captivity they seek to leaven with whimsicality—true to themselves, unable to help themselves, insouciant, insecure. They body forth inflated claims to translatability only to beg off or betray them, burst as balloons at times do. Sometimes they renege before the fact, backtrack in advance, decide not to show up. Sometimes they make themselves known by their absence, a conspicuous reticence one would need to be dead not to notice. But who knows? Maybe even then one would see or sense it, pick up on it somehow. We know they show up camera shy when they do show up. Could the difference between alive and dead be only that shyness?

I've been listening to "Autumn Leaves" on the *Miles Davis in Europe* album, a record I cut my teeth on as a teenager. The vibratory blade Miles uses the mute to make sound into amounts to a balloonlike adjacency, an off-to-the-side reticence or recoil I can't help hearing as recondite presence and manifest absence's mix or mating dance. What but the implications of that sound could be so there but not there, what but the balloons' adjunct agenda, the occult itinerary none but they seem to know but that, possibly, not even they know? Miles's recourse to flutter early on in his solo might be heard as onomatopoeic by some, the "sound" of autumn leaves, falling leaves. I tend to agree but I take it further. We hear the sound, in hearing it so, of a concession to caption, the hovering fall oblique afflatus turns out to be. We hear that concession's glide into an offhand rumble, a sly glide that will agree to caption only to nudge it toward refractoriness, as if *caption* and *captious* were somehow kin. This, moreover, comes of a sound that could not be more introverted, more introspective. Shy sound. Sly.

I'd say don't get me started but you've gotten me started. Listen, then, if you will, to the hover-and-dip, hover-and-dash dexterity Miles brings to that flutter, a not quite flight-of-the-bumblebee élan and agitation, buzz the recondite balloons' masquerade. Falling leaves' equation with not-quite bee flight is nothing if not a fractious caption, a lateral feint bursting with drift and flotation, bordering on tissue paper and comb though it does, nothing if not wind-aided cascade. That he can go, soon after that, from Gatling-gun staccato to quasi-whimper is what I mean by feint, drift, and flotation, a tremulous resolve to be to the side or get to the side of besetment.

Not as blatant as Dizzy's ballooning cheeks, Miles's autumnal bob and weave imparts a balloon salience nonetheless, a balloon detour from Dizzy's overtness and extroversion, a balloon extenuation or, to use Duke's term, extension. I can imagine listening to this track thirty or forty years from now and still finding it fresh, the advent of my own autumnal prospect lending it all the more relevance and resonance, a time-capsule bubble or balloon loaded with decades of what won't tell itself but does, caption after caption donned and auditioned only to be cast off.

Let me know what you think.

Yours,

N.

Excerpted from *From a Broken Bottle Traces of Perfume Still Emanate*, an ongoing series of letters written by the fictional composer/multi-instrumentalist N., founding member of a band known as the Molimo m'Atet. Volumes one through four are *Bedouin Hornbook, Djbot Baghostus's Run, Atet A.D.,* and *Bass Cathedral.* Volume five is not yet titled.

Jaki Byard
Untitled (Fadism), c. 1996
Graphite on sheet music
11 x 8 ½ inches
Courtesy of Diane Byard

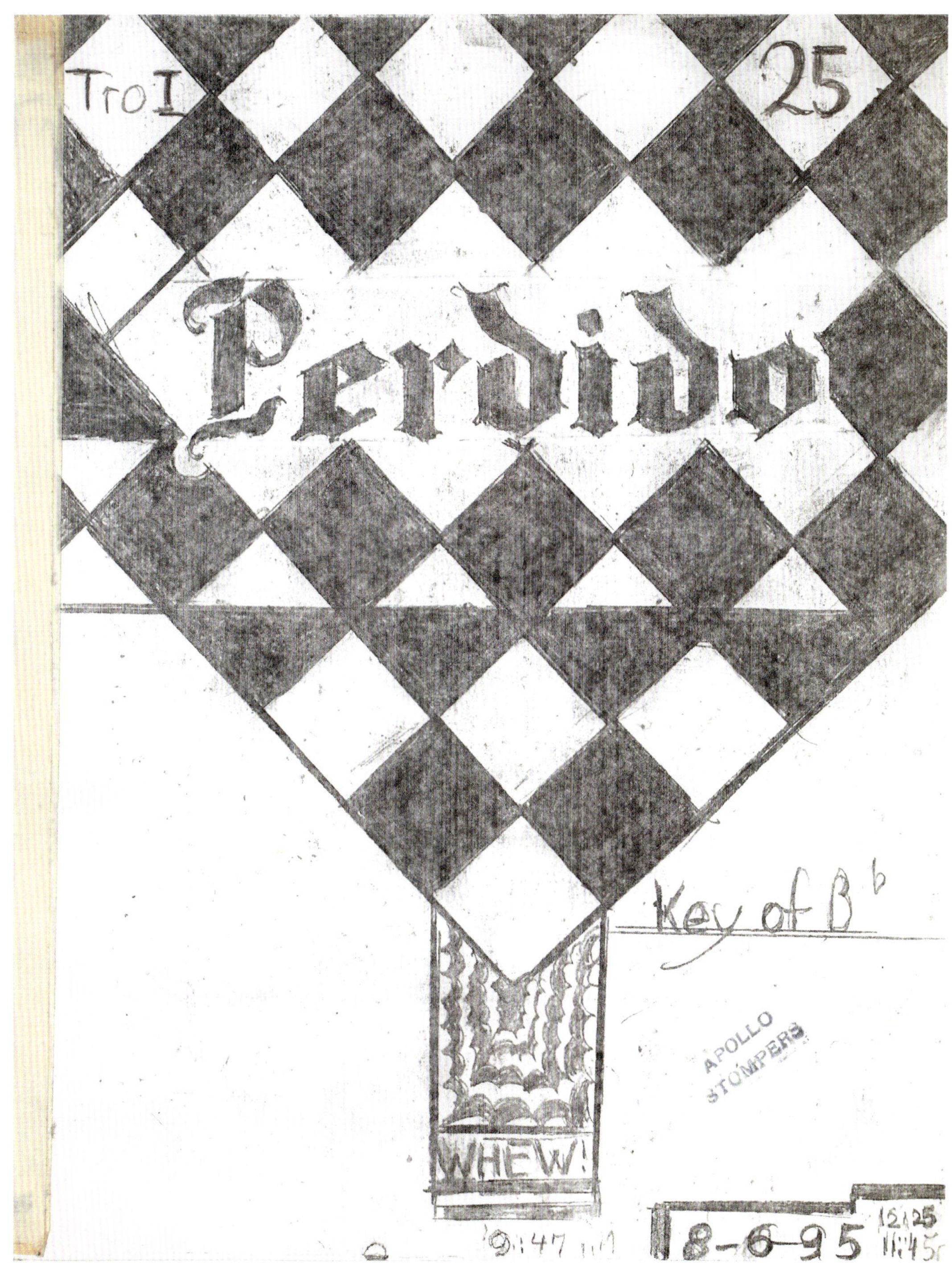

Jaki Byard
Untitled (Perdido), 1995
Graphite on sheet music
11 x 8 ½ inches
Courtesy of Diane Byard

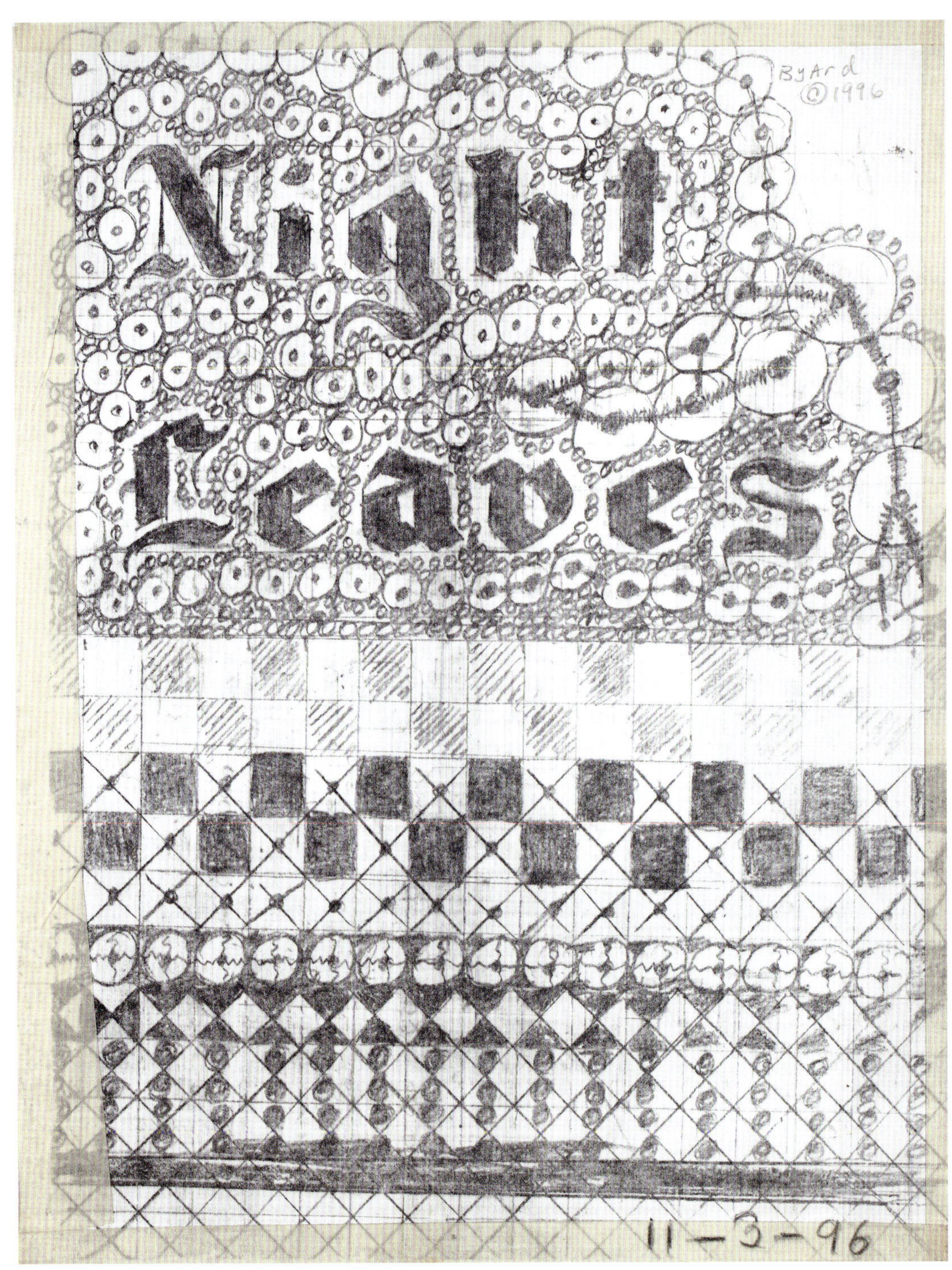

Jaki Byard
Untitled (Night Leaves), 1996
Graphite on sheet music
11 x 8 ¹/₂ inches
Courtesy of Diane Byard

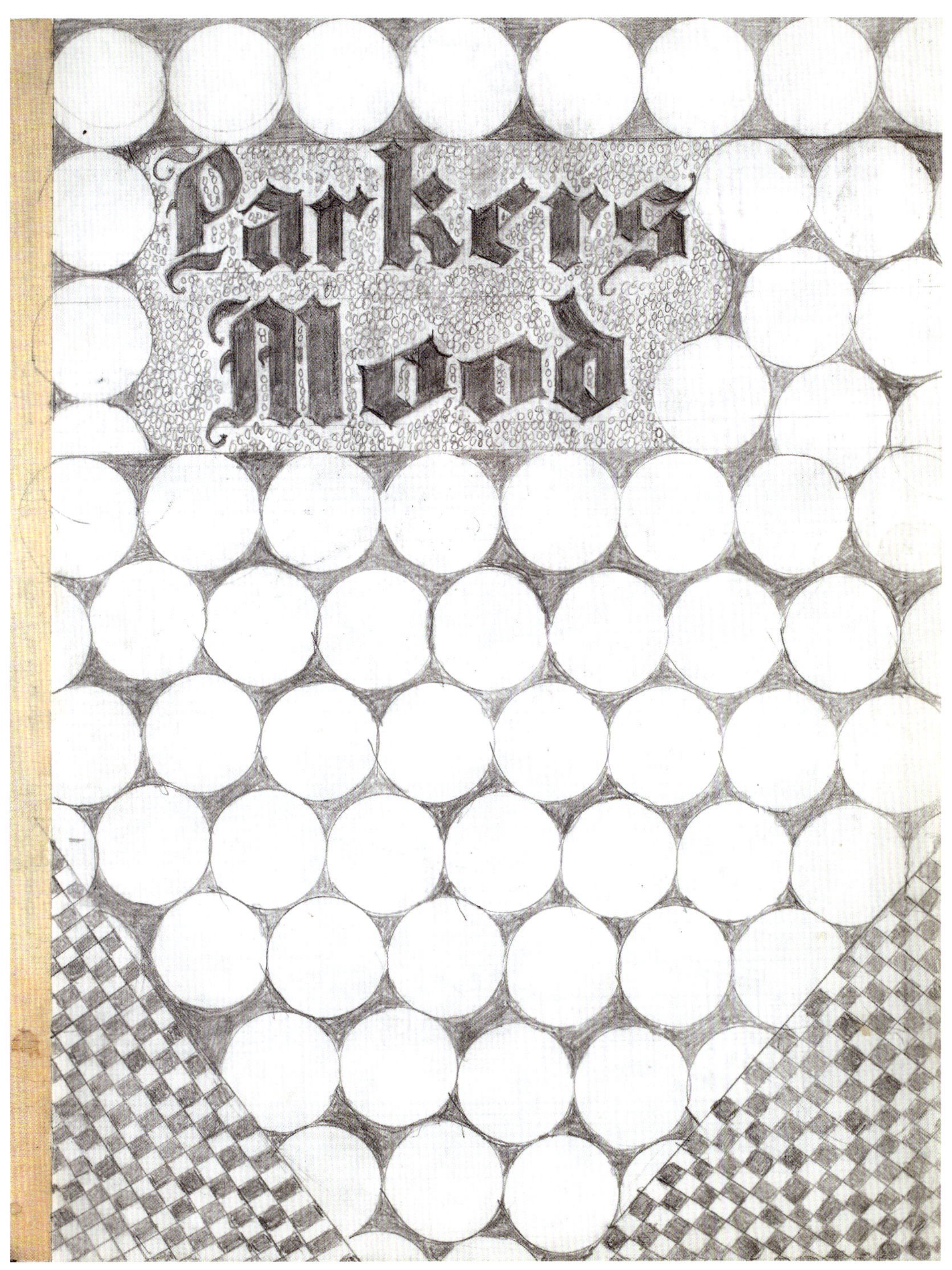

Jaki Byard
Untitled (Parkers Mood), c. 1996
Graphite on sheet music
11 x 8 ¹/₂ inches
Courtesy of Diane Byard

Checklist of the Exhibition

JEAN-MICHEL BASQUIAT
Undiscovered Genius of the Mississippi Delta, 1983
Acrylic, oil-paint stick, and paper collage on canvas
Five panels: 48 x 184 inches overall
The Brant Foundation Inc., Greenwich, Connecticut

ROMARE BEARDEN
Pittsburgh Memory, 1964
Collage of printed papers with graphite on cardboard
8 ¹/₂ x 11 ³/₄ inches
Collection of halley k harrisburg and Michael Rosenfeld, New York

Train Whistle Blues: II, 1964
Collage of various papers with paint and graphite on cardboard
11 x 14 ³/₈ inches
Collection of Robert and Faye Davidson, Los Angeles

Uptown Looking Downtown, 1965
Mixed-media collage on board
11 ³/₄ x 15 ³/₄ inches
Private collection, courtesy of Salon 94, New York

Watching the Trains Go By, c. 1969
Mixed-media collage of various papers and fabric on paperboard, mounted on wood
9 x 12 ¹/₄ inches
Courtesy of Michael Rosenfeld Gallery, New York

Blue Shade, 1972
Collage on Masonite
9 ¹/₂ x 14 inches
Courtesy of Michael Rosenfeld Gallery, New York

GREGG BORDOWITZ
Testing Some Beliefs, 2012
Performance lecture
90 minutes
Courtesy of the artist

MARK BRADFORD
Paris Is Burning, 2010
Mixed-media collage
42 x 200 inches
Private collection, courtesy of the artist and Sikkema Jenkins & Co., New York

EDWARD CLARK
The Stove, 1952
Oil on canvas
44 x 30 inches
Collection of Tom Burrell, Chicago

The Big Egg (Vetheuil Series), 1968
Acrylic on canvas
64 1/2 x 83 inches
Collection of the artist

ROY DECARAVA
117th Street, 1951
Gelatin-silver print
11 x 14 inches
Courtesy of the DeCarava Archives

Billie Holiday, 1952
Gelatin-silver print
14 x 11 inches
Courtesy of the DeCarava Archives

Mary Lou Williams, 1952
Gelatin-silver print
11 x 14 inches
Courtesy of the DeCarava Archives

Shirley embracing Sam, 1952
Gelatin-silver print
14 x 11 inches
Courtesy of the DeCarava Archives

Couple dancing, 1953
Gelatin-silver print
14 x 11 inches
Courtesy of the DeCarava Archives

Hallway, New York, 1953
Gelatin-silver print
14 x 11 inches
Courtesy of the DeCarava Archives

Two couples dancing, group at table, 1953
Gelatin-silver print
11 x 14 inches
Courtesy of the DeCarava Archives

Dancers, New York, 1956
Gelatin-silver print
14 x 11 inches
Courtesy of the DeCarava Archives

Coltrane #24, 1961
Gelatin-silver print
14 x 11 inches
Courtesy of the DeCarava Archives

Coltrane #27, 1961
Gelatin-silver print
14 x 11 inches
Courtesy of the DeCarava Archives

Coltrane looking, 1961
Gelatin-silver print
14 x 11 inches
Courtesy of the DeCarava Archives

Coltrane playing, 1961
Gelatin-silver print
14 x 11 inches
Courtesy of the DeCarava Archives

Trees and subway entrance, 1979
Gelatin-silver print
11 x 14 inches
Courtesy of the DeCarava Archives

Silver fence, 1983
Gelatin-silver print
11 x 14 inches
Courtesy of the DeCarava Archives

Curved branch, 1994
Gelatin-silver print
11 x 14 inches
Courtesy of the DeCarava Archives

BEAUFORD DELANEY
Portrait of a Young Musician, n.d.
Acrylic on canvas
51 x 38 inches
The Studio Museum in Harlem, gift of Ms. Ogust Delaney Stewart, Knoxville, Tennessee

James Baldwin, c. 1955
Oil on canvas board
24 x 18 inches
Private collection, courtesy of Michael Rosenfeld Gallery, New York

Untitled, c. 1958
Oil on canvas
57 ¹/₂ x 45 inches
Courtesy of Michael Rosenfeld Gallery, New York

Portrait of Charlie Parker, 1968
Oil on canvas
28 ³/₄ x 23 ¹/₂ inches
Courtesy of Michael Rosenfeld Gallery, New York

Portrait of Jean Genet, 1972
Oil on canvas
36 ¹/₄ x 28 ³/₄ inches
Courtesy of Michael Rosenfeld Gallery, New York

JEFF DONALDSON
Jampact and Jelly Tite (for Jamila), 1988
Mixed media on canvas
38 x 50 inches
Collection of Jameela Donaldson

STAN DOUGLAS
Hors-champs, 1992
Two-channel video installation with stereo sound
13:40 minutes
Courtesy of the artist

JIMMIE DURHAM
Caliban Codex, 1992
Pencil on paper
Fifteen drawings: 20 $^{13}/_{16}$ x 14 $^{3}/_{16}$
inches each
Collection of Herman J. Daled, Brussels

Untitled (Caliban Mask), 1992
Glass eyes, button, mud, PVC pipe, and glue
9 $^{7}/_{16}$ x 6 $^{1}/_{8}$ x 1 $^{7}/_{8}$ inches
Private collection, Topenga, California, courtesy
of L.A. Louver, Venice, California

MELVIN EDWARDS
Ame Eghan, 1975
Welded steel
12 $^{1}/_{2}$ x 19 $^{1}/_{2}$ x 19 $^{1}/_{2}$ inches
Courtesy of the artist and Alexander Gray
Associates, New York

Fire Blossom, 1991
Welded steel
17 $^{1}/_{2}$ x 13 x 9 $^{1}/_{2}$ inches
Collection of Joel Wachs

Write When You Can, 1991
Welded steel
13 x 10 $^{1}/_{2}$ x 8 inches
Courtesy of the artist and Alexander Gray
Associates, New York

WILLIAM EGGLESTON
Untitled (Morton, Mississippi), c. 1970/2012
Pigment print
20 x 16 inches
Courtesy of the artist and Gagosian Gallery

Untitled (Near Morton, Mississippi),
c. 1970/2012
Pigment print
16 x 20 inches
Courtesy of the artist and Gagosian Gallery

Untitled (Sumner, Mississippi),
c. 1970/2012
Pigment print
16 x 20 inches
Courtesy of the artist and Gagosian Gallery

Untitled, c. 1972/2012
Pigment print
16 x 20 inches
Courtesy of the artist and Gagosian Gallery

Untitled (Eudora Welty's Kitchen),
c. 1982–85
Pigment print
20 x 16 inches
Courtesy of the artist and Gagosian Gallery

*Untitled (Gathering Place at Holly
Springs, Mississippi)*, c. 1982–85
Pigment print
16 x 20 inches
Courtesy of the artist and Gagosian Gallery

Untitled (Holly Springs, Mississippi),
c. 1982–85
Pigment print
20 x 16 inches
Courtesy of the artist and Gagosian Gallery

Untitled (Memphis, Krystal), c. 1982–85
Pigment print
20 x 16 inches
Courtesy of the artist and Gagosian Gallery

Untitled (Near Oxford, Mississippi),
c. 1982–85
Pigment print
16 x 20 inches
Courtesy of the artist and Gagosian Gallery

Untitled (Mississippi), 1992
Pigment print
20 x 16 inches
Courtesy of the artist and Gagosian Gallery

CHARLES GAINES
Untitled (Regression Series: Group 2),
1973–74
Mechanical ink and pen on paper
Seven drawings: 23 x 29 inches each
Courtesy of the artist and Susanne Vielmetter Los
Angeles Projects

Untitled (Regression Series: Group 3),
1973–74
Mechanical ink and pen on paper
Seven drawings: 23 x 29 inches each
Courtesy of the artist and Susanne Vielmetter Los
Angeles Projects

RENÉE GREEN
Import/Export Funk Office, 1992–93
Installation with audio, video, and reading
materials
Dimensions variable
The Museum of Contemporary Art, Los Angeles,
gift of Gaby and Wilhelm Schürmann

DAVID HAMMONS
Chasing the Blue Train, 1989
Mixed media
Dimensions variable
Stedelijk Museum voor Actuele Kunst (S.M.A.K.),
Ghent, Belgium

Rocky, 1990
Stone, hair, and wire
37 x 13 x 13 inches
Eileen Harris Norton Collection

KIRA LYNN HARRIS
Untitled, 2012
Mixed-media installation
Dimensions variable
Courtesy of the artist

Untitled, 2012
Mixed-media installation
Dimensions variable
Courtesy of the artist

RACHEL HARRISON
Hoarders, 2012
Chicken wire, cement, acrylic paint, metal pail,
flatscreen monitor, wireless headphones, video,
and purple runway carpet
Sculpture: 61 x 47 x 45 inches; overall dimensions
variable
Courtesy of the artist and Greene Naftali Gallery,
New York

Untitled, 2012
Colored pencil on paper
19 x 24 inches
Courtesy of the artist and Greene Naftali Gallery,
New York

Untitled, 2012
Colored pencil on paper
19 x 24 inches
Courtesy of the artist and Greene Naftali Gallery,
New York

Untitled, 2012
Colored pencil on paper
19 x 24 inches
Courtesy of the artist and Greene Naftali Gallery,
New York

Untitled, 2012
Colored pencil on paper
19 x 24 inches
Courtesy of the artist and Greene Naftali Gallery,
New York

BARKLEY L. HENDRICKS

Something Like a Bird Double Barbara,
1982
Oil, acrylic, and variegated leaf on canvas
66 x 72 inches
Courtesy of the artist and Jack Shainman Gallery,
New York

LESLIE HEWITT

Riffs on Real Time (1 of 10), 2006–9
C-print
30 x 24 inches
Courtesy of the artist and Sikkema Jenkins & Co.,
New York

Riffs on Real Time (2 of 10), 2006–9
C-print
30 x 24 inches
Courtesy of the artist and Sikkema Jenkins & Co.,
New York

Riffs on Real Time (3 of 10), 2006–9
C-print
30 x 24 inches
Courtesy of the artist and Sikkema Jenkins & Co.,
New York

Riffs on Real Time (4 of 10), 2006–9
C-print
30 x 24 inches
Courtesy of the artist and Sikkema Jenkins & Co.,
New York

Riffs on Real Time (5 of 10), 2006–9
C-print
24 x 30 inches
Courtesy of the artist and Sikkema Jenkins & Co.,
New York

Riffs on Real Time (6 of 10), 2006–9
C-print
24 x 30 inches
Courtesy of the artist and Sikkema Jenkins & Co.,
New York

Riffs on Real Time (7 of 10), 2006–9
C-print
30 x 24 inches
Courtesy of the artist and Sikkema Jenkins & Co.,
New York

Riffs on Real Time (8 of 10), 2006–9
C-print
30 x 24 inches
Courtesy of the artist and Sikkema Jenkins & Co.,
New York

Riffs on Real Time (9 of 10), 2006–9
C-print
30 x 24 inches
Courtesy of the artist and Sikkema Jenkins & Co.,
New York

Riffs on Real Time (10 of 10), 2006–9
C-print
30 x 24 inches
Courtesy of the artist and Sikkema Jenkins & Co.,
New York

MARTIN KIPPENBERGER

New York von der Bronx ausgesehen
(New York Seen from the Bronx), 1985
Bronze
60 $^5/_8$ x 9 $^7/_8$ x 9 $^7/_8$ inches
The Museum of Contemporary Art, Los Angeles,
partial and promised gift of Blake Byrne

Martin, ab in die Ecke und schäm dich
(Martin, Into the Corner, You Should Be
Ashamed of Yourself), 1992
Cast aluminum, clothing, and iron plate
71 $^1/_2$ x 29 $^1/_2$ x 13 $^1/_2$ inches
The Museum of Modern Art, New York, Blanchette
Hooker Rockefeller Fund Bequest, Anna Mari and
Robert F. Shapiro, Jerry I. Speyer, and Michael and
Judy Ovitz Funds, 1992

JUTTA KOETHER

100% (Portrait Robert Johnson), 1990
Oil on canvas
Diptych: 59 $^{13}/_{16}$ x 27 $^3/_{16}$ inches each
Courtesy of the artist and Galerie Daniel Buchholz,
Berlin/Cologne

LIZ LARNER

No M, No D, Only S & B, 1990
Leather, sand, brass zipper, and waxed cotton
thread
36 x 48 x 60 inches
Private collection

Lux Interior (gold plated), 2010
Cast bronze with gold patina
11 x 8 $^1/_2$ x 6 inches
Courtesy of the artist and Regen Projects,
Los Angeles

Octan, 2012
Ceramic and epoxy
39 $^1/_2$ x 24 x 6 inches
Courtesy of the artist and Regen Projects,
Los Angeles

ZOE LEONARD

Untitled, 1994–97
Banana peels, orange peels, stickers, and thread
Dimensions variable
Courtesy of the artist and Galerie Gisela Capitain,
Cologne

1961, 2002–ongoing
Suitcases
Dimensions variable
Courtesy of the artist and Galerie Gisela Capitain,
Cologne

GLENN LIGON

No Room (Gold) #10, 2007
Oil and acrylic on canvas
32 x 32 inches
Courtesy of the artist and Regen Projects,
Los Angeles

No Room (Gold) #12, 2007
Oil and acrylic on canvas
32 x 32 inches
Eileen Harris Norton Collection

No Room (Gold) #15, 2007
Oil and acrylic on canvas
32 x 32 inches
Collection of Shaun Caley Regen, Los Angeles

No Room (Gold) #20, 2007
Oil and acrylic on canvas
32 x 32 inches
Courtesy of the artist and Regen Projects,
Los Angeles

No Room (Gold) #21, 2007
Oil and acrylic on canvas
32 x 32 inches
Courtesy of the artist and Regen Projects,
Los Angeles

No Room (Gold) #22, 2007
Oil and acrylic on canvas
32 x 32 inches
Courtesy of the artist and Regen Projects,
Los Angeles

No Room (Gold) #24, 2007
Oil and acrylic on canvas
32 x 32 inches
Collection of Eugene Sadovoy, Bel Air, California

No Room (Gold) #30, 2007
Oil and acrylic on canvas
32 x 32 inches
Courtesy of the artist and Regen Projects,
Los Angeles

No Room (Gold) #32, 2007
Oil and acrylic on canvas
32 x 32 inches
Collection of Peter Gelles and Eve Steele,
Los Angeles

No Room (Gold) #36, 2007
Oil and acrylic on canvas
32 x 32 inches
Collection of Dallas Price-Van Breda and Bob Van
Breda, Los Angeles

No Room (Gold) #42, 2007
Oil and acrylic on canvas
32 x 32 inches
Courtesy of the artist and Regen Projects,
Los Angeles

KERRY JAMES MARSHALL
Blue Water Silver Moon (Mermaid), 1991
Acrylic and collage on linen
63 x 55 inches
Collection of JoAnn Busuttil, Los Angeles

Souvenir IV, 1998
Acrylic, paper, collage, and glitter on
unstretched canvas
108 x 156 inches
Whitney Museum of American Art, New York,
purchase with funds from the Painting and
Sculpture Committee

BARBARA MCCULLOUGH
*Water Ritual #1: An Urban Rite of
Purification*, 1979
Video; black-and-white and sound
4 minutes
Courtesy of the artist

DAVE MCKENZIE
Portrait as a Ghost, 2004
Clay and paint
2 $^{1}/_{2}$ x 2 x 2 inches
Collection of Bonnie Serkin, Portland

Fear and Trembling, 2009
Conveyer, hanger with text, plastic, timer, and
remote control
73 x 73 x 30 inches
Miller Meigs Collection

Yesterday's Newspaper, 2012
Walnut pedestal and day-old newspaper
20 $^{1}/_{2}$ x 12 x 12 inches
Courtesy of the artist, Susanne Vielmetter Los
Angeles Projects, and Galerie Wien Lukatsch,
Berlin

RODNEY MCMILLIAN
From Asterisks in Dockery, 2012
Mixed-media installation
Dimensions variable
Courtesy of the artist and Susanne Vielmetter
Los Angeles Projects

MARK MORRISROE
Jack with Parakeet and Watching Cats,
c. 1980s
C-print
19 $^{15}/_{16}$ x 15 $^{15}/_{16}$ inches
Whitney Museum of American Art, New York, gift
of Barbara and Eugene Schwartz

Untitled, c. 1981
Gum print
24 $^{15}/_{16}$ x 20 $^{7}/_{8}$ inches
The Estate of Mark Morrisroe (Ringier Collection)
at Fotomuseum Winterthur

Untitled, 1981/84
Silver dye bleach print
19 $^{15}/_{16}$ x 16 inches
Whitney Museum of American Art, New York,
purchase, with funds from the Photography
Committee

*I Dream of Jeanne (Stephen Tashjian's
Head)*, 1983
Silver dye bleach print
20 x 16 inches
Whitney Museum of American Art, New York,
purchase, with funds from the Photography
Committee

*Still Life in the Home of Stephen
Tashjian*, 1985
C-print, negative sandwich
20 x 15 $^{15}/_{16}$ inches
The Estate of Mark Morrisroe (Ringier Collection)
at Fotomuseum Winterthur

Untitled, 1985
C-print
19 $^{7}/_{8}$ x 15 $^{7}/_{8}$ inches
Whitney Museum of American Art, New York,
gift of Barbara and Eugene Schwartz

Untitled, 1985
C-print
22 $^{1}/_{4}$ x 18 $^{1}/_{8}$ inches
Whitney Museum of American Art,
New York, purchase, with funds from
the Photography Committee

Untitled, 1985
C-print
15 $^{15}/_{16}$ x 19 $^{15}/_{16}$ inches
Whitney Museum of American Art,
New York, gift of Pat Hearn Gallery

Dried Arrangement, c. 1986
C-print
15 $^{15}/_{16}$ x 19 $^{15}/_{16}$ inches
Whitney Museum of American Art, New York,
gift of Barbara and Eugene Schwartz

*Blow Both of Us, Gail Thacker and Me,
Summer 1978*, 1986
C-print, negative sandwich, retouched
with ink and inscribed with marker
15 $^{15}/_{16}$ x 15 $^{15}/_{16}$ inches
The Estate of Mark Morrisroe (Ringier Collection)
at Fotomuseum Winterthur

Dismal Boston Skyline, 1986
C-print, negative sandwich, retouched
with ink
15 $^{15}/_{16}$ x 19 $^{15}/_{16}$ inches
The Estate of Mark Morrisroe (Ringier Collection)
at Fotomuseum Winterthur

Light and Shadow, 1986
C-print, negative sandwich, retouched
with ink and inscribed with marker
19 $^{15}/_{16}$ x 15 $^{15}/_{16}$ inches
The Estate of Mark Morrisroe (Ringier Collection)
at Fotomuseum Winterthur

Sweet Raspberry, Spanish Madonna,
1986
C-print
19 $^{15}/_{16}$ x 16 inches
Whitney Museum of American Art,
New York, purchase, with funds from
the Photography Committee

Untitled, c. 1987
Toned gelatin-silver print, photogram of X-ray
10 $^{7}/_{8}$ x 14 inches
The Estate of Mark Morrisroe (Ringier Collection)
at Fotomuseum Winterthur

Untitled, c. 1987
C-print, photogram
14 x 11 inches
The Estate of Mark Morrisroe (Ringier Collection)
at Fotomuseum Winterthur

Untitled, 1988
C-print, negative sandwich
19 $^{15}/_{16}$ x 15 $^{15}/_{16}$ inches
The Estate of Mark Morrisroe (Ringier Collection)
at Fotomuseum Winterthur

MATT MULLICAN
Untitled (Birth to Death List), 1973
Ink on paper
51 $^{3}/_{16}$ x 14 inches
Courtesy of the artist and Mai36 Galerie, Zurich

Untitled (Birth to Death List), 1978
Silkscreen on Fabriano paper
66 $^{1}/_{8}$ x 15 $^{3}/_{4}$ inches
Private collection, Switzerland

SENGA NENGUDI
R.S.V.P., 1975
Nylon mesh and sand
82 $\frac{1}{2}$ x 113 $\frac{1}{2}$ x 4 $\frac{1}{2}$ inches
The Museum of Contemporary Art, Los Angeles,
purchased with funds provided by the Acquisition
and Collection Committee

KORI NEWKIRK
Yall, 2012
Mixed-media installation
Dimensions variable
Courtesy of the artist

LORRAINE O'GRADY
*Body/Ground (The Clearing: Or Cortez
and La Malinche, Thomas Jefferson and
Sally Hemings, N. and Me)*, 1991/2012
Gelatin-silver print (photomontage)
Diptych: 40 x 50 inches each
Courtesy of the artist and Alexander Gray
Associates, New York

Landscape (Western Hemisphere),
2010–11
Video projection; black-and-white and sound
18 minutes
Courtesy of the artist and Alexander Gray
Associates, New York

JOHN OUTTERBRIDGE
California Crosswalk, 1979
Metal, wire, cloth, and mixed media
28 x 36 x 72 inches
California African American Museum, CAAM
Foundation Purchase, with funds provided by the
City of Los Angeles, Cultural Affairs Department

ADRIAN PIPER
Aspects of the Liberal Dilemma, 1978
Gelatin-silver print framed under Plexiglas,
audiotape, and lighting
18 x 18 inches
University of California, Berkeley Art Museum and
Pacific Film Archive, gift of the Peter Norton Family
Foundation

WILLIAM POPE.L
Skin Set Drawings, 2001–5
Mixed media on paper
Twenty drawings: 11 x 8 $\frac{1}{2}$ inches each
The Museum of Contemporary Art, Los Angeles,
purchased with funds provided by the Drawings
Committee

JEFF PREISS
STOP, 1995–2012
16mm film on SD video; color and sound
120 minutes
Courtesy of the artist

TIME WAITS, 2012
16mm film on SD video and digital text; color and
sound
120 minutes
Courtesy of the artist

AMY SILLMAN
DUEL, 2011
Oil on canvas
90 $\frac{1}{2}$ x 84 $\frac{1}{4}$ inches
Courtesy of the artist and Sikkema Jenkins & Co.,
New York

LORNA SIMPSON
Please remind me of who I am, 2009
Ink drawings accompanied by found photobooth
photographs in bronze frames
50 drawings and 50 photographs; dimensions
variable
Collection of Isabelle and Charles Berkovic, Brussels

HENRY TAYLOR
Emelda, 2011
Acrylic on canvas
76 x 80 $\frac{1}{4}$ inches
Collection of the Hudgins Family, New York

Warning Shots Not Required, 2011
Acrylic, charcoal, and collage on canvas
75 x 262 inches
The Museum of Contemporary Art, Los Angeles,
purchased with funds provided by the Aquisition
and Collection Committee

ALMA THOMAS
Late Night Reflections, 1972
Acrylic on canvas
28 $\frac{3}{4}$ x 44 inches
Nasher Museum of Art at Duke University, Fund
for Acquisitions and bequest of Marjorie Pfeffer by
exchange

BOB THOMPSON
Garden of Music, 1960
Oil on canvas
79 $\frac{1}{2}$ x 143 inches
Wadsworth Atheneum, Hartford, Connecticut,
The Ella Gallup Sumner and Mary Catlin Sumner
Collection

WU TSANG
For how we perceived a life (Take 3), 2012
16mm film loop; color and sound
9:34 minutes
Courtesy of the artist and Clifton Benevento,
New York

KARA WALKER
Fall Frum Grace: Miss Pipi's Blue Tale,
2011
Video projection; black-and-white and sound
17 minutes
Courtesy of the artist and Sikkema Jenkins & Co.,
New York

CARRIE MAE WEEMS
Family Pictures and Stories, 1982–84
Gelatin-silver prints
40 prints: 13 x 8 $\frac{1}{2}$ inches each
Courtesy of the artist and Jack Shainman Gallery,
New York

JACK WHITTEN
*Black Table Setting (Homage to Duke
Ellington)*, 1974
Acrylic on canvas
72 x 60 inches
Art Fund, Inc. at the Birmingham Museum of Art,
purchase with funds provided by Jack Drake and
Joel and Karen Piassick

Beta Group Number One, 1975
Acrylic on canvas
40 $\frac{1}{4}$ x 68 $\frac{1}{8}$ inches
Whitney Museum of American Art, New York,
gift of Flora Miller Biddle

Omikron I, 1977
Acrylic on canvas
52 x 64 inches
Collection of Pamela Joyner, San Francisco,
courtesy of Alexander Gray Associates, New York

WILLIAM T. WILLIAMS
Trane, 1969
Acrylic on canvas
108 x 84 inches
The Studio Museum in Harlem, gift of Charles
Cowles, New York

MARTIN WONG
La Vida, 1988
Oil on canvas
96 x 114 inches
Yale University Art Gallery, Charles B. Benenson,
B.A. 1933, Collection

Selected Film and Video in the Exhibition

The date(s) of the footage featured in each film or video is given in parentheses; the release date of the video or DVD is listed with the publisher.

Excerpt from *Hollywood Rhythm Vol. 1: The Best of Jazz and Blues* ("Symphony in Black" performed by Duke Ellington and Billie Holiday, 1935)
123 minutes
Kino Video, 2001

Excerpt from *Berlin Jazz Piano Workshop, 1965* ("Free Improvisation" performed by Jaki Byard, 1965)
51 minutes
Impro-Jazz, 2007

Excerpt from *Piano Legends* (c. 1941–86)
63 minutes
Directed by Dave Chertok; hosted by Chick Corea
Video Artists International, 1999

Devil Got My Woman: Blues at Newport 1966 (1966)
60 minutes
Directed by Alan Lomax
Vestapol, 2002

Excerpt from *The Blues Accordin' to Lightnin' Hopkins* (1969)
41 minutes
Directed by Les Blank and Skip Gerson
Flowers Films, 1992

Excerpt from *Richard Pryor: Live & Smokin'* (1971)
46 minutes
Directed by Michael Blum
The Weinstein Company, 2009

Excerpt from *Wattstax* (1972)
103 minutes
Directed by Mel Stuart
Warner Home Video, 2004

Space Is the Place (1974)
82 minutes
Directed by John Coney
Music arranged, composed, and conducted by Sun Ra
Plexifilm, 2003

Excerpt from *Richard Pryor: Live in Concert* (1979)
78 minutes
Directed by Jeff Margolis
HBO Home Video, 2006

Excerpt from *Anything for Jazz: Jaki Byard* (1980)
25 minutes
Directed by Daniel Algrant
Rhapsody Films, 2005

Excerpt from *Minor Threat: DC Space, Buff Hall, 9:30 Club* (1980–83)
92 minutes
Dischord Records, 2003

The Art Ensemble of Chicago in Concert (1981)
60 minutes
Rhapsody Films, 2005

Excerpt from *Bad Brains: Live at CBGB 1982* (1982)
60 minutes
Produced by Michael Temmer
OT Productions, 2006

Excerpt from *Richard Pryor: Stand-Up Comedy Double Feature: "Here & Now" and "Live on the Sunset Strip"* (1982–83)
176 minutes
Directed by Joe Layton
Sony Pictures Home Entertainment, 2009

Go Go Live at the Capital Centre (1987)
100 minutes
G Street Express, 1987

Excerpt from *Thelonius Monk: Straight, No Chaser* (1988)
90 minutes
Directed by Charlotte Zwerin
Warner Home Video, 2001

Excerpt from *Charles Mingus: Triumph of the Underdog* (1998)
78 minutes
Directed by Don McGlynn
Shanachie Entertainment, 1998

The Wire (2002–8)
60 hours
Created by David Simon
HBO, 2008

Cecil Taylor: All the Notes (2006)
72 minutes
Directed by Christopher Felver
MVD Visual, 2010

The Polymath, or The Life and Opinions of Samuel R. Delany, Gentleman (2007)
75 minutes
Directed by Fred Barney Taylor
Maestro Media, 2009

Selected Bibliography and Recordings

The Selected Bibliography and Recordings
are not meant to constitute a complete
index of works cited in this exhibition, but to
function as a representation of the curator's
process in conceptualizing this project.

Selected Bibliography

1993 Biennial Exhibition. Exh. cat. New
York: Whitney Museum of American
Art, 1993.

Adrian Piper. Exh. cat. Birmingham: Ikon
Gallery, 1991.

Adrian Piper: A Retrospective. Exh. cat.
Edited by Maurice Berger. Baltimore:
Fine Arts Gallery at the University of
Maryland, 1999.

Adrian Piper: Reflections, 1967–1987. Exh.
cat. New York: John Weber Gallery,
1989.

Afro-American Abstraction. Exh. cat. San
Francisco: Art Museum Association,
1982.

*Afro Modern: Journeys through the
Black Atlantic*. Exh. cat. Edited by
Tanya Barson and Peter Gorschluter.
London: Tate Publishing, 2010.

Amy Sillman: Third Person Singular.
Exh. cat. Edited by Ian Berry and
Anne Ellegood. Saratoga Springs,
N.Y.: Frances Young Tang Teaching
Museum and Art Gallery, 2008.

Anastas, Rhea, ed. "The Artist Is a
Currency: A Conversation with Rhea
Anastas, Gregg Bordowitz, Andrea
Fraser, Jutta Koether, and Glenn
Ligon." *Grey Room*, no. 24 (Summer
2006): 110–25.

Anastas, Rhea, with Michael Brenson, eds.
*Witness to Her Art: Art and Writings
by Adrian Piper, Mona Hatoum, Cady
Noland, Jenny Holzer, Kara Walker,
Daniela Rossell, and Eau de Cologne*.
Annandale-on-Hudson, N.Y.: Center for
Curatorial Studies, Bard College, 2006.

*Andrea Fraser: Works, 1984 to
2003*. Exh. cat. Edited by Yilmaz
Dziewior. Cologne: Dumont, 2003.

Archive Fever. Exh. cat. Edited by Okwui
Enwezor. New York: International
Center of Photography, 2008.

The Art of Romare Bearden. Exh. cat.
Washington, D.C.: National Gallery of
Art, 2003.

Attali, Jacques. *Noise: The Political
Economy of Music*. Minneapolis:
University of Minnesota Press, 1985.

Ault, Julie, ed. *Felix Gonzalez-Torres*.
Göttingen, Germany: Steidl/Dangin,
2006.

Baker, Houston A., Jr. *Blues, Ideology,
and Afro-American Literature:
A Vernacular Theory*. Chicago:
University of Chicago Press, 1984.

Baldwin, James. *Another Country*. New
York: Dial Press, 1962.

———. *The Collected Essays*. New York:
Library of America, 1998.

Baraka, Amiri. *Digging: The Afro-
American Soul of American Classical
Music*. Berkeley: University of
California Press, 2009.

———. *The LeRoi Jones/Amiri Baraka
Reader*. New York: Basic Books, 2009.

———. *Transbluesency: Selected Poems
1961–1995*. New York: Marsilio
Publishers, 1995.

Barkley L. Hendricks: Birth of the Cool. Exh.
cat. Edited by Trevor Schoonmaker.
Durham, N.C.: Nasher Museum of Art
at Duke University, 2008.

Bearden, Romare, and Harry Henderson.
*A History of African-American
Artists: From 1792 to the Present*.
New York: Pantheon Books, 1993.

*Beat Culture and the New America,
1950–1965*. Exh. cat. Edited by Lisa
Phillips. New York: Whitney Museum
of American Art, 1995.

Beauford Delaney: A Retrospective. Exh.
cat. New York: Studio Museum in
Harlem, 1978.

*Beauford Delaney: From New York to
Paris*. Exh. cat. Edited by Patricia Sue
Canterbury. Minneapolis: Minneapolis
Institute of Arts, 2004.

*Be-Bomb: The Trans-Atlantic War of
Images and All That Jazz, 1956–
1956*. Exh. cat. Barcelona: Museo
d'Art Contemporani de Barcelona;
Madrid: Museo Nacional Centro de
Arte Reina Sofía, 2008.

Bernadette Corporation. *The Complete
Poem*. Cologne: Walther König, 2010.

Bilderbuch. Exh. cat., Documenta 12.
Edited by Roger M. Buergel and
Ruth Noack. Cologne: Taschen,
2007.

Black Male: Representations of Masculinity in Contemporary American Art. Exh. cat. Edited by Thelma Golden. New York: Whitney Museum of American Art, 1994.

Bob Thompson. Exh. cat. Edited by Thelma Golden. New York: Whitney Museum of American Art, 1998.

Bois, Yve-Alain, and Rosalind E. Krauss. *Formless: A User's Guide.* New York: Zone Books, 1997.

Bordowitz, Gregg. *The AIDS Crisis Is Ridiculous and Other Writings, 1986–2003.* Edited by James Meyer. Cambridge, Mass.: MIT Press, 2004.

———. "Helplessness." *Texte zur Kunst* 17, no. 68 (December 2007): 130–33.

———. *Volition.* New York: Printed Matter, 2010.

Bowles, John P. *Adrian Piper: Race, Gender, and Embodiment.* Durham, N.C.: Duke University Press, 2011.

Brathwaite, Edward. *The Arrivants: A New World Trilogy.* Oxford: Oxford University Press, 1973.

Brathwaite, Kamau. *Ancestors.* New York: New Directions Books, 2005.

———. *Black + Blues.* 3rd ed. New York: New Directions Books, 1995.

———. *Born to Slow Horses.* Middletown, Conn.: Wesleyan University Press, 2005.

———. *ConVERSations with Nathaniel Mackey.* New York: We Press, 1999.

———. *DS (2) dreamstories.* New York: New Directions Books, 2007.

———. *Elegguas.* Middletown, Conn.: Wesleyan University Press, 2010.

———. *Middle Passages.* New York: New Directions Books, 1993.

Brothers, Thomas. *Louis Armstrong's New Orleans.* New York: W.W. Norton, 2006.

Césaire, Aimé. *The Collected Poetry.* Translated by Clayton Eshleman and Annette Smith. Berkeley: University of California Press, 1984.

Charles Gaines: Survey Exhibition 1979–1991. Exh. cat. Santa Monica: Dorothy Goldeen Gallery, 1991.

Charters, Samuel. *The Country Blues.* Cambridge, Mass.: Da Capo Press, 1959.

———. *The Legacy of the Blues: Art and Lives of Twelve Great Bluesmen.* Cambridge, Mass.: Da Capo Press, 1977.

Clay, Mel. *Jazz, Jail, and God.* San Francisco: Androgyne Books, 2001.

Clifford, James. *The Predicament of Culture: Twentieth-Century Ethnography, Literature, and Art.* Cambridge, Mass.: Harvard University Press, 1988.

Cohen, Harvey. *Duke Ellington's America.* Chicago: University of Chicago Press, 2010.

Coleman, Wanda. *African Sleeping Sickness: Stories and Poems.* Santa Rosa: Black Sparrow Press, 1990.

———. *Bathwater Wine.* Santa Rosa: Black Sparrow Press, 1998.

———. *Heavy Daughter Blues: Poems & Stories, 1968–1986.* Santa Rosa: Black Sparrow Press, 1987.

———. *Imagoes.* Santa Rosa: Black Sparrow Press, 1983.

———. *Mercurochrome: New Poems.* Santa Rosa: Black Sparrow Press, 2001.

———. *Native in a Strange Land: Trials and Tremors.* Santa Rosa: Black Sparrow Press, 1996.

———. *The Riot Inside Me: More Trials and Tremors.* Boston: Black Sparrow Books, 2005.

———. *The World Falls Away.* Pittsburgh: University of Pittsburgh Press, 2011.

Coloring: New Work by Glenn Ligon. Exh. cat. Minneapolis: Walker Art Center, 2001.

Connolly, Cynthia, Sharon Cheslow, and Leslie Clague, comps. *Banned in D.C.: Photos and Anecdotes from the D.C. Punk Underground (79–85).* Washington, D.C.: Sundog Propaganda, 1988.

Corbett, John. *Extended Play: Sounding Off from John Cage to Dr. Funkenstein.* Durham, N.C.: Duke University Press, 1994.

Corbett, John, ed. *The Wisdom of Sun Ra: Sun Ra's Polemical Broadsheets and Streetcorner Leaflets.* Chicago: Whitewalls, 2006.

Corbett, John, Anthony Elms, and Terri Kapsalis, eds. *Pathways to Unknown Worlds: Sun Ra, El Saturn, and Chicago's Afro-Futurist Underground 1954–1968.* Exh. cat. Chicago: Whitewalls, 2007.

———. *Traveling the Spaceways: Sun-Ra, The Astro Black, and Other Solar Myths.* Chicago: Whitewalls, 2010.

Critical Inquiry 38, no. 1 (Autumn 2011). Special issue on *The Wire.*

Daáood, Kamau. *The Language of Saxophones.* San Francisco: City Lights Publishers, 2005.

Davey, Moyra. *Long Life Cool White.* Cambridge, Mass.: Harvard University Art Museums, 2008.

———. *The Problem of Reading.* Montpelier, Vt.: Vermont College, 2003.

David Hammons. Exh. cat. New York: Jack Tilton Gallery, 1990.

David Hammons: Blues and the Abstract Truth. Exh. cat. Bern: Kunsthalle Bern, 1997.

David Hammons: In the Hood. Exh. cat. Edited by Robert Sill. Springfield: Illinois State Museum, 1994.

David Hammons: Rousing the Rubble. Exh. cat. Edited by Tom Finkelpearl. Philadelphia: Institute for Contemporary Art, 1991.

Davis, Angela Y. *Blues Legacies and Black Feminism: Gertrude "Ma" Rainey, Bessie Smith, and Billie Holiday.* New York: Vintage Books, 1998.

Davis, Miles, and Scott Gutterman. *The Art of Miles Davis.* New York: Arts, 1991.

Delany, Samuel R. *Dhalgren.* New York: Vintage Books, 2001.

———. *The Motion of Light on Water: Sex and Science Fiction Writing in the East Village, 1957–1965.* 1988. Reprint, Minneapolis: University of Minnesota Press, 2004.

———. *Stars in My Pocket Like Grains of Sand.* Middletown, Conn.: Wesleyan University Press, 2004.

Deleuze, Gilles, and Félix Guattari. *Kafka: Toward a Minor Literature.* Minneapolis: University of Minnesota Press, 1986.

Diederichsen, Diedrich. "The Primary: Political and Anti-Political Continuities between Minimal Music and Minimal Art." In *A Minimal Future? Art as Object 1958–1968.* Exh. cat. Los Angeles: The Museum of Contemporary Art, 2004.

———. "'Selbstdarsteller': Martin Kippenberger between 1977 and 1983." In *Nach Kippenberger*. Exh. cat. Vienna: Museum Moderner Kunst, 2003.

Dislocations. Exh. cat. Edited by Robert Storr. New York: Museum of Modern Art, 1991.

Double Consciousness: Black Conceptual Art since 1970. Exh. cat. Houston: Contemporary Arts Museum, 2005.

Du Bois, W. E. B. *The Souls of Black Folk*. New York: Dover Publications, 1994.

Duncan, Robert. *Bending the Bow*. New York: New Directions Books, 1968.

———. *Selected Poems*. Rev. and enl. ed. New York: New Directions Books, 1997.

———. *A Selected Prose*. 2nd ed. New York: New Directions Books, 2008.

Durham, Jimmie. *A Certain Lack of Coherence: Writings on Art and Cultural Politics*. Edited by Jean Fisher. London: Kala Press, 1993.

Durham, Jimmie, Laura Mulvey, Dirk Snauwaert, and Marc A. Durant. *Jimmie Durham*. London: Phaidon, 1995.

Ed Clark: Master Painter. Exh. cat. New York: G. R. N'Namdi Gallery, 2006.

Edward Clark: For the Sake of the Search. Exh. cat. Edited by Barbara Cavaliere and George R. N'Namdi. Belleville Lake, Mich.: Belleville Lake Press, 1997.

Ellison, Ralph. *The Collected Essays of Ralph Ellison*. Edited by John F. Callahan. New York: Modern Library, 1995.

———. *Invisible Man*. New York: Vintage International, 1995.

———. "Richard Wright's Blues." *Antioch Review* 57, no. 3 (Summer 1999): 263–76.

Energy/Experimentation: Black Artists and Abstraction, 1964–1980. Exh. cat. Edited by Kellie Jones. New York: Studio Museum in Harlem, 2006.

English, Darby. *How to See a Work of Art in Total Darkness*. Cambridge, Mass.: MIT Press, 2007.

Eternal Ancestors: The Art of the Central African Reliquary. Exh. cat. Edited by Alisa Lagamma. New York: Metropolitan Museum of Art, 2007.

Ethridge, Roe. *Rockaway, NY*. Göttingen, Germany: SteidlMack, 2007

Evans, Freddi Williams. *Congo Square: African Roots in New Orleans*. Lafayette, La.: University of Louisiana at Lafayette Press, 2011.

Exposition Zoe Leonard. Exh. cat. Paris: Le Centre National de la Photographie, 1998.

Fahey, John. *How Bluegrass Destroyed My Life*. 3rd ed. Chicago: Drag City, 2000.

Fanon, Frantz. *Black Skin, White Masks*. Rev. ed. Translated by Richard Philcox. New York: Grove Press, 2008.

Ferris, William. *Blues from the Delta*. New York: Da Capo Press, 1984.

———. *Give My Poor Heart Ease: Voices of the Mississippi Blues*. Chapel Hill: University of North Carolina Press, 2009.

The First Show: Painting and Sculpture from Eight Collections, 1940–1980. Exh. cat. Edited by Julia Brown and Bridget Johnson. Los Angeles: Museum of Contemporary Art, 1983.

Flam, Jack, and Miriam Deutch, eds. *Primitivism and Twentieth-Century Art: A Documentary History*. Berkeley: University of California Press, 2003.

Freestyle. Exh. cat. Edited by Thelma Golden. New York: Studio Museum in Harlem, 2001.

Gangitano, Lia, ed. *Boston School*. Boston: Institute of Contemporary Art, 1995.

Gass, William H. *On Being Blue: A Philosophical Inquiry*. 9th ed. Boston: David R. Godine, 2007.

Gates, Henry Louis. *The Signifying Monkey: A Theory of African-American Literary Criticism*. Oxford: Oxford University Press, 1988.

Genet, Jean. *Prisoner of Love*. New York: New York Review of Books, 2003.

———. *The Selected Writings of Jean Genet*. Edited by Edmund White. Hopewell, N.J.: Ecco Press, 1993.

Gilroy, Paul. *The Black Atlantic: Modernity and Double Consciousness*. Cambridge, Mass.: Harvard University Press, 1993.

Gioia, Ted. *West Coast Jazz: Modern Jazz in California 1945–1960*. Berkeley: University of California Press, 1998.

Glenn Ligon: America. Exh. cat. Edited by Scott Rothkopf. New York: Whitney Museum of American Art, 2011.

Glenn Ligon: Some Changes. Exh. cat. Toronto: The Power Plant, 2005.

Glenn Ligon: Text Paintings, 1990–2004. Exh. cat. Los Angeles: Regen Projects, 2004.

Glissant, Édouard. *Caribbean Discourse: Selected Essays*. Charlottesville: University of Virginia Press, 1989.

———. *Faulkner, Mississippi*. Chicago: University of Chicago Press, 2000.

———. *Poetic Intention*. Callicoon, N.Y.: Nightboat Books, 2010.

Graw, Isabelle. *High Price: Art between the Market and Celebrity Culture*. Berlin: Sternberg Press, 2009.

———. "Seen from Here: On Myths of Cologne, Heteronomy, and Scenarios of Withdrawing and Dropping Out in the Face of the Increased Significance of 'Life.'" *Texte zur Kunst* 16, no. 63 (September 2006): 124–32.

———. "You Are Your Potential! An Interview with Paolo Virno by Isabelle Graw." *Texte zur Kunst* 16, no. 63 (September 2006): 140–46.

Graw, Isabelle, Daniel Birnbaum, and Nikolaus Hirsch, eds. *Art and Subjecthood: The Return of the Human Figure in Semiocapitalism*. Berlin: Sternberg Press, 2011.

Green, Renée. *Ongoing Becomings, 1989–2009*. Exh. cat. Zurich: JRP Ringier, 2009.

———. *Shadows and Signals*. Exh. cat. Barcelona: Fundació Antoni Tàpies, 2000.

———. *World Tour*. Exh. cat. Los Angeles: Museum of Contemporary Art, 1993.

Guralnick, Peter. *Feel Like Going Home: Portraits in Blues and Rock 'n' Roll*. New York: Back Bay Books, 1999.

Guralnick, Peter, Robert Santelli, Holly George-Warren, and Christopher John Farley, eds. *Martin Scorsese Presents the Blues: A Musical Journey*. New York: HarperCollins, 2003.

Hartman, Saidiya V. *Scenes of Subjection: Terror, Slavery, and Self-Making in Nineteenth-Century America*. Oxford: Oxford University Press, 1997.

Heffley, Mike. *Northern Sun, Southern Moon: Europe's Reinvention of Jazz*. New Haven, Conn.: Yale University Press, 2005.

Howardena Pindell: Paintings and Drawings. Exh. cat. New York: Roland Gibson Gallery, 1992.

Hughes, Langston. *Selected Poems.* Vintage Classics edition. New York: Random House, 1990.

Hurston, Zora Neal. *Folklore, Memoirs, & Other Writings.* New York: Library of America, 1995.

Information: Zoe Leonard. Exh. cat. Cologne: Galerie Gisela Capitain, 1991.

Isoardi, Steven L. *The Dark Tree: Jazz and the Community Arts in Los Angeles.* Berkeley: University of California Press, 2006.

Jack Whitten. Exh. cat. Antwerp: Zeno X Gallery, 2011.

Jack Whitten: Memorial Paintings. Exh. cat. Atlanta: Atlanta Contemporary Art Center, 2008.

Jones, Kellie. *EyeMinded: Living and Writing Contemporary Art.* Durham, N.C.: Duke University Press, 2011.

Jones, LeRoi. *Blues People: Negro Music in White America.* London: MacGibbon & Kee, 1965.

Josef Strau: A Dissidence Coincidence but W.H.C.T.L.J.S. Exh. cat. Malmö: Malmö Konsthall, 2008.

Joseph, Branden W. *Beyond the Dream Syndicate: Tony Conrad and the Arts after Cage.* New York: Zone Books, 2008.

Josephine Pryde: Valerie. Vienna: Secession, 2004.

Jost, Ekkehard. *Free Jazz.* New York: Da Capo Press, 1994.

Juan Downey: The Invisible Architect. Exh. cat. Edited by Valérie Smith. Cambridge, Mass.: MIT List Visual Arts Center, 2011.

Jutta Koether. Exh. cat. Cologne: DuMont Literatur und Kunst Verlag, 2006.

Kara Walker. Exh. cat. Hannover: Kunstverein Hannover, 2002.

Kara Walker: My Complement, My Enemy, My Oppressor, My Love. Exh. cat. Edited by Philippe Vergne. Minneapolis: Walker Art Center, 2007.

Kaufman, Bob. *The Ancient Rain: Poems 1956–1978.* New York: New Directions, 1981.

———. *Cranial Guitar: Selected Poems.* Minneapolis: Coffee House Press, 1996.

———. *Solitudes Crowded with Loneliness.* New York: New Directions, 1965.

Kelley, Robin D. G. *Africa Speaks, America Answers: Modern Jazz in Revolutionary Times.* Cambridge, Mass.: Harvard University Press, 2012.

———. *Freedom Dreams: The Black Radical Imagination.* Boston: Beacon Press, 2002.

———. *Thelonious Monk: The Life and Times of an American Original.* New York: Free Press, 2009.

Kempton, Arthur. *Boogaloo: The Quintessence of American Popular Music.* New York: Pantheon Books, 2003.

Kerry James Marshall. Exh. cat. Edited by Kathleen S. Bartels and Jeff Wall. Vancouver: Vancouver Art Gallery, 2010.

Kerry James Marshall: Mementos. Exh. cat. Chicago: The Renaissance Society at the University of Chicago, 1998.

Kerry James Marshall: One True Thing, Meditations on Black Aesthetics. Exh. cat. Chicago: Museum of Contemporary Art, 2003.

Kerry James Marshall: Telling Stories, Selected Paintings. Exh. cat. Cleveland: Cleveland Center for Contemporary Art, 1994.

Kippenberger, Martin. *67 Improved Papertigers Not Afraid of Repetition.* New York: Edition Julie Sylvester, 1987.

Koether, Jutta. *The Inside Job.* Graz: Galerie Bleich-Rossi, 1992.

Kofsky, Frank. *Black Nationalism and the Revolution in Music.* New York: Pathfinder Press, 1970.

Konrad Klapheck: Paintings from 1955 to 1998. Exh. cat. Göttingen, Germany: Steidl, 2008

Kori Newkirk: 1997–2007. Exh. cat. Los Angeles: Fellows of Contemporary Art, 2007.

Krebber, Michael. *Außerirdische Zwitterwesen [Alien Hybrid Creatures].* Cologne: Walther König, 2005.

Laplanche, Jean. *Essays on Otherness.* New York: Routledge, 1999.

Lewis, David Levering, ed. *The Portable Harlem Renaissance Reader.* New York: Penguin Books, 1994.

Lewis, George E. "Foreword: After Afrofuturism." *Journal of the Society for American Music* 2, no. 2 (2008): 139–53.

———. "Getting' to Know Y'all: Improvised Music, Interculturalism, and the Racial Imagination." *Critical Studies in Improvisation* 1, no. 1 (2004), available at http://www.criticalimprov.com/article/view/6/15.

———. *A Power Stronger Than Itself: The AACM and American Experimental Music.* Chicago: University of Chicago Press, 2008.

———. "Purposive Patterning: Jeff Donaldson, Muhal Richard Abrams, and the Multidominance of Consciousness." *Lenox Avenue: A Journal of Interarts Inquiry* 5 (1999): 62–69.

———. "Stan Douglas's Suspiria: Genealogies of Recombinant Narrativity." In *Stan Douglas, Past Imperfect: Works 1986–2007.* Exh. cat. Edited by Hans D. Christ and Iris Dressler. Ostfildern, Germany: Hatje Cantz Verlag, 2008.

———. "Too Many Notes: Computers, Complexity and Culture in Voyager." *Leonardo Music Journal* 10 (2000): 33–39.

Ligon, Glenn. "Black Light: David Hammons and the Poetics of Emptiness." *Artforum* 43 (September 2004): 242–49.

———. *Yourself in the World: Selected Writings and Interviews.* New York: Whitney Museum of American Art, 2011.

Liz Larner. Exh. cat. Edited by Russell Ferguson. Los Angeles: Museum of Contemporary Art, 2001.

Lock, Graham. *Blutopia: Visions of the Future and Revisions of the Past in the Work of Sun Ra, Duke Ellington, and Anthony Braxton.* Durham, N.C.: Duke University Press, 1999.

———. *Forces in Motion: The Music and Thoughts of Anthony Braxton.* New York: Da Capo Press, 1988.

Lock, Graham, and David Murray, eds. *The Hearing Eye: Jazz and Blues in*

African-American Visual Art. Oxford: Oxford University Press, 2009.

Lorna Simpson. Exh. cat. New York: Abrams, in association with the American Federation of the Arts, 2006.

Mackey, Nathaniel. *Atet A.D.* San Francisco: City Lights Publishers, 2001.

———. *Bass Cathedral.* New York: New Directions Books, 2008.

———. *Bedouin Hornbook.* Los Angeles: Sun & Moon Press, 1987.

———. *Discrepant Engagement: Dissonance, Cross-Culturality, and Experimental Writing.* Cambridge, England: Cambridge University Press, 1993.

———. *Djbot Baghostus's Run.* Los Angeles: Sun & Moon Press, 2000.

———. *Nod House.* New York: New Directions Books, 2011.

———. "Other: From Noun to Verb." *Representations* 39 (Summer 1992): 51–70.

———. *Paracritical Hinge: Essays, Talks, Notes, Interviews.* Madison: University of Wisconsin Press, 2005.

———. *School of Udhra.* San Francisco: City Lights Publishers, 1993.

———. *Splay Anthem.* New York: New Directions Books, 2006.

Mackey, Nathaniel, and Art Lange, eds. *Moment's Notice: Jazz in Poetry and Prose.* Minneapolis: Coffee House Press, 1992.

Mackey, Nathaniel, and Edward Foster. "An Interview with Nathaniel Mackey." *Talisman: A Journal of Contemporary Poetry and Poetics* 9 (Fall 1992): 48–61.

Major, Clarence. *All-Night Visitors.* Boston: Northeastern University Press, 1998.

———. *Configurations: New and Selected Poems, 1958–1998.* Port Townsend, Wa.: Copper Canyon Press, 1998.

Make Your Own Life: Artists in and out of Cologne. Exh. cat. Edited by Bennett Simpson. Philadelphia: Institute of Contemporary Art, 2006.

Mark Morrisroe, 1959–1989. Exh. cat. Berlin: Neue Gesellschaft für bildende Kunst, 1997.

Marshall, Kerry James. *Kerry James Marshall.* New York: Harry N. Abrams, 2000.

Martin Kippenberger: The Problem Perspective. Exh. cat. Edited by Ann Goldstein. Los Angeles: Museum of Contemporary Art, 2008.

Matt Mullican: Works, 1972–1992. Exh. cat. Edited by Ulrich Wilmes. Cologne: Walther König, 1993.

McMillian, Rodney. "Pain Should Not Be Ignored: On Facing One's Bogeyman." *Afterall* 18 (Summer 2008): 37–44.

Melvin Edwards Sculpture: A Thirty-Year Retrospective, 1963–1993. Exh. cat. Edited by Lucinda H. Gedeon. Purchase, N.Y.: Neuberger Museum of Art, 1993.

Mercer, Kobena, ed. *Discrepant Abstraction.* London: Institute of International Visual Arts, 2006.

———. *Exiles, Diasporas & Strangers.* London: Institute of International Visual Arts, 2008.

Merlin Carpenter, As a Painter I Call Myself the Estate of. Exh. cat. Vienna: Secession, 2000.

Merlin Carpenter: Militant. Exh. cat. Cologne: Galerie Christian Nagel, 2002.

Merlin Carpenter: Nueva Generación. Exh. cat. Madrid: Arte Distrito, 2004.

Meyer-Hermann, Eva, and Susanne Neuburger, eds. *Nach Kippenberger [After Kippenberger].* Vienna: Schlebrügge Editor, 2003.

Mezzrow, Mezz, and Bernard Wolfe. *Really the Blues.* New York: Random House, 1946.

Michael Krebber: Pubertät in der Lehre [Puberty in Teaching]. Exh. cat. Cologne: Walther König, 2008.

Mingus, Charles. *Beneath the Underdog: His World as Composed by Mingus.* Edited by Nel King. New York: Vintage Books, 1991.

Moten, Fred. *B Jenkins.* Durham, N.C.: Duke University Press, 2009.

———. *In the Break: The Aesthetics of the Black Radical Tradition.* Minneapolis: University of Minnesota Press, 2003.

Mullen, Harryette. *Blues Baby: Early Poems.* Lewisburg, Penn.: Bucknell University Press, 2002.

———. *Muse and Drudge.* Philadelphia: Singing Horse Press, 1995.

———. *Recyclopedia: Trimmings, S*PeRM**K*T, and Muse & Drudge.* St. Paul: Gray Wolf Press, 2006.

———. *Sleeping with the Dictionary.* Berkeley: University of California Press, 2002.

Murray, Albert. *The Omni-Americans: Black Experience and American Culture.* New York: Da Capo Press, 1990.

———. *Stomping the Blues.* 1976. New York: Da Capo Press, 2000.

Muyumba, Walton M. *The Shadow and the Act: Black Intellectual Practice, Jazz Improvisation, and Philosophical Pragmatism.* Chicago: University of Chicago Press, 2009.

Neal, Larry. *Hoodoo Hollerin' Bebop Ghosts.* Washington, D.C.: Howard University Press, 1974.

Next Generation: Southern Black Aesthetic. Exh. cat. Winston-Salem, N.C.: Southeastern Center for Contemporary Art, 1990.

Nielsen, Aldon Lynn. *Black Chant: Languages of African-American Postmodernism.* Cambridge Studies in American Literature and Culture. Cambridge, England: Cambridge University Press, 1997.

Now Dig This! Art & Black Los Angeles, 1960–1980. Exh. cat. Edited by Kellie Jones. Los Angeles: Hammer Museum, 2011.

Oehlen Williams 95. Exh. cat. Edited by Catherine Gudis. Columbus, Ohio: Wexner Center for the Arts, 1995.

O'Meally, Robert G., ed. *The Jazz Cadence of American Culture.* New York: Columbia University Press, 1998.

One Planet under a Groove: Hip Hop and Contemporary Art. Exh. cat. New York: Bronx Museum of the Arts, 2001.

Otto, Melanie. *A Creole Experiment: Utopian Space in Kamau Brathwaite's "Video-Style" Works.* Trenton, N.J.: Africa World Press, 2009.

Palmer, Robert. *Deep Blues: A Musical and Cultural History, from the Mississippi Delta to Chicago's South Side to the World.* New York: Penguin Books, 1982.

Perchuk, Andrew, and Rani Singh, eds. *Harry Smith: The Avant-Garde in the American Vernacular.* Los Angeles: Getty Research Institute, 2010.

Piekut, Benjamin. *Experimentalism Otherwise: The New York Avant-Garde at Its Limits.* Berkeley: University of California Press, 2011.

Pindell, Howardena. *The Heart of the Question: The Writings and Paintings of Howardena Pindell.* New York: Midmarch Arts Press, 1997.

Piper, Adrian. *Decide Who You Are: Texts.* New York: Paula Cooper Gallery, 1992.

———. *Out of Order, Out of Sight: Vol. 1.* Cambridge, Mass.: MIT Press, 1996.

Powell, Richard J. *Black Art: A Cultural History.* 2nd ed. London: Thames and Hudson, 2003.

———. *Black Art and Culture in the 20th Century.* London: Thames and Hudson, 1997.

Powell, Richard J., ed. *The Blues Aesthetic: Black Culture and Modernism.* Exh. cat. Washington, D.C.: Washington Project for the Arts, 1989.

Prospect 1 New Orleans. Exh cat. New York: Picturebox, 2008.

Queer Voice. Exh. cat. Edited by Ingrid Schaffner. Philadelphia: Institute of Contemporary Art, 2010.

Radano, Ronald M. *New Musical Figurations: Anthony Braxton's Cultural Critique.* Chicago: University of Chicago Press, 1993.

Rainer, Yvonne. *Feelings Are Facts: A Life.* Cambridge, Mass.: MIT Press, 2006.

Ratliff, Ben. *Coltrane: The Story of a Sound.* 2nd ed. London: Faber, 2008.

Renée Green: Certain Miscellanies, Some Documents. Exh. cat. Amsterdam: De Appel Foundation, 1996.

Renée Green: Partially Buried/Adrian Piper: Hypothesis—Situation Parallel Grid Proposal for Dugway Proving Grounds Headquarters. Exh. cat. 2 vols. in 1. New York: Elizabeth Dee Gallery, 2009.

Rhapsodies in Black: Art of the Harlem Renaissance. Exh. cat. Edited by Richard J. Powell. London: Hayward Gallery, 1997.

Richard Hawkins: Of Two Minds, Simultaneously. Exh. cat. Cologne: Walter König, 2009.

Roberson, Ed. *City Ecologue.* Berkeley, Calif.: Atelos, 2006.

———. *To See the Earth Before the End of the World.* Middletown, Conn.: Wesleyan University Press, 2010.

Roe Ethridge: Le Luxe. London: MACK, 2011.

Romare Bearden in Black-and-White. Exh. cat. New York: Whitney Museum of American Art, 1997.

Ross, Alex. *The Rest Is Noise: Listening to the Twentieth Century.* New York: Picador, 2008.

Roy DeCarava: A Retrospective. Exh. cat. Edited by Peter Galassi. New York: Museum of Modern Art, 1996.

Roy DeCarava: Photographs. Exh. cat. Edited by James Alinder. Carmel, Calif.: The Friends of Photography, 1981.

Ruf, Beatrix, and Thomas Seelig, eds. *Mark Morrisroe.* Zurich: JRP Ringier, 2010.

Russell, Ross. *Bird Lives! The High Times and Hard Life of Charlie (Yardbird) Parker.* Cambridge, Mass.: Da Capo, 1996.

Sackheim, Eric, ed. *The Blues Line: A Collection of Lyrics.* New York: Grossman Publishers, 1969.

Sadie Benning: Suspended Animation. Exh. cat. Columbus, Ohio: Wexner Center for the Arts, 2007.

Shadows and Other Signs of Life: Anniversary Notes for Andy Warhol. Exh. cat. Edited by Benjamin H. D. Buchloh. Cologne: Walther König, 2008.

Siegel, Katy, ed. *High Times, Hard Times.* New York: Independent Curators International, 2006.

Sillman, Amy. "Ab-Ex and Disco Balls: In Defense of Abstract Expressionism II." *Artforum* 49, no. 10 (Summer 2011): 321–25.

Simpson, Bennett. "And Your Mind Will Follow." *Artforum* 50, no. 2 (October 2011): 238–39.

———. "Heeling." In *Cosima von Bonin: Roger and Out.* Exh. cat. Los Angeles: Museum of Contemporary Art, 2007.

———. "Pryor Versions." In *Glenn Ligon: America.* Exh. cat. Edited by Scott Rothkopf. New York: Whitney Museum of American Art, 2011.

Simpson, Lorna, Kellie Jones, Thelma Golden, and Chrissie Iles. *Lorna Simpson.* London: Phaidon, 2002.

Spellman, A. B. *Four Lives in the Bebop Business.* New York: Limelight Editions, 2004.

Sroggins, Mark. *The Poem of a Life: A Biography of Louis Zukofsky.* Berkeley, Calif.: Counterpoint Press, 2007.

Stan Douglas. Exh. cat. Edited by Daina Augaitis. Vancouver: Vancouver Art Gallery, 1999.

Sweet Oblivion: The Urban Landscape of Martin Wong. Exh. cat. New York: New Museum of Contemporary Art, 1998.

Sylvester, Julie, ed. *John Chamberlain: A Catalogue Raisonné of the Sculpture, 1954–1985.* New York: Hudson Hills Press, 1986.

Szwed, John F. *Space Is the Place: The Lives and Times of Sun Ra.* Cambridge, Mass.: Da Capo Press, 1998.

Tapscott, Horace. *The Musical and Social Journey of Horace Tapscott.* Durham, N.C.: Duke University Press, 2001.

Tate, Greg, ed. *Everything but the Burden: What White People Are Taking from Black Culture.* New York: Harlem Moon and Broadway Books, 2003.

The Theater of Refusal: Black Art and Mainstream Criticism. Exh. cat. Edited by Charles Gaines. Irvine, Calif.: Fine Arts Gallery of the University of California, Irvine, 1993.

Thomas Eggerer: "O Pioneers." Exh. cat. Cologne: Galerie Daniel Buchholz, 2007.

Thomas, Lorenzo. *Chances Are Few.* Berkeley, Calif.: Blue Wind Press, 2003.

———. *Dancing on Main Street.* Minneapolis: Coffee House Press, 2004.

Thompson, Robert Farris. *Flash of the Spirit: African and Afro-American Art and Philosophy.* New York: Vintage Books, 1984.

Tim Rollins and K.O.S.: A History. Exh. cat. Edited by Ian Berry. Saratoga Springs, N.Y.: Frances Young Tang Teaching Museum and Art Gallery, 2009.

Wald, Elijah. *Escaping the Delta: Robert Johnson and the Invention of the Blues.* New York: Amistad, 2004.

Wallace, Michele. *Black Popular Culture.* Dia Center for the Arts: Discussions in Contemporary Culture, no. 8, ed. Gina Dent. Seattle: Bay Press, 1992.

Weems, Carrie Mae. *Carrie Mae Weems: Social Studies.* Seville: Centro Andaluz de Arte Contemporáneo, 2010.

West Coast 74: The Black Image. Exh. cat. Sacramento: E. B. Crocker Art Gallery, 1974.

Widener, Daniel. *Black Arts West: Culture and Struggle in Postwar Los Angeles.* Durham, N.C.: Duke University Press, 2010.

Wilkerson, Isabel. *The Warmth of Other Sun: The Epic Story of America's Great Migration.* New York: Random House, 2010.

William Eggleston. Exh. cat. Edited by Hervé Chandès. London: Thames & Hudson, 2002.

William Eggleston: The Democratic Forest. New York: Doubleday, 1989.

William Eggleston's Guide. New York: Museum of Modern Art, 1976.

William Eggleston's Stranded in Canton. Santa Fe: Twin Palms Publishers, 2008.

William Pope.L: The Friendliest Black Artist in America. Exh. cat. Edited by Mark Bessire. Cambridge, Mass.: MIT Press, 2002.

William T. Williams: An Exhibition of Paintings from 1974–1985. Exh. cat. Winston-Salem, N.C.: Southeastern Center for Contemporary Art, 1985.

Williams, Jonathan. *Blues & Roots/Rue & Bluets, A Garland for the Southern Appalachians.* Durham, N.C.: Duke University Press, 1985.

Wilmer, Valerie. *As Serious As Your Life: John Coltrane and Beyond.* London: Serpents Tail, 1992.

Wondrich, David. *Stomp and Swerve: American Music Gets Hot,* 1843–1924. Chicago: Chicago Review Press, 2003.

Yardbird Suite: Hammons 93. Exh. cat. Edited by Deborah Menaker Rothschild. Williamstown, Mass.: Williams College Museum of Art, 1994.

Young, Kevin. *Jelly Roll (A Blues).* New York: Knopf, 2003.

———. *To Repel Ghosts: Five Sides in B Minor.* Cambridge, Mass.: Zoland Books, 2001.

Young, Kevin, ed. *Blues Poems.* Everyman's Library Pocket Poets. New York: Knopf, 2003.

———. *Jazz Poems.* Everyman's Library Pocket Poets. New York: Knopf, 2006.

Zoe Leonard. Exh. cat. Vienna: Secession, 1997.

Zoe Leonard: Photographs. Exh. cat. Edited by Urs Stahel. Göttingen, Germany: Steidl, 2007.

Zukofsky, Louis. *A. 1978.* Baltimore: Johns Hopkins University Press, 1991.

———. *All: The Collected Short Poems, 1923–1958.* New York: W.W. Norton, 1965.

———. *Complete Short Poetry.* Baltimore: Johns Hopkins University Press, 1997.

Selected Recordings

The 13th Floor Elevators. *Easter Everywhere*. Collectables 553, 1993. Originally released in 1967.

20 Years of Dischord. Dischord Records 125, 2002.

Abrams, Muhal Richard. *Afrisong*. 3D MTCJ-2003, 2000. Originally released in 1975.

———. *Blues Forever*. Black Saint 120061, 1993. Originally released in 1982.

———. *Colors in Thirty-Third*. Black Saint 1200912, 1993. Originally released in 1987.

———. *Duet*. Featuring Amina Claudine Myers. Black Saint 1200512, 1993. Originally released in 1981.

———. *Family Talk*. Black Saint 1201322, 1993.

———. *Levels and Degrees of Light*. Delmark DD413, 1991. Originally released in 1968.

———. *Sightsong*. Featuring Malachi Favors. Black Saint 120003, 1993. Originally released in 1976.

———. *Sound Dance*. Pi Recordings B004NTMNJO, 2011.

———. *Think All, Focus One*. Black Saint 1201412, 1996.

———. *Things to Come from Those Now Gone*. Delmark 430, 2000. Originally released in 1972.

———. *Young at Heart/Wise in Time*. Delmark DE423, 1996. Originally recorded in 1969.

———. *see also* Muhal Richard Abrams Orchestra.

Abrams, Muhal Richard, George Lewis, and Roscoe Mitchell. *Streaming*. Pi Recordings 22, 2006.

Ade, King Sunny. *The Best of the Classic Years*. Shanachie SHANCD 66034, 2003.

Ahmed, Mahmoud. *Ethiopiques*. Buda Musique 82979, 1999.

Air. *Air Lore*. Bluebird RCA 6578-2-RB, 1979.

———. *Air Song*. PJL 2002, 1975.

———. *Air Time*. Nessa 12, 2008. Originally released in 1978.

Albert Ayler Trio. *Spiritual Unity*. ESP Disk 1002, 2002. Originally released in 1964.

———. *see also* Ayler, Albert.

Alexandria, Lorez. *Alexandria the Great*. Impulse! UCCI9062, 2001. Originally released in 1964.

Amina Claudine Myers Trio. *The Circle of Time*. Black Saint Records, 1984.

———. *see also* Myers, Amina Claudine.

Anderson, Fred, Hamid Drake, Edward "Kidd" Jordan, and William Parker. *2 Days in April*. Eremite 23, 2005.

Andy, Horace. *Dance Hall Style*. Wackie's 1383, 2005.

Armstrong, Louis. *1925–1926. Masters of Jazz, Volume 8*. Classics 600, 1996.

———. *Hot 5's and 7's, 1925–1928*. Laserlight 15721, 1991.

Art Ensemble of Chicago. *A.A.C.M., Great Black Music: Reese and the Smooth Ones*. Varese 061247, 2002. Originally released in 1969.

———. *Art Ensemble: 1967/1968*. Nessa 2500, 1993.

———. *Bap-tizum*. Koch Jazz 8500, 1999. Originally released in 1972.

———. *Chi Congo*. Varese Sarabande (USA) VSD 3020615282, 2005.

———. *Les Stances à Sophie*. Universal Sound, 2000. Originally released in 1970.

———. *Live in Paris*. Snapper 512, 2006. Originally released in 1969.

———. *Nice Guys*. ECM 827876, 2000. Originally released in 1979.

Ashley, Robert. *Ashley: Automatic Writing/Purposeful Lady Slow Afternoon/She Was a Visitor*. Lovely Music 1002, 1996.

Ashley, Robert, and Paul de Marinis. *In Sara, Mencken, Christ and Beethoven There Were Men and Women*. Gut Bounce 1207, 2007.

Ayler, Albert. *New Grass*. Impulse! 9884219, 2005. Originally released in 1969.

———. *New York Eye and Ear Control*. ESP Disk ESPCD1016, 2008. Originally released in 1964.

———. *Slugs' Saloon, May 1, 1966*. ESP Disk 4025, 2005. Originally released in 1966.

———. *Spirits*. Breathless 52006, 2005. Originally released in 1964.

———. *Spirits Rejoice*. ESP Disk 1020, 2003. Originally released in 1965.

———. *see also* Albert Ayler Trio.

Bad Brains. *Rock for Light*. Caroline Distribution CAROL 16132, 1991. Originally released in 1983.

Badu, Erykah. *New Amerykah Pt. 1: 4th World War*. Universal Motown 001080002, 2008.

Bailey, Derek. *Ballads*. Tzadik Records TZA 7607, 2002.

Bailey, Derek, and Susie Ibarra. *Daedal*. Incus INCUS CD36, 1999.

Barker, Blue Lu. *1938–1939*. Classics 704, 1997.

Basie, Count. *Dance Session, Vol. 1*. Universal Distribution 9132, 2004. Originally released in 1954.

Bastro. *Sing the Troubled Beast*. Homestead 164, 1996.

Big Star. *#1 Record/Radio City*. Stax 60025, 2004. *#1 Record* originally released in 1972; *Radio City* originally released in 1974.

Bill Evans Trio. *Portrait in Jazz*. Fantasy/OJC 0882, 1990. Originally released in 1959.

———. *see also* Evans, Bill.

Black Flag. *Damaged*. SST 36100072, 1990. Originally released in 1981.

Blake, Ran, with Jaki Byard. *Improvisations*. Soul Note (Italy) 121022, 2002.

Bley, Paul. *Blood*. Fontana 883911, 1966.

———. *Footloose!* Savoy 9050, 1993.

———. *see also* Paul Bley Trio.

Blythe, Arthur. *Bush Baby*. Adelphi Records AD 5008, 1977.

Bobby Bradford and the Mo'tet. *Lost in L.A.* Soul Note (Italy) 121068, 1993.

———. *see also* Bradford, Bobby.

Bobo, Willie. *Spanish Grease*. Verve 666, 2002.

———. *Uno Dos Tres 1-2-3*. Verve B000W26BSG, 1994.

Bonnie "Prince" Billy. *Sings Great Palace Music*. Drag City 252, 2004.

Boogie Woogie and Blues Piano. Mosaic 30, 2009.

Bowie, Lester. *Fast Last*. Muse MR-5055, 1974.

Boykins, Ronnie. *The Will Come, Is Now*. ESP Disk 3026, 2009.

Bradford, Bobby. *One Night Stand*. Soul Note (Italy) 121168, 1990.

———. *see also* Bobby Bradford and the Mo'tet.

Braxton, Anthony. *Beyond Quantum.* Tzadik Records 7626, 2008.

———. *The Complete Arista Recordings of Anthony Braxton.* Mosaic 242, 2008.

———. *For Alto.* Delmark Records DE420, 2000. Originally released in 1968.

———. *New York, Fall 1974.* Arista AI4032, 1974.

———. *Quartet (Dortmund).* Hatology 557, 2001. Originally released in 1976.

Braxton, Anthony, with Ran Blake. *A Memory of Vienna.* Hatology HATO 687, 2009.

Brown, James. *In the Jungle Groove.* Polydor 8296242, 2003.

———. *Live at the Apollo I & II.* Universal/Polydor 90572, 2007.

———. *Messing with the Blues.* Polydor 847258, 1995.

Bullwackies All Stars. *Dub Unlimited.* Wackie's 0036, 2006. Originally released in 1976.

Byard, Jaki. *Blues for Smoke.* Candid 79018, 2007. Originally released in 1960.

———. *Here's Jaki.* Prestige/New Jazz 1874, 1995. Originally released in 1961

———. *Hi-Fly.* New Jazz/OJC 1879, 1996. Originally released in 1962.

———. *The Jaki Byard Experience.* Prestige/OJC 1913, 1999. Originally released in 1968.

———. *Jaki Byard with Strings.* Prestige Records 24246, 2000. Originally released in 1968.

———. *A Matter of Black and White.* Highnote Records, 2011.

———. *Out Front!* Prestige/OJC 1842, 1994. Originally released in 1964.

———. *Parisian Solos.* Musica 2008, 1971.

———. *Sunshine of My Soul.* Prestige/OJC 1946, 2001. Originally released in 1967.

———. *To Them—To Us.* Soul Note (Italy) 121025, 1993. Originally released in 1981.

Cannibal Ox. *The Cold Vein.* Def Jux DJX072, 2001.

Carter, Betty. *At the Village Vanguard.* Verve 314-519851-2, 1993. Originally released in 1970.

Carter, John. *Self-Determination Music.* Flying Dutchman FDS 128, 1970.

Carter, John, and Bobby Bradford. *Mosaic Select.* Mosaic Select MS-036, 2010.

Cecil Taylor Quartet. *Looking Ahead!* Original Jazz Classics 452, 1990. Originally released in 1958.

Cecil Taylor Unit. *Cecil Taylor Unit.* New World Records NW2012, 1992. Originally released in 1979.

———. *Dark to Themselves.* ENJA 2084, 2001. Originally released in 1976.

———. *Live in Bologna.* Leo Records 100, 2000. Originally released in 1987.

———. see also Taylor, Cecil.

Central Avenue Sounds: Jazz in Los Angeles, 1921–1956. Rhino 75872, 1999.

Charles Mingus and Eric Dolphy Sextet. *Complete Live in Amsterdam.* Jazz Collectors JC 429, 2009.

———. see also Mingus, Charles; Dolphy, Eric.

Cherry, Don. *"Mu" First Part, "Mu" Second Part.* Varese 061147, 2001.

———. *Where Is Brooklyn?* Blue Note 3114362, 2005. Originally released in 1966.

Chrome. *Alien Soundtracks.* Noiseville 77, 2007. Originally released in 1978.

———. *Half Machine Lip Moves/Alien Soundtracks.* Noiseville 78, 2007. Originally released in 1979.

Cohran, Philip, and the Artistic Heritage Ensemble. *The Malcolm X Memorial (A Tribute in Music).* Katalyst Entertainment 00440, 2007.

———. *On the Beach.* Aestuarium Records, 2001.

———. *The Spanish Suite.* Katalyst Entertainment 00348, 2010.

Coleman, Anthony. *Freakish: Anthony Coleman Plays Jelly Roll Morton.* Tzadik 7631, 2009.

Coleman, Ornette. *The Complete Science Fiction Sessions.* Sony Music Distribution C-2K63569, 2000. Originally released in 1972.

———. *Dancing in Your Head.* Polygram 5435192, 2000. Originally released in 1976.

———. *The Shape of Jazz to Come.* Rhino 8122723982, 2001. Originally released in 1958.

———. *Something Else: The Music of Ornette Coleman.* OJC Remasters 32845, 2011. Originally released in 1958.

———. *Sound Grammar.* Sound Grammar SG 001, 2006.

———. see also Ornette Coleman Quartet.

Coltrane, John. *Ascension.* Impulse! 5434132, 2000. Originally released in 1965.

———. *Coltrane Jazz.* Atlantic SD-1354-2, 1992. Originally released in 1960.

———. *Coltrane Plays the Blues.* Rhino 8122737532, 2004. Originally released in 1962.

———. *Giant Steps.* Rhino 1311, 1987. Originally released in 1960.

———. *Interstellar Space.* Impulse! 543415, 2000. Originally released in 1967.

———. *A Love Supreme.* Impulse! 155, 1995. Originally released in 1964.

———. see also John Coltrane Sextet.

Coltrane, John, and Don Cherry. *The Avant-Garde.* Atlantic 90041-2, 1990. Originally released in 1967.

The Congos. *Heart of the Congos.* VP 1287, 1992. Originally released in 1977.

Congotronics 2: Buzz 'n' Rumble from the Utb'n Jungle. Crammed Discs 230010, 2006.

Connors, Loren Mazzacane. *The Little Match Girl.* Road Cone ROCO 029CD, 2001.

———. *Night Through: Singles and Collected Works, 1976–2004.* Family Vineyard CD 54036, 2002.

———. *Portrait of a Soul.* Fbwl 201, 2000.

Connors, Loren, and David Grubbs. *Arborvitae.* Häpna 13, 2003.

Conrad, Tony. *Early Minimalism Volume One.* Table of the Elements, 329764, 1997.

Creative Construction Company. *CCC, Vol. 1.* Muse 5071, 1970.

———. *CCC, Vol. 2.* Muse 5097, 1971.

Crossfaderz. Moonshine Music 80131, 2000.

D'Angelo. *Voodoo.* Virgin 445058, 2000.

David Holland Quartet. *Conference of the Birds.* ECM Records 8293732, 2000. Originally released in 1972.

Davis, Anthony. *Of Blues and Dreams.* Sackville (Canada) 3020, 2001. Originally released in 1978.

Davis, Betty. *Is It Love or Desire.* Light in the Attic Records LITA047, 2009.

———. *Nasty Gal.* Light in the Attic Records LITA045, 2009. Originally released in 1975.

Davis, Miles. *Birth of the Cool.* Blue Note CDP 7928622, 1990. Originally released in 1956.

———. *Bitches Brew.* Sony Music Distribution 4606022, 1994. Originally released in 1970.

———. *In a Silent Way.* Columbia/Legacy 86556, 2002. Originally released in 1969.

———. *Kind of Blue.* Columbia 64935, 1999. Originally released in 1959.

———. *On the Corner.* Sony Music Distribution 63980, 2000. Originally released in 1972.

———. *'Round about Midnight.* Sony Music Distribution SRCS-9725, 2001. Originally released in 1957.

———. *Sorcerer.* Sony Music Distribution 4743692, 1994. Originally released in 1967.

Dickerson, Walt. *To My Queen.* Prestige Records VICJ60683, 2000.

Dinosaur Jr. *You're Living All Over Me.* Merge 244, 2005. Originally released in 1987.

Dischord 1981: The Year in Seven Inches. Dischord Records, 1994.

DJ Spooky. *Riddim Warfare.* Out Post 30031, 1998.

Dolphy, Eric. *At the Five Spot, Vol. 1.* Prestige Records 30656, 2008. Originally released in 1961.

———. *Far Cry.* Original Jazz Classics OJCCD 4002, 1995. Originally released in 1960.

———. *Iron Man.* Celluloid 5015, 2010. Originally released in 1963.

———. *Out There.* Prestige Records 1881012, 2006. Originally released in 1960.

———. *Out to Lunch.* Blue Note 98793, 1999. Originally released in 1964.

Dolphy, Eric, and John Lewis. *Play Kurt Weill.* Lonehill LHJ 10349, 2008.

Duke Ellington and His Orchestra. *Black, Brown and Beige.* Featuring Mahalia Jackson. Sony Music Distribution 65566, 1999. Originally released in 1958.

Ellington, Duke. *Blues in Orbit.* Sony Music Distribution 4608232, 2004. Originally released in 1960.

———. *The Ellington Suites.* Universal 1864462, 1992. Originally released in 1976.

———. *Live at Newport, 1958.* Mosaic 1014, 2007. Originally released in 1958.

———. *Never No Lament: The Blanton-Webster Band.* BMG 38049/51, 2006.

———. *Piano in the Foreground.* Sony Music Distribution 87042, 2009. Originally released in 1961.

———. see also Duke Ellington and His Orchestra.

Ellington, Duke, with Charles Mingus and Max Roach. *Money Jungle.* Blue Note 5382272, 2002. Originally released in 1962.

Ellington, Duke, and John Coltrane. *Duke Ellington and John Coltrane.* Impulse! 166, 1995. Originally released in 1962.

Evans, Bill, Roy Haynes, Eric Dolphy, Oliver Nelson, Paul Chambers, and Freddie Hubbard. *The Blues and the Abstract Truth.* Universal Distribution 9544, 2004. Originally released in 1961.

———. *Sunday at the Village Vanguard.* Riverside Records 9376, 2001. Originally released in 1961.

———. *Waltz for Debby.* Universal Distribution 9536, 2004.

———. see also Bill Evans Trio.

Evora, Cesaria. *Cabo Verde.* Elektra 79450, 1997.

Fahey, John. *Days Have Gone By, Vol. 6.* Takoma 6509, 2001. Originally released in 1967.

———. *Sea Changes & Coelacanths: A Young Person's Guide to John Fahey.* Table of the Elements 10185, 2006.

———. *The Transfiguration of Blind Joe Death.* Takoma 6504, 1997. Originally released in 1965.

———. see also John Fahey and His Orchestra.

The Faith and Void. *The Faith/Void.* Split LP. Dischord Records 87, 1993.

The Fall. *Dragnet.* Sanctuary Fontana CMRCD 848, 2008. Originally released in 1979.

———. *Grotesque (After the Gramme).* Sanctuary 81202, 2002.

———. *Hex Enduction Hour.* COG Sinister 151, 2002. Originally released in 1982.

———. *Live at the Witch Trials.* Resurgent Music 4107, 1997. Originally released in 1979.

———. *Perverted by Language.* Castle Music Ltd. CLACD 392, 1994. Originally released in 1983.

———. *Totale's Turns (It's Now or Never).* Castle Music Ltd. DOJOCD 83, 1994. Originally released in 1980.

Flynt, Henry. *Back Porch Hillbilly Blues: Vol. 1.* Locust 16, 2002.

———. *Back Porch Hillbilly Blues: Vol. 2.* Locust 14, 2002.

———. *I Don't Wanna.* Locust 39, 2004.

———. *Nova Billy.* Locust 101, 2007.

———. *Raga Electric: Experimental Music, 1963–1971.* Locust 6, 2002.

Freeman, Von. *Serenade and Blues.* Nessa N-11, 1979.

Fugazi. *13 Songs.* Dischord Records DIS 36CD, 1990.

Funkadelic. *Maggot Brain.* Westbound 2007, 1989. Originally released in 1971.

Gastr del Sol. *Crookt, Crackt, or Fly.* Drag City, 1994.

———. *Mirror Repair EP.* Drag City DC 54CD, 1995.

———. *Upgrade & Afterlife.* Drag City 90, 1996.

Gaye, Marvin. *What's Going On.* Motown 530883, 1998. Originally released in 1971.

Goodbye, Babylon. Dust-to-Digital 713587, 2004.

Grubbs, David, and Mats Gustafsson. *Off-Road.* Blue Chopsticks BC 11CD, 2003.

Grubbs, David, and Susan Howe. *Souls of the Labadie Tract.* Drag City BC 17CD, 2007.

Hemphill, Julius. *Reflections.* Freedom 268364, 1995.

Hemphill, Julius, and K. Curtis Lyle. *The Collected Poems for Blind Lemon Jefferson.* Ikef B00006AL9G, 2002.

Henry Threadgill Sextet. *Rag, Bush and All.* Novus 3052, 1989.

Henry Threadgill Very Very Circus. *Spirit of Nuff … Nuff.* Black Saint 1201342, 1991.

Henry Threadgill Zooid. *This Brings Us To, Volume 1.* Pi Recordings 03123, 2009.

————. see also Threadgill, Henry.

Hill, Andrew. *Black Fire*. Blue Note BCT-84151, 1987. Originally released in 1963.

————. *Dance with Death*. Blue Note 8667412, 2004. Originally released in 1968.

————. *Hommage*. East Wind UCCJ-4019, 2000. Originally released in 1975.

————. *Point of Departure*. Blue Note 7841672, 1989. Originally released in 1964.

————. *Smoke Stack*. Blue Note 4160, 2004. Originally released in 1963.

————. *Verona Rag*. Soul Note 121110, 1993. Originally released in 1986.

Holiday, Billie. *Lady Day*. Mbb VBM0077, 2010.

————. *Lady in Autumn: The Best of the Verve Years*. Verve 8494342, 1991.

————. *Singin' the Blues*. Universal Special Products 589570, 2002.

Holland, David. see David Holland Quartet.

Hooker, John Lee. *Plays the Blues*. Universe 138, 2004.

Hopkins, Lightnin'. see Lightnin' Hopkins.

House, Son. *Father of the Delta Blues: The Complete 1965 Sessions*. Columbia/Legacy 122826, 1992.

Howlin' Wolf. *The Definitive Collection*. Geffen 8784, 2007.

————. *His Best*. Chess' 50th Anniversary Collection. MCA/Chess MCD 9375, 1997.

Hudson, Keith. *Flesh of My Skin, Blood of My Blood*. Honest Jones 1005, 2004. Originally released in 1974.

————. *Play It Cool & Playing It Right*. Basic Channel 9, 2005.

Hudson, Keith, and the Soul Syndicate. *Nuh Skin Up*. Pressure Sounds 53, 2007.

Hurt, Mississippi John. *Avalon Blues*. Rounder ROUCD 1081, 1992. Originally released in 1963.

The Ikettes. *Can't Sit Down … 'Cos It Feels So Good! The Complete Modern Recordings*. Kent 276, 2007.

James, Etta. *The Best of Etta James*. Spectrum 5443672, 1999.

James, Skip. *Today!* Ace 79219, 1995. Originally released in 1965.

Jarman, Joseph. *Song For*. Delmark 401, 1991. Originally released in 1966.

Jay, Abner. *The Backbone of America Is a Mule and Cotton*. Brandie B005NCML3E, 1976.

————. *True Story of Abner Jay*. Mississippi Records R1550912, 2009.

————. *The True Story of Dixie*. Brandie SON96001/2, 1968.

John Coltrane Sextet. *Blue Train*. Blue Note 9005, 1998. Originally released in 1957.

————. see also Coltrane, John.

John Fahey and His Orchestra. *After the Ball*. Import 10307, 2001. Originally released in 1973.

————. *Of Rivers and Religion*. Import 10357, 2001. Originally released in 1972.

————. see also Fahey, John.

Johnson, James P. *Carolina Shout*. ASV/Living Era CDAJA 5355, 2000.

Johnson, Linton Kwesi. *In Concert with the Dub Band*. Shanachie 43034/5, 1990.

Johnson, Robert. *Robert Johnson: King of the Delta Blues Singers*. Sony Music Distribution 4844192, 1996. Originally released in 1961.

Kagel, Mauricio. *Mauricio Kagel 1*. Montaigne, MO789004, 1997.

————. *Schwarzes Madrigal*. Winter & Winter, 9100902, 2002.

Kimbrough, Junior. *Meet Me in the City*. Fat Possum 80333, 1999.

————. *Most Things Haven't Worked Out*. Fat Possum 80309, 1997.

————. *You Better Run: The Essential Junior Kimbrough*. Fat Possum 3402, 2002.

Kippenberger, Martin. *Musik /1979–1995*. Edition Krothenhayn EK 004CD, 2010.

Lacy, Steve. *Futurities, Part II*. HatART 6032, 1995.

Lake, Oliver, and Julius Hemphill. *Buster Bee*. Sackville Recordings SKCD 23018, 2002. Originally released in 1978.

Leadbelly. *The Blues: Bourgeois Blues, 1933–1946*. Frémeaux et Associés FA 269, 2005.

————. *Borrow Love and Go*. Masked Weasel 311, 2006.

Lee, Jeanne. *Natural Affinities*. Emarcy 0183522, 2003.

Lee, Jeanne, and Ran Blake. *The Newest Sound Around*. BMG 74321221122, 2000. Originally released in 1961.

Lewis, George E. *Endless Shout*. Tzadik Records 7054, 2000.

————. *Homage to Charles Parker*. Black Saint 1200292, 2003. Originally released in 1979.

————. *Les Exercises Spirituels*. Tzadik Records TZA 8081CD, 2011.

————. *Sequel (For Lester Bowie)*. PID B000H5U2KQ, 2011.

————. *The Solo Trombone Record*. Sackville Recordings SKCD 23012, 2001. Originally released in 1976.

Lightnin' Hopkins. *Double Blues*. Fantasy FCD-24702-2, 1989. Originally released in 1973.

Lincoln, Abbey. *Abbey Is Blue*. Riverside Records 1153, 2005. Originally released in 1959.

Little Richard. *The Very Best of Little Richard*. Specialty Records 30748, 2008.

Lomax, Alan. *Deep River of Song: Virginia and the Piedmont*. Rounder 611827, 2000.

Love. *Forever Changes*. Rhino 74013, 2007. Originally released in 1967.

Love Joys. *Lovers Rock*. Wackie's 2383, 2006. Originally released in 1982.

Mapfumo, Thomas. *The Chimurenga Singles*. Shanachie 43066, 1984.

McDowell, Fred Mississippi. *Long Way from Home: The Blues of Fred McDowell*. Milestone/Original Blues Classics OBCCD 5352, 1990.

Mekuria, Getatchew, and The Ex and Guests. *Moa Anbessa*. Terp R943189, 2006.

Mengelberg, Misha. *Two Days in Chicago*. HAT HUT Records R466083, 1999.

Messiaen, Olivier. *L'Ascension, for Organ (arr. from orchestral piece), I/12b*. Meyer Media 07007, 2008.

Mingus, Charles. *Blues & Roots*. Atlantic SD-1305-2, 1990. Originally released in 1959.

————. *Let My Children Hear Music*. Sony Music Distribution 40509, 2007. Originally released in 1972.

————. *Mingus Ah Um*. Sony Music Distribution 4504362, 1994. Originally released in 1959.

————. *Mingus, Mingus, Mingus, Mingus, Mingus*. 1963. Verve 1703696, 2007. Originally released in 1963.

————. *Mingus Plays Piano: Spontaneous Compositions and Improvisations*.

Impulse! 217, 1997. Originally released in 1963.

———. *Mysterious Blues*. Candid CCD 79042, 1990. Originally released in 1960.

———. *Newport Rebels*. King 8386, 2001.

———. *Oh Yeah*. Rhino 8122755892, 1999. Originally released in 1962.

———. *see also* Charles Mingus and Eric Dolphy Sextet.

Minor Threat. *Complete Discography*. Dischord Records 1314, 1988.

Minott, Sugar. *Wicked Ago Feel It*. Wackies EFA566122, 2002. Originally released in 1984.

Minutemen. *Double Nickels on the Dime*. SST SST 028CD, 1987.

Mitchell, Roscoe. *Before There Was Sound*. Nessa 34, 2011.

———. *L-R-G, the Maze, S II Examples*. Nessa 14, 1989. Originally released in 1978.

———. *Nonaah*. Nessa 9, 2008. Originally released in 1977.

———. *see also* Roscoe Mitchell and the Sound Ensemble; Roscoe Mitchell Art Ensemble; Roscoe Mitchell Sextet.

Monk, Thelonius. *At the Blackhawk*. Original Jazz Classics 305, 1991. Originally released in 1960.

———. *Brilliant Corners*. Universal Distribution UCCO9220, 2008. Originally released in 1957.

———. *Criss-Cross*. Proper Records PVCD-114, 2003. Originally released in 1963.

———. *Genius of Modern Music, Volume 1*. Blue Note 81510, 1989. Originally released in 1952.

———. *Genius of Modern Music, Volume 2*. Blue Note 81511, 1989. Originally released in 1952.

———. *Misterioso*. Original Jazz Classics 206, 1992. Originally released in 1958.

———. *Plays Duke Ellington*. Riverside Records 201, 2004. Originally released in 1955.

———. *Thelonius Himself*. Riverside Records 30510, 2008. Originally released in 1957.

———. *Underground*. Sony Music Distribution 63535, 2003. Originally released in 1968.

———. *The Unique Thelonius Monk*. Riverside/OJC 64, 1991. Originally released in 1956.

———. *see also* Thelonius Monk Orchestra; Thelonius Monk Septet; Thelonius Monk Trio.

Moran, Jason. *TEN*. EMI Music Distribution 4571862, 2010.

Morton, Jelly Roll. *Mr. Jelly Roll*. Tomato TOM 2034, 2003. Originally released in 1956.

Muhal Richard Abrams Orchestra. *Blu Blu Blu*. Black Saint 120117, 1991.

———. *see also* Abrams, Muhal Richard.

Myers, Amina Claudine. *Amina Claudine Myers Salutes Bessie Smith*. Leo Records, 1996. Originally released in 1980.

———. *see also* Amina Claudine Myers Trio.

Nichols, Herbie. *The Complete Blue Note Recordings*. Blue Note 8593522, 1997.

———. *Love, Gloom, Cash, Love*. Bethlehem High Fidelity 9624, 2005. Originally released in 1957.

Niney the Observer. *Niney and Friends: Blood & Fire, 1970–1978*. Sanctuary 80359, 2003.

Ornette Coleman Quartet. *Complete Live at the Hillcrest Club*. Gambit 69272, 2007.

———. *This Is Our Music*. Sepia Tone 2, 2002. Originally released in 1961.

———. *see also* Coleman, Ornette.

O'Rourke, Jim. *Bad Timing*. Drag City DC 120CD, 1997.

———. *Eureka*. Drag City 162, 1999.

———. *Insignificance*. Domino WIGCD 104, 2001.

Pablo, Augustus. *Dub, Reggae & Roots from the Melodica King*. Ocho 004, 2000.

Parker, Charlie. *Charlie Parker on Dial*. Definitive Classics 11149, 2000.

———. *The Complete Savoy and Dial Master Takes*. Savoy Jazz 17149, 2002.

Parks, Van Dyke. *Discover America*. Rhino/Warner Bros., 2007. Originally released in 1972.

———. *Song Cycle*. Rhino/Warner Bros., 2007. Originally released in 1968.

Parliament. *Chocolate City*. Mercury AA4400770272, 2003. Originally released in 1975.

Parsons, Gram. *G.P.* Vivid Sound 3219, 2004. Originally released in 1973.

———. *Grievous Angel*. Vivid Sound 3221, 2004. Originally released in 1974.

Patton, Charley. *Complete Recordings, 1929–1934*. JSP Records R 1191108, 2006.

Paul Bley Trio. *Closer*. ESP Disk 1021, 2008. Originally released in 1965.

———. *see also* Bley, Paul.

Perry, Lee "Scratch." *Lord God Muzick*. Zensor 858102, 1991.

Perry, Lee "The Upsetter." *Roast Rish Collie Weed & Corn Bread*. VP VPCD 1000, 1992.

Peterson, Oscar. *Oscar Peterson Plays for Lovers*. Prestige Records PRST-7649, 1969.

Powell, Bud. *The Amazing Bud Powell, Vol. 1*. Blue Note 5321362, 2001. Originally released in 1951.

———. *The Amazing Bud Powell, Vol. 2*. Blue Note 5321372, 2003. Originally released in 1955.

Public Enemy. *It Takes a Nation of Millions to Hold Us Back*. Ral R 28187, 1988.

———. *Yo! Bum Rush the Show*. Def Jam 40658, 1990.

Ra, Sun. *see* Sun Ra.

Rail Band. *Belle Epoque 1: Soundiata*. Sterns Africa B0000AUHPA, 2007.

———. *Belle Epoque 2: Mansa*. Sterns Africa B0006IIO9U, 2008.

The Raincoats. *Odyshape*. We Three 4, 2011. Originally released in 1981.

Rainey, Ma. *Ma Rainey's Black Bottom*. Yazoo 89401, 2006.

Red Krayola. *Amor and Language*. Drag City DC 53CDX, 1995.

———. *Five American Portraits*. Drag City DC384, 2010.

———. *Hazel*. Drag City DC 98CD, 1996.

———. *Introduction*. Drag City 39083041, 2006.

———. *The Parable of Arable Land*. Collectables 551, 1993.

———. *The Red Krayola*. Drag City DC 52CD, 1994.

———. *Soldier-Talk*. Drag City 79, 2007.

Red Krayola with Art & Language. *Black Snakes*. Drag City 104, 1997.

———. *Corrected Slogans*. Drag City 96, 1997.

———. *Kangaroo?* Drag City 80, 1995.

———. *Sighs Trapped by Liars.* Drag City 39083432, 2007.

———. *Singles: 1968–2002.* Drag City 257, 2004.

R.E.M. *Murmur.* I.R.S. Records 44797-0014-2, 1983.

Rites of Spring. *End on End.* Dischord Records DIS 16CD, 2002. Originally released in 1985.

Rivers, Sam. *Crystals.* Universal Distribution 5897602, 2002. Originally released in 1974.

———. *Fuchsia Swing Song.* Blue Note 593-8742, 2003. Originally released in 1964.

Roscoe Mitchell and the Sound Ensemble. *Snurdy McGurdy and Her Dancin' Shoes.* Nessa N20, 1981.

Roscoe Mitchell Art Ensemble. *Congliptious.* Nessa NES2CD, 2009. Originally released in 1968.

———. *Old/Quartet Sessions.* Nessa NCD27/28, 2011. Originally released in 1975.

Roscoe Mitchell Sextet. *Sound.* Delmark 408, 1996. Originally released in 1966.

———. *see also* Mitchell, Roscoe.

Royal Trux. *Royal Trux.* Drag City 5, 1993.

Schweizer, Irène, and Pierre Favre. *Irène Schweizer and Pierre Favre.* Intakt Records 009, 1990.

Scott, Little Jimmy. *All the Way.* Sire 7599269552, 1992.

Shabazz Palaces. *Black Up.* Sub Pop 70900, 2011.

Shepp, Archie. *Attica Blues.* Universal Distribution 5073, 2003. Originally released in 1972.

———. *Four for Trane.* Universal Distribution 5268, 2005. Originally released in 1964.

Shudder to Think. *Curses, Spells, Voodoo, Mooses.* Sammich Records 5, 1989.

———. *Funeral at the Movies.* Dischord Records DIS 54C, 1995.

Silver Jews. *The Arizona Record.* Drag City 28, 1995.

———. *Send in the Clouds.* Domino RUG 077CD, 1998.

Simone, Nina. *The Best of Nina Simone.* BMG 37297, 2002.

Sissy Man Blues: 25 Authentic Straight and Gay Blues and Jazz Vocals. Jass Records J-CD-13, 1989.

Slint. *Spiderland.* Touch & Go TG-64CD, 1991.

Smith, Bessie. *Chicago Bound Blues.* Quadromania Klassik 222480, 2005.

Smith, J. B. *Ever Since I Have Been a Man Full-Grown & Two Other Prison Songs Sung Unaccompanied.* Takoma B003TVGSA8, 1966.

Smith, Leo. *Spirit Catcher.* Nessa 19, 2009. Originally released in 1980.

Smith, Wadada Leo. *Kabell Years: 1971–1979.* Tzadik Records 7610, 2004.

———. *Reflectativity.* Tzadik TZA 7060, 2000.

Smith, Willie "The Lion." *Pork and Beans.* Black Lion 8776712, 2009.

Son Cubano NYC: Cuban Roots, New York Spices, 1972–82. Honest Jon's 8743762, 2005.

Sonic Youth. *Confusion Is Sex.* SST 096, 1983.

———. *Daydream Nation.* DGC 24515, 1993.

———. *EVOL.* DGC 24513, 1994.

———. *Sister.* DGC 24514, 1994.

Squirrel Bait. *Skag Heaven.* Drag City 103, 1997.

Stanley, Ralph. *Ralph Stanley and the Clinch Mountain Boys, 1971–1973.* Rebel 1613, 1995.

Sun Ra. *Disco 3000.* Art Yard R 706859, 2007. Originally released in 1978.

———. *Lanquidity.* Evidence 22220, 2000. Originally released in 1978.

———. *Nothing Is.* ESP-Disk 1045, 1993. Originally released in 1966.

———. *Space Is the Place.* GRP AAIMPD249, 1993. Originally released in 1972.

———. *Spaceship Lullaby (1954–60).* Atavistic Records 243, 2003.

Sun Ra and His Arkestra. *Some Blues but Not the Kind That's Blue.* Unheard Music Series/Atavistic R 1290305, 2008. Originally released in 1977.

Sun Ra and His Astro Infinitiy Arkestra. *Holiday for Soul Dance.* Evidence ECD 220112, 1991. Originally released in 1960.

Sun Ra and His Intergalactic Infinity Arkestra. *The Night of the Purple Moon.* Atavistic Records 264, 2007. Originally released in 1970.

Sun Ra and His Solar-Myth Arkestra. *The Solar-Myth Approach, Vol. 1.* Sunspots SPOT509, 2004. Originally released in 1970.

———. *The Solar-Myth Approach, Vol. 2.* Sunspots SPOT520, 2004. Originally released in 1971.

Sun Ra Quartet. *Other Voices, Other Blues.* Horo 23-24, 1978.

Tapscott, Horace. *The Dark Tree.* HatOLOGY 630, 2009.

———. *Dial "B" for Barbra.* Nimbus NS 1147, 1981.

———. *West Coast Hot.* Jive/Novus R167394, 1991. Originally released in 1969.

Tatum, Art. *20th-Century Piano Genius.* Polygram 5317632, 1996.

Taylor, Cecil. *Cecil Taylor: 3 Phasis.* New World Records NWR 803032, 1979.

———. *Cell Walk for Celeste.* Candid 79034, 2006. Originally released in 1961.

———. *Chinampas.* Leo Records 153, 2000. Originally released in 1987.

———. *Conquistador!* Blue Note 5767492, 2004. Originally released in 1966.

———. *For Olim.* Soul Note (Italy) 121150, 1993. Originally released in 1986.

———. *Garden Pt. 1.* HatART 6050, 1981.

———. *Garden Pt. 2.* HatART 6051, 1981.

———. *The Great Paris Concert.* Black Lion 760201, 1999. Originally released in 1966.

———. *Jazz Advance.* Blue Note 7844622, 1991. Originally released in 1956.

———. *Jumpin' Punkins.* Candid CCD-79013, 1987.

———. *Leaf Palm Hand.* Jazzwerkstatt 6, 2001. Originally released in 1988.

———. *Live at the Café Montmartre.* Fantasy 6014, 1964.

———. *One Too Many Salty Swift and Not Goodbye.* Hat Hut Records 6090, 1994. Originally released in 1978.

———. *Silent Tongues.* Black Lion 8776332, 2001. Originally released in 1975.

———. *Unit Structures.* Blue Note BNZ 218, 1987. Originally released in 1966.

———. *The World of Cecil Taylor.* Candid CCD-79006 1989. Originally released in 1960.

———. *see also* Cecil Taylor Quartet; Cecil Taylor Unit.

Taylor, Cecil, and Buell Neidlinger. *New York City R&B.* Candid CCD 79017, 1989. Originally released in 1961.

Taylor, Hound Dog, and the House Rockers. *Natural Boogie.* Alligator

Records ALCD-4704, 1989. Originally released in 1973.

Thelonius Monk Orchestra. *At Town Hall.* Essential Jazz Classics EJC 55525, 2011.

Thelonius Monk Septet. *Monk's Music.* Universal 7232689, 2011. Originally released in 1957.

Thelonius Monk Trio. *Thelonius.* Prestige Records 7230164, 2007. Originally released in 1954.

———. *see also* Monk, Thelonius.

Thompson, Mayo. *Corky's Debt to His Father.* Drag City 49, 1994.

Threadgill, Henry, and Make a Move. *Everybody's Mouth's a Book.* Pi Recordings PI 01CD, 2001.

———. *see also* Henry Threadgill Sextet; Henry Threadgill Very Very Circus; Henry Threadgill Zooid.

Tropicália: Ou Panis et Circencis. Lilith LR 150CD, 2008. Originally released in 1968.

Trouble Funk. *Droppin' Bombs: The Definitive Trouble Funk.* Harmless Recordings 014, 1998.

Turner, Otha, and the Afrossippi Allstars. *From Senegal to Senatobia.* Birdman Records BMR 025, 1999.

Ulmer, James "Blood." *Odyssey.* Columbia 64934, 1996. Originally released in 1984.

Unrest. *Fuck Pussy Galore and All Her Friends.* Matador OLE 0242, 1994.

Van Oehlen. *Rock and Roll Is Here to Die.* Blue Chopsticks BC 10CD, 2000.

———. *We are Eggsperienced.* Blue Chopsticks BC 3CD, 2000.

Verlaine, Tom. *The Wonder.* Fontana Distribution 842420, 2004.

The Walker Brothers. *Nite Flights.* Sony Music Distribution 4844382, 1999.

Warwick, Dionne. *Here I Am.* Collectors' Music Choice CCM 755, 2007. Originally released in 1965.

Waters, Muddy. *The Anthology, 1947–1972.* MCA/Chess 1126492, 2001.

Wells, Junior, Muddy Waters, Elmore James, and Otis Spann. *Blues Hit Big Town.* Delmark 640, 1998. Originally released in 1977.

White, Bukka. *Sky Songs: Vols. 1 and 2.* Arhoolie ARHCD 323, 1991.

White Mice. *Vocals.* Basic Replay R 1238551, 2006.

The Wildflowers. *Wildflowers: Loft Jazz New York, 1976.* Douglas Music DG 28, 2009.

Williams, Mary Lou. *Town Hall '45: Zodiac Suite.* Jazz Classics 6002, 1996.

Wolf, Howlin'. *see* Howlin' Wolf.

Womack, Bobby. *The Best of Bobby Womack: The Soul Years.* Toshiba EMI 70490, 2008.

Womack & Womack. *Love Wars.* Elektra 6029322, 2003. Originally released in 1983.

Workshop. *Yog Sothoth.* Sonig 37, 2004.

Wu-Tang Clan. *Enter the Wu-Tang (36 Chambers).* Loud/RCA 66336-4, 1993.

Wyatt, Robert. *Comicopera.* Domino WIGCD 202, 2007.

Young, Lester. *Classic Columbia, Okeh and Vocalion: Lester Young with Count Basie (1936–1940).* Mosaic 4239, 2008.

———. *Lester Young Trio.* Mercury 521650, 1994. Originally released in 1951.

———. *Lester Young with Oscar Peterson Trio.* Giants of Jazz Recordings CD 53391, 2003.

Afterword

The blues, in all its diversity, has been called one of the greatest cultural inventions to emerge from the American twentieth century. Along with jazz, it has been considered this country's classical music. But what could the blues mean for visual art, and where might it be found today? Including works in a variety of media by approximately fifty artists from the past half century, as well as a range of musical, filmic, and cultural materials, "Blues for Smoke" is ambitious in scope and conception. Rather than narrating a history of the blues as we have come to expect it, the exhibition turns to moments in culture and art when ideas and forms of the blues become relevant. The exhibition positions the blues not simply as a musical category, but as an artistic sensibility and worldview informing multiple generations of artists. Moving across expectations of discipline, art history, race, and culture, "Blues for Smoke" argues for the vitality and innovation of the blues within modern and contemporary art.

Inspired by a rich tradition of scholarship, the exhibition foregrounds the expansiveness and flexibility of the blues, finding in it a language perfectly suited to topics resonant in visual art: articulations of daily life; modes of abstraction and repetition; self-performance and extravagant subjectivity; ecstatic and cathartic expression; an impulse toward archiving and referencing; and metaphors of hauntedness and memory. Bringing together diverse artworks and contexts, "Blues for Smoke" contributes significantly to the ongoing definition of the blues aesthetic.

In presenting "Blues for Smoke," the Museum of Contemporary Art, Los Angeles (MOCA), continues to break new ground in terms of critical discourse and theory around contemporary art. Over the past three decades, the museum's venerable history of important thematic exhibitions has contributed to—and in some cases helped to redefine—popular understanding of developments in art. Speculative shows such as "A Forest of Signs: Art in the Crisis of Representation" (1989), "Ecstasy: In and About Altered States" (2005), and "The Painting Factory: Abstraction After Warhol" (2012) have each in their own way provided an opportunity to focus on an aspect of current thinking about contemporary art in order to reveal something new or yet untold. At the same time, MOCA's groundbreaking historical surveys, which include "A Minimal Future? Art as Object 1958–1968" (2004), "WACK! Art and the Feminist Revolution" (2007), and "Ends of the Earth: Land Art to 1974" (2012), have consistently challenged the conventional notions and narratives about established art topics and movements.

"Blues for Smoke" was organized by MOCA Curator Bennett Simpson, who brought a tremendous amount of intelligence, rigor, and sensitivity to the process of conceiving and researching this project. His ongoing commitment to the artists in the exhibition is admirable, as is his compelling articulation of the blues as a relevant force in contemporary visual art. A number of individuals and institutions have helped to make this exhibition possible. First and foremost I thank MOCA's Board of Trustees for their steadfast commitment to contemporary art. I am especially grateful to Founding Chairman and Life Trustee Eli Broad, Co-Chairs Maria Arena Bell and David G. Johnson, and President Jeffrey Soros for their leadership and support. I would also like to acknowledge the incredible generosity of the Andy Warhol Foundation for the Visual Arts, Carolyn and William Powers, Sol Republic, Blake Byrne and Justin Gilanyi, Karyn Kohl, Shaun Caley Regen, Susanne Vielmetter Los Angeles Projects, and John Rubeli, who provided crucial financial support. I also thank the Whitney Museum of American Art, New York, and Alice Pratt Brown Director Adam D. Weinberg, for their participation in the exhibition's tour.

I am grateful to the numerous lenders who have parted with important works from their collections to support this groundbreaking exhibition, as well as to all those who offered their time, expertise, and energy to its realization. Finally, I am profoundly indebted to the artists featured in "Blues for Smoke," whose inspiring works and generous participation have made this important project possible.

Jeffrey Deitch, Director
The Museum of Contemporary Art, Los Angeles

Acknowledgments

"Blues for Smoke" has been in the works a long time—since before I arrived at the Museum of Contemporary Art, Los Angeles (MOCA), and throughout my six years in Los Angeles. Needless to say, the process of realizing this exhibition, one so near to my heart and thoughts, has benefited from the extraordinary generosity of many people. Foremost, I express my profound gratitude to Glenn Ligon. Glenn was the first artist I approached about this exhibition, in 2006—not, initially, to be a participant, but to help in its conception as a co-curator (a role that shifted to something like "lead advisor" when his schedule became increasingly consumed by a midcareer retrospective at the Whitney Museum of American Art). Glenn is among the most sensitive "readers" of contemporary culture, and indeed it was his September 2004 *Artforum* article "Black Light: David Hammons and the Poetics of Emptiness," which performed a meditation on the work and influence of Hammons through the examples of a younger generation of artists, that in many ways prompted my early thinking about this show. Without his timely and strategic input on matters both practical and theoretical, without his introductions, encouragement, and ongoing willingness to engage me on the complex issues at stake, "Blues for Smoke" would be a very different exhibition. I would also like to acknowledge several other individuals whose own work, thinking, and perceptions have fundamentally inspired my imagination of what "the blues" has been and could be, and without whose support I would be at a tremendous loss: Gregg Bordowitz, Stan Douglas, Charles Gaines, Thelma Golden, Renée Green, George E. Lewis, Nathaniel Mackey, Rodney McMillian, Fred Moten, Jeff Preiss, Mayo Thompson, Hamza Walker, and Jack Whitten.

One of the premises of this exhibition is that the proposal and revision of culture are often most striking in the work of artists—that artists might always exceed the bounds of what culture is and how it is named. Having looked to artists to show me a blues that has not yet been fully understood, I am most grateful to all of the participants for their trust and collaboration. I am also greatly appreciative of the generosity of the exhibition's many lenders, whose willingness to part with works for an extended period has meant everything to the realization of this project, and of the galleries and individuals who assisted in locating and securing works.

At MOCA, I wish to thank Director Jeffrey Deitch for his support of this exhibition since his arrival in 2010, as well as former Director Jeremy Strick and former Chief Executive Officer Charles E. Young for their commitment to it during the early stages of its organization. I am grateful to former Chief Curator Paul Schimmel for his constant embrace of the project, and to former Senior Curator Ann Goldstein, now Director of the Stedelijk Museum in Amsterdam, for her ongoing friendship and council. Paul and Ann brought me to MOCA in 2007 with this exhibition in hand, and I will forever appreciate their faith in its relevance to the institution's history and program. I also wish to thank MOCA's Board of Trustees for their support, in particular Maria Arena Bell, Co-Chair; David G. Johnson, Co-Chair; Jeffrey Soros, President; and Fred Sands, Vice-Chair. I extend special gratitude to Trustee Carolyn Powers for her enthusiastic investment in the success of the exhibition.

As always, MOCA's dedicated staff worked tirelessly to see this exhibition to completion. Director of Exhibition Management Susan Jenkins and Co-Directors of Development Jill Haynie and Veridiana Pontes-Ring as well as former Director of Development Jennifer Arceneaux all played crucial roles during a period of fund-raising and planning challenges. Curatorial Research Assistant Mia Locks was an invaluable and integral partner thoughout this exhibition's development and in all aspects of its organization. I am eternally grateful for her considerable skills, foresight, and good nature. Thanks are due, as well, to Curatorial Associate Lily Siegel and former Curatorial Assistant Christine Robinson, each of whom worked closely on this project, and to my colleagues in the Curatorial Department: Senior Curator Alma Ruiz, former Senior Curator Philipp Kaiser, and Associate Curator Rebecca Morse. Very special acknowledgment goes to Technical Manager, Exhibitions David Bradshaw, Exhibition Production Coordinator Stacie B. London, and Director of Exhibition Production Jang Park for gracefully addressing the challenges of the exhibition design and installation. I am also thankful to Associate Registrar Melissa Sapsford for her dedicated efforts to ensure the safe transport of the works. For their many and various contributions to this project I acknowledge Receptionist Patricia Bell, Logistics Associate Aldo Espina, former Grants Manager Elizabeth Greenway, Chief Financial Officer Michael Harrison, Public Relations Coordinator Nancy Lee, Assistant Director of Development for Institutional Giving Kris Lewis, Exhibition Management Coordinator Carolyn Lifsey, former Senior Designer Nicholas Lowie, Web Initiatives Manager Bret Nicely, Associate Director of Security and Maintenance Sergio Ramirez, former Senior Education Program Manager Aandrea Stang, Director of Communications Lyn Winter, and former Writer/Editor Erica Wrightson, and our partners at MOCA TV, Emma Reeves and John Toba.

This publication would not have been possible without the expertise and professionalism of MOCA's exceptional Senior Editor and Publications Manager Elizabeth Hamilton, who worked closely with me and our many writers to guide the book to its fullest potential. I would also like to acknowledge former Director of Publications Lisa Gabrielle Mark, who was a crucial sounding board and advisor not just on the book, but on the exhibition as a whole. Her friendship and intellectual generosity are priceless. I am grateful for the enthusiasm and commitment of MOCA's publishing partner, Mary DelMonico of DelMonico Books, and for the gifted editorial eye of Michelle Piranio, whose input was essential in honing the book's contents. I am indebted to Michael Worthington of Counterspace, Los Angeles, for lending his as-always extraordinary talents to the book's design. This is the third MOCA book I have done with Michael, after *Dan Graham: Beyond* (2009) and *William Leavitt: Theater Objects* (2011), and I count myself lucky to have had such a sympathetic collaboration. I am very proud of this publication's range of contents as well, which includes critical essays commissioned for the occasion and a broad assortment of poetry, fiction, and artist's statements. For their deeply original contributions and willingness to engage, I wish to thank Gregg Bordowitz, Wanda Coleman, George E. Lewis, Glenn Ligon, Nathaniel Mackey, Fred Moten, Harryette Mullen, and Jack Whitten.

MOCA is most fortunate to collaborate once again with the Whitney Museum of American Art, New York, where "Blues for Smoke" will travel after its presentation in Los Angeles. I am extremely grateful to Alice Pratt Brown Director Adam D. Weinberg and Chief Curator and Deputy Director for Programs Donna De Salvo for their faith and interest in this exhibition. And I am thrilled to work, for a second time (following our 2009 exhibition *Dan Graham: Beyond*), with my great friend and colleague Chrissie Iles, the Whitney's Anne and Joel Ehrenkranz Curator of Contemporary Art, as well as with Curator Jay Sanders. I extend special thanks to Curator Scott Rothkopf for his advocacy and support over many years.

A further word of thanks is due to all those who, in many other ways, have helped me prepare this exhibition and catalogue: Terry Adkins; Matthew Bakkom; Eric Banks; Nicholas Baume; Susanne Bennett; David Berman; Beatrice von Bismarck; Cosima von Bonin; Jennifer Bornstein; Mark Bradford; Connie Butler and Ann Temkin, The Museum of Modern Art, New York; Diane Byard; Tom Chasteen; Huey Copeland; John Corbett; Claire Daigle; Joshua Decter; Diedrich Diederichsen; Anthony Elms; Roe Ethridge; Will Fowler; Andrea Fraser; Malik Gaines; Roger Gastman; Thelma Golden, Naima Keith, and Thomas Lax, The Studio Museum in Harlem; Claudia Gould; Dan Graham; Alexander Gray; Renée Green and Javier Anguera; Carol Greene and Alexandra Tuttle, Greene Naftali Gallery, New York; Tim Griffin; David Grubbs; David Hammons; Rachel Harrison; Leslie Hewitt; Patricia Hickson; A. C. Hudgins; Steven Isoardi; Janet Jenkins; Branden Joseph; Craig Kalpakjian; Robin Kelly; John Kelsey; Peter Kirby; Nicole Klagsbrun; John Knight and Michelle Saylor; Jutta Koether; Karyn Kohl; Michael Krebber; Lisa Lapinski; William Leavitt; Mary Leclere; Annette Leddy; Bill Lester, Dockery Farms Foundation; Ian MacKaye, Dischord Records; Carter Mathes; Deborah McLeod, Gagosian Gallery, Beverly Hills; Jill Medvedow; Jen Mergel; Nicole Miller; Helen Molesworth; John Morace and Tom Kennedy; Jason Moran; Eileen Harris Norton; Benjamin Piekut; Ed Pollard; Isaac Preiss; Josephine Pryde; R. H. Quaytman; Jeremy Rall; Shaun Caley Regen, Jennifer Loh, and Miranda Siegel, Regen Projects, Los Angeles; Jock Reynolds; Jeanne Greenberg Rohatyn; Michael Rosenfeld; Allen Ruppersberg; Mark von Schlegell; Trevor Schoonmaker; Amy Sillman; Ralph Simpson; Franklin Sirmans; Nancy Soto; Susanne Vielmetter; Maria Vogelauer; Joel Wachs; Tom Watson; Andrew Weiss; Charlie White; and Christopher Williams.

A final, impossible thank you goes to Rhea Anastas, my wife and fiercest interlocutor. Before all else, her openness to moving to Los Angeles many years ago made the present exhibition a reality, and I am forever humbled by her grace.

Bennett Simpson, Curator
The Museum of Contemporary Art, Los Angeles

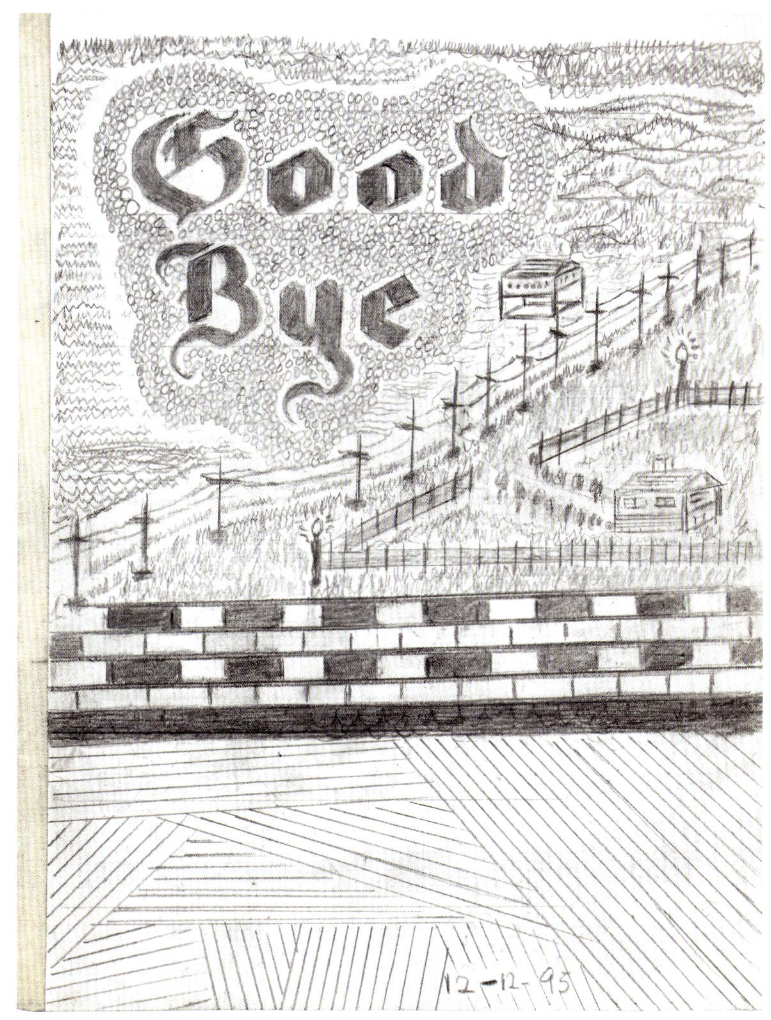

Jaki Byard
Untitled (Goodbye), 1995
Graphite on sheet music
11 x 8 ½ inches
Courtesy of Diane Byard

This publication accompanies the exhibition "Blues for Smoke," organized by Bennett Simpson and presented at The Museum of Contemporary Art, Los Angeles, The Geffen Contemporary at MOCA, October 20, 2012–January 7, 2013, and at the Whitney Museum of American Art, New York, February 7–April 28, 2013.

"Blues for Smoke" is made possible by the Andy Warhol Foundation for the Visual Arts. Major support is provided by Carolyn and William Powers. Generous support is provided by Sol Republic. Additional support is provided by Blake Byrne and Justin Gilanyi, Karyn Kohl, Shaun Caley Regen, Susanne Vielmetter Los Angeles Projects, and John Rubeli.

Managing Editor: Elizabeth Hamilton
Editor: Michelle Piranio
Photo editor: Mia Locks
Designer: Counterspace, Los Angeles
Color separations: Echelon, Los Angeles
Printer: C&C, China

Published in 2012 by The Museum of Contemporary Art, Los Angeles, and DelMonico Books • Prestel

Prestel is a member of Verlagsgruppe Random House GmbH

Prestel Verlag
Neumarkter Strasse 28
81673 Munich Germany
Tel: 49 89 41360
Fax: 49 89 41362335
prestel.de

Prestel Publishing Ltd.
4 Bloomsbury Place
London WC1A 2QA
United Kingdom
Tel: 44 20 7323 5004
Fax: 44 20 7636 8004

Prestel Publishing
900 Broadway, Suite 603
New York, NY 10003
Tel: (212) 995 2720
Fax: (212) 995 2733
sales@prestel-usa.com

Library of Congress Cataloging-in-Publication Data

Blues for smoke / organized by Bennett Simpson.
     pages cm
  This publication accompanies the exhibition "Blues for Smoke," organized by Bennett Simpson and presented at The Museum of Contemporary Art, Los Angeles, The Geffen Contemporary at MOCA, October 20, 2012–January 7, 2013.
  Includes bibliographical references.
  ISBN 978-3-7913-5253-4 (hardback)
  1. Arts, Modern—20th century—Exhibitions. 2. Arts, Modern—21st century—Exhibitions. 3. Blues (Music) in art—Exhibitions. I. Simpson, Bennett. II. Museum of Contemporary Art (Los Angeles, Calif.)
  NX456.B58 2012
  700.9'0407479494—dc23
                     2012025362

Cover: Mark Morrisroe, detail from *Light and Shadow*, 1986
Endsheets: Jeff Preiss, stills from *STOP*, 1995–2012

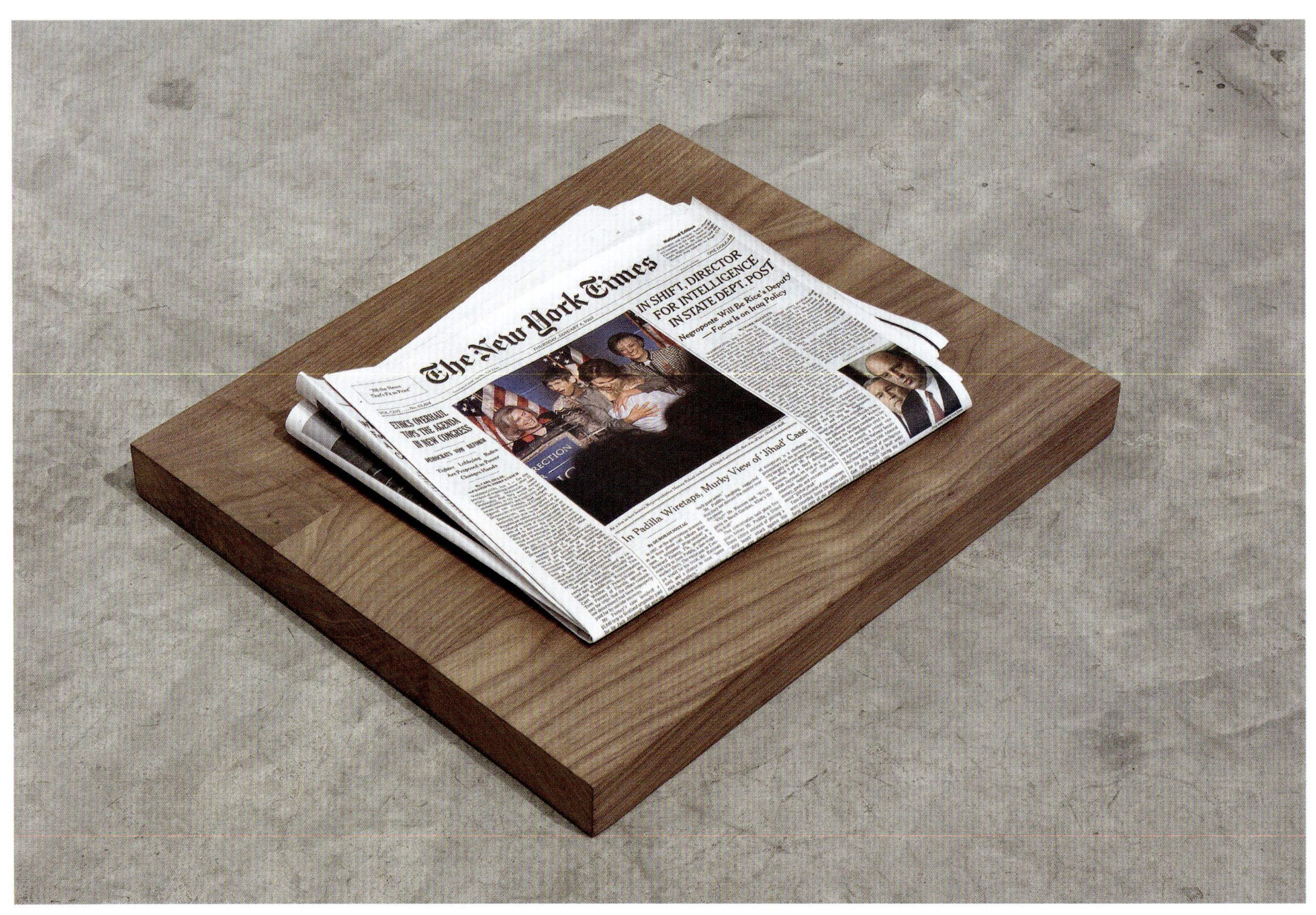

Dave McKenzie
Yesterday's Newspaper, 2012

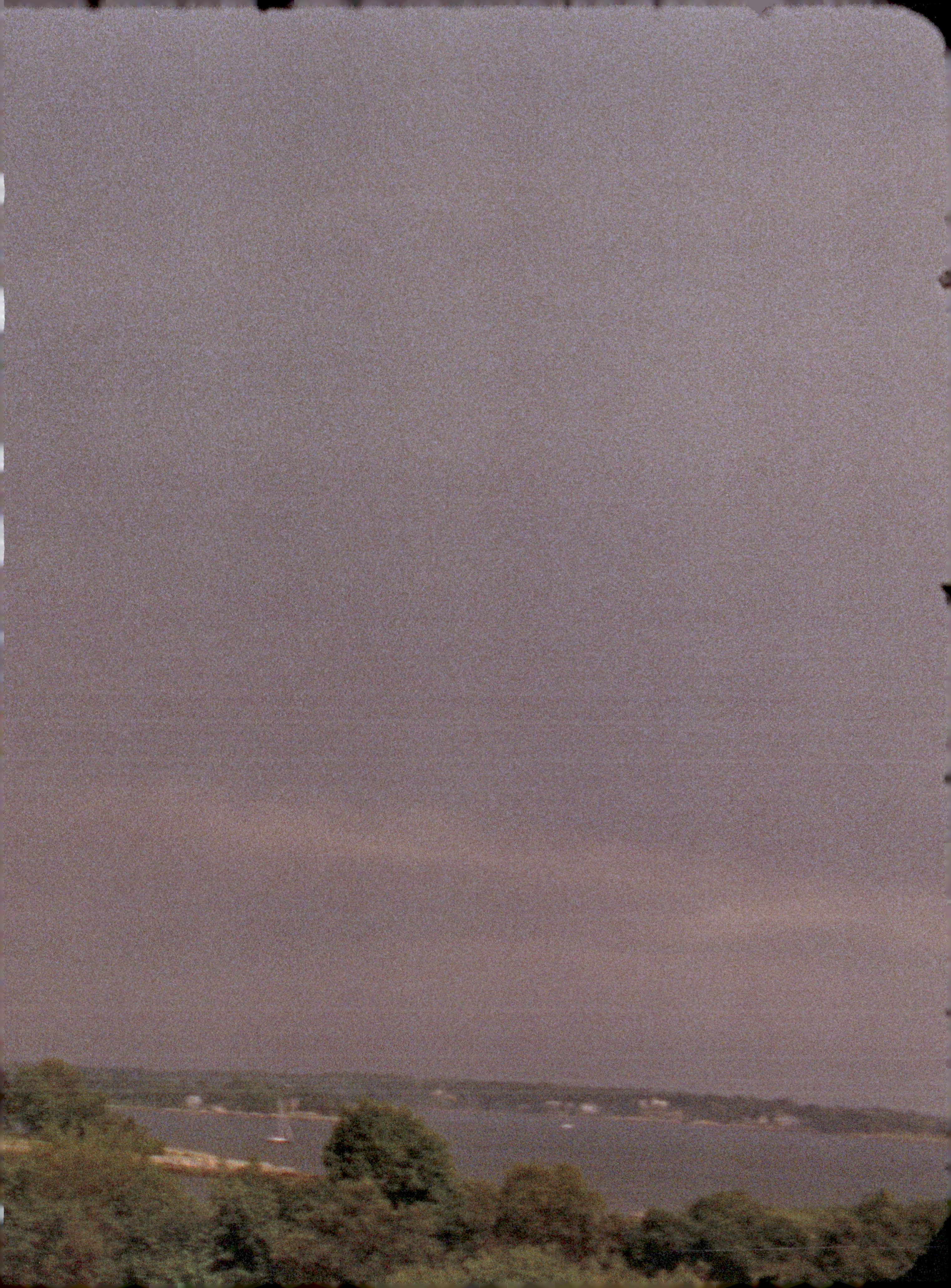